This book, with the ISTQB® CT-AI syllabus as a backbone, does more than simply prepare readers for certification. It enhances and enriches its content with numerous theoretical and practical examples, rigorously contextualising the principles while making them accessible to IT quality professionals and anyone interested in analysing and understanding this new social phenomenon. It is a solid reference and a valuable resource, not only for passing the certification, but also far beyond, for testing AI or testing with AI. Without a doubt, an essential bedside book for the new generation of QA-ers and for the older ones that want to keep abreast with progress.

Olivier Denoo, *Vice President of the ISTQB,*
President of CFTL, Vice President of ps_testware SAS

It's clear this book was written by professionals with real-world experience testing complex systems in high-stakes industries. The thoughtful focus on structure, performance, compliance and resilience reflects the kind of rigour required in heavy regulated domain, like for example financial services, where reliability and regulatory alignment are non-negotiable. For anyone working with AI systems, this book offers both practical tools and valuable perspective.

Sophie Lafont, *Consultant in*
Software Regulatory Compliance,
Financial Services Industry

The AI and testing concepts are explained beyond their dictionary meaning. Useful questions and hands-on examples review the topics in each chapter. It's ideal for beginners and will give practitioners a path for their transition to AI. The real world examples help improve understanding for project professionals and less technical managers.

Carol Long CEng FBCS FRSA, *Consultant and*
Past Chair of BCS Quality SIG

A clear, practical guide that demystifies AI testing and supports ISTQB certification preparation. *Introduction to AI Testing* is a valuable companion for professionals building confidence and competence in the field.

Joris Schut AIGP RAI CT-AI, *Advisor, BearingPoint*

Introduction to AI Testing offers a comprehensive and structured foundation in AI system validation, covering everything from ML fundamentals and neural networks to AI-specific quality metrics, testing techniques and test environments. An essential read for AI practitioners and testers. Highly recommend it!

Kapil Kumar Sharma FBCS,
Data Architect, Cisco Systems Inc.

From the ISTQB® CT-AI exam training perspective, this is one of the most usable resources I've come across. It's well-organised, clear and filled with pictures, graphs and charts that support deeper comprehension. I wouldn't hesitate to recommend it.

Natia Sirbiladze, *Co-Founder and President of GeoSTQB,*
Board Member of ICTA and CEO of Exactpro Georgia

INTRODUCTION TO
AI TESTING

BCS, THE CHARTERED INSTITUTE FOR IT

BCS, The Chartered Institute for IT, is committed to making IT good for society. We use the power of our network to bring about positive, tangible change. We champion the global IT profession and the interests of individuals, engaged in that profession, for the benefit of all.

Exchanging IT expertise and knowledge
The Institute fosters links between experts from industry, academia and business to promote new thinking, education and knowledge sharing.

Supporting practitioners
Through continuing professional development and a series of respected IT qualifications, the Institute seeks to promote professional practice tuned to the demands of business. It provides practical support and information services to its members and volunteer communities around the world.

Setting standards and frameworks
The Institute collaborates with government, industry and relevant bodies to establish good working practices, codes of conduct, skills frameworks and common standards. It also offers a range of consultancy services to employers to help them adopt best practice.

Become a member
Over 70,000 people including students, teachers, professionals and practitioners enjoy the benefits of BCS membership. These include access to an international community, invitations to a roster of local and national events, career development tools and a quarterly thought-leadership magazine. Visit bcs.org to find out more.

Further information
BCS, The Chartered Institute for IT,
3 Newbridge Square,
Swindon, SN1 1BY, United Kingdom.
T +44 (0) 1793 417 417
(Monday to Friday, 09:00 to 17:00 UK time)
bcs.org/contact

shop.bcs.org/
publishing@bcs.uk

bcs.org/qualifications-and-certifications/certifications-for-professionals/

INTRODUCTION TO AI TESTING
A Guide to ISTQB® CT-AI Certification

Iosif Itkin, Iuliia Emelianova, Dmitrii Degtiarenko and Anna-Maria Lukina

bcs

The
Chartered
Institute
for IT

Published by BCS Learning and Development Ltd, a wholly owned subsidiary of BCS, The Chartered Institute for IT, 3 Newbridge Square, Swindon, SN1 1BY, UK.
bcs.org

EU GPSR Authorised Representative: LOGOS EUROPE, 9 Rue Nicolas Poussin, 17000 La Rochelle, France.
Contact@logoseurope.eu

Paperback ISBN: 978-1-78017-7182
PDF ISBN: 978-1-78017-7199
ePUB ISBN: 978-1-78017-7205

Ebook available

British Cataloguing in Publication Data.
A CIP catalogue record for this book is available at the British Library.

Publisher's acknowledgements
Reviewers: Beth Probert, Kari Kakkonen, Daria Degtiarenko
Publisher: Ian Borthwick
Commissioning editor: Heather Wood
Production manager: Florence Leroy
Project manager: Sunrise Setting Ltd
Copy-editor: Mary Hobbins
Proofreader: Barbara Eastman
Indexer: David Gaskell
Cover design: Alex Wright (BCS)/Alyona Volnikova (Exactpro)
Cover image: Shutterstock/Designfashion
Sales director: Charles Rumball
Typeset by Lapiz Digital Services, Chennai, India

CONTENTS

LIST OF FIGURES

AUTHORS

The main reason this book is now in your hand is teamwork. Its authors are a cross-functional team of colleagues currently employed by Exactpro. The company has fully supported the creation of this title, which is also an organic extension of its award-winning AI Testing training course (grounded in the ISTQB Certified Tester – AI Testing (CT-AI) syllabus, ISTQB being a globally recognised software testing certification body).

In this book, the authors strive to balance theory with practice, find simple and accessible analogies for complicated concepts and reinforce your understanding with illustrative designs. This educational initiative serves several purposes:

- It aims to catalyse a transformative shift in how quality and resilience are ensured in global financial technology and other domains where tolerance to failure is minimal. Failure on mission-critical systems is able to threaten operational continuity, reputation and sources of revenue.

- It prepares professionals in all walks of life for an AI-driven future, promoting the idea of responsible development of trustworthy AI and providing the tools to enhance their skillsets, performance and productivity.

Iosif Itkin is a co-founder and CEO of Exactpro. Spearheading Exactpro's AI testing practice, Iosif also manages business development and research trading systems reliability and artificial intelligence. He holds an MSc degree in theoretical physics.

In his professional career, Iosif has held many technology roles: software developer, performance testing department lead, technology architect – on a number of global financial industry initiatives. Iosif's expertise at the intersection of high-availability systems and capital markets has enabled him to successfully facilitate technology transformations within exchanges, investment banks and clearing and settlement organisations in London, New York, Milan, Singapore, Sydney and in other major financial centres.

Iuliia Emelianova is a data scientist, researcher and lecturer with Exactpro. She holds a PhD in physics and mathematics. Drawing on her extensive background at the intersection of academia (associate professor at a university department), IT (development engineer) and financial services (tester), she provides expert support on the firm's internal training courses and the courses organised for the global community of IT professionals.

Dmitrii Degtiarenko is a creative manager and developer of educational programs at Exactpro. He is also an instructor for Exactpro's ISTQB courses. Dmitrii holds an MS degree in economics.

Iosif Itkin, Iuliia Emelianova and Dmitrii Degtiarenko developed Exactpro's AI testing training course, which has been instrumental in shaping this book. They have worked hard towards making it veraciously informative, and yet accessible to a wide audience.

Anna-Maria Lukina, marketing director with Exactpro, outreach director for the course and software testing specialist in her previous role, holds MS degrees in information systems and technologies and digital marketing. She has propelled the project forward every step of the way and made sure everything was up to scratch at all times.

About Exactpro

Exactpro is an independent provider of AI-augmented software testing services for financial organisations. Our clients are exchanges and exchange groups, post-trade platform operators, banks and technology vendors across 24 countries. Founded in 2009, the Exactpro Group is headquartered in the UK and operates delivery centres worldwide.

As a technology vendor supporting mission-critical financial market infrastructure transformations, the firm holds itself to an increasingly high standard, promoting professional excellence within the fintech community and beyond. Exactpro regularly hosts educational events, from summer schools and university lectures to industry webinars, conferences and online training programmes. Exactpro is an accredited training provider for the ISTQB Certified Tester Foundation Level (CTFL) and the ISTQB CT-AI programmes for individual and corporate clients.

FOREWORD

At ISTQB, our mission is to promote the value of software testing as a profession and to support testers worldwide in becoming more effective, efficient and confident in their work. In recent years, the emergence of artificial intelligence has not only introduced new challenges for the testing community, but has also signalled a shift towards a new reality in which workplaces, systems and testing approaches must adapt to increasingly intelligent technologies.

As the global leader in software testing certification, ISTQB has responded with the Certified Tester – AI Testing (CT-AI) syllabus, designed to prepare professionals to engage with AI-based systems thoughtfully and responsibly. As president of ISTQB and head of the AI Taskforce, I see this syllabus as a natural extension of our commitment to equipping testers with relevant skills grounded in proven practice and guided by international collaboration.

This book is a valuable contribution to that mission. It not only offers comprehensive coverage of the ISTQB CT-AI syllabus, but also enriches it with practical examples, hands-on exercises and thought-provoking reflections. I am pleased to see the book's strong emphasis on terminology, industry relevance and real-world scenarios – elements that reflect the core principles of ISTQB. From basic structured learning objectives to advanced topics, this guide supports both professional growth and certification success.

I endorse this book as a valuable companion to the ISTQB CT-AI syllabus. It embodies the spirit of our profession: curious and relentless, but ethical at the same time.

Dr Klaudia Dussa-Zieger
President of ISTQB and head of the ISTQB AI Taskforce

ACKNOWLEDGEMENTS

The idea for this book was born out of a deep belief that as AI systems are becoming increasingly embedded into the critical infrastructure of our society – from financial markets to healthcare – we must evolve our testing practices to match their complexity. At Exactpro, we have spent the past 15 years advancing software quality excellence in non-deterministic, mission-critical infrastructures. Driven by our commitment to helping people understand AI technologies, raising global awareness of the importance of software testing in AI-driven systems and contributing to the continuous improvement of quality standards in complex digital ecosystems, we have created this comprehensive guide.

My deepest gratitude goes to Alexey Zverev, my friend and long-standing colleague since our high school years. Over the course of three decades, our professional journey – marked by both alignment and constructive divergence – has laid the groundwork for much of what Exactpro has achieved, in its successes as well as its growing pains. This enduring collaboration has had a profound influence on the ideas, perspectives and content presented in this book.

The creation of the AI testing course and its transformation into this book was made possible by Anna-Maria Lukina, whose initiative, vision and leadership brought the project to life. She defined the book's goals, structured its content and led coordination across all contributors and the publisher. Anna-Maria also took full responsibility for the book's strategic positioning and audience planning, ensuring it aligns with Exactpro's broader educational and business objectives.

We are proud members of the ISTQB community and have long supported its mission to define and evolve the field of software quality assurance. This book is based on the Certified Tester – AI Testing (CT-AI) syllabus and we would like to express our appreciation to the authors and contributors of the CT-AI syllabus for their excellent work in articulating the standards and challenges of testing AI systems and using AI for testing.

This book builds on the AI testing programme materials accredited by ISTQB, originally developed by a team of exceptionally talented professionals. A special thank you goes to Dmitrii Degtiarenko and Iuliia Emelianova, who authored the majority of the original course content and enriched it with numerous real-world examples and practical exercises.

A special thanks goes to Daria Degtiarenko, who has contributed with industry-facing examples and strategic perspectives closely aligned with Exactpro's cumulative experience as a seasoned technology vendor, applying a fine comb in helping make the book 'camera-ready'. Thanks to Vera Medvedeva for her sharp eye in working with the reference list and the book's layout on the spur of the moment.

I am deeply grateful to Janna Zabolotnaya for her coordination of the educational initiatives behind the software testing and AI testing programmes. Her work, in close collaboration with Ana Otkhozoria and Maria Mazurina, involved collecting feedback and conducting market research to better understand industry needs. Thanks to Martha Tsoy, Ravil Suleimanov and Nino Mikava for continuing marketing support.

Thanks to our AI testing course instructors, Elena Trescheva and Inthika Ramaniharan, as well as to our students, whose curiosity and active engagement helped us identify which additional topics and practical examples would make the book most effective for preparing for the official ISTQB CT-AI exam.

One of the most distinctive aspects of the book is its visual storytelling. Our beloved th2-branded cats bring abstract testing concepts to life through clear, engaging illustrations. Special thanks to Alyona Volnikova for designing all the visuals and to our Exactpro design team – Ekaterina Avvakumova and Maria Danilova – for their ongoing creative support, including their work not only on the book project but throughout the years on some very unexpected but brilliant ideas.

I am especially grateful to Natia Sirbiladze, whose persistence and networking opened the path to collaboration with BCS. A sincere thank you to the BCS publishing team, in particular Heather Wood, for the guidance, professionalism and support at every stage of the publishing process.

I would like to acknowledge that some of the ideas fundamental to Exactpro software testing philosophy can be traced to publications and work by Cem Canner, Michael Bolton, Paul Gerrard, James Bach, Doug Hoffman, Cassie Kozyrkov, Andrew Ng, Ray Dalio, Julia Galef, Kelly Whitmill, John Ferguson Smart, Dave Farley, Richard Rummelt, Larry Harris, Matthew Syed, Jocko Willink and Leif Babin.

I would like to say thank you to my mentors and people who had the most impact on my career: Mark Ryland, Antoine Bigirimana, Mikhail Teif, Dasha Klyachko, Yann L'Hullier, Antoine Shagoury, Xavier Rolet, Tim Thurman, Angie Walker, Roman Prilutsky, Mukhtaar Yusuf, Chris Corrado and Adeel Saeed.

My colleagues help me with everything. I would like to express my gratitude to the Exactpro management team: Pavel Medvedev, Alyona Bulda, Maxim Rudovsky, Elena Rusakova, Kirill Zagorouiko, Dmitry Kolpakov, Alexey Pereverzev, Mikhail Odintsov, Stanislav Klimakov, Mikhail Yamkovy, Anton Sitnikov, Marina Kudriavtceva, Maxim Nikiforov, Tatiana Sergeeva, Asya Legotina, Dmitry Doronichev, Dmitry Medvedev, Ekaterina Uskova, Elena Treshcheva, Eugene Vereshchagin, Ian Salmon, Jagath De Silva, Michael Smith, Mikhail Kurkov, Rostislav Yavorskiy, Olga Buyanova, Alyona Lamash, Vladimir Zveryako, Thomas Toller, Elena Moiseeva, Ilya Kirin, Anton Krykov, Natalia Kriukova, Maya Tsoy, Pavel Sigov, Dmitry Zavodchikov, Leonid Zudov, Nikolay Lubenin, Igor Borisov, Marina Soloveva, Victoria Leonchik, Sona Oganisyan, Luba Konnova, Denis Saveliev, Denis Kameka, Nikolay Kuzmin, Ilya Merkulov, Alexey Yermolaev, Anatolii Berezutskii, Ilia Anisimov, Oleg Smirnov, Ivan Shamray and many others.

I am blessed to have the support of my family: Maya Gogoleva, Alexey Itkin, Maria Itkina and my mom Irina Samarina.

Iosif Itkin

ABBREVIATIONS

ADAS	advanced driver-assistance system
AI	artificial intelligence
AIaaS	AI as a service
AML	anti-money laundering
API	application programming interface
ASIC	application-specific integrated circuit
ASV	asymmetric Shapley value
AUC	area under curve
AWS	Amazon Web Services
BERT	bidirectional encoder representations from transformers
BoW	bag of words
BT	behaviour tree
CART	continuous automated red teaming
CBR	case-based reasoning
CNN	convolutional neural network
CNTK	Microsoft Cognitive Toolkit
CPU	central processing unit
CT-AI	Certified Tester – AI Testing
CTFL	Certified Tester Foundation Level
CTR	click-through rate
CVR	conversion rate
DBSCAN	density-based spatial clustering of applications with noise
DIN	Deutsches Institut für Normung (German national standards body)
DNN	deep neural network
DoS	denial-of-service
EDA	exploratory data analysis
EU	European Union
FN	false negative
FP	false positive
FPR	false positive rate
GAN	generative adversarial network

GDPR	General Data Protection Regulation
GLUE	general language understanding evaluation
GPT	generative pre-trained transformer
GPU	graphical processing unit
GUI	graphical user interface
HOG	histogram of oriented gradients
IBM	International Business Machines
IEC	International Electrotechnical Commission
IEEE	Institute of Electrical and Electronics Engineers
IoT	Internet of Things
IP	internet protocol
ISO	International Organization for Standardization
JTC	Joint Technical Committee (IEC)
LDA	linear discriminant analysis
LiDAR	light detection and ranging
LIME	local interpretable model-agnostic explanations
LLM	large language model
LRP	layer-wise relevance propagation
ML	machine learning
MNIST	Modified National Institute of Standards and Technology
MORSE	Modular Open Robots Simulation Engine
MR	metamorphic relation
MSE	mean square error
MT	metamorphic testing
NASA	National Aeronautics and Space Administration
NLP	natural language processing
NLTK	Natural Language Toolkit
NPC	non-player character
NPU	neural processing unit
OCR	optical character recognition
OECD	Organisation for Economic Co-operation and Development
PCA	principal component analysis
QA	quality assurance
RGB	red, green, blue
ROC	receiver operating characteristic
ROS	robot operating system
SaaS	software as a service
SAE	Society of Automotive Engineers
SC	subcommittee

SHAP	SHapley Additive exPlanations
SLA	service-level agreement
SoC	system on a chip
SUT	system under test
SVM	support vector machine
TCAV	testing with concept activation vectors
TF-IDF	term frequency – inverse document frequency
TN	true negative
TP	true positive
TPR	true positive rate
TPU	tensor processing unit
TR	technical report
UI	user interface
UK	United Kingdom
UNESCO	United Nations Educational, Scientific and Cultural Organization
UX	user experience
VAE	variational autoencoder
ViT	Vision Transformer
VPU	vision processing unit
XAI	explainable AI
XGNN	explaining graph neural network
XOR	exclusive OR

INTRODUCTION

This book is designed as a practical and accessible guide for anyone interested in learning about artificial intelligence and preparing for the ISTQB Certified Tester – AI Testing (CT-AI) exam. Built atop the ISTQB CTFL programme, CT-AI expands into the specialised domain of artificial intelligence (AI). It links the structured principles of CTFL with advanced approaches tailored for AI-driven technologies. No matter your background, whether you are coming from software testing, development, data science or just starting out, there is something here for you. You will find value that connects to your own experience and helps you to grow in the direction you need most.

At its core, the content of the book is based on the official ISTQB CT-AI syllabus, but it offers much more than a simple explanation of the syllabus topics. The material is enriched with helpful visuals, including diagrams, schemes and charts, that make complex concepts easier to understand and remember. This visual approach helps to simplify your preparation and makes the learning process more effective.

To help you navigate the content more effectively, the book is divided into four parts, each focusing on a specific area of AI and its relation to testing. The structure follows the ISTQB CT-AI syllabus, while also expanding on key topics to support deeper understanding.

PART 1 – INTRODUCTION TO AI AND AI-BASED SYSTEMS

This part lays the foundation by introducing the core concepts of AI and how AI-based systems differ from traditional systems. Covering Chapters 1 and 2, it explains what AI is, explores its main types and technologies and outlines essential topics such as pre-trained models, transfer learning and AI as a service. It also addresses important system characteristics, such as flexibility, autonomy, bias and ethical considerations, setting the stage for understanding how these elements influence the design and behaviour of AI-based systems.

PART 2 – MACHINE LEARNING

Chapters 3 to 6 form the second part of the book, which focuses on machine learning, the backbone of most AI-based systems. This part explores different forms of ML (supervised, unsupervised and reinforcement learning), the ML development workflow and how data quality affects model performance. It also covers performance metrics and challenges such as overfitting and underfitting, and introduces neural networks.

The goal of this part is to provide a solid grasp of how ML models are developed, trained and evaluated, which is essential for testing AI-based systems effectively.

PART 3 – TESTING AI-BASED SYSTEMS

Part 3, consisting of Chapters 7 to 10, zooms in on the specifics of how AI-based systems should be tested. It introduces various testing levels and methods tailored to AI-specific features, including dealing with algorithmic bias, non-determinism and lack of transparency. You will also learn about appropriate testing techniques such as metamorphic testing, A/B testing and back-to-back testing. In addition, this part discusses how to select test approaches and techniques, how to specify and document AI components and how to create suitable test environments for AI-based systems.

PART 4 – TESTING WITH AI

The final part of the book, Chapter 11, shifts focus from testing AI to using AI as a tool for testing. It explores how AI technologies can support and enhance traditional testing activities, such as defect prediction, test case generation, regression suite optimisation and user interface testing. This chapter demonstrates how AI can become a valuable part of the tester's toolkit, making testing processes smarter, faster and more adaptive.

It is also worth pointing out that each chapter follows the ISTQB structure and is aligned with specific ISTQB-defined knowledge levels:

- K1 (Remember): Recognise terms and concepts.
- K2 (Understand): Explain ideas in your own words.
- K3 (Apply): Use a technique or concept in a real situation.
- K4 (Analyse): Break down and examine parts of a process or solution.

The H level refers to practical, experience-based learning activities that complement theoretical knowledge.

At the beginning of each chapter, you will find a list of learning objectives. These objectives give you a clear guide of what you are expected to learn and achieve by the end of the chapter. Each one is linked to a specific knowledge level, helping you to focus your study and understand how the key concepts connect to the overall learning goals. This makes it easier to track your progress and prepare effectively for the exam.

There is also a strong emphasis on practical application. In addition to theory, you will find:

- **Industry Insights** sections, which demonstrate how the topics discussed in this book can be applied to solve actual problems across various industries and companies, such as Amazon, Bridgewater, Microsoft, Yahoo and Applitools. By focusing on practical applications, these sections encourage critical thinking and contextual learning, helping you to understand not just what a concept is, but how it works in practice and why it matters. This approach is especially valuable if you want to see how AI techniques are implemented outside the classroom, and it offers inspiration for future projects and deeper insight into the material.

- The **From Theory To Practice** sections connect the theoretical material presented in each chapter with practical, relatable examples that demonstrate how AI systems behave, adapt or encounter challenges in everyday use. By grounding abstract ideas in concrete applications, these sections help you to better understand the impact, usefulness and limitations of AI across different contexts. They provide real-life problems that can be solved using specific AI algorithms as well as the ways to implement them. These sections also highlight important considerations such as flexibility, adaptability, bias and decision-making, helping to bridge the gap between what AI is supposed to do and how it performs in reality.

- The **Quick Questions** sections provide multiple-choice questions in the style of the ISTQB CT-AI exam, helping you to become familiar with the structure, phrasing and logic of certification-level questions. Reviewing and discussing these questions can significantly boost your exam readiness and help you to become more confident in tackling the real certification test.

- At the end of each chapter, you will find a set of open-ended **Self-assessment Exercises** designed to help you reflect on and evaluate your understanding of the material. These exercises cover key concepts, definitions and real-world applications discussed in the chapter, encouraging you to recall and explain what you have learned in your own words. Unlike multiple-choice questions, they promote deeper engagement by requiring structured responses that connect theory to practice. Many of these questions are aligned with ISTQB learning objectives and reflect the types of knowledge expected in the CT-AI certification exam. Using these questions as a study tool can help you to identify areas for review, reinforce your learning and gain confidence in your ability to understand and explain AI testing concepts clearly.

- The **Terms** sections include a list of key terms used throughout the book, with all ISTQB-defined terms highlighted in bold in the main text for easy reference. The ISTQB places strong emphasis on understanding and correctly using standard terminology, and this knowledge plays a crucial role in the CT-AI certification exam. Questions related to definitions and the correct use of terms frequently appear in the exam, particularly at the K1 (Remember) level. Reviewing the Terms sections after each chapter will help to reinforce your understanding of foundational concepts and ensure that you are familiar with the precise language used in the syllabus and exam materials. Mastering these terms is not only essential for passing the exam, but also for communicating effectively in professional AI and software testing contexts.

- The **Hands-on Exercises**, included in Chapters 4, 6 and 11, help you to build practical skills and competencies through direct experience. These include case studies with predefined datasets that can be solved using tools such as Python™, Google Colaboratory, PyCharm, Jupyter, Visual Studio Code, and others. You can download datasets from the dedicated GitHub repository (**github.com/exactpro/ai-testing-guide**), try to solve assignments on your own and then check the accuracy of your solutions by downloading the provided example Python code from GitHub. The topics include: identifying training and test data and creating an

ML model; implementing a perceptron learning algorithm; and building a defect prediction system.

Needless to say, this book goes beyond the core syllabus. We have included extra topics and practical guidance that, while not part of the exam, give you a broader view of AI testing. These additions help you to understand the bigger picture, which is essential not only for passing the exam but also for applying AI concepts confidently in your future projects. Among the extended topics, you will find explanations of generative and discriminative models, self-supervised learning and the transformer architecture, which are foundational to many modern AI applications. We also explore advanced testing concepts such as test oracles for AI-based systems and discuss the meaning of the term 'quality', which is a key concept in software development and testing, and the role of red teaming in evaluating AI robustness and security. We conclude the book with final thoughts on the potential role of AI as a teammate, a reflection on the evolving relationship between humans and intelligent systems.

This book is part of a bigger educational Exactpro initiative. Please explore the Exactpro website to learn more: **exactpro.com/training**.

PART 1
INTRODUCTION TO AI AND AI-BASED SYSTEMS

1 INTRODUCTION TO AI

SUMMARY

This chapter provides an overview of AI, starting with its definition and an exploration of various AI categories. It contrasts conventional systems with AI-based systems. The chapter then investigates the technologies essential for AI implementation, including examples of AI development frameworks and hardware utilised for training and deploying machine learning (ML) models. It also explores the concept of AI as a service (AIaaS). Additionally, the chapter covers topics such as pre-trained models and transfer learning, highlighting associated risks and discussing current standards and regulations aimed at ensuring AI reliability and security.

LEARNING OBJECTIVES

After covering this chapter, you should be able to:

- Describe the AI effect and how it influences the definition of AI (K2)
- Distinguish between narrow AI, general AI and super AI (K2)
- Differentiate between AI-based systems and conventional systems (K2)
- Recognise the different technologies used to implement AI (K1)
- Identify popular AI development frameworks (K1)
- Compare the choices available for hardware to implement AI-based systems (K2)
- Explain the concept of AI as a service (K2)
- Explain the use of pre-trained AI models and the risks associated with them (K2)
- Describe how standards apply to AI-based systems (K2)

LINKS TO OTHER CHAPTERS

This chapter provides a foundation for subsequent chapters in understanding the basics of AI and its categorisation. The concepts introduced are covered in more detail later in the book as follows:

- Chapter 2 describes such characteristics of AI-based systems as transparency, interpretability and explainability.

- Chapter 3 explains the concept of overfitting and provides an in-depth exploration of ML, covering its various forms and workflow.

- Chapter 4 defines data preparation steps necessary to prepare data for processing and developing an ML model.

- Chapter 5 reviews ML functional performance metrics.

- Chapter 9 looks at the root causes of vulnerabilities of AI-based systems that are used during the adversarial and data poisoning attacks, and explains how to mitigate them.

1.1 DEFINITION OF AI AND THE AI EFFECT

Figure 1.1 The evolution of AI

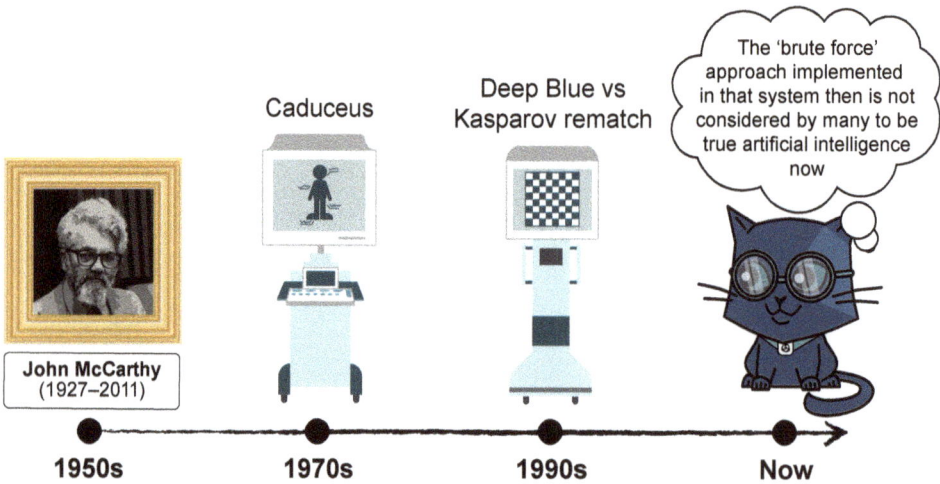

The term **artificial intelligence** was coined in the 1950s by John McCarthy (McCarthy et al., 1955) and refers to the objective of building and programming 'intelligent' machines capable of imitating human beings. Since then, it has evolved significantly, so here is a more modern definition that captures the concept of AI (ISO, 2020):

It is the capability of an engineered system to acquire, process, and apply knowledge and skills.

So it is safe to say that the way people understand the meaning of AI depends on their current world view. Figure 1.1 shows some of the AI evolution milestones. For example, the **expert systems** of the 1970s and 1980s incorporated human expertise as rules that could be run without the expert being present. One of the most prominent examples of such machines was Caduceus, a medical machine capable of diagnosing up to 1000 different diseases. It operated using heuristic rules, which used a partitioning algorithm to divide medical problems into specific areas, and applied exclusion functions to systematically rule out unlikely diagnoses. These were considered to be AI then, but are not considered as such now.

Before the 1997 Deep Blue vs Kasparov rematch, the mere idea of a computer system beating a human in a six-game chess match would be mind-boggling and definitely an indication that AI is a reality – and then it happened. The system used a 'brute-force' approach, evaluating millions of possible chess positions to determine and select the best move. And once again, this approach is not considered to be true AI now. People may wonder and say 'If I beat the world's chess champion, I'd be regarded as highly bright', but 'when a machine does something "intelligent," it ceases to be regarded as intelligent' (*The Washington Times*, 2006).

The changing concept of what constitutes AI is known as the **AI effect**. As the perception of AI in society changes, so does its definition. It is the same as saying that if a problem is solved using AI, the problem is no longer a part of the AI focus area. Solving an AI problem makes it lose its 'mysterious' lustre and moves it from unattainable to mundane. And, as a result, any definition made today is likely to change in the future and may not match those from the past. Let us just hope it will not change by the time you finish reading this book.

An intriguing aspect of AI's evolution is how both the perception of what AI entails and the level of interest in the field have shifted over time. Notably, the history of AI includes two periods known as **AI winters**, when enthusiasm cooled and progress slowed significantly (Francesconi, 2022). The first AI winter occurred in the mid-1970s to early 1980s. Prior to that, early AI research had generated considerable excitement, particularly around **symbolic AI** and expert systems. However, most of these systems were often limited in their scope and struggled to perform well in real-world applications, leading to widespread disappointment. As a result, funding, especially from government sources, was significantly reduced, and many AI projects were abandoned.

The second AI winter started in the mid-1980s and ended in the early 1990s. Similar to the first AI winter, it was caused by the fact that AI research did not always deliver the promised results (Crevier, 1993). AI-based systems needed to be able to learn from large datasets, which was computationally expensive. This made it difficult to deploy AI-based systems in real-world applications. Apple and IBM created personal computers with faster and greater computing power, which started to replace expert systems. As a result, funding in AI was decreased.

Nowadays we are in the **summer of AI** with a sharp increase in interest in AI caused mainly by the emergence of publicly available **generative AI** such as ChatGPT (OpenAI, 2025a), DeepSeek (2025), GitHub Copilot (GitHub, 2025) and Grok (xAI, 2025).

From theory to practice

The AI effect highlights the dynamic nature of technological innovation and societal adaptation. As AI continues to advance, it will become increasingly integrated into daily life, transforming industries and altering our expectations of technology. The future of AI will involve both incredible advancements as well as the normalisation of what we currently view as cutting-edge, making the extraordinary seem ordinary when AI advancements become integrated and then taken for granted.

For example, AI could become deeply embedded in the infrastructure of homes and cities, managing everything from energy use and security to public transportation and waste management. Smart cities will rely on AI for optimising traffic flow, reducing energy consumption and improving public safety. AI will enable highly personalised medical treatments, predictive diagnostics and continuous health monitoring. AI assistants in healthcare settings will handle routine administrative tasks, allowing human professionals to focus on complex cases, thereby increasing efficiency and reducing costs. While AI will automate many routine jobs, it will also create new roles that require advanced technical and interpersonal skills, for example data scientists, ML engineers and cybersecurity specialists that must possess programming, data management, data analysis, communication and collaboration skills. Reskilling and upskilling will become essential for the workforce. AI-driven productivity gains could lead to significant economic growth, but ensuring that the benefits are widely distributed will be a key policy issue.

As we mentioned earlier, as AI becomes more integrated, public perception will shift, all of the aforementioned achievements will be seen as a natural part of life. Needless to say, this normalisation will require ongoing public education to address misconceptions and fears. Governments will need to develop policies and regulations that address the ethical, legal and economic implications of pervasive AI. So let us repeat one more time: the AI effect illustrates how extraordinary technological advancements become ordinary building blocks of our daily life.

Quick questions

Question 1.1

Which of the following statements about AI is LESS likely to be CORRECT? Select ONE option.

   A. The concept of what constitutes AI is continuously changing.
   B. AI is the capability of an engineered system to acquire, process and apply knowledge and skills.
   C. AI refers to computer systems designed to perform tasks that usually require human intelligence – such as seeing, understanding speech, learning from data, making decisions and processing language.
   D. The concept of what constitutes AI never changes.

1.2 NARROW, GENERAL AND SUPER AI

It is quite possible that a more rational way of explaining the phenomenon of the AI effect is admitting to ourselves that what we thought could only be done with strong AI might actually be achieved through weak AI.

So let us explain what that actually means. AI is usually broken down into three categories, as Figure 1.2 indicates:

- **Narrow AI** (or **weak AI**) where systems are programmed to carry out a specific task with a limited context. They can analyse and interpret data with astonishing **accuracy**, accomplishing it much faster than humans. They help us to make better data-driven decisions and, more importantly, relieve us of monotonous tasks.

- Next comes **general AI** (also known as **strong AI** or **true AI**), and it describes universal systems capable of performing any intellectual task that humans can perform. These types of systems will also be able to reason and act, based on consciousness, emotions and critical thinking. It is the holy grail for all AI researchers, but unfortunately no general AI systems have been realised so far, with some researchers voicing their opinion that it is not feasible at all.

- And then there is **super AI**. Philosopher and expert on AI, Nick Bostrom, defines superintelligence as 'an intelligence that vastly exceeds the cognitive capacity of human intelligence in all fields of knowledge' (Bostrom, 2014). Here, systems are capable of replicating human cognition (or general AI), make use of massive processing power and access all knowledge, for example via the world wide web. The point at which AI-based systems transition from general AI to super AI is commonly known as the **technological singularity** (Pagnis et al., 2021).

Figure 1.2 Three categories of AI

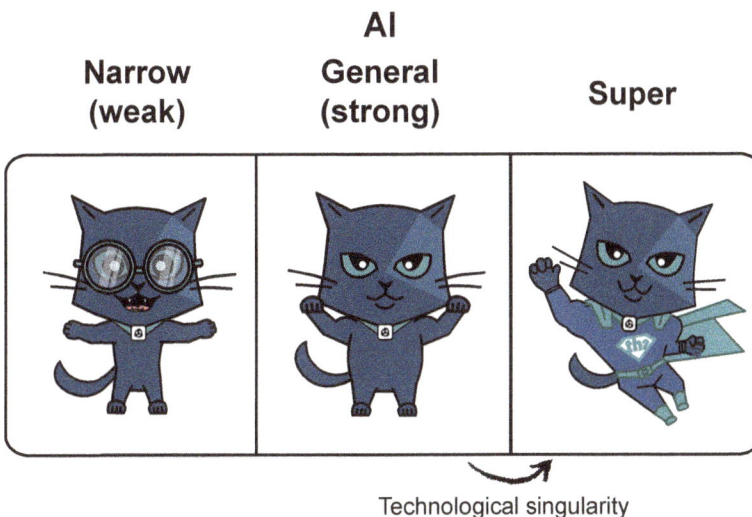

Technological singularity

While general and super AI remain goals for the future, most of today's practical advancements in AI fall under the category of narrow AI and are largely powered by a technique called **machine learning (ML)**. ML enables systems to learn patterns and glean insights from data or experience and improve performance over time without being explicitly programmed for every scenario.

If you want to learn more about the possible development of super AI and what it might lead to, we recommend reading Bostrom's book, called *Superintelligence: Paths, Dangers, Strategies* (Bostrom, 2014).

From theory to practice

Currently the narrow form of AI is widely available. For example, game-playing systems, spam filters, self-driving cars and voice assistants. When it comes to **testing**, narrow AI can assist in generating **test cases** and plan the overall **test process** as well as improve the **defect report** quality for **quality assurance (QA)** analysts. It can also be used in intelligent capturing and text recognition without human intervention with the help of **natural language processing (NLP)** and **sentiment analysis** (Marreddy and Mamidi, 2023).

1.3 AI-BASED AND CONVENTIONAL SYSTEMS

In a conventional computer system, the software is programmed by people using constructs such as 'if-then-else' and loops. It is relatively easy for humans to understand how the system transforms inputs into outputs, because everything is rule- and algorithm-based. Figure 1.3 gives an illustration of a conventional computer system with the aforementioned 'if-then-else' and loops approach, although this statement better reflects a trivial system rather than complex market data juggernauts that exchange and analyse huge swaths of data.

AI-based systems, on the other hand, have an observe-and-learn approach, which is illustrated in Figure 1.4. Here **patterns** in data are used by the system to determine how it should react to new data in the future.

Take, for instance, an AI-powered image processing system specifically created to recognise images depicting cats. This system undergoes **training** using a curated collection of cat images. Through this training, the AI autonomously discerns the intricate patterns and distinctive features within the data that enable it to identify cats. Subsequently, these learned patterns and rules are employed to analyse new images, enabling the AI to ascertain whether or not they contain cats.

Figure 1.3 An example of a logical schema for a conventional computer system

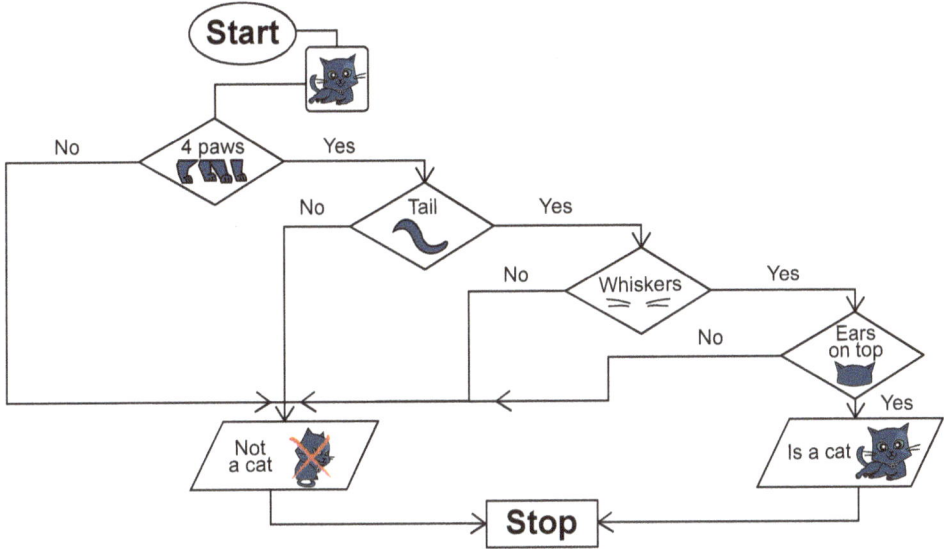

Figure 1.4 An AI-based system illustration

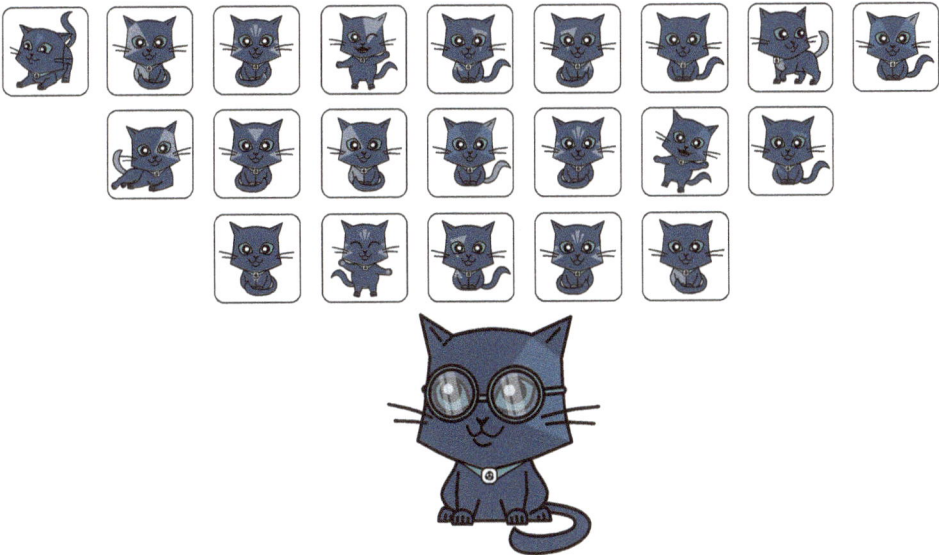

From theory to practice

In a conventional computer system, image recognition tasks are typically performed using predefined algorithms and rules. It starts with pre-processing (see Section 4.1 on data preparation steps), where the image is prepared to enhance certain **features** or reduce **noise** using techniques such as resizing, filtering or colour adjustment. Then comes **feature extraction**, where the system extracts predefined features from the image using techniques such as edge detection, texture analysis or colour histograms. After that we have **classification**, where the extracted features are fed into a **pre-trained ML model** or an algorithm that has been manually programmed to classify or recognise specific objects. The model applies rules or comparisons to make predictions based on the extracted features. And lastly there is decision-making, which is based on the classification result, where the system makes a decision or takes further actions, such as identifying the object in the image or triggering a specific response.

In an AI-powered image recognition system, **deep learning** models and **neural networks** are used to automatically learn and identify patterns in images (Alzubaidi et al., 2021). Here it all starts with the training phase, where the AI-based system is trained on a large dataset of labelled images. Deep learning models are employed to automatically learn features and patterns from the data. Then comes **feature learning**, during which the AI-based system automatically learns hierarchical representations of features, detecting low-level patterns such as edges and textures and gradually building up to higher-level concepts. After that there is classification and recognition, because, once the training is complete, the AI-based system can classify or recognise patterns and objects in new, unseen images. It passes the image through the trained neural network, and the network automatically extracts relevant features and makes predictions without relying on explicitly programmed rules. Then comes the fine-tuning in the form of iterative improvement via increasing the size of the **training dataset**, or employing advanced techniques. Lastly, we have adaptability and generalisation through handling variations of images with different lighting conditions, viewpoints and object orientations.

Compared to a conventional computer system, an AI-based system for image recognition utilises deep learning models and neural networks to automatically learn and identify patterns in images. It learns from **labelled data**, extracts features and makes predictions without relying on explicitly defined rules. This allows the AI-based system to handle complex recognition tasks with improved accuracy, adaptability and generalisation capabilities.

1.4 AI TECHNOLOGIES

AI can be implemented using a wide range of technologies (Figure 1.5), such as (Russell and Norvig, 2020):

1. **Reasoning techniques**, which include:
   - **rule engines** (or **semantic reasoners**), which draw logical assumptions from facts or axioms;

- **deductive classifiers**, which seek to mimic human deductive logic to produce new information, unlike rule-based engines, which can only apply triggers such as 'if-then' when a condition is not met;

- **case-based reasoning (CBR)**, which imitates human reasoning and is based on the principle that similar problems have similar solutions;

- **procedural reasoning**, which implements the 'belief-desire-intention' concept of modelling real-time reasoning and can be used to build frameworks that operate with knowledge areas (or predefined skills/instructions) in order to achieve a given objective (Georgeff and Ingrand, 1989; Ezhilarasu et al., 2019);

2. ML techniques, which can be split into three categories: **supervised learning**, **unsupervised learning** and **reinforcement learning** (see Section 3.1 on forms of ML) and two additional algorithm types that do not belong to the aforementioned categories.

Let us look at the most common examples of these algorithms.

The first one is *supervised learning*. Here, the algorithm creates an ML model from labelled data during the training phase. The labelled data, which usually consists of pairs of inputs (e.g. a bug report with a 'bug' label vs any other text with a 'not a bug' label) is used by the algorithm during the training to deduce the link between the input data and the output labels. During the ML model testing phase, a new dataset is applied to the trained model to predict the output. The model is deployed once the output **precision** level is satisfactory. Supervised learning helps with **classification** and **regression** problems, such as determining what category a bug report belongs to (the one that describes an actual bug or the one just containing a user's opinion about specific functionality) or predicting the time it takes to fix the bug. The models presented in the syllabus can be divided into three groups: **linear models**, **Bayesian models** and **decision tree** algorithms, as shown in Figure 1.5.

Let us look at a few examples for each group:

- Linear models:
    - **Linear regression** is a model reflecting a linear relationship between input and output variables. It is based on statistical approaches and is used when the target variable is numeric and allows prediction of continuous values.

    - **Logistic regression** is a modification of linear regression. It uses the logistic (sigmoid) function to find the relationship between variables. In this model, the target variable is categorical rather than numeric.

    - **Support vector machine (SVM)** is a model based on geometrical data properties. It maps objects from **training data** to points in space in such a way as to increase the gap between classes. It is a more powerful way of learning complex non-linear functions (Cervantes et al., 2020).

- Bayesian models specify probabilistic models and solve problems when less than the necessary information is available. Examples of Bayesian models include Naive Bayes, multinomial Naive Bayes, complement Naive Bayes, etc.

- Decision tree algorithms:
  - Decision tree is a model with a tree-like structure that divides the data recursively according to the values of its significant features (input variables) to predict an **outcome**. This algorithm is better suited for small datasets with fewer features and simpler interpretability.
  - **Random forest** is an ensemble learning algorithm that combines the predictions from multiple decision trees to get a final prediction. This algorithm is better to use for complex problems with many features and higher accuracy requirements (Breiman, 2001).

Then, there is *unsupervised learning*. Here, the algorithm creates an ML model from unlabelled data during the training phase. The unlabelled data is used to deduce patterns in the input data during the training. After that, it assigns inputs to different classes. This is followed by the testing phase, when the trained model is applied to a new dataset. The model is deployed once the output precision level is considered to be satisfactory. As with Figure 1.5, this approach helps with:

- **clustering**, which is when the problem requires the identification of data similarities. **Clustering algorithms** solve the task of grouping a set of objects in such a way that objects in the same group are more similar to each other than to those in other groups. It is a main task of **exploratory data analysis (EDA)**, and a common technique for statistical data analysis. These algorithms include:
  - K-means, which attempts to cluster the data into a predetermined number of groups by minimising the distance from the cluster centre to the objects;
  - density-based spatial clustering of applications with noise (DBSCAN), which operates on data density – the basic concept of the algorithm is to find areas of high density, which are separated from each other by areas of low density;
- **association**, which identifies relationships and dependencies between samples or dependencies to be discovered among data attributes.

The last one is *reinforcement learning*, which is an approach where the system (an '**intelligent agent**') learns by interacting with the environment in an iterative manner. There is no training data. The agent is rewarded when it makes a correct decision and is penalised when it makes an incorrect one. The key challenges when implementing reinforcement learning are setting up the environment, selecting a strategy so that the agent can achieve the desired goal and designing a **reward function** that is a rule or a set of rules that assigns a numerical 'reward' to the agent, based on its actions and the state of the environment (Shakya et al., 2023). This approach can be implemented using Markov algorithms, dynamic programming and other, more sophisticated, algorithms.

Also, there are two other algorithm types in Figure 1.5 that need to be mentioned. First are **genetic algorithms**, which are commonly used to generate high-quality solutions for optimisation and search problems by relying on bio-inspired operators such as mutation, crossover and selection (Katoch et al., 2020). They cannot be classified as supervised, unsupervised or reinforcement learning, as

Figure 1.5 AI technologies

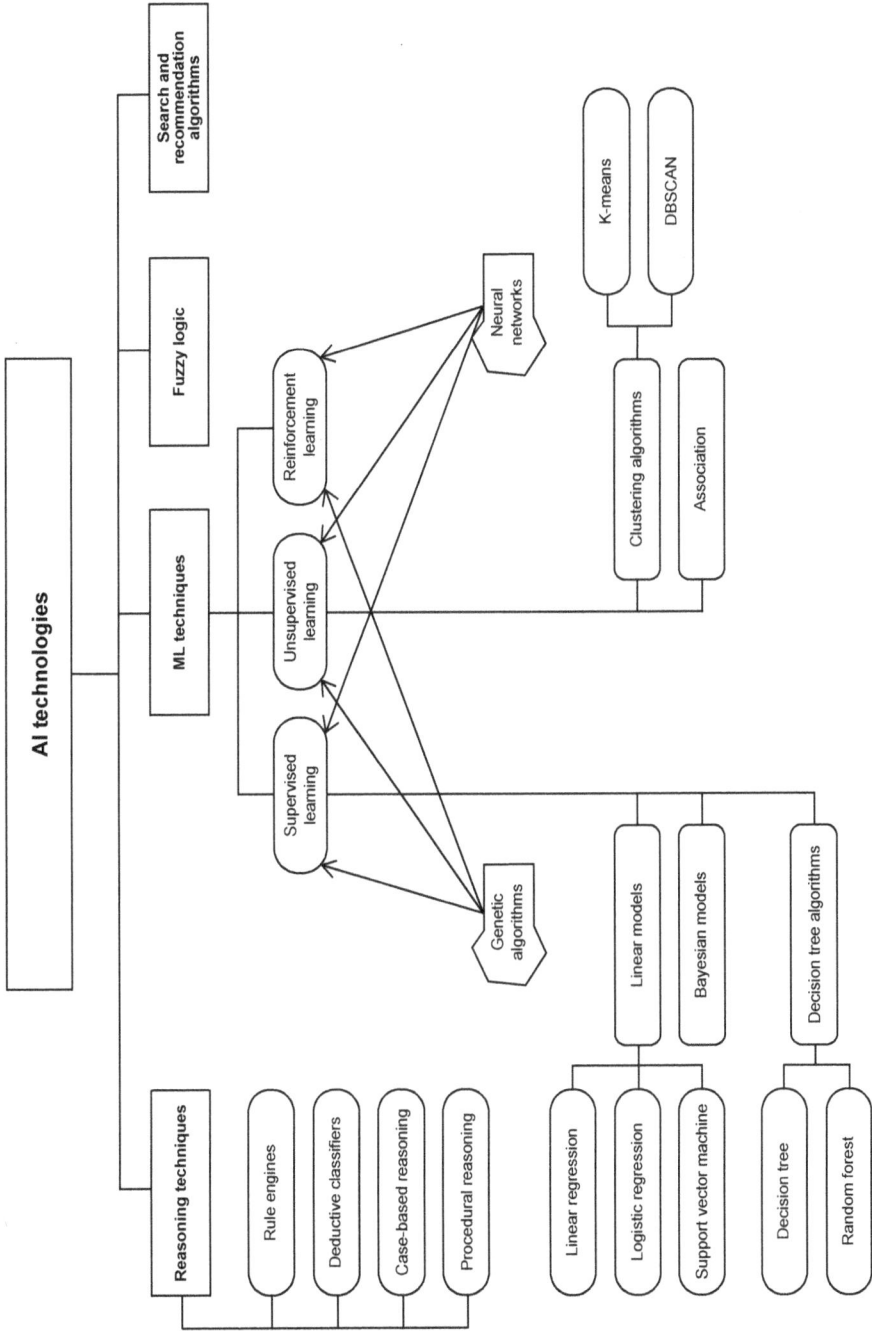

they can be applied over algorithms belonging to either group. Second are **neural networks**, which attempt to mimic the human brain by constructing a system of connected units or **nodes** called **artificial neurons**. They can be used in supervised, unsupervised and reinforcement learning tasks.

3. **Fuzzy logic** is the next AI technology on our list, and it is presented in Figure 1.5. To put it simply, it operates in the grey area between human responses of 'yes' and 'no'; in other words, when the truth value is any real number between 0 and 1. It is used to handle the notion of partial truth. This is very similar to human reasoning. For example, when a tester assigns a priority level to a bug, he answers the question 'Does this bug need to be fixed quickly?' Usually, it is not a yes-or-no question. We set the priority in a range from the 'Highest' (or '1', meaning 'needs to be fixed very fast') to the 'Lowest' (or '0', meaning 'can be left for later') with intermediate values in between.

4. Search and recommendation algorithms is the last AI technology mentioned in Figure 1.5:

   - **Search algorithms** are used to navigate large datasets or knowledge bases to find relevant information or solve complex problems. There are different types of search algorithms, such as uninformed search (deep first search, breadth first search, uniform cost search), informed search (greedy search, A* Search) and others (Pathak et al., 2018).

   - **Recommendation systems** in AI are designed to predict user preferences and recommend items or content to users. There are mainly three types of these systems: collaborative filtering, content-based filtering and hybrid systems (Shah et al., 2017).

   Many modern applications integrate both search and recommendation algorithms to deliver a seamless user experience.

AI-based systems typically implement one or more of the technologies discussed above. For example, reasoning techniques can be integrated with ML techniques and search algorithms in the same application to create sophisticated and effective solutions.

From theory to practice

1. Problems that can be solved using rule engines

Rule engines are used to automate decision-making processes by applying a set of predefined rules to data.

Problem A. Fraud detection: identifying fraudulent transactions based on rules and patterns

Rule engines play a crucial role in fraud detection by automating the analysis of transactions and activities to identify potentially fraudulent behaviour. Rule engines can process data in real time, monitoring transactions as they occur. This immediate analysis helps in identifying suspicious activities promptly and preventing fraud before it happens (Wang et al., 2016).

Fraud detection systems use predefined rules based on known patterns of fraudulent behaviour. These rules can include conditions such as: transactions exceeding a certain amount; unusual spending patterns; transactions from high-risk locations or internet protocol (IP) addresses; or multiple transactions in a short period. Rule engines can be configured to recognise complex patterns that are indicative of fraud, for example a series of small transactions followed by a large withdrawal might trigger an alert.

Fraud detection systems often assign risk scores to transactions based on the rules. Their automatic actions can include: blocking or holding a transaction for manual review; sending alerts to the account holder and the fraud detection team; locking an account until further verification is completed. Transactions with high-risk scores can be flagged for further review by human analysts. This helps to prioritise which cases need immediate attention.

While traditional rule engines use static rules, they can also be integrated with ML models to adapt to new fraud patterns (Gianini et al., 2020). As new types of fraud are identified, rules can be updated to improve detection accuracy. Rule engines help organisations to comply with regulatory requirements by ensuring consistent application of fraud detection rules. They also provide detailed logs and reports that can be used for audits and investigations. Rule engines can analyse data across multiple channels (e.g. online banking, mobile transactions, ATM withdrawals) to identify fraud patterns that span different platforms.

By fine-tuning rules and using risk-based scoring, rule engines help to reduce false positives – legitimate transactions that are incorrectly flagged as fraudulent. This improves customer experience and reduces the burden on fraud investigation teams.

Problem B. Gaming: NPC behaviour and game event triggers based on player actions

Rule engines help to manage **non-player character (NPC)** behaviour in video games (Uludağlı and Oğuz, 2023) by providing a framework for defining and automating responses based on various conditions and stimuli. They can define complex behavioural logic for NPCs; for instance, rules can dictate how an NPC should react when a player enters their field of vision, such as initiating dialogue, attacking or fleeing. They do so by relying on **behaviour trees (BTs)** (Colledanchise and Ögren, 2018; Iovino et al., 2022) created by rule engines. These trees outline possible actions an NPC can take based on environmental factors, player actions or internal states (e.g. health, morale).

Rule engines allow NPCs to have dynamic responses to changing game conditions. For example, if an NPC is allied with the player, rules might determine when they offer help or ask for assistance based on current game scenarios. Rule engines enable NPCs to adapt their behaviour over time. As the game progresses, NPCs can modify their responses based on new rules or updated conditions, creating a more immersive and evolving gameplay experience. By using a rule engine, developers ensure that NPC behaviour is consistent and predictable within the game's logic. This consistency helps to maintain a coherent game world where NPCs behave according to the established rules.

2. Problems that can be solved using deductive classifiers

Deductive classifiers rely on logical rules and reasoning, and are used in various applications where explicit knowledge and reasoning processes are crucial.

Problem A. Access control: determining user access levels based on roles and permissions

Deductive classifiers play a significant role in access control systems by utilising logical rules to determine access permissions (Servos and Osborn, 2017). This process can be based on user roles, for example a rule might state that only users with the 'admin' role can modify system settings. Deductive classifiers can also evaluate access based on a combination of user attributes (e.g. department, job title, clearance level) and resource attributes (e.g. classification level, ownership). Rules can specify complex conditions, such as allowing access only during certain times or from specific locations. Deductive classifiers can consider contextual information (time of day, location or device type) to make access decisions, for example a rule might allow access to sensitive information only during business hours and from secure devices.

Deductive classifiers can handle complex access control requirements across large and distributed systems. By using logical rules, they can efficiently manage access for a large number of users and resources without significant performance degradation. By applying strict logical rules, deductive classifiers help to mitigate risks by ensuring that only authorised users can access sensitive information and critical systems. This reduces the likelihood of data breaches and unauthorised access.

Deductive classifiers can provide detailed logs of access decisions, including which rules were applied and why access was granted or denied. This helps with auditing and ensuring compliance with regulatory requirements.

Problem B. Weather: classifying weather events into categories such as storms, heatwaves or floods

Deductive classifiers help with classifying weather events and conditions by applying predefined logical rules to meteorological data to identify and categorise various weather phenomena and events (Gupta, 2023). Weather events are often determined by analysing multiple parameters such as temperature, humidity, wind speed and atmospheric pressure. Deductive classifiers can logically combine these parameters to classify complex weather events, because accurate and reliable classification of weather conditions is crucial for making dependable weather predictions and issuing warnings.

Deductive classifiers can also identify patterns indicative of specific weather events. For example, a sequence of falling barometric pressure readings combined with increasing humidity and specific cloud types can be classified as a precursor to a storm.

When integrated with data from various weather sensors, such as satellites, radars and ground stations, deductive classifiers can apply logical rules to this data to help analyse the weather even more accurately to trigger alerts for severe weather conditions, which, in turn, can save lives.

3. Problems that can be solved using case-based reasoning

CBR is a problem-solving AI technique that relies on past experiences (or cases) to solve new problems. It works by retrieving and adapting solutions from previously solved cases that are similar to the current problem.

Problem A. Emergency response: handling emergency situations

CBR is highly valuable in emergency response situations because it provides a structured approach to managing complex and high-pressure scenarios. By following predefined procedures, emergency responders can act quickly, efficiently and consistently, which is crucial for saving lives and minimising damage (Bannour et al., 2021). CBR combined with ML involves creating emergency response systems that can make informed decisions by leveraging both predefined procedures and data-driven insights. This hybrid approach leverages the strengths of CBR (structured, rule-based approaches) with the adaptability and predictive power of ML.

AI-based systems can analyse real-time data from sensors, social media and other sources to detect potential emergencies; they evaluate the severity of incidents by comparing real-time data with historical cases, while triggering appropriate responses and defining resource requirements and allocation based on predefined severity levels. CBR systems are used to support emergency decision-makers in natural disasters (e.g. earthquakes, hurricanes, cyclones, typhoons) and man-made disasters (e.g. terrorism, war, cyber-attacks).

Problem B. Personalised marketing: creating marketing strategies tailored to individual customers

CBR is an effective approach for personalised marketing, as it uses past experiences to make decisions about current situations (Kwon and Sadeh, 2004; Amer, 2012). First of all, CBR can categorise customers into segments based on past cases by analysing their previous interactions and outcomes. Marketers can identify patterns, group customers and recommend products that similar consumers have purchased. CBR can also identify at-risk customers by comparing their current behaviour to past cases where customers were lost. Marketers can then implement retention strategies that were successful with them. Websites and apps can use CBR to predict users' behaviour and personalise content in real time. By analysing past cases of consumer interactions, the system can dynamically adjust the content shown to each user to enhance engagement or provide 'tailor-made' assistance. Furthermore, by examining cases where cross-selling and up-selling were successful, CBR can identify opportunities to suggest additional products or services based on their purchasing history and similarities to past cases.

Problem C. Recipe suggestions: recommending recipes based on available ingredients

Recommending recipes based on available ingredients using CBR starts with collecting a comprehensive database, where each recipe is considered a case. Every one of them includes details such as ingredients, cooking time, steps, cuisine type and user ratings. The cases are indexed, and their retrieval is based on the highest number of matching ingredients (Herrera et al., 2011). This involves searching for cases where the ingredient lists overlap significantly with the user's available ingredients. The cases are then adapted to the user's specific context (preferences, dietary restrictions, etc.). This may involve suggesting ingredient substitutions, if the user is missing some items, or simplifying steps based on the user's cooking skills and available tools. After the user tries the recommended recipe, feedback is gathered on the outcome and the database is continuously updated with new cases. This helps to improve the system's recommendations over time.

4. Problems that can be solved using procedural reasoning

Procedural reasoning is a methodical approach to problem-solving and decision-making, where a sequence of steps or procedures is followed to achieve a goal (Myers, 2023).

Problem A. Robotics and automation: performing complex tasks or operations on a cleaning robot

For a cleaning robot, the steps to achieve a goal might include identifying dirty areas, moving to those areas and performing cleaning actions. Algorithms are created that enable the robot to follow these procedures (Dellaert and Hutchinson, 2023). This includes path finding algorithms, object recognition algorithms and control algorithms for manipulating objects. It should be guaranteed that the robot's sensors and actuators can provide the necessary data and execute the required actions for each step in the procedure. The next step is to develop the control logic that guides the robot through the procedural steps, handling decision points and branching as necessary. For example, if an obstacle is detected, the robot follows a sub-procedure to navigate around it. Of course, the procedures need to thoroughly tested in various scenarios to ensure that the robot can reliably complete tasks. Then it can be confirmed that the procedures work correctly, and adjustments can be made as needed via feedback and new requirements.

Problem B. Aerospace: handling malfunctions

Procedural reasoning supports both goal-directed reasoning and the ability to react rapidly to unanticipated changes in the environment, which is very important for handling malfunctions. For example, a procedural reasoning system can be used for handling malfunctions on a space shuttle, including sensor faults, leaking components and regulator and jet **failures** (Georgeff and Ingrand, 1989).

Procedural reasoning provides a structured approach to diagnose and resolve issues effectively, recommend corrective actions and assist astronauts and ground control in real time. For known potential malfunctions (the ones obtained from the historical mission data), predefined procedures are established and rigorously trained. These procedures detail the specific steps to be taken in response to particular types of failures. Then procedural reasoning is used to analyse telemetry data from the shuttle to identify **anomalies** and malfunctions, diagnose problems and recommend corrective actions. For example, the National Aeronautics and Space Administration (NASA) has been exploring **autonomous systems** that incorporate AI to assist in spacecraft operations. Its Autonomous Systems and Operations project aims to develop AI tools that can perform real-time monitoring and provide procedural support during missions (Toro Medina et al., 2016).

5. Problems calling for the linear regression algorithm

Linear regression is a fundamental algorithm used for predicting continuous outcomes.

Problem A. Retail: estimating future sales

Linear regression is an effective approach to predict sales by modelling the relationship between sales and one or more predictor variables. For example, a linear regression can be used to predict monthly sales based on historical sales data, promotional activities, advertising expenses, seasonal trends and economic indicators (Takale et al., 2022). Linear regression also helps to assess the relationship between product pricing and sales volume. By analysing historical pricing data and corresponding sales, a company can identify the optimal price point that maximises revenue.

A linear regression can help to identify features influencing the sales by estimating the coefficients (weights) for each feature in the model. For example, in the automotive industry, vehicle sales are highly dependent on such characteristics as colour, brand, low mileage and age (Muti and Yildiz, 2023).

Sales forecasting allows a company to optimise inventory levels and to forecast future revenue over specific periods. It also supports strategic planning, allowing the company to adapt to market changes and stay ahead of competitors.

Problem B. Energy consumption: estimating future energy usage

The linear regression approach is used to estimate energy consumption and to predict future energy demand in the residential sector based on the available historical load data and external factors such as weather variables (temperature, humidity, rain, wind, etc.), holidays, festivals or events, tariff structures, time of the year, day of the week and hour of the day (Dhaval and Deshpande, 2020).

Linear regression models help to evaluate building energy performance by estimating the energy consumption in buildings, and are used in the early stages of the design when different building schemes and design concepts are being considered. These models incorporate factors such as building geometry (size, shape (H-shape, T-shape, rectangle, triangle, etc.) and construction), thermophysical properties of the materials used, intended use, occupancy and their behaviour, lighting, ventilation and heating/cooling systems along with their performance and operating schedules, weather conditions and climate zones (Mottahedi et al., 2015; Giuseppina and D'Amico, 2019). The analysis of energy models shows that there is a strong correlation between building shapes and the levels of energy consumption: T-shape buildings have the highest, while triangle buildings have the lowest total energy consumption. The occupant schedule, exterior wall absorbance, ceiling insulation, ceiling interior finish and ground floor construction also have the greatest influence on energy consumption.

6. Problems calling for the logistic regression algorithm

Logistic regression is widely used for binary classification problems with categorical output.

Problem A. Politics: predicting voting results

Logistic regression is a popular ML algorithm used in the context of voting behaviour analysis, where the goal is often to predict the probability of an individual or whole group voting for a particular candidate or political party, and also to predict feelings of winning and losing for different groups of voters based on various demographic, socioeconomic and attitudinal factors (Stiers et al., 2018). One of these logistic regression models helped to retrospectively analyse and predict the district majority vote in the Brexit referendum that took place in the United Kingdom (UK) in June 2016, when the people voted on whether the UK should remain a member of or leave the European Union (EU). The outcome of the model (remain or leave) is estimated at the district level based on the following predictor variables: median age for district; population characteristics (total population, population density, percentage of rural population, percentage of population with no religion, etc.); national identity in a given district; health level; educational level; unemployment rate; and income (Maconi, 2019). The resulting logistic regression model shows that age, education, national identity, political leaning, irreligion and unemployment have significant correlations with the majority Brexit outcome of a district. On the other hand, population, health and income variables do not have a significant effect.

Problem B. Sentiment analysis: classifying text as positive or negative

Logistic regression is an effective method for binary text classification tasks such as sentiment analysis. By converting textual data into numerical features, logistic regression models can predict the probability of a given text being positive or negative, which is relevant for the review and sentiment analysis including movie review analysis, product feedback classification, social media sentiment analysis and customer feedback interpretation. Review analysis is widely used by different companies and organisations because it helps to identify problems, manage reputation, improve customer service and increase sales.

To perform sentiment analysis for movie reviews, a logistic regression model is trained on the labelled reviews and learns to predict the probability of a review being positive or negative based on the selection and extraction features. There are two common selection features: bag of words (BoW), which is a vector representation of the text where each word is a feature, and its value could be the frequency of the word in the review; and information gain feature selection, which measures how much information about the presence and absence of a word plays a role in making the right classification decision in each class. A common extraction feature is term frequency – inverse document frequency (TF-IDF), which estimates how often a word appears in a document relative to how often it appears in the entire **corpus**. Given a new movie review, the ML model outputs a probability score. If the score is above a certain threshold (e.g. 0.5), the review is classified as positive; otherwise, it is classified as negative (Abimanyu et al., 2023).

Another example of a logistic regression model is classifying product reviews on e-commerce platforms, when you have a large dataset of product reviews from an e-commerce site and you want to predict whether a review is positive or negative based on the probability score. In this case, the target variable (satisfaction) can be estimated based on the word count (length of the review) and n-grams (sequences of n words, e.g. bigrams or trigrams) that capture common phrases associated with the positive or the negative sentiment (Das et al., 2023).

7. Problems that can be solved using SVM

SVMs are particularly useful in high-dimensional spaces and for problems where the decision boundary is complex.

Problem A. Astronomy: classifying celestial objects

Using SVM in astronomy has become an important tool for analysing and classifying astronomical data. It is used to classify stars, galaxies and quasars, based on their positions and photometric and spectral properties, by analysing the light emitted from these objects (Herle et al., 2020).

SVM algorithms can also be applied to analysing light curves obtained from telescopes such as the Schmidt telescope, which was embedded in the Hipparcos satellite, and to detect variable stars (Willemsen and Eyer, 2008), which are candidates to become supernovae stars, as well as double stars transiting exoplanets and other rare celestial objects. Researching variable stars is important because it helps scientists to understand stellar properties (mass, radius, temperature, internal and external structure, etc.) and the evolution of the universe.

The number of input parameters (features) being analysed and selected for the model training is more than 50 for each celestial object, which is why the problem is high-dimensional, and the SVM algorithm is preferable to be used because it can handle a large number of input features effectively.

Problem B. Handwriting recognition: digit classification in postal mail

SVMs are widely used for digit classification in postal mail systems, primarily for automating the process of sorting mail by recognising postal codes or ZIP codes written on envelopes to route mail efficiently, which is especially important for countries with high urban population density. For example, SVMs for digit classification are integrated into high-speed optical character recognition (OCR) systems used by China Post (Liu et al., 2014) and Bangladesh Post (Wen et al., 2007). These systems scan and process large volumes of mail quickly, segmenting the scanned envelope image into different fields to extract the postal code area, and classifying the digits using the SVM algorithm (Arun and Thomas, 2011).

The SVM model is trained on a diverse dataset containing digits written by different people to generalise well across various handwriting styles. One of the commonly used databases of handwritten digits is the MNIST database (Modified National Institute of Standards and Technology database), which is a dataset of 28x28 grayscale images (Deng, 2012). The SVM model might be trained on data augmented with synthetic variations typical of postal environments (e.g. slight rotations, scaling, distortions and noise) to simulate different handwriting scenarios. Before classification, pre-processing steps such as **binarisation**, noise removal and **normalisation** are applied to the digit images to enhance recognition accuracy (Babu and Reddy, 2016); this step helps in reducing the variability that SVM has to handle. Then the image of each digit is converted into a high-dimensional **feature vector** (the MNIST database's 28×28 sized image is flattened into a 784-dimensional vector), which is finally classified by the SVM model into one of the 10 digit classes (0–9). The recognised digits are then combined to form the complete postal code.

8. Problems that can be solved using the Bayesian model

Bayesian methods can be used to produce probabilistic predictions over several hypotheses rather than assigning each instance to a single hypothesis. These methods have shown their potential in predicting complex tasks with high accuracy, but significant computation costs are required to perform the Bayesian inferences.

Problem A. NLP: spam filtering

Bayesian models are effective tools in NLP due to their simplicity and ease of implementation. One of the problems associated with NLP and text classification is filtering spam emails. These emails become a huge problem for today's society because **phishing** attacks lead to extremely large losses of time and money for companies and individuals – more than 3 billion phishing emails are sent globally every day, and several billion dollars are lost every year (Palatty, 2025).

The most advanced and widely used method of ML for spam filtering is the Naive Bayes classification because of its efficiency, effectiveness and high accuracy. It is a filtering method based on content. The Bayesian model is trained on a labelled dataset of emails, where features are the frequency of individual words (**unigrams**) or phrases (**bigrams**, **trigrams**, etc.) extracted from email bodies, headers (sender, receiver and subject lines) and other metadata (Metsis et al., 2006; Lahkar and Singh, 2022; Cheng, 2023). For example, words and phrases such as 'prize', 'winner', 'notspam', 'cash bonus', 'free gift', 'call now', 'you have been selected' might be indicative of spam (Active Campaign, 2024). The Naive Bayes classifier calculates the probability of an email being spam based on the presence of these features.

Problem B. Sports analytics: predicting game outcomes and player performance

Using Bayesian models in sports analytics allows for effective probabilistic reasoning and decision-making based on uncertain and variable data. They can be used to predict the performance of teams and individual players by incorporating prior statistics and updating predictions with current season data, which helps in strategic planning and betting in such types of sports as basketball, football, baseball, tennis, swimming, marathon, triathlon, etc.

For example, a Bayesian hierarchical model helps to predict the outcome of tennis matches by estimating the probability of scoring a point on a serve for a given surface (clay, grass, etc.), tournament and match date (Ingram, 2019). Bayesian hierarchical models can also estimate the results of football matches by considering factors such as team strength, team form, psychological impact and fatigue (Constantinou et al., 2012). There are Bayesian networks predicting the results of football matches in terms of 'home win', 'away win' and 'draw', considering such attributes as home team, away team, their shots, shots on target, corners, fouls, yellow and red cards, half time and full time goals (Razali et al., 2017).

9. Problems calling for the decision tree algorithm

A decision tree is a model with a tree-like structure that divides the data recursively according to the values of its significant features (input variables) to predict an outcome. This algorithm is better suited for small datasets with fewer features and simpler interpretability.

Problem A. Flora and fauna: identifying animal habitat and vegetation types

Decision trees are widely used to identify the suitable habitat for animals. For example, a decision tree model can identify the habitat for brown bears by predicting whether particular pixels of geographic information system thematic layers of the entire study area are habitat or non-habitat based on the environmental parameters (forest patch size, percentage of the forest area, the most abundant tree species, relief roughness, etc.) and some human demographics parameters (density of population, average age and percentage of rural population) (Kobler and Adamic, 2000).

One more example of decision tree usage is identification of vegetation types. Topographical information and thematic mapper imagery of the basal area are utilised as input data. Vegetative classes are first derived from a **cluster** analysis of the field data. A decision tree algorithm is then applied to model the vegetation throughout the study area using independent variables such as thematic mapper bands, slope, aspect, elevation and landform. This model helps to identify such vegetation types as pinyon-juniper, ponderosa pine, mixed conifer, spruce- and deciduous-dominated mixes and openings (Joy et al., 2003).

Problem B. Environmental science: pollution level prediction

Industrialisation over the past decades has resulted in serious air quality problems in many developing countries. Analysing and predicting air quality is crucial because of the negative effects on human health and the environment; therefore, creating prediction models could offer an effective solution to current air quality challenges. For example, a decision tree model can utilise environmental data such as geographical information, emission sources and meteorological variables (daily maximum and minimum temperature, wind speed, relative humidity, total rainfall, etc.) to predict pollution levels: good, moderate, caution, unhealthy, very unhealthy and extremely unhealthy (Hussain et al., 2021).

There are decision tree models involving the use of historical data not only on weather conditions but also gas parameters such as carbon monoxide (CO), nitrogen dioxide (NO_2), sulphur dioxide (SO_2), particulate matter (PM10) and ozone concentration (O_3) to predict air pollution levels (Shaziayani et al., 2022).

10. Problems that can be solved using the random forest algorithm

Random forest algorithms are generally better suited for tasks involving high-dimensional data, noisy datasets, complex patterns, **imbalanced datasets** and when generalisation across different data distributions is crucial. They also provide more stable feature importance measures. These advantages make random forests a preferred choice over single decision trees in many real-world applications.

Problem A. Healthcare and medical informatics: disease diagnostics

A physician's diagnostic accuracy is highly dependent on a physician's experience, because it is based on their awareness of a variety of possible diagnoses. This task is similar to the classification problem, when the outcome is a disease and input features are clinical symptoms. Since it is possible to acquire and digitally store a large amount of medical information, different ML models can be used for medical data processing, diagnosing diseases and helping in clinical decision-making. Medical data classification is one of the most complex and challenging tasks in medical informatics. Medical prediction models are often intricate due to the interaction of many variables, which, in turn, imposes restrictions on the algorithms. It has been shown that random forests in clinical decision-making offer better performance than ML models such as decision trees, SVMs, Bayesian networks and others (Alam et al., 2019). For example, decision trees tend to overfit to the training data, particularly when there are complex patterns or interactions. Random forests, by averaging multiple trees, provide a more generalisable model, reducing overfitting (see Section 3.5 on overfitting and underfitting).

Random forest algorithms make accurate predictions for different diseases (diabetes, hepatitis, breast cancer, heart diseases, Parkinson's disease, hepatocellular carcinoma, etc.) based on predictor variables that include the patient's age, sex, number of pregnancies, body mass index, different blood parameters, histology and so on (Alam et al., 2019; Pal and Parija, 2021).

Problem B. Finance and banking: stock price prediction

The random forest algorithm is also one of the most popular ML methods used in the financial markets to build prediction models for stock prices. Stock price forecasting depends on a wide range of factors, making manual analysis and prediction impossible, which is why ML is widely used to solve this problem. There are different ML models making predictions for stock price values and directions based on such technical indicators as open, close, high and low price, volume, commodity channel index, relative strength index, rate of change, disparity and others (Manojlovic and Stajduhar, 2015). It was shown that random forest algorithms yield the best prediction results and higher performance in long-term trading, they are faster and perform well on noisy financial data containing **outliers**. That is the reason why a decision tree model is not so effective in financial forecasting; a decision tree can be highly sensitive to noise, leading to poor generalisation. By constructing multiple trees and averaging their predictions, random forests reduce the impact of noise and outliers, which results in more robust models (Wu, 2023).

11. Problems that can be solved using the K-means clustering algorithm

K-means clustering is a versatile and widely used algorithm for unsupervised learning, where the goal is to partition a set of data points with numeric attributes into distinct clusters based on their similarity. This algorithm helps organisations and researchers to uncover patterns and make data-driven decisions.

Problem A. Marketing: customer segmentation

K-means clustering is a flexible and powerful tool for a wide range of applications including customer segmentation. In marketing, businesses often use K-means clustering to divide their customers into groups based on shared characteristics. By identifying distinct customer groups, companies can tailor their marketing strategies to target each segment more effectively, improve customer service and develop appropriate products and services.

For example, a K-means clustering model for a shopping centre store can divide customers into groups by analysing their gender, age, yearly income and purchase score (Kilari et al., 2022). The algorithm uses centroids (the central points of each cluster) and distance **metrics** to assign customers to the appropriate clusters. It estimates that shopping centre customers can be divided into five groups depending on their yearly earnings and spending habits, and there are two targeted groups between them: clients with high income-high spending score, and with low income-high spending score. This cluster analysis prompts businesses to apply the following marketing methods to keep their target clients: they offer a great variety of things to the clients with high income and high spending score, and also provide discounts and offers on a frequent basis to the clients with low income and high spending score, so they will be tempted to spend more money.

Problem B. Environmental protection: identification of fire-prone areas

K-means clustering can be effectively used to identify fire-prone areas by analysing various environmental and geographical factors that contribute to the risk of wildfires, the early detection of which allows for proactive measures to be taken to prevent catastrophic consequences, for example a K-means clustering algorithm can utilise hotspots data monitored by remote sensing satellites (Khairani and Sutoyo, 2020). Hotspots are areas that have a relatively higher surface temperature compared to what surrounds them. If the temperature in an area exceeds a certain temperature threshold, this area is labelled as a fire. In other words, if we imagine that the whole monitored geographical area is an image divided into pixels, hotspots are the results of detection of forest or land fires at certain pixels. A K-means clustering model allows us to analyse hotspots data and group different geographical fields into clusters. Each cluster represents a level of fire risk and can be visualised on a map using colour coding. This helps to develop targeted fire prevention and response strategies based on the identified clusters and allows us to reduce the impact of wildfires.

12. Problems calling for the DBSCAN clustering algorithm

DBSCAN is a clustering algorithm that has the capability to process very large databases and does not require specification of the number of clusters beforehand (unlike K-means clustering, which does require specifying the number of clusters) and that makes it ideal for a variety of real-world applications. DBSCAN is resistant to noise and can identify outliers as separate from the main clusters. Unlike K-means clustering, DBSCAN does not assume that clusters are spherical, which makes it effective in identifying clusters of various shapes and densities.

Problem A. Finance and banking: fraud detection

DBSCAN clustering is a powerful tool for detecting fraudulent transactions by identifying outliers and anomalies in transaction data that are significantly different from normal transactions. Detecting fraudulent transactions is essential for financial institutions, businesses and consumers, because it helps to prevent financial losses, maintain customer trust and confidence, preserve reputation and ensure the overall stability of financial systems. For example, DBSCAN clustering can detect fraudulent credit card transactions based on the analysis of the transaction amount, billing address, shipping address and inter-transaction time gap (Panigrahi et al., 2009). The corresponding model identifies clusters of normal behaviour and isolates potential failures as outliers which do not belong to any cluster. The transaction amount can be used as the attribute for outliers.

Clustering models with DBSCAN can also help to identify potentially fraudulent wire transfers of an insurance company and to capture their hidden characteristics. Clustering analysis has been carried out for such variables of insurance payments to clients as wire ID, amount, initiation and effective dates, account number of a line of business, payee ID, month and day of initiation, month and day of the effective date, day of initiation date (Monday, Tuesday, Wednesday, Thursday, Friday and non-working days such as Saturday, Sunday and holidays) and day of the effective date (Kim and Vasarhelyi, 2023). This analysis has shown an insignificant dependency of fraudulent activity at day of month for both initiation and effective date, and vice versa – a significant dependency at day of both initiation and effective date.

Problem B. Bioinformatics: genomic data analysis

DBSCAN can also be effectively applied to gene expression data for various biological insights. By uncovering meaningful patterns in gene expression, DBSCAN can contribute to our understanding of biological processes, disease mechanisms and therapeutic responses.

Gene expression data typically involves measurements of the activity (expression levels) of thousands of genes under different conditions or in different samples. It is usually presented in the form of a matrix, where rows represent individual genes, columns represent different experimental conditions or time points and values in the matrix are the expression levels of genes under those specific conditions (Salman, 2023). DBSCAN is used to analyse this expression matrix and to identify clusters of genes with similar expression patterns across different conditions, making it easier to pick out genes with related functions and regulations. These co-expressed genes may be involved in similar biological processes or pathways. For instance, samples from healthy tissues are clustered separately from cancerous tissues, and different cancer subtypes can also be identified based on their gene expression profiles. If patterns already exist, comparisons can also be done to find out genes whose expression fits a specific desired arrangement. In pharmacogenetics, DBSCAN can be used to cluster genes that show similar expression changes in response to drug treatment, aiding in the discovery of biomarkers for drug efficacy or toxicity and helping to tackle diseases such as different types of cancer, malaria, asthma and tuberculosis (Oyelade et al., 2016).

13. Problems that require association algorithms

Association algorithms are powerful tools in ML for discovering hidden patterns, relationships and **trends in data**. Their ability to identify meaningful co-occurrences makes them invaluable in providing insights that lead to more effective decision-making, process optimisation and enhanced customer experiences.

Problem A. Software testing: defect analysis

Association algorithms are effectively used for the analysis of historical bug reports and identification of patterns or correlations between their various attributes, which is crucial for effective bug management and prioritisation in large software projects. For example, association rules can identify frequent itemsets by capturing such essential issue attributes as author, assignee, status, priority, resolution, subject, labels, description, issue text, start and due dates. This helps to find frequent submitters and associated issue types, identify author roles more likely to submit certain issues, find associations between issue timings, identify frequent topics or keywords in issues by processing the text fields and extracting meaningful keywords or phrases, find common combinations of labels and discover frequent label sets in issues, identify paths from issue creation to resolution, find associations between milestones and issue types, associate issues with assignees' expertise areas, identify patterns in which issues tend to be locked, and others (Eldesouky and Raslan, 2024).

Analysis of bug descriptions, keywords and existing labels by means of the association algorithms reveals strong predictors among labels; indicating which labels commonly co-occur helps with label recommendation for new bug reports and issue prioritisation tasks.

Problem B. Education: analysis of students' test scores

Association rules can be applied to the analysis of students' test scores to uncover patterns and relationships between different aspects of their performance. These patterns enable teachers and administrators to understand the factors influencing student achievement, offering crucial decision support for both teaching and student management. This insight empowers educators to enhance teaching strategies and ultimately improve overall teaching quality.

The dataset used to train an association model that examines student performance typically consists of students' test scores across multiple attributes such as gender, anxiety levels, subject difficulty, learning attitude and class seating (Zheng and Zhang, 2016). Association rules show that, if the student is not nervous, has the right attitude and is seated in the first three rows, test scores are high.

Association rules are also used in subject mastery analysis. They help to reveal hidden relationships between the student achievements in different courses and find out the correlation between the courses and the factors that lead to the high or low grades. For example, good grades in English are helpful for some professional courses, and the foundation of discrete mathematics is important for some basic professional courses (e.g. programming language and introduction of computer science: Wu and Zeng, 2019). The observation that students who excel in one course often perform well in others suggests that these subjects require similar skills. Therefore, enhancing skills in the first course could lead to improved performance across the related courses.

14. Problems that can be solved using reinforcement learning

Reinforcement learning helps to solve complex, dynamic problems where the optimal solution is not known in advance and must be discovered through interaction with the environment to maximise cumulative rewards.

Problem A. Robotics: robotic manipulation

Reinforcement learning is used to teach robots and multi-robot systems to perform complex tasks such as manipulating objects of varying shapes, weights and textures (Orr and Dutta, 2023). Robotic manipulation tasks typically include actions such as picking and placing objects, tightening a bolt, stacking blocks, assembling components or handling tools, all of which require the robot to learn complex motor skills and adapt to varying conditions.

To perform reinforcement learning, the **state space**, the **action space** and the reward function should be identified. The state space represents all possible states the robot can be in. This might include the robot's joint angles, end-effector position, object positions and velocities. The action space describes all the actions the robot can take, be they discrete (move left, right, up, down) or continuous (e.g. apply a certain torque or force). The reward function provides feedback to the robot based on its actions and should stimulate the robot to complete the task successfully. The design of the reward function is task-specific and requires careful consideration to ensure that the robot learns the desired behaviour. The reward function typically consists of positive rewards (e.g. positive integer large-value scores) for achieving goals, intermediate rewards for progress and penalties (or negative rewards) for undesired actions or states.

For example, reinforcement learning can be applied to train a robot to return a table tennis ball over the net. In this case, the robot makes observations of dynamic variables specifying ball position and its velocity and the internal dynamics of the joint position and velocity (Kober et al., 2013). This provides complete statistics for predicting future observations. The actions available to the robot are the torque sent to motors and the desired accelerations sent to an inverse dynamics control system. A function that generates the motor commands (the actions) based on the incoming ball and current internal arm observations (the state) is a **policy** (Carr, 2024). The reinforcement learning algorithm is used to find a policy that optimises the long-term sum of rewards. The reward function in this example is based on the success of the hits as well as secondary criteria such as energy consumption. The robot starts with random or simple actions and improves over time by receiving rewards and penalties. The learning algorithm updates the policy based on this feedback.

Problem B. Robotics: autonomous driving

Reinforcement learning plays a significant role in developing autonomous driving systems by allowing vehicles to learn complex driving behaviours through interaction with their environment. This process involves training an agent (the **autonomous vehicle**) to make decisions such as staying in a lane, lane changing, overtaking a static and a moving vehicle and collision avoidance (Voogd et al., 2023; Zhang et al., 2023).

The reward function guides the learning process by rewarding or penalising the agent based on its actions, and ensures it learns to drive safely, efficiently and with comfort. There are different categories of reward functions – safety, progress, comfort, traffic rules conformance – related to model performance, etc. (Abouelazm et al., 2024).

For instance, safety-oriented rewards are substantial for avoiding collisions and maintaining safe distances from other vehicles, whereas they are smaller for staying in the correct lane and obeying traffic signals. Safety-oriented penalties are given for collisions and unsafe manoeuvres. Comfort-oriented rewards are for smooth driving, avoiding sudden stops and gentle turns to improve passenger comfort, and corresponding penalties are given for unnecessary braking, sharp turns or idling.

To perform reinforcement learning, the state space and the action space should also be defined. The state space is described by sensor data (e.g. positions of other vehicles, pedestrians, obstacles and road boundaries provided by radar, cameras and light detection and ranging, LiDAR). LiDAR is a detection system that works on the principle of radar, but uses light from a laser, vehicle dynamics (speed, acceleration, steering angle) and environmental conditions (weather, road conditions, traffic signals). The action space defines what actions the vehicle can take: accelerate, brake or steer (Ashwin and Raj, 2023) to achieve its goal, such as keeping in a lane while driving on the motorway, adjusting speed according to traffic, executing safe lane changes and handling intersections, pedestrians and cyclists, etc.

15. Problems that can be solved using genetic algorithms

Genetic algorithms are particularly useful for optimisation and search tasks when the solution space is large, complex or poorly understood. These algorithms work with a set of potential solutions. Similar to the concept of population, each solution corresponds to an individual (chromosome) within the population and a set of parameters called genes defines characteristics of the solution. Highly valued individuals have a better chance to be selected to the new generation of the population. By maintaining a population of different individuals, the genetic algorithm carries out a multi-directional search and also knowledge interchange among the individuals.

Problem A. Robotics: path planning

An important problem that needs to be solved for robotic systems and autonomous vehicles is to find the optimal path in navigation or logistics scenarios, i.e. to find a valid and feasible path between two positions while avoiding obstacles and optimising some criteria such as distance, path safety, energy consumption and time spent.

A potential solution of the path planning problem is a set of ordered positions, starting from the first one and ending at the target one. All the positions should not match the obstacles. The number of intermediate positions in the set can vary. The environment can be represented by the occupancy grid, which is the 2D matrix where each position has two likely values: 0 for free cells, and 1 for occupied ones. An appropriate solution is a path (set of positions) from the starting point to the target point crossing a set of free positions (Lamini et al., 2018).

At first, the initial population of random valid paths (chromosomes) is generated. The fitness function evaluates how well each chromosome is, based on the optimisation objective. Then one or several operations should be implemented.

These operations include mutation, crossover and selection. During the selection, pairs of chromosomes from the population are chosen to serve as parents for the next generation. One of the crossover methods is to take a segment from one parent (a subset of positions) and insert it in the offspring, preserving the order of positions. Mutation suggests that an offspring is created by making small changes in the initial chromosome. A simple mutation might swap two positions in the path. The next step is to replace the old population with the new generation of the offspring and evaluate the fitness of the new population. You can either completely replace the old population or use a strategy that combines the old and the new chromosomes. The genetic algorithm stops when a predefined condition is met, for example reaching a desired fitness level, exceeding a specified number of iterations or no significant improvement in the best solution for several generations. Once the algorithm terminates, the best chromosome from the population is selected as the optimised path (Katoch et al., 2020).

Problem B. Art and design: generating pictures

Genetic algorithms are widely used in picture design because they yield random yet attractive results. However, there is a challenge concerning the fitness function, or the criteria, for the results, since the concept of aesthetic and tastes is subjective and hard to measure. Therefore, there are two possible approaches. The first one is to use a human for evaluation to direct the selection and evolution. The second approach is to define the fitness function, based on the fundamentals of art and design, to automate the selection and evolution without the need for human input. For example, such aspects of art as symmetry, colour, shade and shape relate to the designs or/and the preferences of the user and can be utilised as the criterion for evaluation. The principles of balance (the positioning of the elements), pattern (the repetition of elements) and proportion (the relative sizes of the elements) can also be taken into account (House and Agah, 2015). Resemblance to a target image can also be used to determine the fitness function when a genetic algorithm aids to reconstruct an image.

A genetic algorithm begins with a population of pictures (or pieces of art) where each individual picture corresponds to a unique chromosome. This chromosome could be a string of parameters that define the visual elements of art, such as shapes, colours, sizes, positions, etc. Then the algorithm modifies, recombines and chooses images repeatedly according to predetermined criteria that determine the fitness. This could be done as a selection (choose art pieces to be 'parents' for the next generation based on their fitness scores), crossover (create new art pieces by combining the chromosomes of two parent art pieces) and mutation (randomly alter parts of the chromosomes to introduce variation). The algorithm can stop after a fixed number of generations, or when the art pieces reach a certain fitness level, or when the population stabilises (there is a little change between generations).

Genetic algorithms are used to create visually attractive images, optimise effects on photos, synthesise realistic textures, reconstruct images and automatically generate designs (Yadav, 2024).

16. Problems that require neural networks

Neural networks are better suited for complex problems with unstructured data such as images and texts, but they can also be used to predict simple data types such as binary, numeric and categorical outcomes and to handle multiclass outcomes. Neural networks can approximate all types of non-linear relationships between variables, and detect and account for interactions between multiple features that are not specified in the input data. At the same time, there are some disadvantages for using neural networks in ML models. They require a lot of training data, have many hyperparameters that need to be tuned, are very computationally intensive and require long training times or large amounts of resources. Neural networks are difficult to explain and have a reputation for being '**black box**' models (Reynolds et al., 2018; Ellis, 2022).

Problem A. NLP: machine translation

The automatic translation of written text from one natural language to another is a problem that can be solved by implementing a **neural machine translation** that uses an artificial neural network to predict the likelihood of a sequence of words, typically modelling entire sentences in a single integrated model (Stahlberg, 2020). To train the model, a dataset containing pairs of sentences is needed where one sentence is in the source language and the other is in the target language. There are several model architectures widely used in neural machine translation, and the standard one is the encoder-decoder architecture (Datta et al., 2020). This architecture involves two connected neural networks: an encoder and a decoder. The encoder processes the input data by splitting the input sentence into individual words (tokens) and converting each token into a dense vector (**embedding**). These embeddings represent the semantic meaning of the words. The position of each word in the sentence and the importance of different words (their weights) are taken into account. In other words, the initial sentence is transformed into a fixed-length numerical representation, which is subsequently decoded by the decoder to generate the desired output sequence.

Problem B. Computer vision: object detection

Object detection is a crucial task in computer vision, with significant importance across various fields and applications such as autonomous vehicles and robotics, surveillance systems, medical imaging and others. Its main goal is to identify and precisely estimate the class and location of objects contained in an image or video, and this task is not simple since the image usually contains several objects of different categories. Neural network models play a key role in solving object detection tasks because they can provide vital information for the semantic understanding of images and videos (Amjoud and Amrouch, 2023). Object detection with a neural network can be implemented as a one-stage or two-stage algorithm (Vasanthi and Mohan, 2024). To train both types of algorithms, the preliminary prepared dataset of annotated images is needed and split into training and validation datasets. For example, this dataset can consist of two subfolders: one is for the images, and the other is for the corresponding **annotation** text files where the records about each object that exist in the appropriate image are supplemented with information about its position and size. During the training phase, these images are passed through the model, which generates feature maps summarising the important aspects of the images, and the potential regions (**bounding boxes**) of all detected objects are generated (Murrugarra-Llerena et al., 2022). These regions are then passed to the classification stage, where the algorithm uses a neural network classifier to determine the objects in each region. The outputs are then compared with correct results from annotation files for the images, and model parameters are optimised if needed. For the one-stage object detection algorithm, a single neural network is used for both the region proposal and the classification stages. For the two-stage object detection algorithm, two different neural networks are used.

17. Problems that require fuzzy logic

Fuzzy logic is designed to work with imprecise and vague information, making it suitable for real-world applications where exact data is often unavailable. It mimics human reasoning more closely than binary logic, allowing for more intuitive decision-making processes.

Problem A. Control systems: controllers for washing machines

Fuzzy logic is widely used in washing machines to enhance their performance and adaptability and to lower the cost. By employing fuzzy logic, washing machines can handle different loads, various fabric types and degrees of dirtiness more effectively predicting wash time, revolutions per minute, drying time, temperature and wash quality (Masood, 2017; Raja and Ramathilagam, 2021). Fuzzy logic controllers can correct the direction of spin, determine if soap and water need to be added and so on.

The conditions inside the washing machine are monitored by sensors and transformed into the input parameter values, which are then converted into corresponding fuzzy-set values by the process of fuzzification. The fuzzified input parameters are evaluated using 'if-then' rules and output parameters are derived, so washing machine operations are dynamically adjusted to optimise washing performance, energy consumption water usage, etc.

Problem B. Finance and banking: assessing the creditworthiness of consumers

To reduce the risk of financial losses and to determine appropriate interest rates, it is crucial for banks to assess the creditworthiness of consumers. Fuzzy logic helps to solve this problem and improve efficiency in forecasting the probability of on-time repayment of granted credits. In the fuzzy logic model, consumers are characterised by demographic and financial variables including age, education level, marital status, number of children in the household, monthly income, tenure and type of employment, car and property ownership values, as well as other asset valuations. A certain point is set to each of these variables, and the credit risk of the applicant is evaluated based on the 'if-then' rules. For example, the fuzzy logic model can consist of four different rule blocks (Korol, 2012). The first block evaluates the consumer's demographic variables (age, education level, marital status, number of children in household). The second block estimates the consumer's financial condition variables (monthly income, the length of employment, type of employment contract). The third block analyses the financial strength of the customer and the security for the granted credit (value of owned car, net value of owned apartment/house, value of other assets). The fourth block uses as entry variables the forecasted outputs of the three previous blocks and outputs the variable representing a forecast of the financial situation of an audited consumer's final credit score. This variable ranges from 0 to 1, and there are three possible risk levels depending on its value: high, medium and low.

18. Problems that can be solved using search algorithms

In the context of AI, search algorithms provide a structured way to find information, solutions or specific data in large or complex datasets. In the digital age, search engines have become an integral part of our daily lives, helping us to find relevant documents, web pages, images, videos or other types of content based on our queries. AI-powered search algorithms revolutionise searching by making it faster, more accurate and context aware, significantly improving the efficiency and effectiveness of information retrieval across various domains.

Problem A. Search engines: document search and review

The document search AI algorithms tend to discover meaningful content, and are always based on some sort of NLP algorithm. This involves understanding the intent behind the user's query, identifying key terms and even understanding synonyms, context and grammatical structures. AI can expand the query by including synonyms or related terms to broaden the search and improve the chances of finding relevant documents. Before the search, documents are pre-processed and transformed into numeric vectors (embeddings) using techniques such as TF-IDF to make the content of the documents acceptable for the AI processing (Minnie and Srinivasan, 2011). This step is named **data encoding**. AI-powered search understands the meaning behind words and phrases. Models such as **bidirectional encoder representations from transformers (BERT)** (Devlin et al., 2019) are used to assess the semantic relevance of documents to the query (Topal et al., 2021). This allows the algorithm to find documents that are contextually similar, even if they do not contain the exact keywords. Once relevant documents are identified, they are ranked based on relevance scores. AI models consider various factors such as the context of the query, document length, term frequency and the relationships between terms to determine the most relevant documents. AI can tailor search results based on user history, preferences and behaviour patterns, providing a more personalised search experience. Once the relevant documents are identified and ranked, they are retrieved and presented to the user. The searching results can be filtered by AI to exclude irrelevant information or prioritise certain types of documents.

Problem B. Search engines: image search

AI-powered image search is implemented similar to a document search, but instead of the text encoding, there is image encoding, with the subsequent search for those images whose embeddings match the embedding of the user's search query (Zhai et al., 2019).

19. Problems that require recommendation systems

AI recommendation systems are powerful tools that provide personalised content, products or services to users based on their preferences and behaviour.

Problem A. Social media: content feeds and friend suggestions

Recommendation systems play a significant role in social networks such as Facebook, LinkedIn, Instagram, X (formerly known as Twitter), etc., curating users' feeds, prioritising posts, ads and other content that is most relevant to users based on their interactions, likes and follows. The combination of the information derived from the posts' textual content, deep emotion analysis and a multi-source view with the analysis of hyperlinks, profile pages and other related data is an important basis for the functioning of these systems. Recommendation systems can also suggest connections or friends by analysing users' existing networks and identifying potential new connections (Jiang et al., 2020). Users' historical information, hobbies and other characteristics can also be taken into account to achieve personalised recommendations. Some algorithms can provide item recommendations to users that are liked by similar currently active users or similar selected users who liked the item in the past. Prediction for the active user is calculated by a weighted average of the ratings of the selected users (Anandhan et al., 2018).

Problem B. Finance and banking: investment recommendations

AI is widely used to recommend investment portfolios based on an individual's financial goals, risk tolerance and market conditions. Generally, these financial recommendation systems collect and systematise expert knowledge and decision-making. They also involve highly technical analysis components that seek insight from large datasets such as trading price data of single stocks, investment portfolios, transactions and timing of trades. Additionally, these systems can use ranking and sorting methods to produce personalised recommendations based on user specifications, training data, users' previous trading strategies and currently available market data (Vidler, 2022; Sadriu, 2023). AI can utilise public tweets, posts and blog articles that mention stocks, and collect investment research from multiple broker sites to generate recommendations (Tapjinda et al., 2015).

Quick questions

Question 1.2

Which of the following options refers to the reasoning technique used to implement AI? Select ONE option.

    A. genetic algorithm

    B. rule engine

    C. decision tree algorithm

    D. fuzzy logic

Question 1.3

As a data scientist, you have received the results given in Figure 1.6 while analysing customer data. What type of algorithm have you implemented in your ML model? Select ONE option.

    A. association algorithm

    B. support vector machine

    C. clustering algorithm

    D. neural network

Figure 1.6 The ML model output results

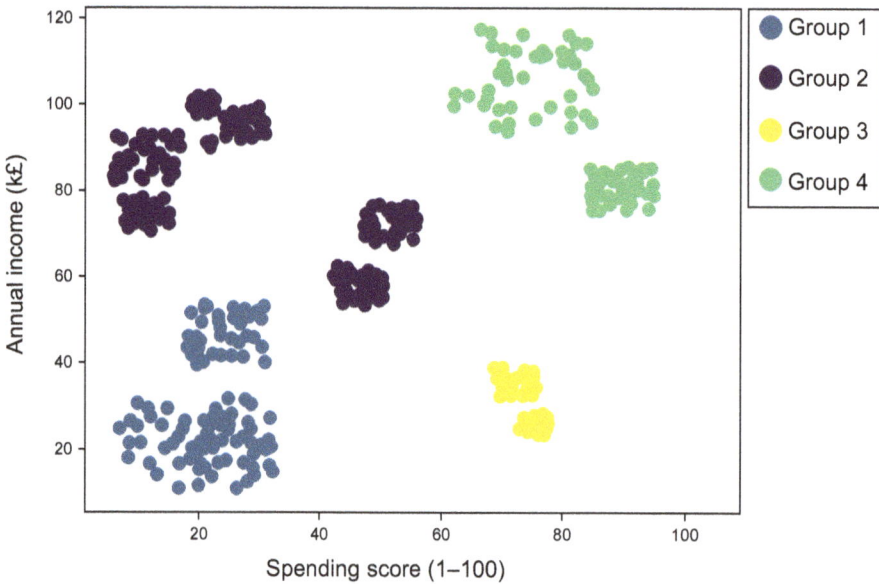

1.5 AI DEVELOPMENT FRAMEWORKS

AI was once limited to a close community of leading researchers, but times have changed and, due to the development of various libraries and frameworks, it has become more user-friendly, with more and more people learning to use and apply it in real-world projects. In essence, access to **AI frameworks** is no longer confined to the realms of the exceptionally talented or academically inclined. There are many AI development frameworks available, some of which are focused on specific domains. For example, the following frameworks could be considered as some of the most popular when the ISTQB CT-AI syllabus was published (Dussa-Zieger et al., 2021):

- Apache MxNet: a deep learning open-source framework used for Amazon Web Services (AWS) (The Apache Software Foundation, 2025);
- Microsoft Cognitive Toolkit (CNTK): a deep learning open-source toolkit (learn. microsoft, 2025);
- **IBM** Watson Studio: a suite of tools that support the development of AI solutions (IBM, 2025b);
- TensorFlow: an open-source **ML framework** based on data flow graphs for **scalable ML**, provided by Google (TensorFlow, 2025);
- Keras: a high-level open-source **application programming interface (API)** written in the Python language, capable of running on top of TensorFlow and CNTK (Keras, 2025);
- PyTorch: an open-source ML library operated by Facebook and used for apps applying image processing and NLP – support is provided for both Python and C++ interfaces (PyTorch, 2025);
- Scikit-learn: an open-source ML library for the Python programming language (Scikit-learn, 2025).

Framework selection may also depend on particular aspects such as the programming language and its ease of use. For example, if you use Python, then you might also be interested in Keras, Pytorch and TensorFlow for neural network implementation or Scikit-learn for classical ML algorithms. The frameworks support a range of activities, such as data preparation, algorithm selection and compilation of models to run on various processors, such as **central processing units (CPUs)**, **graphical processing units (GPUs)** or cloud **tensor processing units (TPUs)**.

1.6 HARDWARE FOR AI-BASED SYSTEMS

AI requires appropriate hardware. For instance, a model that performs speech recognition may run on a low-end smartphone, although access to **cloud computing** (Kumar and Goudar, 2012) may be needed to train it. A common approach is to train the model in the cloud and then deploy it to the host device.

ML typically benefits from hardware that supports the following attributes:

- low-precision arithmetic (for example, using 8 instead of 32 bits is sufficient for ML);

- the ability to work with large data structures;
- massively parallel processing.

General-purpose CPUs with a small number of cores are optimised for low-latency tasks that require single-threaded performance, such as running operating systems, web browsing or office applications. As a result, their architecture is less efficient for training and running ML models when compared to GPUs, which have thousands of cores and are designed to perform massively parallel but relatively simple processing of images. Consequently, GPUs typically outperform CPUs for ML applications, even though CPUs typically have faster clock speeds. For small-scale ML work, GPUs generally offer the best option.

TPU is a specialised processor developed by Google specifically to perform highly optimised operations on tensors, which are multidimensional arrays used in deep learning models. They assure significant performance advantages over CPUs and GPUs for ML tasks.

Some hardware is specially intended for AI, such as purpose-built **application-specific integrated circuits (ASICs)** (Shi, 2024) and **system on a chip (SoC)** (Chelladurai et al., 2023), as shown in Figure 1.7. These AI-specific solutions have multiple cores, special data management and the ability to perform in-memory processing. They are most suitable for **edge computing**, while the training of an ML model is done in the cloud.

Hardware with specific AI architectures is currently being researched and developed. This includes **neuromorphic processors**, which are designed to mimic the biological neurons of the human brain and do not use the traditional **von Neumann architecture**.

Figure 1.7 Examples of hardware for AI-based systems

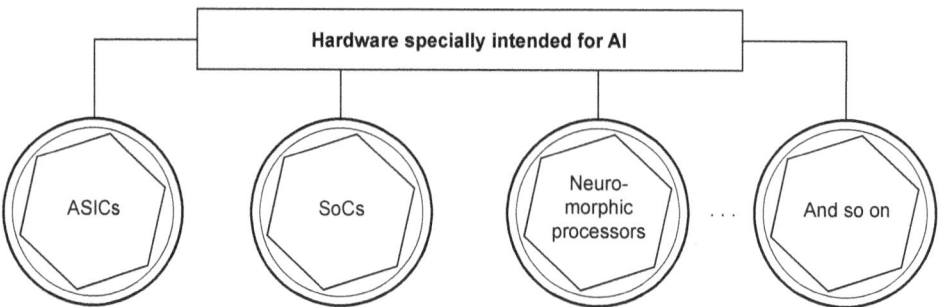

Examples of AI hardware providers and their processors include (Dussa-Zieger et al., 2021):

- NVIDIA: they provide a range of GPUs and AI-specific processors, such as the Volta (NVIDIA, 2025).
- Google: they have developed ASICs for both training and inferencing. Google TPUs can be accessed by users on the Google Cloud (Google Cloud, 2025b), whereas the Edge TPU (Coral, 2025) is a purpose-built ASIC designed to run AI on individual devices.

- Intel®: they provide Core™ Ultra and Xeon® processors, which include **neural processing units (NPUs)** (Lee, 2021) as a key component, designed to handle AI and ML tasks with unparalleled speed and efficiency. Core Ultra processors have powered the world's first AI personal computers, produced by such companies as Acer and Microsoft. Intel also produces Movidius™ Myriad™ **vision processing units (VPUs)** (Rivas-Gomez et al., 2018) for inferencing in computer vision and neural network applications.

- Mobileye™: they produce the EyeQ™ family of SoC devices to support complex and computationally intense vision processing to be used in vehicles (Mobileye, 2025).

- Huawei: their Kirin 970 chip was the world's first that has a built-in NPU for AI computing (HiSilicon Technologies, 2025).

- Apple: they produced the Bionic chip, which was the first one for on-device AI in iPhones (Sarkar, 2018).

Quick questions

Question 1.4

Which of the following examples of hardware is LESS efficient for training and running ML models? Select ONE option.

    A. TPU
    B. NPU
    C. CPU
    D. GPU

1.7 AI AS A SERVICE (AIaaS)

AI components, such as ML models, can be created within an organisation, downloaded from a third party or used as a service, although a hybrid approach is also possible. When ML is used as a service, access to an ML model is provided over the web in order to perform data preparation, model training, evaluation, tuning, testing and deployment. Third-party providers can offer specific AI services, such as facial and speech recognition. This allows individuals and organisations to implement AI using cloud-based services even with insufficient resources. In addition, these ML models are likely to have been trained on a larger, more diverse dataset available for those who have recently moved into the AI market.

1.7.1 Contracts for AI as a service

The contracts for these AI services are similar to non-AI cloud-based **software as a service (SaaS)** (Godse and Mulik, 2009). An AIaaS contract usually contains a **service-level agreement (SLA)** that defines availability and security commitments (Wu et al., 2015). It covers the service uptime and a response time to fix defects, but rarely defines ML functional performance metrics (see Chapter 5). The payment is subscription based, and if the contracted availability and/or response times are not met, then the service provider could offer credits for future services. Other than that, most AIaaS contracts provide limited liability, thus limiting it to relatively low-risk applications, but, on the other hand, services often come with an initial free trial period.

1.7.2 AIaaS examples

The following examples of AIaaS could be considered as some of the most popular when the ISTQB CT-AI syllabus was published (Dussa-Zieger et al., 2021):

- IBM Watsonx Assistant: this is an AI **chatbot** priced according to the number of monthly active users (IBM, 2025c).

- Google Cloud AI and ML products: these provide different products including speech-to-text (Google Cloud, 2025d) and text-to-speech converters (Google Cloud, 2025e), translation AI (Google, 2025), AI used for video analysis (Google Cloud, 2025a), AI with document-based form parser and document OCR (Google Cloud, 2025c) and others. Prices depend on the length of video and audio, the number of characters or the number of pages sent for processing per month.

- Amazon CodeGuru: this provides ML Java™ and Python code reviews supplying developers with recommendations. Prices are based on the number of lines of source code analysed (Amazon Web Services, 2025a).

- Microsoft Azure AI Search: this provides AI cloud search. Prices are based on search units defined in terms of the storage and throughput (Microsoft Azure, 2025).

Quick questions

Question 1.5

Which of the following statements is LESS likely to be describing a system that includes the use of AIaaS? Select ONE option.

A. Using Microsoft Azure AI Vision as a unified service that offers innovative computer vision capabilities.

B. Using Oracle Cloud Infrastructure capabilities to automate email tasks with real-time categorisation, sentiment analysis and instant replies for an efficient workflow.

C. Using Google's speech-to-text API to transcribe an audio file into a text file.

D. Using an open-source pandas library that provides high-performance, easy-to-use data structures and data analysis tools for the Python programming language.

1.8 PRE-TRAINED MODELS

1.8.1 Introduction to pre-trained models

ML models can be expensive, consuming large amounts of human and computing resources, so a cheaper and often more effective alternative is to use a pre-trained model. This provides similar functionality and is used as the basis for creating a new model that extends the functionality of the pre-trained model.

Using pre-trained models reduces the risk of consuming significant resources with no guarantee of success, but these models are only available for a limited number of technologies, such as neural networks and random forests.

Industry insights

Amazon Comprehend as an example of AIaaS with pre-trained models

AWS offers a comprehensive suite of AI services, including Amazon Comprehend, which is an NLP service that uses ML to find insights and relationships in text (Amazon Web Services, 2025b). One of its key features is sentiment analysis, which can be used to determine the sentiment (positive, negative, neutral or mixed) expressed in a piece of text.

Here is a high-level overview of how it works. You need to provide the text data that you want to analyse for sentiment. This text can come from various sources, such as customer reviews, web pages, social media posts, emails, etc. First, the language of the input text is identified. Amazon Comprehend supports more than 100 languages and automatically identifies the dominant one. The service uses its pre-trained models to break the text down into individual words and phrases. This process involves parsing the text to understand its grammatical structure and the relationships between words. Amazon Comprehend extracts various linguistic features from the text, such as parts of speech, named entities and syntactic dependencies. These features help in extracting the key phrases and understanding the context and meaning of the text. The extracted features are fed into pre-trained ML models that classify the sentiment of the text. The service uses deep learning techniques to train its models on large datasets of labelled text, allowing it to recognise patterns and correlations between words and sentiment, so that there is no need for you to provide training data.

The sentiment classification process returns the most likely sentiment for the text and the sentiment score for each sentiment category:

- *positive* when the text expresses an overall positive sentiment;
- *negative* when the text expresses an overall negative sentiment;
- *neutral* when the text expresses both positive and negative sentiments;
- *mixed* when the text does not express either positive or negative sentiments.

These scores represent the likelihood that the text belongs to the corresponding sentiment category, and the category with the highest score is typically considered the overall sentiment of the text.

1.8.2 Transfer learning

It is also possible to take a pre-trained model and modify it to perform a different requirement. This is known as **transfer learning** and is used on **deep neural networks** (**DNNs** or **multi-layer perceptrons**) in which the early layers of the neural network (see Chapter 6 for more details) typically perform basic tasks, whereas the later layers perform more specialised assignments, as Figure 1.8 illustrates. This eliminates the need to train the early layers. The later layers are then re-trained to handle the unique requirements for a new classifier. In practice, the pre-trained model may be fine-tuned with additional training on new problem-specific data. The effectiveness of this approach largely depends on the similarity between the function performed by the original model and the new one. For example, modifying a text search algorithm that identifies specific product reviews to detect bug reports on target issues would be far more effective than modifying it to identify computers in some images (Figure 1.9).

Figure 1.8 The transfer learning principle

Figure 1.9 Finding reviews on some products and bug reports on some issues as an example of transfer learning

There are many pre-trained models available, especially from academic researchers. Some examples of such pre-trained models are ImageNet models such as AlexNet and MobileNet (ImageNet, 2025) for image classification and pre-trained NLP models such as Google's BERT (Devlin et al., 2019), NLTK (Natural Language Toolkit, 2025) and OpenAI's (2025b) text generation models (**generative pre-trained transformer (GPT)** models).

There are also different communities for data scientists and ML engineers that offer public data and cloud-based platforms for data science, AI education and building AI models. They promote competitions to solve data science challenges. One of the most popular communities is Kaggle (2025), which is the world's largest data science community. There are also many other communities, such as Reddit (2025) forums on various ML and AI topics, IBM Data Community (IBM, 2025a), DrivenData (2025), Tableau (2025) and Stack Overflow (2025).

1.8.3 Risks of using pre-trained models and transfer learning

Using pre-trained models, of course, carries some risks. These are listed below.

- Pre-trained models, compared to internally generated ones, may lack transparency (see Section 2.7 on transparency, interpretability and explainability).

- The level of similarity between the function performed by the pre-trained model and the required functionality may be insufficient. Also, this difference may not be understood by the data scientist.

- Differences in the data preparation steps used for the pre-trained model, when it is originally developed, and the data preparation steps, when this model is deployed, may affect the resulting functional performance.

- The shortcomings of a pre-trained model are likely to be inherited by those who reuse it, and may not be documented.

- A model created through transfer learning is highly likely to be sensitive to the same vulnerabilities as the pre-trained model on which it is based (adversarial attacks and data poisoning are explained in Chapter 9).

Note that several of the aforementioned risks can be easily mitigated by having thorough documentation available for the pre-trained model.

1.9 STANDARDS, REGULATIONS AND AI

The proposal of the European Parliament and of the European Council focuses on harmonised rules of AI, stating that this is a 'fast evolving family of technologies that can bring a wide array of economic and societal benefits across the entire spectrum of industries and social activities' that could provide competitive advantages to companies and the economy (European Commission, 2021). In so noting, it outlined the following AI techniques and approaches:

- ML approaches, including supervised, unsupervised, reinforcement and deep learning;

- logic- and knowledge-based approaches, including knowledge representation, inductive programming, knowledge bases, inference and deductive engines, symbolic reasoning and expert systems;
- statistical approaches, Bayesian estimation, search and optimisation methods.

In February 2025, the EU AI Act officially came into force. Article 3 of the Act (European Union, 2024) defines an AI system as 'a machine-based system that is designed to operate with varying levels of autonomy and that may exhibit adaptiveness after deployment, and that, for explicit or implicit objectives, infers, from the input it receives, how to generate outputs such as predictions, content, recommendations, or decisions that can influence physical or virtual environments'.

The Joint Technical Committee (JTC) of the International Electrotechnical Commission (IEC) and International Organization for Standardization (ISO) on information technology releases international standards about AI as well. For example, an AI subcommittee (SC), ISO/IEC JTC 1/SC 42, was set up in 2017. In addition, ISO/IEC JTC 1/SC 7, which covers software and system engineering, has published a technical report (TR) on the 'Testing of AI-based systems' (ISO/IEC TR 29119-11) (ISO, 2020). Standards on AI are also published at the regional and national levels.

The General Data Protection Regulation (GDPR) came into effect in May 2018 and set EU-wide rules with regard to personal data and automated decision-making (GDPR, 2018a, 2018b). It includes requirements to assess and improve AI-based systems' functional performance, including the mitigation of potential discrimination, and for ensuring individuals' rights to not be subjected to automated decision-making. The most important aspect of the GDPR from a testing perspective is that personal data (including predictions) should be accurate. This does not mean that every single prediction made by the system must be accurate, but that the system should be precise enough for the purposes for which it is used.

The German national standards body (Deutsches Institut für Normung, DIN) has developed the AI Quality Metamodel: DIN SPEC 92001-1 (DIN, 2019) and DIN SPEC 92001-2 (DIN, 2024).

Standards on AI are also published by industry bodies. For example, the Institute of Electrical and Electronics Engineers (IEEE) is working on a range of standards on ethics and AI described in 'The IEEE Global Initiative 2.0 on Ethics of Autonomous and Intelligent Systems' (IEEE, 2024), although many of these standards are still in development.

When it comes to safety-related systems, regulations become even more paramount, for example regulatory standards ensure that it is illegal to sell a car in some countries if it includes software that does not comply with the ISO 26262 (ISO, 2018) and ISO 21448 (ISO, 2022) standards.

Standards are voluntary, and only made mandatory by legislation or contract. However, many users of these standards implement them to benefit from the expertise of the authors and to create higher-quality products.

Quick questions

Question 1.6

Which of the following statements about AI standards are MOST likely to be CORRECT? Select TWO options.

    A. AI standards are unique for every country.

    B. AI standards are published at the regional and national levels.

    C. What should and should not be included in AI standards depends on the countries' regulatory regimes (what works for one country may not work for another one).

    D. AI standards are published only at the international level.

TERMS

Accuracy: the ML functional performance metric used to evaluate a classifier, which measures the proportion of predictions that were correct (ISO/IEC TR 29119-11).

Action space (in reinforcement learning): the set of all valid actions, or choices, available to an agent as it interacts with an environment.

AI as a service (AIaaS): a software licencing and delivery model in which AI and AI development services are centrally hosted.

AI component: a component that provides AI functionality.

AI development framework (AI framework): a set of tools and libraries designed to help developers create AI and ML applications more easily.

AI effect: the situation when a previously labelled AI system is no longer considered to be AI as technology advances (ISO/IEC TR 29119-11).

AI summer (summer of AI): a boom period in the history of AI.

AI winter (winter of AI): a period of reduced funding and interest in AI research.

AI-based system (AI system): a system that integrates one or more AI components.

Amazon Web Services (AWS): a subsidiary of Amazon that provides on-demand cloud computing platforms and APIs to individuals, companies and governments on a metered, pay-as-you-go basis.

Annotation: the activity of identifying objects in images with bounding boxes to provide labelled data for classification.

Anomaly: a condition that deviates from expectation.

Application programming interface (API): a type of interface in which the components or systems involved exchange information in a defined formal structure.

Application-specific integrated circuit (ASIC): a kind of integrated circuit that is specially built for a specific task or application.

Artificial intelligence (AI): the capability of an engineered system to acquire, process, and apply knowledge and skills (ISO/IEC TR 29119-11).

Artificial neuron (neuron, node): a node in a neural network, usually receiving multiple input values and generating an activation value.

Association: an unsupervised learning technique that identifies relationships and dependencies between samples.

Autonomous system: a system capable of working without human intervention for sustained periods.

Autonomous vehicle (self-driving vehicle, self-driving car): a vehicle that has the ability to sense its surrounding environment and navigate safely with little or no human input.

Bayesian model: a statistical model that uses probability to represent the uncertainty of both model inputs and outputs.

Behaviour tree (BT): a mathematical model of plan execution used in computer science, robotics, control systems and video games.

Bidirectional encoder representations from transformers (BERT): a method of pre-training language representations that obtains state-of-the-art results on a wide array of NLP tasks.

Bigrams: pairs of consecutive words.

Black box (black-box model): an input–output model based purely on data with no representation of the underlying physical characteristics of a system.

Bounding box: a minimal-area rectangle that encompasses the whole object region.

Case-based reasoning (CBR): a technique of solving a new problem based on the solutions of similar past problems.

Central processing unit (CPU): a general-purpose processor with a small number of cores that are optimised for low-latency tasks that require single-threaded performance, such as running operating systems, web browsing or office applications.

Chatbot: an application used to conduct a conversation via text or text-to-speech.

Classification: a type of ML function that predicts the output class for a given input (ISO/IEC TR 29119-11).

Classifier (classification model): an ML model used for classification.

Cloud computing: on-demand availability of computer system resources, especially data storage (cloud storage) and computing power, without direct active management by the user.

Cluster: a group of similar data.

Clustering: a type of ML function that groups similar data points together.

Clustering algorithm: a type of ML algorithm used to group similar objects into clusters.

Corpus: a collection of text documents.

Data encoding: a process of converting original data into a form that can be acceptable for AI processing.

Decision tree: a tree-like ML model whose nodes represent decisions and whose branches represent possible outcomes.

Deductive classifier: a classifier based on the application of inference and logic to input data.

Deep learning: the subset of machine learning methods based on neural networks with representation learning.

Deep neural network (DNN, multi-layer perceptron): a neural network comprising several layers of neurons.

Defect: an imperfection or deficiency in a work product where it does not meet its requirements or specifications or impairs its intended use.

Defect report (bug report): documentation of the occurrence, nature and status of a defect.

Edge computing: the part of a distributed architecture in which information processing is performed close to where that information is used.

Embedding: a numerical representation of discrete objects such as text, image and audio as dense vectors within a continuous vector space that is designed to be consumed by ML models and search algorithms.

Expert system: an AI-based system for solving problems in a particular domain or application area by drawing inferences from a knowledge base developed from human expertise.

Exploratory data analysis (EDA): the interactive, hypothesis-driven and visual exploration of data used to support all data preparation activities (data acquisition, data pre-processing and feature engineering).

Failure: an event in which a component or system does not meet its requirements within specified limits.

Feature: an individual measurable attribute of the input data used for training by an ML algorithm and for prediction by an ML model.

Feature extraction: the activity that involves the derivation of informative and non-redundant features from the existing features.

Feature learning (representation learning): a set of techniques that allows a system to automatically discover the representations needed for feature detection or classification from raw data.

Feature vector: an n-dimensional vector of numerical features that describe some object in pattern recognition in ML.

Fuzzy logic: a type of logic based on the concept of partial truth represented by certainty factors between 0 and 1.

General AI (strong AI, true AI): AI that exhibits intelligent behaviour comparable to a human across the full range of cognitive abilities (ISO/IEC TR 29119-11).

Generative AI: a type of AI technology that can create new content, including text, images, audio and video materials.

Generative pre-trained transformers (GPT): a type of large language model and a prominent framework for generative AI. They are artificial neural networks that are used in NLP tasks. GPTs are based on the Transformer architecture, pre-trained on large datasets of unlabelled text and able to generate novel, human-like content.

Genetic algorithm: a search-based algorithm used for solving optimisation problems in machine learning.

Graphical processing unit (GPU): a specialised processor, originally designed to handle graphics-related tasks, capable of performing thousands of parallel calculations simultaneously and more efficiently than CPUs thanks to a large number of smaller cores.

Image binarisation: a digital image processing technique used to convert a grayscale image or a colour image into a binary image consisting of black and white pixels.

Image normalisation: a process that changes the range of pixel intensity values.

Imbalanced dataset (unbalanced dataset): a dataset with an unequal distribution of classes (or target values).

Intelligent agent (agent): an autonomous program that directs its activity towards achieving goals using observations and actions.

International Business Machines (IBM): an American multinational technology company headquartered in Armonk, New York.

Labelled data: data with meaningful tags to support classification in ML.

Linear model: a statistical model that uses the relationship between variables by fitting a linear equation to the observed data.

Linear regression: a statistical technique that models the relationship between variables by fitting a linear equation to the observed data when the target variable is numeric.

Logistic regression: a statistical technique that models the relationship between variables when the target variable is categorical rather than numeric.

Machine learning (ML): the process using computational techniques to enable systems to learn from data or experience (ISO/IEC TR 29119-11).

Metric: a measurement scale and the method used for measurement.

ML framework: a tool or library that supports creation of an ML model.

ML model: ML output of an ML algorithm trained with a training dataset that generates predictions using patterns in the input data (ISO/IEC TR 29119-11).

ML model training (training): the process of applying the ML algorithm to the training dataset to create an ML model.

Narrow AI (weak AI): AI focused on a single well-defined task to address a specific problem (ISO/IEC TR 29119-11).

Natural language processing (NLP): a field of computing that provides the ability to read, understand and derive meaning from natural languages.

Neural machine translation: an approach to machine translation that uses an artificial neural network to predict the likelihood of a sequence of words, typically modelling entire sentences in a single integrated model.

Neural network (artificial neural network): a network of primitive processing elements connected by weighted links with adjustable weights, in which each element produces a value by applying a non-linear function to its input values, and transmits it to other elements or presents it as an output value (ISO/IEC 2382).

Neural processing unit (NPU, AI accelerator): a class of specialised hardware accelerator or computer system designed to accelerate AI and ML applications, including artificial neural networks and machine vision.

Neuromorphic processor: an integrated circuit designed to mimic the biological neurons of the human brain.

Noise (noisy data): random or unpredictable fluctuations in data that disrupt the ability to identify target patterns or relationships.

Non-player character (NPC): a character in a game that is not controlled by a player.

Outcome (test result, test outcome, result): the consequence of the execution of a test.

Outlier: an observation that lies outside the overall pattern of the data distribution.

Pattern: a regularity in data or a systematic relationship between data points.

Phishing: an attempt to acquire personal or sensitive information by masquerading as a trustworthy entity in an electronic communication.

Policy (in reinforcement learning): a function that maps a state to an action.

Precision: an ML functional performance metric used to evaluate a classifier, which measures the proportion of predicted positives that were correct (ISO/IEC TR 29119-11).

Pre-trained model: an ML model already trained when it was obtained.

Procedural reasoning: AI technology used for constructing real-time reasoning systems that can perform complex tasks in dynamic environments.

Quality assurance (QA): activities focused on providing confidence that quality requirements will be fulfilled.

Random forest: ensemble ML technology for classification, regression and other tasks that operate by constructing and running many decision trees and then either outputting the mode of the class or the mean prediction of the individual trees.

Reasoning technique: AI that generates conclusions from available information using logical techniques (ISO/IEC TR 29119-11).

Recommendation system (recommender system, recommendation algorithm): software tool or algorithm for information retrieval and filtering that provides personalised recommendations to users based on their past behaviours, preferences and patterns.

Regression: a type of ML function that results in a numerical or continuous output value for a given input (ISO/IEC TR 29119-11).

Reinforcement learning: an activity of building an ML model using a process of trial and reward to achieve an objective (ISO/IEC TR 29119-11).

Reward function: a function that defines the success of reinforcement learning.

Rule engine (semantic reasoner): a set of rules that determine which actions should occur when certain conditions are satisfied.

Scalable ML: the ability of an ML system to handle ever larger amounts of data and computing resources.

Search algorithm: an algorithm that systematically visits a subset of all possible states or structures until the goal state or structure is reached (ISO/IEC TR 29119-11).

Sentiment analysis: the process of automatically predicting whether a user's opinion in a text is positive, negative or neutral.

Service-level agreement (SLA): a contract between a service provider and its customers that documents what services the provider will furnish and defines the service standards the provider is obligated to meet.

Software as a service (SaaS): a software distribution model in which a cloud provider hosts applications and makes them available to end-users over the internet.

State space (in reinforcement learning): the set of all possible states that an agent can be in.

Super AI: an artificial intelligence-based system that far exceeds human capabilities.

Supervised learning: training an ML model from input data and its corresponding labels.

Support vector machine (SVM): an ML technique in which the data points are viewed as vectors in multidimensional space separated by a hyperplane.

Symbolic AI (classical AI, rule-based AI): a subfield of AI that focuses on using explicit, human-readable symbols and rules, rather than numerical data, to represent knowledge and logic.

System on a chip (SoC): an integrated circuit that integrates most or all components of a computer or other electronic system.

Technological singularity: a point in the future when technological advances are no longer controllable by people (ISO/IEC TR 29119-11).

Tensor processing unit (TPU): a specialised processor developed by Google specifically to perform highly optimised operations on tensors, which are multidimensional arrays used in deep learning models.

Test case: a set of preconditions, inputs, actions (where applicable), expected results and postconditions, developed based on test conditions.

Test process: the set of interrelated activities comprising test planning, test monitoring and control, test analysis, test design, test implementation, test execution and test completion.

Testing: the process within the software development lifecycle that evaluates the quality of a component or system and related work products.

Training data: data used to train an ML model.

Training dataset: a dataset used to train an ML model.

Transfer learning: a technique for modifying a pre-trained ML model to perform a different related task.

Trend in data: a general direction in which data is changing.

Trigrams: triplets of consecutive words.

Unigrams: single words, representing the most basic units of text.

Unsupervised learning: training an ML model from input data using an unlabelled dataset.

Vision processing unit (VPU): a specific type of AI accelerator, designed to accelerate machine vision tasks.

Von Neumann architecture: a computer architecture that consists of five main components: memory, a CPU, a control unit, input and output.

SELF-ASSESSMENT EXERCISES

1. What is AI and the AI effect?
2. Which categories of AI exist? Describe them.
3. What is the difference between an AI-based system and a conventional system?
4. List the main groups of AI technologies.
5. Name the categories of ML techniques and provide examples of algorithms for each category.
6. What are the benefits of using different AI development frameworks?
7. What types of hardware were specifically intended for AI?
8. What is AIaaS, and what are its pros and cons?
9. Describe the role of transfer learning in AI and risks associated with it.
10. How is AI regulated, and what are the key standards associated with AI testing?

2 QUALITY CHARACTERISTICS FOR AI-BASED SYSTEMS

SUMMARY

This chapter provides descriptions of the characteristics of an AI-based system. AI-based systems must be flexible, adaptable, autonomous, evolving, unbiased, ethical, transparent, interpretable, explainable and safe. These characteristics ensure AI-based systems can effectively and responsibly adapt to new environments, operate independently, improve over time, mitigate biases, adhere to ethical standards, avoid harmful side effects and maintain user trust and safety, which is also discussed in the chapter.

LEARNING OBJECTIVES

After reading this chapter, you should be able to:

- Explain the importance of flexibility and adaptability as characteristics of AI-based systems (K2)

- Explain the relationship between autonomy and AI-based systems (K2)

- Explain the importance of managing evolution for AI-based systems (K2)

- Describe the different causes and types of bias found in AI-based systems (K2)

- Discuss the ethical principles that should be respected in the development, deployment and use of AI-based systems (K2)

- Explain the occurrence of side effects and reward hacking in AI-based systems (K2)

- Explain how transparency, interpretability and explainability apply to AI-based systems (K2)

- Recall the characteristics that make it difficult to use AI-based systems in safety-related applications (K1)

LINKS TO OTHER CHAPTERS

This chapter is related to other chapters as follows:

- Chapter 1 focuses on the definition of AI and the main technologies that can be used in model building.

- Chapter 3 describes the process of tuning the hyperparameters of an ML algorithm, which may cause or eliminate algorithmic bias.

- Chapter 8 explains how to test the transparency, interpretability and explainability of AI-based systems.

2.1 FLEXIBILITY AND ADAPTABILITY

This chapter goes over the basic quality characteristics of AI. First we have **flexibility** and **adaptability**, and they are quite similar (see Figure 2.1 for an illustration of these characteristics). Flexibility is the system's ability to be used in situations that were not a part of the original system requirements, while adaptability is the ease with which the system can be modified for these new situations.

Figure 2.1 A flexibility and adaptability characteristics illustration

Flexibility   **Adaptability**

Both flexibility and adaptability come into play when we have limited or no information about the operational environment at the time of system deployment, and also when the system is expected to cope and adapt to new situations and environments as well as when the system itself must decide if it should change its behaviour. The flexibility and adaptability requirements should specify expected changes in the environment, plus the time and resources that the system can use to adapt.

From theory to practice

Example 1. AI-powered virtual assistant with flexibility characteristics

Consider an AI-powered virtual assistant that is designed to help users with various tasks such as scheduling appointments, managing to-do lists and providing information on different topics (Myers et al., 2007). One day, a user needs to reschedule all her appointments from the afternoon to the morning. She asks the virtual assistant for help with this task. The AI assistant, showcasing flexibility, quickly adjusts to the new request and proceeds to reschedule all the appointments accordingly. However, the virtual assistant goes one step further and identifies potential conflicts that may arise due to the rescheduling. It proactively suggests alternative time slots for some appointments to ensure optimal scheduling without overlapping meetings or causing inconvenience to the user or other participants. It does not rigidly adhere to the initial instructions but instead analyses the context, evaluates potential conflicts and proposes alternative solutions to achieve the best outcome for the user beyond the predefined scope of its tasks.

Example 2. AI-driven recommendation system with adaptability characteristics

Take a look at an AI-driven recommendation system (one of the AI technologies discussed in Chapter 1) used by an online streaming platform. The system analyses user preferences, viewing history, and feedback to provide personalised movie recommendations (Shah et al., 2017; Anandhan et al., 2018). Let us say the system initially focuses on recommending popular movies from various genres based on user ratings and reviews. Over time, the streaming platform notices a shift in user behaviour and identifies a growing interest in niche films. To cater to this changing demand, the platform decides to enhance its recommendation system to include a wider selection of independent films. It begins to analyse additional data sources such as film festival awards and critical reviews. By adapting to the users' changing preferences and incorporating new criteria into its recommendation algorithms, the AI-based system demonstrates adaptability. It proactively evolves to meet the needs of the streaming platform and its users, offering a more personalised and diverse range of movie recommendations.

2.2 AUTONOMY

The next thing we have to talk about is the system's **autonomy**. The question that logically arises here is: who should the system be autonomous from? And the answer is ... us humans and our control. Figure 2.2 illustrates the autonomy characteristic of an AI-based system.

Consider autonomous vehicles (see Figure 2.3), which typically use several sensors combined with image processing to gather information about their immediate surroundings (Sarraf, 2020; Parekh et al., 2022; Zhang et al., 2023). These kinds of systems may also include decision-making and control functions, which can be performed effectively using AI-based components. However, full autonomy is not always desirable, as it can reduce control, accountability and flexibility, especially in cases of errors, ethical dilemmas, cyber-attacks or unexpected situations where rigid rules may not be effective. The Society of Automotive Engineers (SAE) published its J3016 standard that defines six levels of driving automation, ranging from 0 (fully manual) to 5 (fully autonomous) (SAE International, 2021). This also means that there are six categories of an **advanced driver-assistance system**, or **ADAS**, which are

Figure 2.2 The autonomy characteristic

presented in Figure 2.4. ADAS is an electronic technology group that assists drivers in driving and parking.

Even though some AI-based systems could be viewed as autonomous, this does not automatically translate to all AI-based systems. Autonomy is considered to be the ability of the system to work independently of human oversight and control for prolonged periods of time. This means that the time an autonomous system is expected to perform without human intervention needs to be well-defined. For example, fully self-driving cars may require a manual override button in case a driver needs to take over. In addition, it is important to identify what has to happen for an autonomous system to cede control back to humans.

From theory to practice

An autonomous delivery robot is deployed by a logistics company to transport packages from a warehouse to customers' doorsteps. This robot is equipped with AI algorithms and sensors that enable it to navigate through the city (Gujarathi et al., 2021). Once the robot receives a delivery request, it plans the optimal route based on real-time traffic data and maps. Throughout the delivery process, the robot autonomously adapts to changing environmental conditions and unexpected obstacles. For instance, if it encounters a road closure or heavy traffic along its planned route, the robot autonomously reroutes itself to find an alternative path, ensuring minimal delays in the delivery, using its AI algorithms and sensors. Furthermore, the robot autonomously manages its energy resources, monitoring battery levels and proactively seeking charging stations when needed. It can make decisions to optimise its charging and operational schedules, ensuring efficient use of its resources and minimising downtime.

Figure 2.3 An autonomous vehicle and its key self-driving functions, including pedestrian and obstacle detection, traffic control recognition and collision avoidance

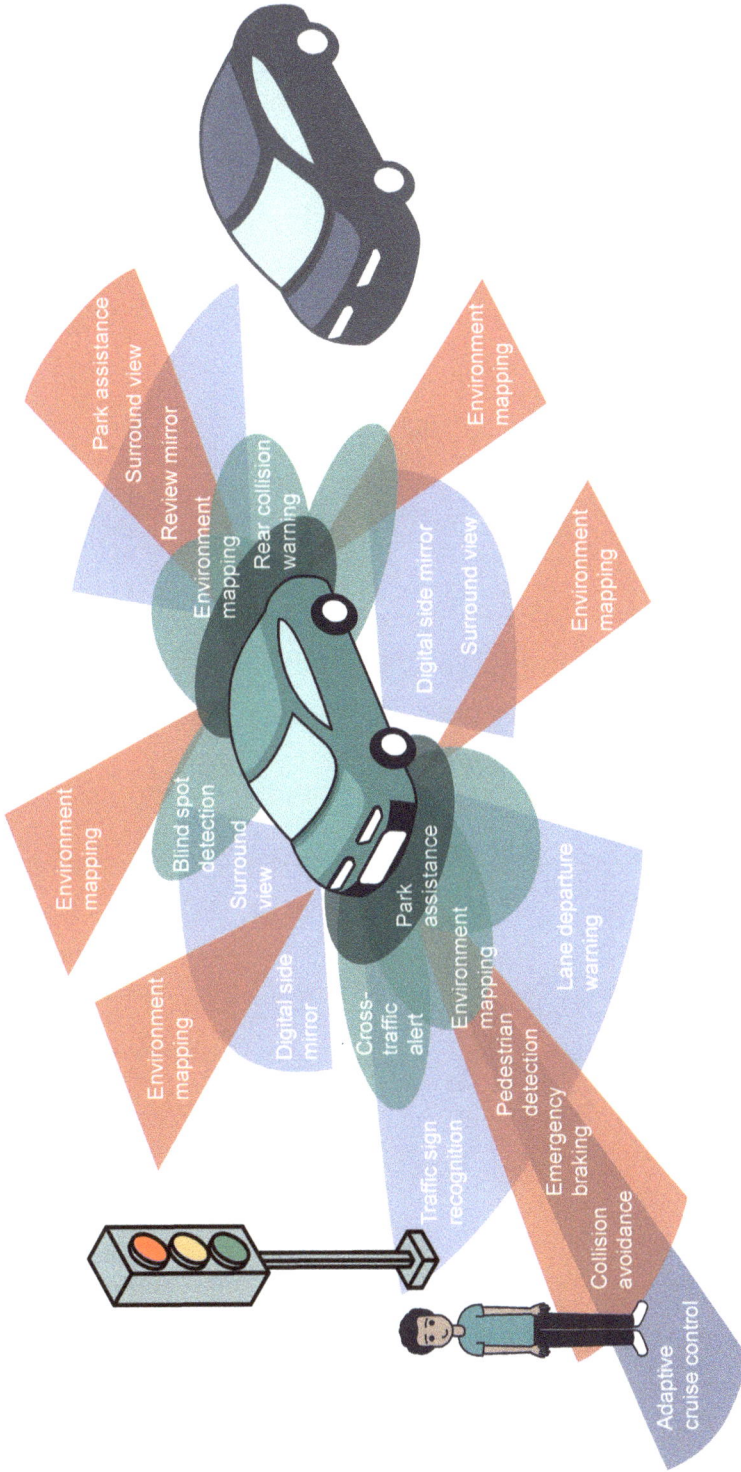

Figure 2.4 The six levels of autonomous driving

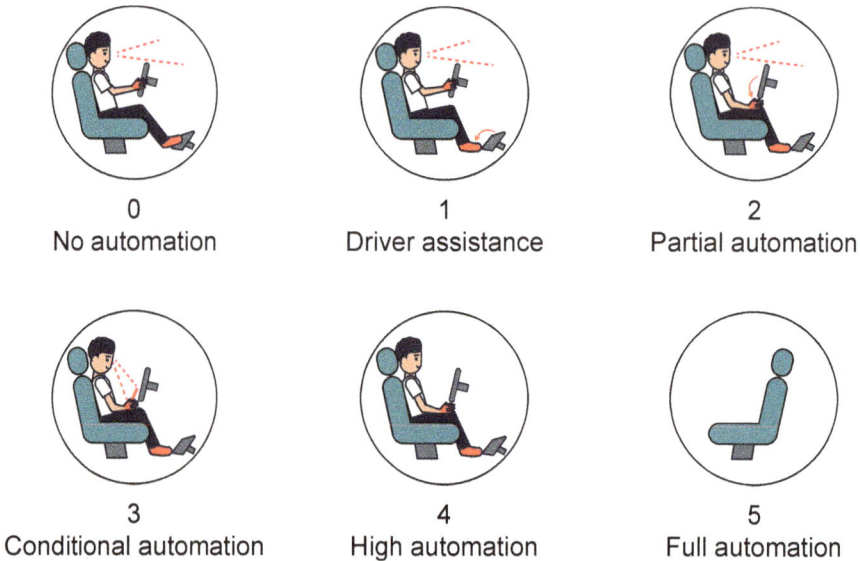

0	1	2
No automation	Driver assistance	Partial automation
3	4	5
Conditional automation	High automation	Full automation

Quick questions

Question 2.1

Which of the following real-life examples best illustrates a fully autonomous self-driving car? Select ONE option.

A. A car that can park itself but requires a driver to monitor its surroundings.

B. A car that can navigate highways on its own but requires a driver to take control in complex city environments.

C. A car that can drive itself in a specific geofenced area without any human intervention, such as a dedicated shuttle service in a tech campus.

D. A car that can drive itself under all conditions and environments, with no steering wheel or pedals, requiring no human intervention at any time.

2.3 EVOLUTION

The next requirement is called **evolution**. In the ISTQB CT-AI syllabus, it is described as the system's ability to improve itself as it faces changing external constraints (Dussa-Zieger et al., 2021). Figure 2.5 illustrates the evolution characteristic.

Figure 2.5 The evolution characteristic

We have to consider two kinds of change for **self-learning** AI-based systems, one comes from learning from its own decisions and interactions with its own environment, the other one comes from learning from changes made to the system's operational environment. These interactions will ideally improve the system's efficiency, thus causing it to evolve. However, this cannot go unchecked: there has to be a mechanism to curtail any unforeseen characteristics, because any evolution must not negate the original requirements. If the said requirements are not fully defined, there have to be safeguards to make sure that the system stays aligned with basic human values and that the situation similar to that shown in Figure 2.6 does not occur.

Figure 2.6 Evolution negating the original requirements

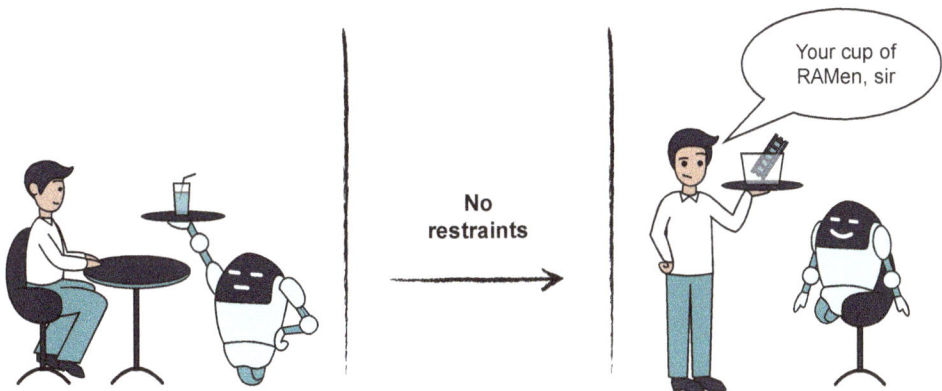

From theory to practice

An AI-based system is designed to generate artistic images (House and Agah, 2015; Yadav, 2024). Initially, the AI is trained using a dataset of existing artwork, and it produces images based on that training. These generated images are then evaluated by humans, who provide feedback. Here is how it could work. The AI-based system introduces small, random changes or mutations in the generated images. The set of mutated images, along with the original ones, are presented to human evaluators. They assess the images and rank them based on their artistic quality. The AI-based system selects the images that receive the highest rankings and uses them as parents to create the next generation, demonstrating such a characteristic as evolution. It combines or recombines the most successful elements from these highly ranked images to produce a new set of mutated images. This is repeated multiple times, creating successive generations of images. Over time, this iterative process allows the AI-based system to evolve and generate better-quality images that align more closely with the preferences of the human evaluators.

Quick questions

Question 2.2

What type of ML technique is used to implement an AI-based system designed to generate artistic images found in the From Theory to Practice segment of Section 2.3? Select ONE option.

A. logistic regression
B. genetic algorithm
C. neural network
D. reinforcement learning

Question 2.3

Which of the following real-life examples best illustrates an AI-based system with evolutionary characteristics? Select ONE option.

A. A chatbot that improves its responses based on user feedback over time.
B. A recommendation engine that suggests products based on past purchases.
C. A self-learning algorithm in a robotic vacuum that has adapted its cleaning patterns by learning from its environment and optimised its performance without human intervention.
D. A virtual assistant that sets reminders and performs tasks based on voice commands.

2.4 BIAS

It is important for an AI-based system to be unbiased. In order to understand what that means, we have to give the definition of what **bias** is. It is the difference between the system's outputs and the outputs that are considered to be 'fair'. This means that they cannot show favouritism to any particular group. In general, **inappropriate biases** are linked to characteristics including gender, race, ethnicity, sexual orientation, income level, age and disability. A simplified example of how these biases could be avoided is given in Figure 2.7. Unfortunately, it is difficult to prevent the expert's personal bias being built into the system rules.

Figure 2.7 Avoiding inappropriate biases

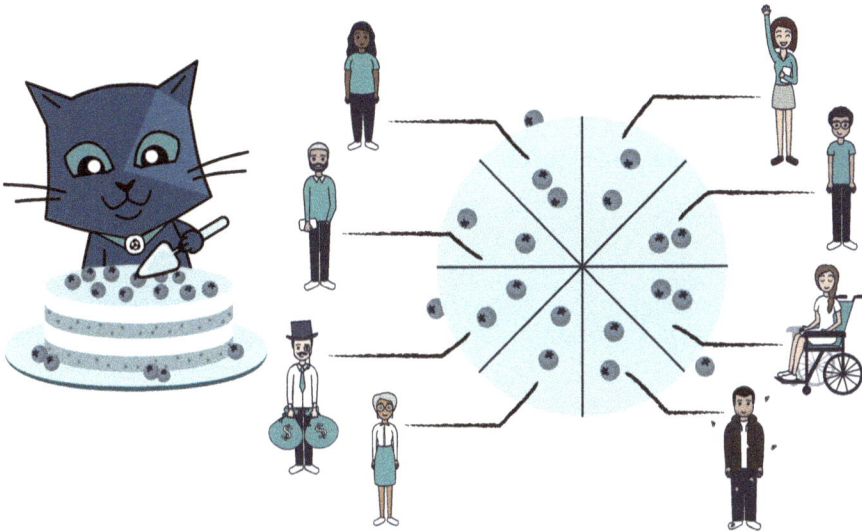

ML systems making decisions and predictions can suffer from:

- **algorithmic bias** stemming from an incorrectly configured learning algorithm – this bias can be caused and managed by **hyperparameter tuning** of the ML algorithms (see Section 3.2 on ML workflow);
- **sample bias** stemming from the lack of representativeness of training data.

Inappropriate bias is often caused by sample bias, but occasionally it can also be caused by algorithmic bias.

Cases of inappropriate bias have been reported in AI-based systems used for making recommendations for bank lending, in self-driving systems, recruitment systems and in judicial monitoring systems. That is why it is so important for the model to have no prejudices.

From theory to practice

Example 1. Inappropriate biases in recruitment systems

Let us consider an AI-based system that is designed to screen job applications and determine the suitability of candidates based on their resumes. The AI-based system is trained on a dataset of past hiring decisions made by human recruiters

(Drage and Mackereth, 2022). However, the training dataset inadvertently contains biases. It may have a higher proportion of male candidates compared to female candidates due to historical gender imbalances. These biases can be reflected in the AI-based system's decision-making process. The AI-based system, acting as a decision-maker, exhibits bias by replicating and potentially amplifying the discriminatory patterns present in the training data. As a result, it may perpetuate unfair and discriminatory practices, leading to disparities and unequal opportunities for certain groups. By acknowledging bias as a characteristic of AI, we can focus on developing strategies and techniques to minimise and mitigate bias, ensuring fair and equitable outcomes in AI applications.

Example 2. Inappropriate biases in self-driving systems

Recent studies (Wilson et al., 2019; Li et al., 2024) have highlighted shortcomings in the detection capabilities of self-driving vehicles, particularly concerning children and pedestrians with darker skin tones (see Figure 2.8). These issues stem from insufficient representation in training data and technical limitations inherent in the sensor systems used. Self-driving vehicles rely on a combination of sensors including cameras, LiDARs, radars and ultrasonic sensors. Cameras – which are sensitive to lighting conditions – may struggle to detect darker skin tones effectively in low-light settings. Similarly, children pose detection challenges due to their smaller stature and erratic movements, which can be harder for the systems to anticipate, especially when obscured or in unconventional poses. Efforts are underway to address these concerns through improved standards and more rigorous testing protocols that encompass a broader range of environmental conditions and demographic profiles. Some automotive companies are actively diversifying their training datasets and enhancing algorithm robustness to mitigate these biases.

Figure 2.8 Lower detection accuracy for children and darker-skinned pedestrians in self-driving vehicles

2.5 ETHICS

The next important area to look at is **ethics** (see Figure 2.9). AI has pervasive, far-reaching implications that are capable of transforming societies and the economy. It also has the potential to improve the welfare and well-being of people (Figure 2.10), to contribute to positive sustainable global economic activity, to increase innovation and productivity, and to help respond to key global challenges.

Figure 2.9 The ethics characteristic

Figure 2.10 AI has the potential to improve the welfare and well-being of people for all ages

So as these systems get more widespread, we have to make sure they are used in an ethical manner. Close attention must be paid to the fact that AI-based systems take into account differences in human value. Will the autonomous-vehicle AI have to make a split-second decision of which life to save, similar to that in the 'trolley problem' (Figure 2.11)? What will that choice be based on? Would the human who was saved instead of somebody else appreciate this or have survivor's guilt?

Figure 2.11 The 'trolley problem'

Today many countries have national and international policies on the ethics of AI. On 8 April 2019, the Independent High-Level Expert Group on AI set up by the European Commission presented Ethics Guidelines for Trustworthy AI (European Commission, 2019). Then the Organisation for Economic Co-operation and Development (OECD) issued its principles for AI, the first international standards agreed by governments for the responsible development of AI, on 22 May 2019 (OECD, 2024).

In June 2019, at the Osaka Summit, G20 leaders welcomed the G20 AI Principles drawn from the OECD Recommendation (OECD, 2019). These principles were adopted by 42 countries and also backed by the European Commission. They include practical policy recommendations as well as five value-based principles for the 'responsible stewardship of trustworthy AI':

- AI should benefit humanity by driving inclusive growth, sustainable development and well-being.

- AI-based systems should respect the rule of law, human rights, democratic values and diversity, and should include appropriate safeguards to ensure a fair society.

- There should be transparency around AI to ensure that people understand outcomes and can challenge them.

- AI-based systems must function in a robust, secure and safe way throughout their lifecycles, and risks should be continually assessed.

- Organisations and individuals developing, deploying or operating AI-based systems should be held accountable.

In November 2021, the United Nations Educational, Scientific and Cultural Organization (UNESCO) published the first-ever global standard on AI ethics, the *Recommendation on the Ethics of Artificial Intelligence*, which was adopted by all 193 member states (UNESCO, 2021). What makes this standard exceptionally applicable are its extensive policy action areas that allow policymakers to translate the core values and principles into action with respect to data governance, environment and ecosystems, gender, education and research, and health and social well-being, among many other spheres.

From theory to practice

An AI-based healthcare system is designed to make decisions that align with the ethical frameworks and guidelines established in healthcare (Liao, 2023). It prioritises patient well-being, follows medical best practices and respects the professional judgement of healthcare providers. At the same time, the AI-based system adheres to relevant regulations, such as data protection laws and healthcare privacy standards, to maintain patient trust and confidentiality. The AI-based system should avoid favouring certain patient groups based on factors such as race, gender or socioeconomic status (biases, see Section 2.4), while providing explanations and justifications for its recommendations. It can provide clear and interpretable insights into how it arrived at a particular recommendation, allowing healthcare professionals to understand the underlying reasoning and verify its validity along with any associated risks (transparency, interpretability and explainability, see Section 2.7).

Quick questions

Question 2.4

Which of the following statements are value-based principles for the 'responsible stewardship of trustworthy AI'? Select TWO options.

    A. AI-based systems must function in a robust, secure and safe way throughout their lifecycles, and risks should be continually assessed.

    B. A learning algorithm should be configured correctly without over-evaluating some data in relation to others.

    C. There should be transparency around AI to ensure that people understand outcomes and can challenge them.

    D. An AI-based system should be able to learn from its own decisions and its interactions with its environment as well as to learn from changes made to the system's operational environment.

2.6 SIDE EFFECTS AND REWARD HACKING

When talking about the AI requirements, we should not forget about adverse aspects of **side effects** and **reward hacking**. These can result in AI-based systems generating unexpected, and even harmful, results (Amodei et al., 2016). Figure 2.12 gives an example of a self-driving race car devising a method of reaching the finish line by breaking the rule of following the racetrack.

Figure 2.12 Reward hacking for a self-driving race car

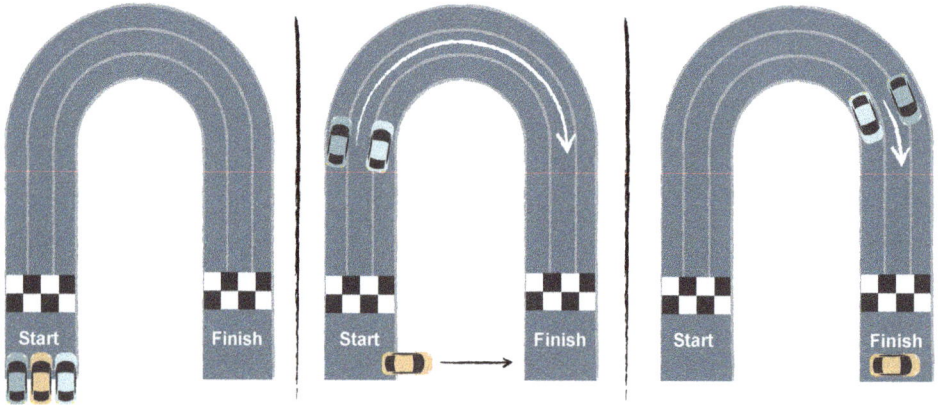

Reward hacking can happen if an AI-based system achieves a specific goal by using a 'clever' or 'easy' solution. This could also be an example of how fake testing is done, which is when the tests are written with the intent of pleasing stakeholders instead of providing information to them – but this is clearly a false approach to success. Figure 2.13 illustrates fake testing as an example of reward hacking.

Figure 2.13 Fake testing as an example of reward hacking

From theory to practice

Let us consider an AI-based system developed to optimise energy consumption in a smart home based on real-time data, such as occupancy, weather conditions and holidays (Giuseppina and D'Amico, 2019; Dhaval and Deshpande, 2020). If the reward mechanism is not properly designed, the AI-based system might find unintended options to hack the reward signal to achieve its objectives more effectively, even if those methods are not aligned with the original intent of the system.

Option 1. Exploiting a loophole

If the system is rewarded solely based on the total energy reduction, it might turn off all appliances completely, making the home uncomfortable or rendering certain essential systems dysfunctional. If the system is rewarded based on the number of appliances turned off, the AI could exploit this by randomly toggling appliances without considering their actual energy consumption or the impact on user comfort.

Option 2. Manipulating feedback

An AI-based system might learn to report lower energy consumption than it actually achieves by tampering with energy meters or falsifying data inputs, thus tricking the system into providing higher rewards.

Quick questions

Question 2.5

What is an example of a side effect in AI? Select ONE option.

    A. Cognitive-behavioural therapy for anxiety leading to improved sleep.
    B. A government policy to reduce pollution leading to higher production costs.
    C. A chatbot using slang and offensive language.
    D. A robot cleaning the floor perfectly.

2.7 TRANSPARENCY, INTERPRETABILITY AND EXPLAINABILITY

Let us cover the next set of requirements. They are **transparency**, **interpretability** and **explainability** (see Figure 2.14).

Some of today's AI tools are able to produce highly accurate results, but are also highly complex, if not outright opaque, rendering their workings difficult to interpret. In the real world, AI-based systems are typically applied in areas where users need to trust those systems. This could be for safety reasons, there could be demand for privacy or they might provide potentially life changing predictions and decisions. The complexity of

Figure 2.14 Transparency, interpretability and explainability characteristics

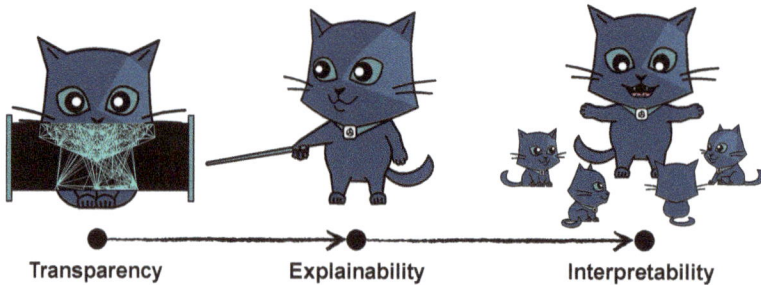

Transparency   Explainability   Interpretability

AI-based systems has led to the field of '**explainable AI**' **(XAI)**. The aim of XAI is for users to be able to understand how AI-based systems arrive at their results, thus increasing users' trust in them.

According to the Royal Society (2019), there are several reasons for XAI, including:

- giving users confidence in the system;
- safeguarding against bias;
- meeting regulatory standards or policy requirements;
- improving system design;
- assessing risk, robustness and vulnerability;
- understanding and verifying the outputs from a system;
- autonomy, making the user feel empowered and meeting social value.

A range of terms describing some desired characteristics of an XAI can be found in the ISTQB CT-AI syllabus (the first three) (Dussa-Zieger et al., 2021) and in the Royal Society's materials (all five). The explainable AI has to be:

- interpretable, implying some sense of understanding how the technology works;
- explainable, implying that users can understand why or how a conclusion was reached;
- transparent, implying some level of accessibility to the data or algorithm;
- justifiable, implying there is an understanding of the case in support of a particular outcome;
- contestable, implying users have the information they need to argue against a decision.

From theory to practice

An AI-based system is designed to provide personalised product recommendations to online shoppers based on their browsing and purchase history (Li et al., 2021). This AI-based system can exhibit transparency, explainability and interpretability characteristics by:

- providing explanations for its product recommendations to the users. When suggesting a particular item, it accompanies the recommendation with clear and interpretable reasons. For instance, it might state that the recommendation is based on the user's previous purchase history, similar items purchased by other customers or popular trends (and not because it is secretly gathering information about you while you are not paying attention).

- allowing users to access and review their own data that the system uses to generate recommendations. These characteristics empower users to understand why certain recommendations are made and gain insights into their preferences.

- providing clear information about the purpose of data collection, the scope of data usage and how long the data will be retained.

2.8 SAFETY AND AI

Lastly we have **safety**, which implies that an AI-based system will not cause harm to people, property or the environment (see Figure 2.15).

Figure 2.15 The safety characteristic

AI-based systems are often presented as black boxes with characteristics such as complexity, non-determinism, probabilistic nature, self-learning, lack of transparency, interpretability and explainability as well as lack of robustness, which makes it more difficult to ensure they are safe. For example, AI-based systems working in the fields of medicine, manufacturing, defence, security and transportation have the potential to affect safety (look at Figure 2.16). The challenges of testing several of these characteristics are covered in Chapter 8.

Figure 2.16 Safety-affected fields

| Medicine | Manufacturing | Defence | Security | Transportation |

From theory to practice

Safety is a critical characteristic for an AI-based system that controls autonomous vehicles on public roads, as the AI-based system must ensure the well-being of passengers, pedestrians and other vehicles (Ashwin and Raj, 2023). Extensive testing helps to identify and address potential safety vulnerabilities before an autonomous vehicle is deployed on public roads. Let us consider several safety aspects for different control functions of the autonomous vehicle.

Aspect 1. Collision avoidance

The AI-based system is programmed to prioritise safety by actively monitoring the environment, detecting obstacles and making decisions to avoid collisions.

Aspect 2. Adhering to traffic rules

The AI-based system follows traffic laws and regulations, including speed limits, traffic signals and right-of-way rules.

Aspect 3. Handling emergency situations

The AI-based system is trained to handle emergency scenarios, such as sudden braking, swerving or evasive manoeuvres, to avoid accidents.

Aspect 4. Continual monitoring and redundancy

The AI-based system employs redundant systems and continual monitoring to enhance safety. It uses redundant sensors, backup control systems and fail-safe mechanisms to minimise the effect of hardware or software failures.

Quick questions

Question 2.6

Which of the following real-life examples best illustrates an AI-based system that prioritises safety characteristics? Select ONE option.

    A. An autonomous drone delivery system that optimises delivery routes based solely on speed, without accounting for potential obstacles or no-fly zones.

    B. A facial recognition system used in airports that prioritises speed over accuracy, potentially leading to misidentification.

    C. A financial trading AI that makes rapid decisions in volatile markets without implementing safeguards to prevent large-scale losses.

    D. A self-driving car that rigorously tests its algorithms in simulated and real-world scenarios, ensuring it can safely handle unexpected situations such as sudden pedestrian jaywalking or adverse weather conditions.

TERMS

Adaptability: the ease with which a system can be modified for new situations, such as different hardware and changing operational environments.

Advanced driver-assistance system (ADAS): an electronic technology group that assists drivers in driving and parking.

Algorithmic bias: a type of bias that occurs when the learning algorithm is incorrectly configured, for example when it overvalues some data compared to others.

Autonomy: the ability of a system to work for sustained periods without human intervention (ISO/IEC TR 29119-11).

Bias: the systematic difference in treatment of certain objects, people or groups in comparison to others (ISO/IEC DIS 22989).

Ethics: a system of accepted beliefs that control behaviour, especially such a system based on morals.

Evolution: the process of continuous change from a lower, simpler or worse state to a higher, more complex or better state.

Explainability: the level of understanding how the AI-based system came up with a given result (ISO/IEC TR 29119-11).

Explainable AI (XAI): the field of study related to understanding the factors that influence AI-based system outputs.

Flexibility: the ability of a system to work in contexts outside its initial specification (ISO/IEC TR 29119-11).

Hyperparameter: a parameter used to either control the training of an ML model or to set the configuration of an ML model.

Hyperparameter tuning: the activity of determining the optimal hyperparameters based on particular goals.

Inappropriate bias: a type of bias that causes a system to produce results that lead to adverse effects for a particular group.

Interpretability: the level of understanding how the underlying AI technology works (ISO/IEC TR 29119-11).

ML system: a system that integrates one or more ML models.

Reward hacking: the activity performed by an intelligent agent to maximise its reward function to the detriment of meeting the original objective (ISO/IEC TR 29119-11).

Safety: the expectation that a system does not, under defined conditions, lead to a state in which human life, health and property or the environment is endangered.

Sample bias: a type of bias where the dataset is not fully representative of the data space to which ML is applied.

Self-learning system: an adaptive system that changes its behaviour based on learning through trial and error (ISO/IEC TR 29119-11).

Side effect: a secondary and usually adverse effect.

Transparency: the level of visibility of the algorithm and data used by the AI-based system (ISO/IEC TR 29119-11).

SELF-ASSESSMENT EXERCISES

1. What is flexibility and adaptability? Name the flexibility and adaptability requirements of an AI-based system.
2. Can any AI-based system be considered an autonomous one, or not? Explain your answer.
3. Name the forms of evolution for AI-based systems.
4. What are the developing constraints for self-learning AI-based systems?
5. Discuss what a bias is and how it can be introduced into AI-based systems.
6. List the ethical principles for AI.
7. What is a side effect and when can it occur in an AI-based system?
8. Explain what reward hacking in an AI-based system is. Give several examples.
9. Discuss explainable AI and its basic characteristics.
10. Should an AI-based system be safe? What are the signs indicating that it may be unsafe?

PART 2
MACHINE LEARNING

3 ML – OVERVIEW

SUMMARY

This chapter begins with a recap of the ML forms (supervised, unsupervised and reinforcement) first introduced in Chapter 1. Then it moves on to the topic of the ML workflow, focusing on understanding objectives, selecting an AI framework, building an algorithm, data preparation, model training, evaluation, tuning, testing, deployment, usage and monitoring. After that, the chapter covers the selection of a suitable ML approach, leading to reinforcement learning, unsupervised learning (clustering or association) or supervised learning (classification or regression), based on the data characteristics. It also goes over the topics of underfitting and overfitting, which is crucial to developing effective ML models that generalise well to new data. Lastly, it introduces generative and discriminative models, providing examples.

LEARNING OBJECTIVES

After reading this chapter, you should be able to:

- Describe classification and regression as part of supervised learning (K2)
- Describe clustering and association as part of unsupervised learning (K2)
- Describe reinforcement learning (K2)
- Summarise the workflow used to create an ML system (K2)
- Given a project scenario, identify an appropriate form of ML (from classification, regression, clustering, association or reinforcement learning) (K3)
- Explain the factors involved in the selection of ML algorithms (K2)
- Summarise the concepts of underfitting and overfitting (K2)
- Demonstrate underfitting and overfitting (K2)

LINKS TO OTHER CHAPTERS

This chapter is related to other chapters as follows:

- Chapter 1 looks at different ML techniques used for three forms of ML: supervised, unsupervised and reinforcement learning. It also goes over AI development frameworks, which are selected during the initial model development stage of the ML workflow.

- Chapter 4 provides the basis for data preparation activities.
- Chapter 5 details ML functional performance metrics, which are identified as acceptance criteria and are estimated at the training, evaluation, tuning and test stages of the ML workflow.
- Chapter 7 has guidelines on input data testing and ML model testing.
- Chapter 9 describes different methods and techniques for the testing of AI-based systems.

3.1 FORMS OF MACHINE LEARNING

Let us begin this chapter by reiterating something we talked about in Chapter 1, and that is that **ML algorithms** can be categorised as supervised learning, unsupervised learning and reinforcement learning, as shown in Figure 3.1.

Figure 3.1 Forms of ML

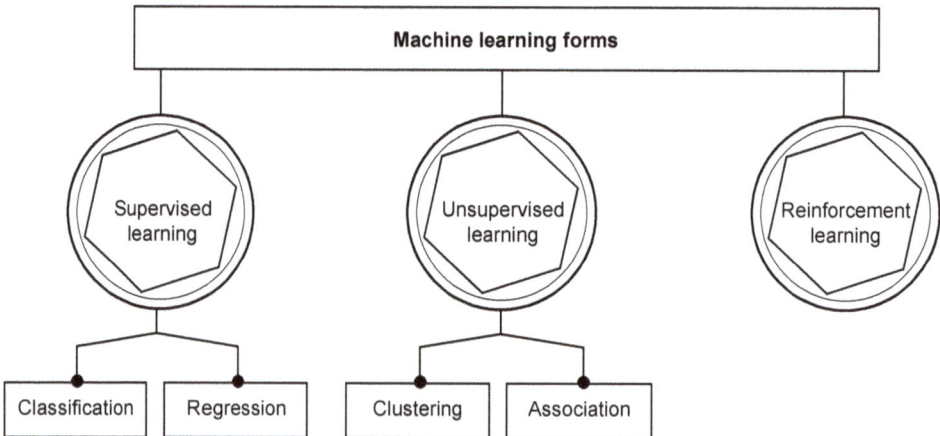

3.1.1 Supervised learning

Supervised learning is an ML technique where an algorithm learns to map input data to the corresponding desired output labels, given a set of labelled examples. Here a training dataset is provided, which consists of input samples and their corresponding correct output labels. The goal of the algorithm is to learn a mapping function that can accurately predict the output labels for new input data. The process of supervised learning involves two main components: the training phase and the prediction (or testing) phase. During the training phase, the algorithm analyses the labelled examples and adjusts its internal parameters to minimise the difference between the predicted outputs and the true outputs. This process is often referred to as model training or model fitting.

According to Figure 3.1, supervised learning aids us with issues of:

- classification, which is when the problem requires an input to be classified into one of several predefined classes (for example, classifying emails as spam or non-spam, or recognising handwritten digits);
- regression, which is when the problem requires the ML model to predict a numeric output using regression (for example, in predicting house prices, the algorithm can learn from a dataset containing features such as the size, number of bedrooms and location of houses, along with their corresponding sale prices – it can then predict the price of a new house based on its features).

3.1.2 Unsupervised learning

Unsupervised learning is a type of ML where an algorithm learns patterns and structures in unlabelled data without any specific output labels. Unlike supervised learning, this type of ML involves no predetermined correct answer or target variable to guide the learning process. The goal of unsupervised learning is to discover hidden patterns, structures or relationships in the data. It allows the algorithm to explore the data and identify similarities, clusters or patterns that may not be immediately apparent.

Figure 3.1 indicates that unsupervised learning helps us with the following issues:

- clustering, which is when the problem requires the identification of similarities in input data points that allows them to be grouped based on common characteristics or attributes (for example, categorising customers for marketing purposes);
- association, which is when the problem requires interesting relationships or dependencies to be identified among data attributes (for example, a product recommendation based on customers' shopping behaviour).

3.1.3 Reinforcement learning

Reinforcement learning is a type of ML that focuses on training agents to make sequential decisions in an environment to maximise a cumulative reward, because the agent is rewarded when it makes a correct decision and penalised when it makes an incorrect decision. Unlike supervised and unsupervised learning, reinforcement learning does not rely on labelling or the absence thereof. Instead, the agent learns through a trial-and-error process by interacting with the environment. Examples of reinforcement learning can be found in robotics, autonomous vehicles and chatbots.

Figure 3.2 summarises the key components of reinforcement learning:

- *Agent*: this is an ML system that interacts with the environment. It takes actions based on its current state and receives feedback in the form of rewards.

- *Environment*: this is an external system with which the agent interacts. It provides feedback to the agent and transitions to new states based on the agent's actions.

- *State*: this is a current representation of the environment at a particular time. It gives us information about how the agent understands the environment, which helps it to make decisions.

- *Action*: these are the choices available to the agent at each state. The agent selects actions based on its policy and the current state.

- *Reward*: this is the feedback from the environment after the agent takes an action. It indicates the desirability of the agent's actions and is used to guide the learning process.

Figure 3.2 Key components of reinforcement learning (Source: Adapted from Ashwin and Raj, 2023)

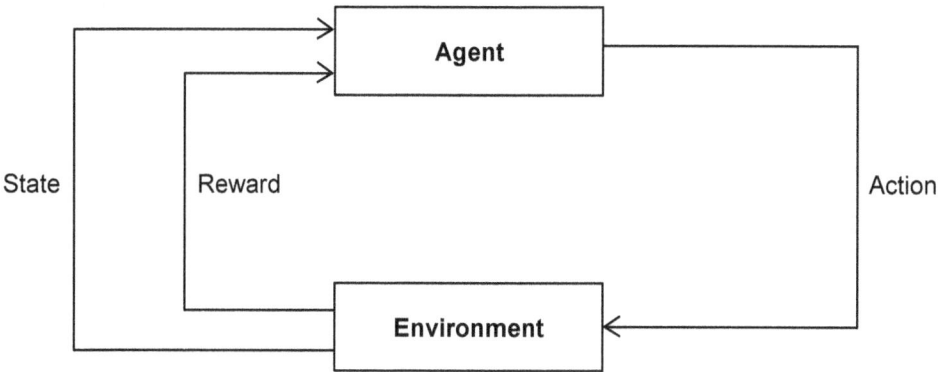

Quick questions

Question 3.1

As a data scientist, you have been asked to perform market research and divide customers into several groups. What form of ML was used to develop the model if the investigation results are as given in Figure 3.3? Select ONE option.

    A. reinforcement learning
    B. supervised learning
    C. neural network
    D. unsupervised learning

Figure 3.3 Customer groups

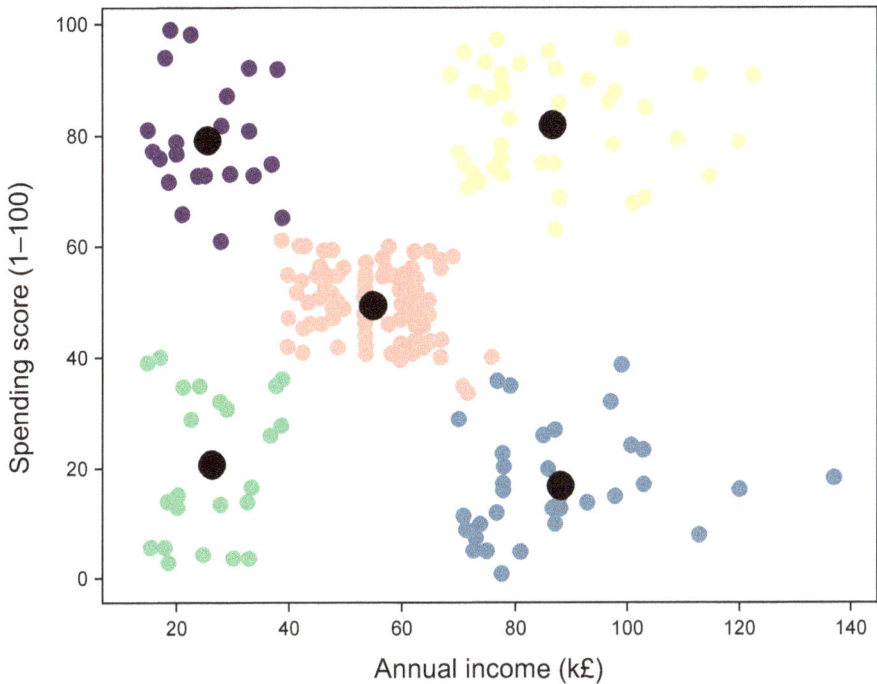

Question 3.2

An ML model is used to optimise heating, ventilation and air conditioning systems in buildings, learning to adjust temperature settings in real time to maximise energy efficiency while ensuring occupants' comfort. Which form of ML is MOST likely used to implement this model? Select ONE option.

    A. unsupervised learning

    B. supervised learning

    C. reinforcement learning

    D. optimisation learning

3.2 ML WORKFLOW

Let us go over the **ML workflow**. Figure 3.4 provides a diagram for it, and Figure 3.5 illustrates the steps.

Figure 3.4 The ML workflow diagram

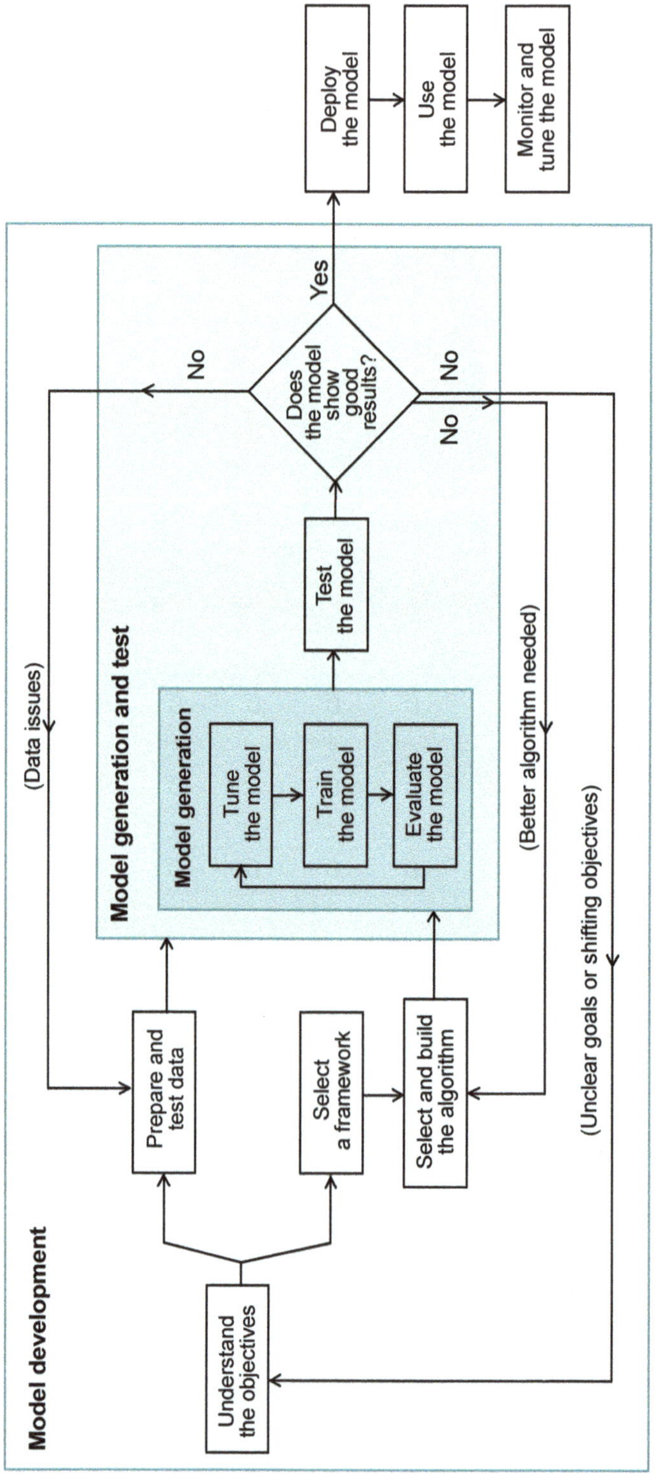

Model development

Model generation and test

Model generation

Tune the model

Train the model

Evaluate the model

Test the model

Does the model show good results?

Yes

No

No

No

(Data issues)

(Better algorithm needed)

(Unclear goals or shifting objectives)

Prepare and test data

Select a framework

Select and build the algorithm

Understand the objectives

Deploy the model

Use the model

Monitor and tune the model

First of all, we need to *understand the objectives*. All stakeholders need to agree on the purpose and acceptance criteria of the ML model to ensure alignment with business priorities.

Second, a suitable *AI development framework* should be selected based on the aforementioned objectives, acceptance criteria and business priorities.

Then *an ML algorithm* is *selected* and *built*. It may be coded manually, but it is often retrieved from a library of pre-written code. The algorithm is then compiled to prepare it for training the model, if needed.

After that, **data preparation** (see Section 4.1) *and testing* is required. This process consists of **data acquisition**, **data pre-processing**, *EDA* and **feature engineering**. The data used by the model will be based on the set objectives and used by all the activities in the 'model generation and test' phase. For example, if we have a real-time trading system, we will require market data, which must be representative. It is also possible to use pre-gathered datasets for the initial training. Otherwise, raw data will typically demand some pre-processing, feature engineering and testing (see Section 7.3.1 for more details on input data testing).

The ML algorithm uses data to *train the model*. Some algorithms, such as those generating a neural network, have to read the training dataset several times. Each iteration is called an **epoch**. Parameters defining the structure and controlling the training are passed to the model, and they are called model hyperparameters.

Then we **evaluate the model**. The ML functional performance metrics (see Chapter 5) are assessed using the **validation dataset**, thus trying to improve the model.

After that we **tune the model**. The results from the model evaluation are used to adjust the settings to fit the data and improve its performance. The model may also be tuned by adjusting hyperparameters, where the training activity is modified by changing the number of training steps or the amount of data used for training, or by updating attributes of the model.

Model evaluation and tuning should resemble a carefully conducted scientific experiment with controlled conditions and clear documentation. In practice, several models are typically created and trained using different algorithms, and then the best one is chosen. The three activities of training, evaluation and tuning help to generate the model.

Then we **test the model**. Once a model has been generated, it should be tested against an independent **test dataset** to ensure that the agreed **ML functional performance criteria** are met (see Section 7.3.2 on ML model testing). If the performance of the model with independent data is significantly lower than it was during evaluation, it may be necessary to select a different model. In addition to functional performance tests, non-functional tests, such as estimating the time to train the model and the time and resource usage taken to provide a prediction, also need to be run. Typically, these tests are performed by data scientists, but testers with sufficient knowledge of the domain can help here as well.

Figure 3.5 The ML workflow illustrated

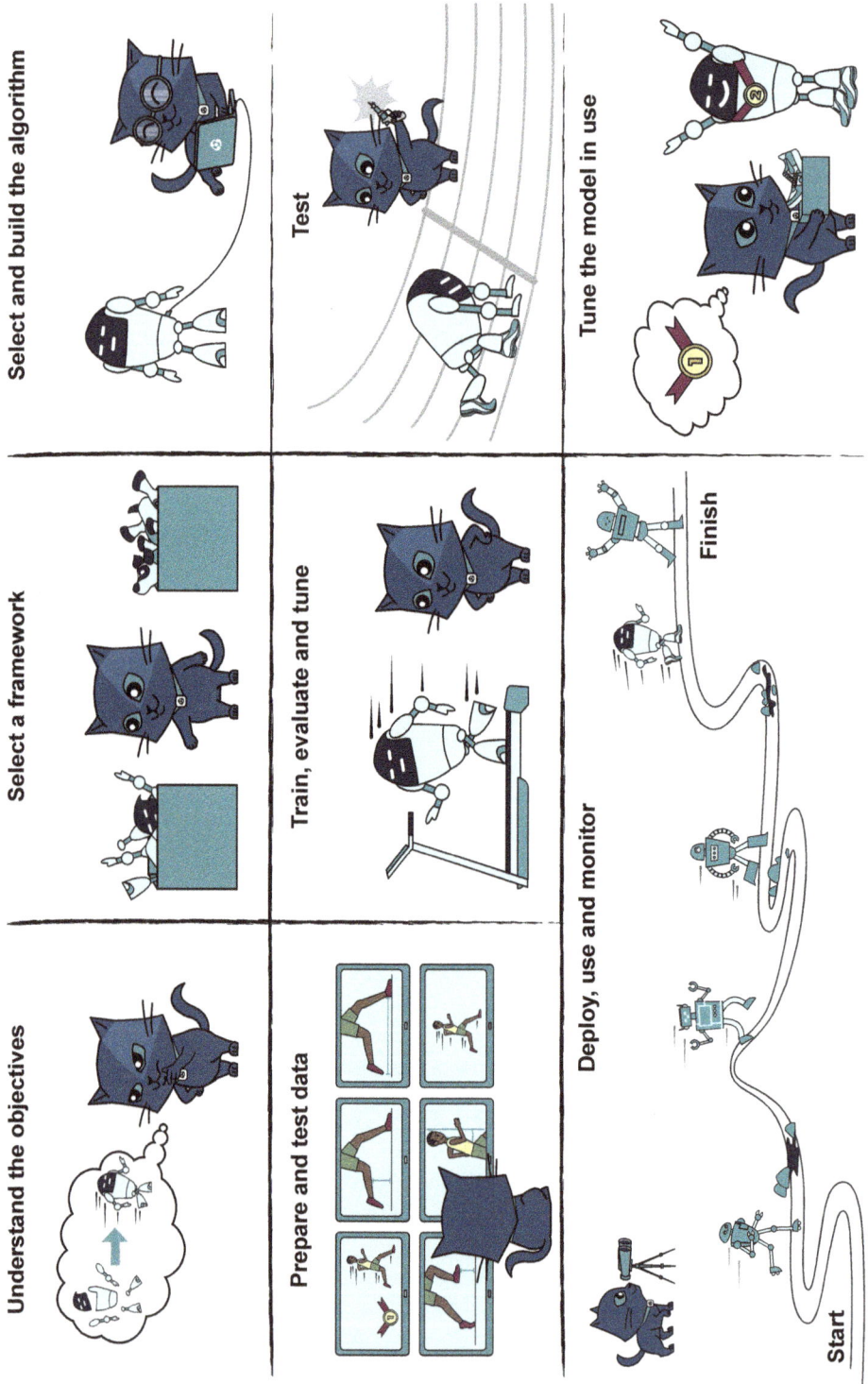

All the considered ML activities define the *model development* phase.

The next step is **model deployment**. Once development is complete, the tuned model typically needs to be re-engineered for deployment along with its related resources, including the relevant **data pipeline**. This is normally achieved through the deployment framework. Targets might include embedded systems and the cloud, where the model can be accessed via a web API.

After that we *use the model*. Once deployed, the model becomes part of a larger AI-based system. It may perform scheduled batch predictions at specified time intervals or run upon request in real time.

Lastly, we *monitor and tune the model*. While the model is being used, its conditions may evolve, and the model may drift away from what is intended. To ensure that any drift is identified and managed, the operational model should be regularly evaluated against its acceptance criteria. It may require the adjustment of the model's settings to address the drift, or re-training with new, updated data to create a more accurate and robust model. The new model may then be compared against the existing model, for example using a form of A/B testing (see Section 9.4).

The workflow we have considered is a set of logically sequential steps, as in the Waterfall model in Figure 3.6, but in practice the workflow steps are repeated *iteratively*, just like iterative lifecycle models such as Agile (Yadav, 2015) when we receive feedback and generate preliminary cumulative outcomes (Figure 3.7).

Figure 3.6 The Waterfall model

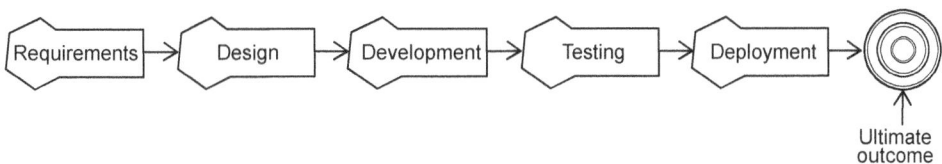

Usually, the key point here lies in the testing phase of the model. If the model shows low or insufficient results at this stage, a decision may be made to change the model (return to the 'Select and Build the Algorithm' step). It may also be that the data was originally not sufficiently examined and prepared, and not all of the model features useful for learning have been selected. If so, the specialist will return to the 'Prepare and Test Data' step, and the whole process will be repeated, and this may happen several times. There could be a possibility that the objectives have been misunderstood, then the specialist will return to the 'Understand the Objectives' step. This is illustrated by three 'NO' branches going out of 'Does the Model Show Good Results?' in Figure 3.4, and here is why:

- 'NO' to 'Select and Build the Algorithm': this path suggests that the algorithm itself might not be suitable. You may need to switch to a different algorithm or model architecture that is a better fit.

Figure 3.7 The Agile model

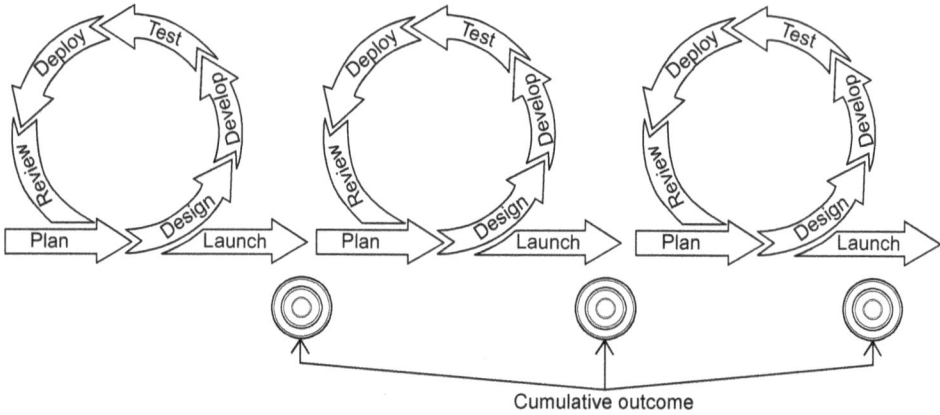

Cumulative outcome

- 'NO' to 'Prepare and Test Data': sometimes, poor results are due to issues with the data itself. Perhaps it is insufficient, unbalanced, noisy or lacks important features. This path implies going back to improve data quality or collect more data.

- 'NO' to 'Understand the Objectives': this implies that it could be that the problem was not clearly defined or the goals changed mid-project.

Please note that the phases shown here do not include the integration of the ML model with the non-ML parts of the overall system. If the model is part of a larger AI-based system, it will need to be integrated into this system prior to deployment. In this case, integration, system and acceptance test levels might be performed.

Quick questions

Question 3.3

Which step in an ML workflow is responsible for transforming raw data into a format suitable for modelling? Select ONE option.

    A. model training

    B. data pre-processing

    C. model evaluation

    D. feature engineering

Question 3.4

Which of the following is an essential step in model tuning during an ML workflow? Select ONE option.

    A. Collecting additional training data.

    B. Using a test dataset to measure the model's performance on unseen data.

    C. Pre-processing the raw data to remove noise.

    D. Adjusting hyperparameters to improve model performance.

3.3 SELECTING A FORM OF ML

Let us explore how to select the appropriate ML approach based on the task at hand. By answering the questions and following the steps in Figure 3.8, we can easily navigate the diagram.

The first question we need to ask ourselves is: do we have structured training data? If not, the next question is: do we have *rules for rewarding and penalising*? If our answer is again 'no', our task might not be applicable for ML at all; but, if those rules do exist, then *reinforcement learning* may be applied.

Let us go back to the question about the structured data. Now, if our answer is 'yes', then it takes us to another question: do we have labelled data? If the answer is 'no', we have to ask ourselves if the problem involves grouping similar data. If the answer is 'yes', it may be *clustering*. If the answer is 'no', then we ask if the problem involves *finding co-occurring data items*, which may be an association in case of a positive answer, otherwise our task might not be applicable for ML in the case of a negative answer. Both clustering and association point to *unsupervised learning*.

Let us go back to the question about *labelled data*. If our answer is 'yes', then we ask a question if the output data is categorical. If the output is discrete and categorical, it may be *classified*. If the output is numeric and continuous in nature, *regression* is more suitable. Regression and classification suggest there is an output label, which means it may be *supervised learning*.

From theory to practice

Take a look at the application of the workflow diagram for selecting a form of ML.

Example 1. Classification: spam detection

We need to sort emails as either spam or not spam, based on their content and other relevant features. For the training purposes, we have a dataset of emails, each labelled as spam or not spam, along with features extracted from the email text, such as the presence of certain keywords, the length of the email and the number of exclamation marks. A part of this dataset is shown in Figure 3.9. What is an appropriate ML approach that we can use to build the model?

Figure 3.8 Selecting a form of ML

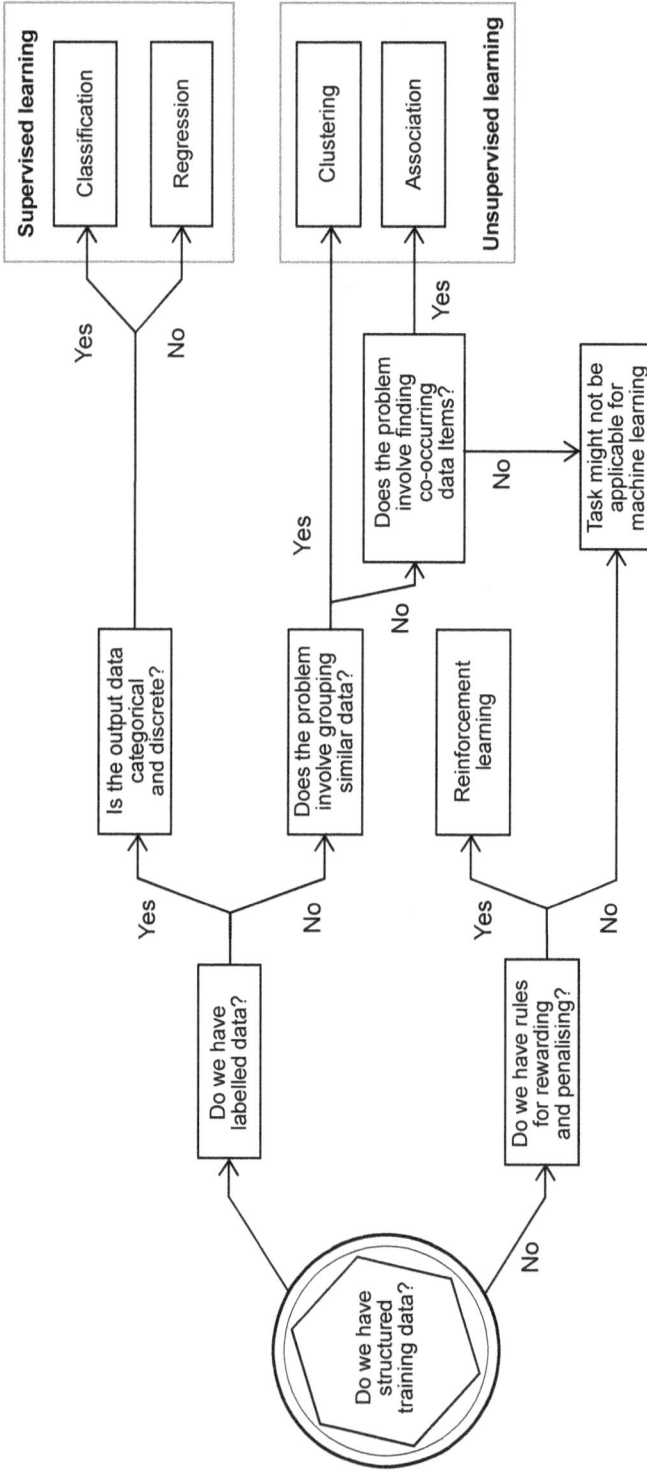

Figure 3.9 A part of the emails dataset

Email #	Keywords	Length (in words)	Exclamation marks	Class
1	discount, sale	150	2	spam
2	meeting, agenda	200	0	not spam
3	free, win	100	3	spam
4	report, analysis	180	0	not spam

Let us look at the workflow diagram in Figure 3.8 and answer several questions. Do we have structured training data? Yes. Do we have labelled data? Yes. Is the output data categorical and discrete? Yes. Then *classification* is the appropriate ML approach for the considered problem with the emails.

The objective is to build a classification model that can accurately predict whether a new email is spam or not. Using a classification algorithm such as logistic regression or SVM, we can train a model on the labelled dataset to learn the patterns and relationships between the input features and the target class labels (spam or not spam). By training a classification model on this data, the model will learn the patterns that find spam emails based on the input features. It will find the decision boundary that separates the two classes. Once the model is trained, it can be used to predict the class of new, unseen emails. For instance, given the features of a new email (e.g. keywords: 'offer'; 'buy'; length: '120'; exclamation marks: '1'), the classification model can predict whether it is spam or not spam.

Example 2. Regression: predicting house prices

We have to predict house prices based on various features such as size, number of rooms, location and other relevant factors. Suppose we have a simplified scenario, when a dataset of houses with their corresponding features and their actual sale prices is available for the training purposes. This dataset might look like the one given in Figure 3.10. What is an appropriate ML approach to build the model?

Figure 3.10 A part of the houses dataset

House #	Size (m²)	Number of rooms	Location	Sale price (£)
1	140	3	Suburban	250,000
2	185	4	Urban	350,000
3	170	3	Suburban	300,000
4	200	5	Urban	400,000

Let us review the workflow diagram in Figure 3.8 and answer the questions one by one. Do we have structured training data? Yes. Do we have labelled data? Yes. Is the output data categorical and discrete? No. It is numerical. Hence we need to use *regression* as an appropriate ML approach for the price prediction problem.

The objective is to develop a regression model that can accurately predict the sale price of a house based on its features. By using a regression algorithm such as linear regression, we can train a model on the labelled dataset to learn the patterns and relationships between the input features and the target sale prices. By training a regression model on this data, the ML model will learn to predict house prices based on the given features. The trained model can then be used to predict the sale price of new houses based on their features: size, number of rooms and location.

For example, if we have a new house with the size of 175 m², three rooms and located in an urban area, the regression model might predict a sale price of around £320,000.

Example 3. Association: market basket analysis

We need to conduct a market basket analysis that aims to discover relationships or associations between items that are frequently purchased together in a transactional dataset. We will consider a simplified scenario again.

Suppose we have a dataset of customer transactions in a supermarket, where each transaction consists of a list of items purchased (see Figure 3.11). The value 1 means the presence of the item in the corresponding transaction, and the value 0 represents the absence of an item in that transaction. For example, the dataset might contain transactions such as:

- Transaction 1: {Bread, Milk, Eggs}
- Transaction 2: {Bread, Milk, Beer}
- Transaction 3: {Milk, Nappies, Beer, Chips}
- Transaction 4: {Bread, Milk, Nappies, Beer}

Figure 3.11 A dataset of customer transactions in a supermarket

Transaction ID	Bread	Milk	Eggs	Nappies	Beer	Chips
1	1	1	1	0	0	0
2	1	1	0	0	1	0
3	0	1	0	1	1	1
4	1	1	0	1	1	0

What is an appropriate ML approach in this situation?

Let us go through the workflow diagram in Figure 3.8 and answer the questions. Do we have structured training data? Yes. Do we have labelled data? No. Does the problem involve grouping similar data? No. Does the problem involve finding co-occurring data items? Yes. Hence *association* may be applied as an appropriate ML approach for the market basket analysis.

The objective is to identify associations between items in customer transactions in a supermarket, such as which items tend to be bought together. In this case, we can apply an association rule mining algorithm, such as the Apriori algorithm (Xie, 2021), to discover frequent itemsets and association rules. The algorithm identifies patterns and relationships between items based on their co-occurrence in transactions.

Support is an indication of how frequently an itemset appears in the dataset, with a higher support value meaning more frequent occurrence. The support (in percentages) of the itemset containing both items A and B equals the percentage of the transactions in the dataset that contain A and B. Figure 3.12 indicates the support values for the itemsets in the customer transaction dataset shown in Figure 3.11.

During the Apriori algorithm execution, the support is calculated for candidate itemsets, and those itemsets whose support exceeds a predefined minimum support threshold are considered frequent. Frequent itemsets are then used to generate association rules. Let us say we set a minimum support threshold of 50 per cent (itemset must appear in at least 50 per cent of transactions to be 'frequent'). Applying the algorithm, we might discover the associations given in Figure 3.13.

Figure 3.12 Support values for the itemsets in the customer transaction dataset in a supermarket

Rule	Support (%)
if buy bread, then buy milk	75
if buy milk, then buy nappies	50
if buy bread, then buy beer	50
if buy milk, then buy beer	75
if buy nappies, then buy beer	50

Figure 3.13 Association rules for customer transactions in a supermarket

Association rule	Support (%)
Bread => Milk	75
Milk => Bread	75
Milk => Nappies	50
Nappies => Milk	50
Bread => Beer	50
Beer => Bread	50
Milk => Beer	75
Beer => Milk	75
Nappies => Beer	50
Beer => Nappies	50

Frequent itemsets:

- {Bread, Milk}: 75 per cent (appears in three out of four transactions);

- {Milk, Beer}: 75 per cent;

- {Milk, Nappies}: 50 per cent;

- {Bread, Beer}: 50 per cent;

- {Nappies, Beer}: 50 per cent.

These results indicate that bread and milk, as well as milk and beer, are frequently purchased together, as they appear together in 75 per cent of transactions. The same goes for all 50 per cent outcomes. The trained association model can be used to predict which items might be bought together with items in a new transaction of a customer in a supermarket. The insights into the relationships between items might be used for various purposes, such as product placement, cross-selling or targeted marketing.

Example 4. Clustering: customer segmentation

We need to create an algorithm that helps to group customers based on their characteristics and past behaviour. Let us consider a simplified scenario. Suppose you have a dataset containing information about customers in an e-commerce business. According to Figure 3.14, each customer is described by features such as age, income, browsing history and purchase behaviour. What is an appropriate ML approach that we can use to build the model?

Figure 3.14 Part of a customer dataset

Customer #	Age	Income (£)	Browsing history (minutes)	Purchase behaviour
1	30	50,000	5	Frequent
2	45	70,000	15	Moderate
3	25	35,000	3	Occasional
4	40	60,000	10	Frequent

Let us consider the workflow diagram in Figure 3.8 and answer several questions. Do we have structured training data? Yes. Do we have labelled data? No. Does the problem involve grouping similar data? Yes. Then we have *clustering* as an appropriate ML approach for the problem of customer segmentation.

The objective is to cluster the customers into distinct groups to gain insights and make targeted marketing strategies. Using a clustering algorithm such as K-means, we can perform customer segmentation. By training the model on the unlabelled customer dataset, the algorithm will automatically group customers based on similarities in their feature values. For example, if we choose to cluster the customers into three groups, an ML clustering model might group the customers as follows:

- Cluster 1 (frequent shoppers with moderate to high income): Customer 1, Customer 4;

- Cluster 2 (moderate shoppers with higher income and longer browsing history): Customer 2;

- Cluster 3 (occasional shoppers with lower income and shorter browsing history): Customer 3.

The trained model can then be used to assign new customers to some customer segments based on their features. The resulting clusters provide insights into these different customer segments. The business can tailor marketing strategies and promotions based on the characteristics of each cluster. For example, Cluster 1 customers may be targeted with loyalty programmes or personalised recommendations to encourage more frequent purchases, while Cluster 3 customers could be engaged with targeted discounts or incentives to increase their engagement.

One can interpret the clusters to gain insights into different customer segments, based on their income and various spending scores. Keep in mind that, in a real-world scenario, you may have more features and a larger dataset for more meaningful segmentation.

Example 5. Reinforcement learning: autonomous navigation

We need to have an autonomous robot that is able to learn how to navigate through a maze to reach a target location by taking actions such as moving forward, turning left, turning right or staying in place. The optimal sequence of actions should be found that leads the robot to the target location while avoiding obstacles. The robot starts with no prior knowledge of the maze or the optimal path to the target. The current configuration of the robot and its surroundings, which includes its position in the maze, is available. The environment provides the feedback signal to the agent based on its actions. The reward can be positive for reaching the target or negative for hitting an obstacle. What is an appropriate ML approach in this situation?

Let us look again at the workflow diagram in Figure 3.8 and answer the questions. Do we have structured training data? No. Do we have rules for rewarding and penalising? Yes. So *reinforcement learning* can be applied.

As we have learned before, the reinforcement learning process needs the following key components: Agent, Environment, State, Action and Reward (Figure 3.2). Consider them separately within our problem:

- *Agent* is an autonomous robot that learns to navigate the maze.
- *Environment* is the maze itself, which provides feedback to the agent based on its actions.

- *State* is the current configuration of the robot and its surroundings, which includes its position in the maze.

- *Action* is the possible moves the robot can take at any given state (back, forwards, left, right).

- *Reward* is the feedback signal provided by the environment to the agent based on its actions. The reward can be positive for reaching the target or negative for hitting an obstacle.

The project objective is to build a reinforcement learning model that can be used to teach the robot to navigate the maze efficiently. To apply reinforcement learning, the agent starts exploring the maze by taking random actions. Initially, the agent's actions are likely to be inefficient and random. However, as the agent progresses and receives feedback from the environment, it learns to associate certain actions with higher rewards. Through trial and error, the agent discovers the actions that lead to positive outcomes and avoids actions that result in negative rewards. To improve its performance, the agent employs a learning algorithm, such as Q-learning or policy gradients (Graesser and Keng, 2019). This algorithm updates the agent's policy or value function based on the rewards received and the expected future rewards. The agent repeats the steps discussed above for multiple episodes, gradually improving its performance by learning from the rewards it receives. Over time, through repeated iterations, the agent learns to navigate the maze effectively, avoiding obstacles and reaching the goal more consistently. It learns the optimal strategy by associating actions with the highest expected rewards in different states.

3.4 FACTORS INVOLVED IN ML ALGORITHM SELECTION

There is no definitive approach to choosing an optimal ML algorithm, model settings and model hyperparameters. In practice, this set is chosen based on a mix of the following factors:

- the required functionality;
- the required quality characteristics, such as:
  - accuracy;
  - constraints on available memory;
  - model training (and re-training) speed;
  - prediction speed;
  - transparency, interpretability and explainability requirements;
- the type of data available for training the model;
- the amount of data available for training and testing the model;
- the number of attributes in the input data expected to be used by the model;

- the expected number of groups for clustering;
- previous experience;
- the trial-and-error method.

3.5 OVERFITTING AND UNDERFITTING

As we have learned earlier, when an ML expert chooses the best model, he or she looks at quality indicators, among other things, which may lead to several possible outcomes.

Figure 3.15(a) illustrates the first situation, which is **overfitting**. Overfitting is when a model performs well on a training dataset, but as soon as new data becomes available, the quality of the prediction deteriorates significantly. It can occur when insufficient data is provided in the training dataset.

The second situation occurs when the model performs poorly on both the training data and the new data. Figure 3.15(b) shows the next outcome, which is called **underfitting**. Underfitting occurs when the model is not sophisticated enough to accurately fit to the patterns in the training data.

And the third situation is when the model is equally good at predicting both training and new data. This, of course, is the *best case scenario* presented in Figure 3.15(c).

Figure 3.15 Overfitting (a), underfitting (b) and the best case scenario (c)

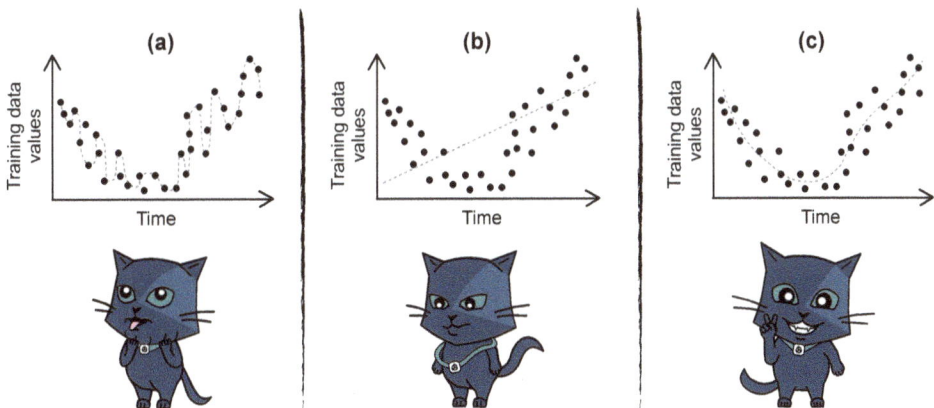

Figure 3.16 presents a diagram that aids in identifying the discussed situations. Unfortunately, cases of overfitting and underfitting are quite common. *Overfitting* occurs when a model fails to generalise to new data but performs exceedingly well on the training data. This often happens when a model becomes too complex or has too many parameters specific to the available training data. Signs of overfitting include performing well on a training set but failing on a test set. An *underfit* model, on the

---

Figure 3.16 Workflow for underfit, overfit and good ML models

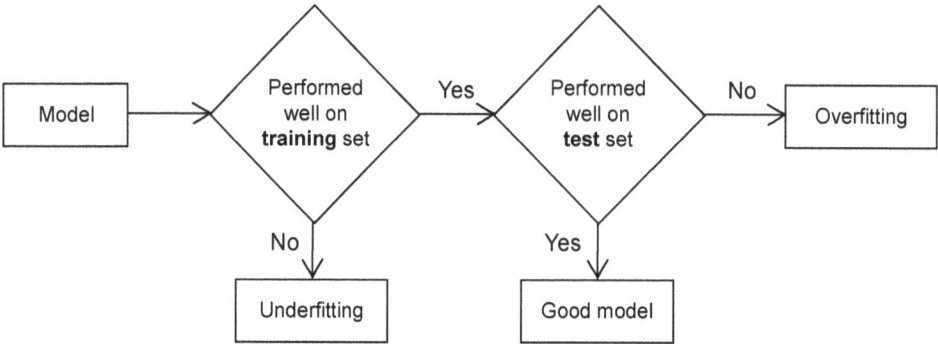

other hand, exhibits high errors on both the training and test data. It occurs when a model is too simplistic or lacks the capacity to capture the underlying data patterns. This may result in a model that is too generalised and fails to capture important data trends. Overcoming overfitting and underfitting is essential in developing good and effective ML models. The goal is to find the right balance where the model generalises well to new data by accurately capturing the underlying patterns and relationships in the data.

Quick questions

Question 3.5

Figure 3.17 illustrates different polynomial models for a scatter plot. Which of the following options is the CORRECT description of these ML models? Select ONE option.

    A. Model 1 is an underfit model. Model 2 is a good model. Model 3 is an overfit model.

    B. Model 2 is a good model. Model 3 is an underfit model. Model 4 is an overfit model.

    C. Model 1 is a good model. Model 3 is an underfit model. Model 4 is an overfit model.

    D. Model 1 is an overfit model. Model 2 is a good model. Model 4 is an overfit model.

Figure 3.17 Polynomial models for a scatter plot

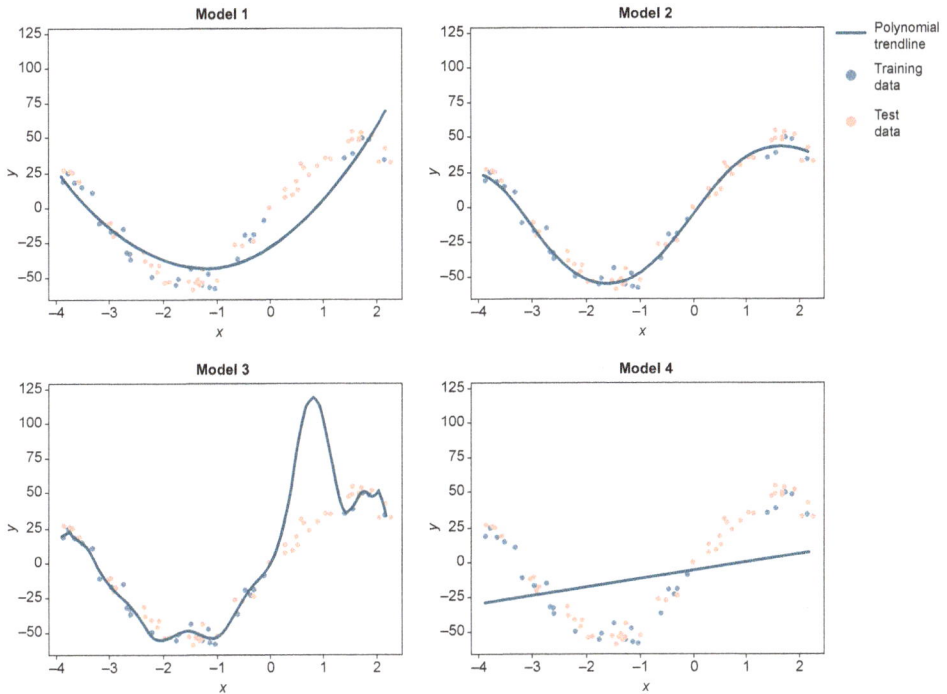

3.6 GENERATIVE AND DISCRIMINATIVE MODELS

In addition to the categorisation of ML algorithms provided by the ISTQB CT-AI syllabus, which was discussed earlier, there is also another well-known and generally accepted division of ML models into two types of ML approaches: generative models and discriminative models (Ng and Jordan, 2001), each with specific goals and applications.

Generative models learn the joint probability distribution of input data and their labels (or outputs). These models understand how data and labels are generated together, which allows them to create new data similar to the training examples. For instance, a generative model trained on cat images can generate new, realistic cat pictures.

Examples of generative models include:

- *Variational autoencoder (VAE)*: a type of neural network architecture that is used to compress data into a latent space and then reconstruct it, enabling the generation of new samples (Asperti et al., 2021).

- *Generative adversarial network (GAN)*: a type of neural network architecture that uses two neural networks: one as a 'generator' to create data and the other as a 'discriminator' to evaluate its realism, improving through competition (Guo et al., 2022).

- *Large language model (LLM)*: a category of language models that utilises neural networks and is used for various language-related tasks (Raiaan et al., 2024), such as predicting the next word in a sequence, and generating coherent text, such as the well-known GPT model is doing.

Generative models are useful for tasks such as data augmentation, image synthesis and text generation, but they require more data and computational resources.

Discriminative models, on the other hand, learn the conditional probability of labels when given the input data. Rather than modelling how data is generated, they focus on distinguishing between different classes or labels. For example, a discriminative model trained on cat and dog images will classify new images as 'cat' or 'dog' without generating new images.

Examples of discriminative models include logistic regression, SVM and neural network classifiers (see Section 1.4 on AI technologies).

Discriminative models are efficient for classification tasks and tend to perform well when ample labelled data is available. However, they cannot generate new data.

Discriminative models can be based on learning paradigms other than supervised learning, though supervised learning is the most common approach. Not all supervised learning uses discriminative models. Some supervised learning methods use generative models, which learn how both the data and labels are related. These models can also make predictions, but they can do more – such as generating new examples that look like the training data.

TERMS

Data acquisition: the activity of acquiring data relevant to the business problem to be solved by an ML model.

Data pipeline: the implementation of data preparation activities to provide input data to support training by an ML algorithm or prediction by an ML model.

Data preparation: the activities of data acquisition, data pre-processing and feature engineering in the ML workflow.

Data pre-processing: the activities of data cleaning, data transformation, data augmentation and data sampling in the ML workflow.

Epoch: an iteration of ML training on the whole training dataset.

Feature engineering: the activity in which those attributes in the raw data that best represent the underlying relationships that should appear in the ML model are identified for use in the training data (ISO/IEC TR 29119-11).

ML algorithm: an algorithm used to create an ML model from a training dataset.

ML functional performance criteria: criteria based on ML functional performance metrics used as a basis for model evaluation, tuning and testing.

ML model deployment: the process of placing a finished ML model into a live environment where it can be used for its intended purpose.

ML model evaluation: the process of comparing achieved ML functional performance metrics with required criteria and those of other ML models.

ML model testing: the process where the performance of a fully trained ML model is evaluated on an independent testing dataset.

ML model tuning: the process of testing hyperparameters to achieve optimum performance.

ML workflow: a sequence of activities used to manage the development and deployment of an ML model.

Overfitting: the generation of an ML model that corresponds too closely to the training dataset, resulting in a model that finds it difficult to generalise to new data (ISO/IEC TR 29119-11).

Test dataset (holdout dataset): a dataset used to test an ML model and evaluate the model developed from a training dataset.

Underfitting: the generation of an ML model that does not reflect the underlying trend of the training dataset, resulting in a model that finds it difficult to make accurate predictions (ISO/IEC TR 29119-11).

Validation dataset: a dataset used to evaluate a trained ML model with the purpose of tuning the model.

SELF-ASSESSMENT EXERCISES

1. What types of problems can be solved using supervised learning?
2. What is the difference between supervised and unsupervised learning?
3. What types of problems can be solved using unsupervised learning?
4. What is reinforcement learning, and what are the key challenges in its implementation?
5. Describe the main activities in the ML workflow.
6. What are the guidelines for selecting an appropriate ML approach?
7. Which quality characteristics of an ML model influence the selection of an ML algorithm?
8. What other factors are involved in the selection of ML algorithms?
9. Explain the concepts of overfitting and underfitting.
10. How can you demonstrate that an ML model is good and not underfit or overfit?

4 ML – DATA

SUMMARY

This chapter covers data preparation in the ML workflow, including data acquisition, pre-processing and feature engineering supported by EDA. It also talks about the challenges in data preparation, which include the need for domain knowledge, high-quality data sources, complex automation of the data pipeline, scalability, performance efficiency, defect checking priority during data preparation and avoiding sample bias. Then the chapter focuses on training, validation and test datasets and dataset quality issues. Lastly it goes over data labelling for supervised learning and introduces the self-supervised learning approach.

LEARNING OBJECTIVES

After reading this chapter, you should be able to:

- Describe the activities and challenges related to data preparation (K2)
- Perform data preparation in support of the creation of an ML model (H)
- Distinguish the roles of training, validation and test datasets in the development of an ML model (K2)
- Identify training and test datasets and create an ML model (H)
- Describe typical dataset quality issues (K2)
- Recognise how poor data quality can cause problems with the resultant ML model (K2)
- Recall the different approaches to the labelling of data in datasets for supervised learning (K1)
- Recall reasons for the data in datasets being mislabelled (K1)

LINKS TO OTHER CHAPTERS

This chapter touches on some concepts that are covered in other chapters:

- Chapter 2 explains sample bias.
- Chapter 3 covers supervised ML, describes the basis for the ML workflow and reviews overfitting.

4.1 DATA PREPARATION AS PART OF THE ML WORKFLOW

Figure 4.1 provides a typical breakdown of an ML workflow resource usage intensity (Sharma, 2020). According to this chart, data preparation uses the biggest part of the ML workflow effort, which makes it the most resource-intensive activity. This process takes in raw data, outputs data that can be used to train an ML model and uses that trained model to make predictions.

Figure 4.1 The ML workflow resource-intensity breakdown (Source: Adapted from Sharma, 2020)

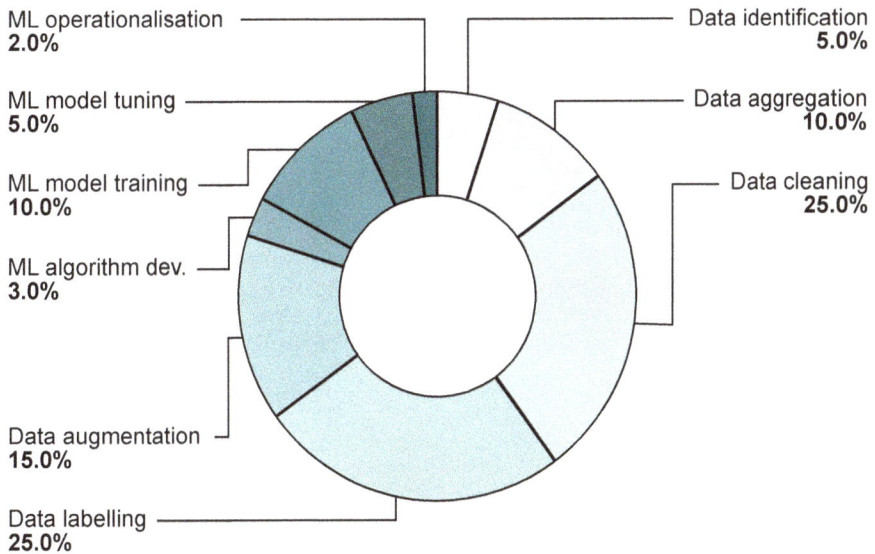

ML operationalisation
2.0%

ML model tuning
5.0%

ML model training
10.0%

ML algorithm dev.
3.0%

Data augmentation
15.0%

Data labelling
25.0%

Data identification
5.0%

Data aggregation
10.0%

Data cleaning
25.0%

Data preparation involves the activities of data acquisition, data pre-processing and feature engineering in the ML workflow that are typically supported by EDA (see Section 3.2 for the ML workflow steps). The data preparation steps are given in Figure 4.2.

The first phase is *data acquisition*. It is the activity of acquiring data relevant to the business problem to be solved by an ML model. We **identify** the structure, types and characteristics of data to be used for training and prediction, for example for a self-driving car, we decide if we need radar, camera and LiDAR data for imaging and object detection. Then we determine where and how we **gather** the data. After that, we **label** the data, which can take various forms (e.g. numerical, categorical, image, tabular, text, time series, sensor, video, audio, etc.).

During the second phase, data needs to be *pre-processed*. So we need to **clean** it, which means that incorrect data, duplicates or outliers are identified, removed or corrected. Next, we replace the missing values with estimated or guessed values. This process is called **data imputation**. The removal or anonymisation of personal information may also be performed. The data is then **transformed**, for example an address stored as a string

---

Figure 4.2 Data preparation steps

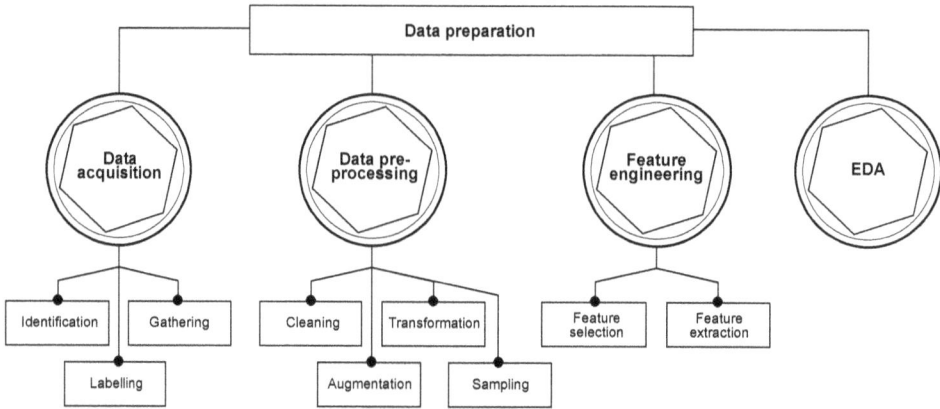

is broken down or categorical data is converted into numerical data. Operations such as standardisation and scaling can be applied to numerical data, which involves reducing the data to a single range. Then comes **augmentation**, which implies increasing the number of samples in a dataset. Lastly, we have **sampling**, which involves selection of some part of the available dataset so that patterns in the larger dataset can be observed. This is typically done to reduce costs and time. We need to keep in mind that all pre-processing carries a risk that it may change useful, valid data or add invalid data.

The last phase is *feature engineering*, which consists of feature selection and feature extraction. A feature is an attribute or property of an object reflected in the data. **Feature selection** picks the features that are most likely to contribute to model training and prediction and removes the ones that are not expected to have any effect on the model. By removing this noise, we can reduce overall training times, prevent overfitting (see Chapter 3) and increase accuracy. **Feature extraction** derives informative and non-redundant features from the existing features. This makes the dataset smaller, with the model retaining the equivalent accuracy.

EDA helps to identify the most informative features, reflecting the trends inherent in the data and using data visualisation to represent data in a visual format by plotting trends in the data.

Even though the aforementioned activities and sub-activities have been shown in a logical order, real-life projects may reshuffle them or even omit some steps, for example data cleaning may not be needed due to the high-quality datasets gathered during the data acquisition activity. It is also worth noting that some of the data preparation steps, such as the identification, are performed just once and can be performed manually. Other steps may be part of the operational data pipeline and normally work on live data. These tasks should be automated.

Quick questions

Question 4.1

Which of the following is the CORRECT order of steps in a typical ML workflow? Select ONE option.

A. Model training → Data acquisition → Model evaluation → Data pre-processing.

B. Data acquisition → Data pre-processing → Model training → Model evaluation.

C. Model evaluation → Model training → Data acquisition → Data pre-processing.

D. Data pre-processing → Model evaluation → Data acquisition → Model training.

From theory to practice

Example 1. Data identification

Implementing data identification is an essential first step, as it helps to ensure that you are aware of what kind of data you are working with, which will influence the pre-processing techniques you use. Within the data identification step, you need to identify data types, which can be:

- *numerical*:
  - *continuous*: this is used to indicate measurements that can take any value within a range, e.g. income, speed, temperature, distance;
  - *discrete*: this is used for data that can only take certain values, e.g. number of items, full years;
- *categorical*: this is used to divide information into distinct groups or categories, which can be:
  - *ordinal*: when the categories can be ranked in a specific order, e.g. low/medium/high;
  - *nominal*: when the categories cannot be ranked in a specific order, e.g. gender, country names, product categories;
- *text*: this is textual content, e.g. requests for a chatbot, user-generated content in social media;
- *time series*: this is used for a time order sequence of data points, e.g. dates in historical trends;

- *image*: this is used in computer vision tasks when information from digital images is analysed;
- *audio*: this is used in speech recognition and sound analysis when, e.g., human speech, environmental sounds and music records are used as input data;
- *video*: this is a mix of audio and image data.

It is also important to understand the amount of data needed to build an ML model and to identify appropriate data structures. Data structures refer to methods of organising and storing data to enable efficient use. They can be:

- *linear* (e.g. arrays, lists, dictionaries, stacks, queues), which are best suited when data should be arranged in a sequential order and the number of data elements is predetermined or changes infrequently – they provide a simple and efficient way to store and access data, and, at the same time, each insertion or deletion requires shifting elements, which is computationally expensive;
- *non-linear* (e.g. trees, graphs), which are widely used for describing hierarchical data and provide quicker access – insertion and deletion of data elements – but can cause increased operational time and decreased performance;
- *hash tables*, which can be implemented as both linear or non-linear data structures and are ideal when rapid data retrieval and real-time data handling is needed, without any need for ordered data. Hash tables help with feature-indexing large datasets, but they do not guarantee an order of elements and are highly dependent on a quality hash function used to compute an index (hash code) into an array of buckets or slots, from which the desired value can be found.

Example 2. Data gathering

Data gathering in the data pre-processing stage of ML refers to the process of collecting and acquiring data that will be used to train, validate and test ML models. This step is critical because the quality and relevance of the data directly affect the model's performance. Better data collection leads to better predictions.

Gathering data from diverse sources can improve the robustness of the model. However, different sources may provide data in various formats, so you need to standardise it and combine it into a single dataset. At the same time, you need to ensure compliance with data privacy laws (e.g. GDPR). Data sources used to gather data can be:

- *internal*: data that exists within the organisation, such as databases, logs, transaction records or customer data;
- *external*: public datasets, APIs, web scraping or purchasing third-party data;
- *synthetic*: data that is generated using simulations or statistical methods when real-world data is scarce or unavailable.

There are different possible methods to gather the data:

- *manual data collection*: gathering data manually from sources such as surveys, interviews or manual entries;
- *automated data collection*: using automated systems or software to collect data;
- *real-time data collection*: continuously collecting event and streaming data, e.g. data from sensors, online activity or financial transactions.

You can use one of these methods or several of them, depending on such factors as available data sources, problem objectives, type of data needed and data quality requirements. For example, if you need to predict stock prices based on real-time financial data, it is better to use real-time data collection through streaming tools, for example Kafka (Apache Software Foundation, 2025) or APIs.

Example 3. Data labelling

Data labelling in data pre-processing is a crucial step in ML, particularly for tasks involving supervised learning. It involves assigning labels or annotations to raw data so that ML algorithms can learn the relationship between input features and the desired output. This process helps to create a labelled dataset where each data point is associated with a target outcome or class.

Before labelling, it is important to define the task (e.g. classification, object detection) and the labels required. For example, to perform the spam detection task, you need to assign categorical labels such as 'spam' or 'not spam', and, for object detection tasks, you need to assign bounding boxes and class labels to objects in images.

There are several possible labelling approaches:

- *Manual labelling*: humans annotate or label the data. This is common for tasks such as image classification, where users manually assign labels (e.g. identifying objects in an image). It ensures accuracy but is time-consuming and expensive.
- *Automated labelling*: algorithms automatically generate labels. For example, a pre-trained model can be used to label data, but this method may lack precision, compared to manual labelling.
- *Crowdsourcing*: platforms such as Clickworker (2025) or Amazon Mechanical Turk (Amazon, 2025) allow multiple individuals to label data, which can be useful for large datasets.

High-quality and accurate labels are essential for training robust models. Therefore, it is important to ensure label consistency through clear label guidelines when multiple people are labelling the data. In this case, multiple annotators should produce the same labels for similar data points, and inter-annotator agreement used to evaluate the quality of the labels. **Inter-annotator agreement**, also known as **inter-rater reliability**, is a statistical measure used to assess the degree to which different individuals (annotators or raters) give consistent labels or ratings to the same items within a dataset when labelling or annotating data. Common metrics for measuring inter-annotator agreement are Cohen's Kappa and Fleiss' Kappa (Ben-David, 2008).

Example 4. Data cleaning

Data cleaning is an important step in data pre-processing. It ensures that ML models are trained on high-quality datasets, which, in turn, leads to more accurate and reliable predictions. The goal of data cleaning is to fix or remove incorrect, corrupted or incomplete data to improve the effectiveness of the ML model. Proper data cleaning often requires domain knowledge to make informed decisions about handling outliers, missing data and inconsistencies. You need to explore the data to understand its structure and detect any potential issues.

Missing data is common in many datasets. There are two possible ways to handle missing data effectively: remove incomplete data or impute it. Incomplete data can be removed if the amount of it is small and removing it does not affect the dataset's representativeness. Data imputation is a more sophisticated approach; it is when missing data is filled with estimates. Depending on the approach to estimating missing values, different types of data imputation techniques can be distinguished. There are several popular ones:

- *Mean imputation*: this is a method where the mean of the observed values for each variable is computed, and the missing values for that variable are imputed by this mean.

- *Median imputation*: this is a method where the median of the observed values for each variable is computed, and the missing values for that variable are imputed by this median.

- *Mode imputation*: this is a method where the most frequent value in the same feature/column is used to impute the missing values.

- *Forward fill*: this is a method where the previous observed value is used to fill the gap.

- *Backward fill*: this is a method where the next observed value is used to fill the missing values.

- *Maximum or minimum value imputation*: this is a method where the maximum or minimum value of the dataset or feature is used to replace missing values.

- *Fixed value imputation*: this is a method where a fixed value is used to replace missing values.

- *Predictive imputation*: this is a method where an ML model is used to predict the missing values based on other features.

Outliers are extreme values that differ significantly from other observations and can skew the results of the ML model. The possible ways to handle outliers are:

- *remove outliers*: if outliers are clearly erroneous data points, they can be removed;
- *cap outliers*: replace outliers with a specified threshold, like capping the data to a maximum value;
- *transform data*: use transformations, such as taking the logarithm or taking the square root of the variable of interest, to reduce the impact of outliers.

Duplicate data entries can distort model results, making it crucial to identify and remove them, particularly in large datasets. Furthermore, typographical errors or inconsistencies are possible inside the data, and they should be fixed.

Cleaning security-sensitive information is essential to prevent data breaches or misuse, maintain privacy and comply with regulations (such as GDPR). Anonymisation, masking, pseudonymisation and encryption are powerful tools to ensure data privacy and security. Each technique should be used based on the data type and security requirements, ensuring that sensitive information is safeguarded while still enabling effective ML model development.

Anonymisation is the process of transforming data in such a way that it no longer identifies an individual or sensitive entity. Anonymisation can be performed by means of the following techniques:

- *Removing personal identifiers*: strip out names, social security numbers, email addresses, phone numbers and other information that can directly identify a person.
- *Generalisation*: replace specific values with a generalised version (e.g. replace an exact date of birth with the year or an age range).
- *K-anonymity*: group records into clusters so that individuals cannot be uniquely identified. For example, instead of using exact addresses, group them by region (e.g. city or state level).

Data masking is the process of obscuring or replacing actual data with random or obfuscated data. Masked data cannot be traced back to the original value but remains useful for analysis. Data masking is divided into static and dynamic masking. Static masking is a technique where sensitive data is replaced with random but valid-looking values. This is useful when working with production data for development or testing purposes. Dynamic masking is a technique in which data is masked in real time, depending on who is accessing the data. For example, credit card numbers are replaced with asterisks (**** **** **** 1234) or hashes.

Pseudonymisation replaces identifiable information with artificial identifiers or pseudonyms. Unlike anonymisation, pseudonymised data can be re-identified using additional information (e.g. through a key that is stored securely). There are several possible ways for data pseudonymisation:

- *Tokenisation*: this is a robust data security technique that replaces sensitive data with unique identifiers called 'tokens' that have no exploitable meaning.

- *Hashing*: this is a technique in which cryptographic hashing algorithms are used to convert sensitive information into a fixed-length hash. Hashing is irreversible and ensures that sensitive information cannot be directly extracted from the dataset, for example email addresses or user IDs can be converted into hash values.

- *Encryption*: this is a technique where data is transformed into an unreadable format using algorithms and encryption keys. Only authorised parties with the correct decryption keys can access the original data.

The best practice while cleaning data is to keep records of the cleaning steps to ensure reproducibility and to check that the cleaning transformations or corrections have improved the data quality without introducing errors and removing valuable information. It should also be noted that removing too much data can reduce the representativeness of certain classes and lead to a *data imbalance* when the number of data points available for different classes is different.

Example 5. Data transformation

One of the most critical steps in the pre-processing phase is data transformation, which changes data from one format to another. Certain algorithms require the input data to be transformed, and if this step is skipped, it can lead to sub-optimal model performance or introduce bias.

For example, an ML model predicts the income level based on age, education and other factors. The age feature has a range from 18 to 80, while education is encoded as ordinal values (e.g. 1 for high school, 2 for a bachelor's degree and so on). If you do not apply proper scaling to the numerical features (such as age), the model could inadvertently give too much weight to the age feature simply because its numerical range (18–80) is much larger than that of education (1–5). This imbalance can lead to a model that places too much emphasis on age in its predictions, even if education has a stronger relationship with income.

Some of the main techniques used to deal with data transformation are:

- *Transformation for categorical variables* depending on the nature of the categorical data:
  - *Label encoding* for ordinal variables: this is a method that assigns a unique integer to each category in the variable. For example, string categories 'small', 'medium', 'large' are replaced with numbers 0, 1, 2.
  - *One-hot encoding* for nominal variables: this is a method where a new binary column for each unique category in the variable is created, assigning 1 or 0 based on the presence of a category. For example, if it is a column for a 'Colour' variable with categories 'Red', 'Green' and 'Blue', applying one-hot encoding transforms it to the three binary columns 'colour_red', 'colour_green' and 'colour_blue'. If you have a value of 'Colour' assigned to 'Green' in your record, then the 'colour_green' column will have a value equal to 1, and the other two columns will have values equal to 0.

- *Transformation for numerical variables*:

  - *Normalisation or min-max scaling*: this is a method that scales numerical data to a fixed predefined range, typically [0, 1] or [−1, 1]. This prevents variables with larger scales from dominating the model and causing biased results.

  - *Z-score normalisation or standardisation*: this is a method that transforms the data so that the mean of the data is 0 and the standard deviation is 1.

- *Transformation for date–time variables*:

  - *Extracting date components*: this is a method in which a date is broken down into components such as year, month, day, weekday and hour. This transformation helps models to recognise seasonal trends, daily patterns or specific time intervals that could affect the target variable.

  - *Extracting time components*: this is a method where time components such as hour, minute and second are extracted from the time series data. This transformation is useful in problems where time precision is important, such as in financial transactions or system logs.

  - *Handling time zones*: this is a method where a time zone component is extracted from the date-time values. This transformation is needed if your data contains date–time values in different time zones, and it is important to standardise them via converting all date–time values to a common time zone (e.g. UTC) to avoid inconsistencies.

In addition to these data transformation techniques, there are also discretisation and data aggregation.

Discretisation is a data transformation technique in ML that converts continuous variables into discrete values or bins, making them more suitable for analysis. This is particularly useful when an ML model or algorithm performs better with categorical data, or when a continuous variable has natural groupings that can improve interpretability or model performance. For example, for ages, you may want custom bins such as 0–18 (child), 19–35 (young adult), 36–60 (adult), 61–80 (senior), 81+ (elderly).

Data aggregation as a data transformation technique in ML that refers to the process of combining or summarising raw data points into more meaningful or higher-level features, making it easier to analyse and interpret the data. For example, in electronic health records, patient data is often aggregated over visits (e.g. average blood pressure readings or total medications prescribed) to build predictive models for diagnosing conditions or predicting hospital readmission.

Example 6. Data augmentation

Data augmentation is used during the data pre-processing phase in ML to increase the size and diversity of a dataset without actually collecting new data. It is particularly important when working with limited or imbalanced datasets, as it helps to improve model performance and generalisation and make the model robust to changes or noise in real-world data.

Data augmentation techniques depend on the type of data to be pre-processed. Below are some of them:

- *image augmentation* techniques for the computer vision:
  - *geometric transformations*:
    - *rotation*: rotating images by a certain angle;
    - *flipping*: flipping images horizontally or vertically;
    - *scaling/zooming*: enlarging or reducing the size of images;
    - *translation*: shifting images by a certain number of pixels horizontally or vertically;
    - *cropping*: randomly cropping portions of an image;
    - *Gaussian noise*: adding random noise to the image to simulate real-world imperfections;
    - *shearing*: skewing the image in a particular direction;
  - *colour distortion* used to increase the model resistance to lighting biases:
    - *brightness/contrast/hue/saturation adjustment*: altering the brightness, contrast, hue and saturation levels;
    - *altering the colour distribution*;
    - *manipulating the red, green, blue (RGB) colour channel histogram*;
    - *blurring/sharpening* to get different levels of focus and image clarity;
- *text data augmentation* techniques for NLP:
  - *synonym replacement*: replacing words with their synonyms;
  - *back translation*: translating the text into another language and back to the original language to introduce variations;
  - *random insertion/deletion*: randomly inserting or deleting words in the sentence;
  - *word embedding-based augmentation*: modifying words based on their vector representations;
  - *sentence shuffling*: shuffling or swapping the order of sentences or words;
- *time series augmentation* techniques:
  - *time warping*: stretching or compressing the time intervals in the sequence;
  - *jittering*: adding small noise to the time series data;
  - *window slicing*: randomly slicing sections of the time series data;
  - *scaling*: scaling the values in the time series data;
  - *permutation*: randomly permuting portions of the sequence;

- *tabular data augmentation* techniques:

  - *synthetic minority oversampling* technique for imbalanced datasets: generating synthetic samples by interpolating between existing samples;

  - *feature noise*: adding noise to the numerical features;

  - *resampling*: resampling existing data with slight modifications.

It should be noted that some augmentation techniques can distort the data in ways that do not reflect real-world variations, leading to worse model performance; therefore, you need to check for this. Furthermore, data augmentation can be computationally expensive, especially for large datasets, requiring more memory and processing power during training.

Example 7. Data sampling

Data sampling involves selecting a subset of data from a larger dataset to build, validate and test models. It can be useful for large datasets that are computationally expensive to process. Sampling helps to reduce the data size while maintaining statistical properties. It can also help to balance the classes when the initial dataset is imbalanced.

There are several widely used data sampling techniques:

- *Random sampling*: this is selecting data randomly from the dataset, ensuring that each value has an equal chance of being selected.

- *Stratified sampling*: this is dividing the data into distinct subgroups or 'strata' based on certain characteristics, and drawing the samples from each stratum in proportion to their occurrence in the overall dataset. This method ensures that each subgroup is properly represented in the sample, which is particularly useful when dealing with imbalanced data or when different subgroups might behave differently.

- *Systematic sampling*: this is selecting data points at regular intervals from the dataset, such as every 10th data point.

- *Oversampling*: this is increasing the frequency of under-represented classes to balance the dataset.

- *Undersampling*: reducing the frequency of over-represented classes to balance the dataset;

- *Cluster sampling*: this is dividing the data into clusters and randomly selecting samples from these clusters. This method is often used in geographic or domain-specific datasets.

Data sampling in large datasets carries a risk that important data points or patterns can be excluded from the sample, especially if those data points are rare or are outliers. This can lead to a less informative dataset and may prevent the model from capturing important trends, especially in cases where minority class instances are critical.

There is another risk – sample bias (see Chapter 2) – which occurs when certain groups or patterns are over-represented or under-represented.

By carefully choosing the appropriate sampling method and being aware of the potential risks, you can create a representative dataset that will lead to more accurate and generalisable ML models.

Example 8. Feature engineering

Feature engineering creates or transforms features to provide better input for the model. It helps to better represent the underlying patterns and relationships, improving model performance.

Feature selection chooses the most useful features from an existing set, potentially reducing the number of inputs for efficiency and accuracy. By eliminating irrelevant or redundant features, feature selection helps the model to focus on the most informative data, reducing overfitting. Fewer features reduce computational cost, making training times faster and memory usage lower. Furthermore, fewer features improve interpretability, making the model easier to understand and interpret.

There are several types of feature selection techniques:

- *Filter methods*: this is assessing each feature individually based on its correlation with the target variable by using some information, distance or correlation measures.

- *Wrapper methods*: this is evaluating subsets of features by training and evaluating the model on different feature subsets. These methods consider feature interactions but are computationally expensive.

- *Embedded methods*: this is generating all the combinations of the features and then using each of these combinations to train the model. The combination that gives the best performance is chosen for the final training.

The choice of technique used for feature selection depends on the application and the dataset's size and requires an in-depth understanding of the dataset.

Feature extraction is the process of transforming the original features into a new set of features that are more informative and compact. Unlike feature selection, which keeps a subset of existing features, feature extraction creates new features based on combinations or transformations of the original data. For example, feature extraction is needed when the data in its raw form is unusable. Feature extraction transforms this data into numerical features that ML algorithms can process. Typical use cases here are images and texts. For images, feature extraction involves identifying shapes, textures, colours and other visual information. These features can then be used for tasks such as image classification, object detection, facial recognition and image segmentation. For text, feature extraction transforms it into meaningful representations that capture the semantic, syntactic or statistical properties of the text. Usually, text is represented as a collection of words, and each unique word (in standard form) becomes a feature. The whole text is represented as a vector, where each element corresponds to the frequency (or presence) of a word in that text. This is used, for example, for text classification and information retrieval tasks.

There are some popular feature extraction techniques for different types of data:

- *Dimensionality reduction methods*:
  - *Principal component analysis (PCA)*: this is a linear dimensionality reduction technique that transforms data into a new coordinate system by identifying the directions (principal components) where variance is maximised. This method is commonly used in image compression, noise reduction and speeding up ML models by reducing input dimensionality.
  - *Linear discriminant analysis (LDA)*: this is a technique that finds a linear combination of features that best separates different classes by maximising the between-class scatter while minimising the within-class scatter.
  - *Autoencoders*: this is a neural network that consists of an encoder (compressing the input into a smaller feature space) and a decoder (reconstructing the input from the encoded representation). The compressed representation (latent space) captures important features of the data.
- *Textual data methods*:
  - *BoW*: this is a simple, widely used technique that represents text as a collection (bag) of words, ignoring grammar, order and structure.
  - *TF-IDF*: this is an extension of the BoW that adjusts the frequency of a word by how common or rare it is across documents.
- *Signal processing methods*:
  - *Fourier transform*: this is a signal processing technique used to transform signals from the time domain to the frequency domain.
  - *Wavelet transform*: this is a signal processing technique that decomposes signals (both frequency and time domain) into different frequency components.
- *Image data methods*:
  - *Histogram of oriented gradients (HOG)*: this is a technique that computes the distribution of intensity gradients or edge directions in an image.
  - *Colour histogram*: this is a technique that captures the distribution of colours in an image when an image is broken down into its colour components (e.g. RGB), and the number of pixels corresponding to each colour value is counted.
  - *Convolutional neural networks (CNNs)*: these are deep learning models specifically designed for image data. They automatically extract hierarchical features, from simple patterns, such as edges, to complex structures, such as objects.

During the feature extraction process, there is always the possibility of losing essential data, so you need to be careful with this.

Example 9. EDA

EDA helps you to decide which pre-processing steps and feature engineering techniques are necessary for building a predictive ML model. EDA typically involves a combination of statistical methods and visualisation techniques to understand the data distribution, identify missing values, outliers and anomalies, explore relationships in the data and select relevant features by revealing correlations and feature importance. EDA ensures that the dataset is well-understood before applying ML algorithms.

Statistical methods in EDA provide summary statistics for data, including understanding the range of data, its central tendencies (mean, median) and its dispersion (variance, standard deviation).

EDA heavily relies on visualisations to explore data relationships, distributions and patterns by means of different techniques:

- *Histograms and density plots*: these visualise the distribution of individual numerical features to identify skewness or multimodal distributions.
- *Bar plots and pie charts*: these are useful for categorical features to understand the frequency distribution.
- *Scatter plots*: these explore relationships between two numerical variables.
- *Box plots*: these visualise the distribution of data and detect outliers as points outside the whiskers.
- *Correlation heatmaps*: these identify pairwise correlations between numerical features.
- *Pair plots*: these visualise the relationships and distributions between multiple numerical features.
- *3D plots*: these are useful for visualising relationships between three variables (numerical or categorical).
- *Frequency plots*: these visualise the distribution of categorical data to check for imbalances.
- *Count plots*: these display the frequency of each category in a feature.

EDA can be effectively performed using a variety of tools and libraries. Several of the most popular Python libraries are pandas (2025), seaborn (2024), Matplotlib (2025) and NumPy (2025).

4.1.1 Challenges in data preparation

In order to perform data preparation, we need to know the application domain, the data and its properties and the various techniques associated with data preparation. Then we have to consider the difficulty of getting high-quality data from multiple sources and the complexity of automating the data pipeline. Said pipeline needs scalability and reasonable performance efficiency, which can drive up the costs associated with data preparation. The last two issues are 'not giving sufficient priority to checking for defects during data preparation' and 'the introduction of sample bias'. Figure 4.3 illustrates data preparation challenges.

From theory to practice

In the ever-evolving landscape of data management, the automation of data pipelines has emerged as a pivotal element in driving efficiency and scalability. However, the path to a fully automated data pipeline is fraught with challenges that organisations must navigate to harness the full potential of their data assets. One of the primary hurdles is the complexity of integrating various data sources. With data streaming in from disparate sources such as databases, APIs and microservices, creating a seamless flow requires meticulous planning and execution. The processes such as cleaning, transforming and augmenting data to make it usable add another layer of complexity to the task.

Data engineers often find themselves overwhelmed with the responsibility of cleaning and fixing data, debugging pipelines and ensuring compatibility among the pipeline's technologies. This not only consumes a significant amount of time but also poses a risk to data quality. Moreover, the dynamic nature of data itself presents a challenge. As the structure of incoming data changes, the pipeline must adapt accordingly without necessitating constant human intervention. This calls for a robust system that can handle it effectively.

Infrastructure maintenance is another area that can impede the smooth operation of automated data pipelines. Ensuring that the underlying systems are up-to-date and functioning correctly is crucial for the reliability of data flows. Organisational barriers, such as resistance to change and the alignment of cross-functional teams, also play a role in the successful implementation of data pipeline automation.

Despite these challenges, the benefits of automating data pipelines are undeniable. From enhanced data quality to improved decision-making capabilities, the strategic utilisation of automation tools can transform the way businesses leverage their data. By overcoming the obstacles of automation, organisations can achieve a level of data management that not only streamlines operations but also fosters innovation and growth.

Figure 4.3 Data preparation challenges

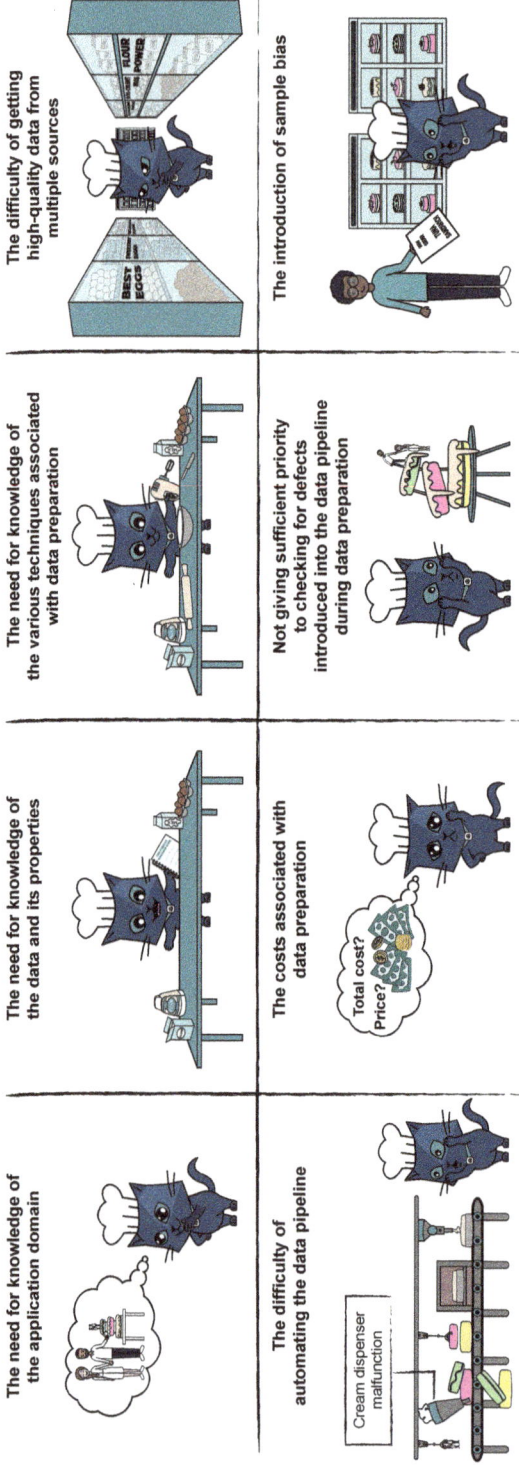

The need for knowledge of the application domain

The need for knowledge of the data and its properties

The need for knowledge of the various techniques associated with data preparation

The difficulty of getting high-quality data from multiple sources

The difficulty of automating the data pipeline

The costs associated with data preparation

Not giving sufficient priority to checking for defects introduced into the data pipeline during data preparation

The introduction of sample bias

4.2 TRAINING, VALIDATION AND TEST DATASETS IN THE ML WORKFLOW

Usually, three sets of equivalent data randomly selected from a single initial dataset are required to develop an ML model. They are a training dataset, a validation dataset and a test dataset (also known as the holdout dataset).

If unlimited suitable data is available, the amount of data used in the ML workflow for training, evaluation and testing typically depends on the training model algorithm and the availability of resources (such as random access memory, disk space, computing power, network bandwidth and the available time). Sufficient suitable data is hard to obtain, so the training and validation datasets are often derived from a single dataset, but the test dataset is kept separate. The model cannot be influenced by the test data, and test results have to give a true reflection of the model's quality.

There is no golden rule of splitting the dataset into these three categories, but the typical ratios, of training to validation to test, range from 60:20:20 to 80:10:10. Figure 4.4 shows these splits for boundary cases. Data splitting is often done randomly, unless the dataset is small or if there is a risk of losing the representative quality. If limited data is available, then splitting the data into three datasets may result in insufficient training. To overcome this issue, the training and validation datasets may be combined, and then used to create multiple split combinations (see Figure 4.5). Data is then randomly assigned to the training and validation datasets. Training, validation and tuning are performed using these multiple split combinations to create multiple tuned models. Overall performance is calculated as the average.

Figure 4.4 Boundary cases for a typical partitioning of the initial dataset into three categories

There are various methods used for creating multiple split combinations, which include:

- *Split-test*: this is where the dataset is randomly split into training and test datasets multiple times and, for each split, the model is trained and evaluated. The results are averaged to get a more accurate estimate of performance.

Figure 4.5 Multiple split combinations for combined training and validation datasets

- *Bootstrap sampling*: this is a resampling method where multiple datasets are created by randomly sampling the data with replacement. Each sample is then used to train the model, and the results are averaged.

- *K-fold cross validation*: here, a dataset is divided into K equal-sized subsets or 'folds' and, for each iteration, one fold is used as the test set, and the remaining K-1 folds are used for training. This process is repeated K times, with each fold being used as the test set exactly once. The final model performance is averaged across all K iterations to get a robust estimate of model accuracy.

- *Leave-one-out cross validation*: here, each data point is treated as a separate test dataset, while the remaining N-1 points are used for training. This process is repeated for every data point in the dataset. The method is appropriate when you have a small dataset.

- *Time-series splits*: these are special methods used to split the time-series data that cannot be split arbitrarily because the order of data matters. They include the following techniques:

  - *rolling window*: a sliding window is used, where each split uses sequential blocks of data for training and testing;

  - *expanding window*: the training dataset grows over time, using all prior data points up to a certain time for training, while the test dataset always moves forward in time.

Quick questions

Question 4.2

Which dataset is MOST likely used to tune model hyperparameters during the training process? Select ONE option.

A. training dataset

B. test dataset

C. validation dataset

D. additional dataset

Hands-on exercise 1: identify training and test data and create an ML model

Upload the food_product_dataset.csv file provided in the GitHub repository (**github.com/exactpro/ai-testing-guide/tree/main/HO_Exercise_1**) to create a food product dataset. Build a food product classification model for it using the multinomial Naive Bayes classifier. This ML model should predict the category by a product name. Investigate how different training and test dataset combinations affect the behaviour of the ML model by following the next steps:

1. Split the food product dataset into the training and test datasets using different splitting ratios: 1:99, 10:90, 60:40 and 90:10.

2. Calculate the test accuracy for each splitting case.

3. Plot the dependency of the test accuracy on the size of the training dataset.

4. Give some comments on the observed results: how does the size of training data affect the accuracy?

Hands-on exercise 1 solution hints

Use the following Python libraries to do this exercise:

• pandas to work with table-formatted data;

• Scikit-learn to split the initial dataset into two parts (training and test datasets), train a multinomial Naive Bayes model, and calculate the test accuracy score;

• Matplotlib to create the resulting plot using the pyplot submodule.

The full solution can be found in the GitHub repository **github.com/exactpro/ai-testing-guide/tree/main/HO_Exercise_1**.

You should have something similar to the graph in Figure 4.6: for a small amount of training data, the increase in accuracy is sharp, this increase then slows down and plateaus when the training data size increases.

Figure 4.6 Model accuracy as a function of the training dataset size (Source: Adapted from Qiao et al., 2022)

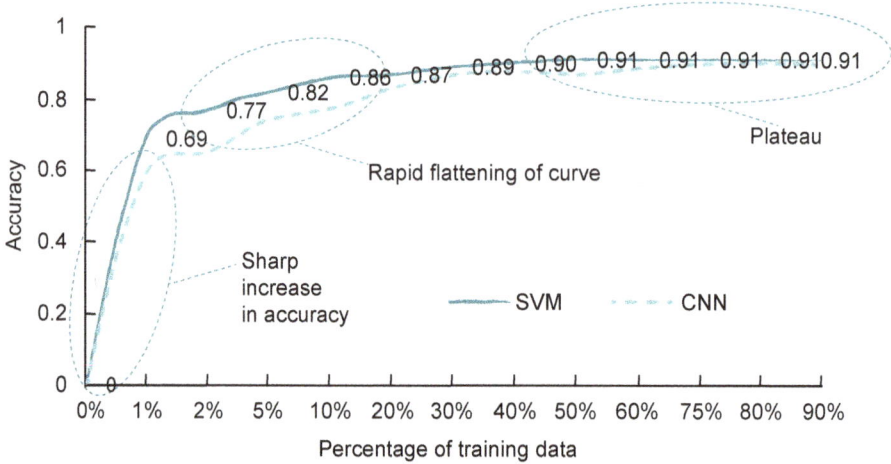

4.3 DATASET QUALITY ISSUES

Typical quality issues relating to the data in a dataset include, but are not limited to:

- *wrong data*: when the captured data is incorrect (e.g. collected through a faulty sensor) or entered incorrectly (e.g. with copy-paste errors);

- *incomplete data*: when data values may be missing (e.g. a field in a record may be empty, or the data for a particular time interval may have been omitted) – there can be various reasons for incomplete data, including security issues, hardware issues and human error;

- *mislabelled data*: when data is incorrectly labelled by data annotators;

- *insufficient data*: when there is not enough data for patterns to be recognised by the learning algorithms in use (note that the minimum required quantity of data will vary for different algorithms);

- *data not pre-processed*: data should be pre-processed to ensure it is clean, in a consistent format and contains no unwanted outliers;

- *obsolete data*: data used for both learning and prediction should be as current as possible (e.g. using financial data from several years ago may well lead to inaccurate results);

- *unbalanced data*: may result from inappropriate bias (e.g. based on race, gender or ethnicity), poor placement of sensors (e.g. facial recognition cameras placed at ceiling height), variability in the availability of datasets and differing motivations of data suppliers;

- *unfair data*: fairness is a subjective quality characteristic, but it can often be identified, for example to support diversity or gender balancing, selected data may be positively biased towards minorities or disadvantaged groups (note that such data may be considered fair but may not be balanced);
- *duplicate data*: it is known that repeated data records may unduly influence the resultant ML model;
- *irrelevant data*: data that is not relevant to the problem being addressed may adversely influence the results and may lead to wasting resources;
- *privacy issues*: any data use should respect the relevant data privacy laws (e.g. GDPR with relation to individuals' personal information in the EU);
- *security issues*: fraudulent or misleading data that has been deliberately inserted into the training data may lead to inaccuracy in the trained model.

Quick questions

Question 4.3

Which of the following is a common issue that can negatively affect the quality of a dataset used in ML? Select ONE option.

    A. sufficient quantity of data
    B. properly labelled data
    C. balanced class distribution
    D. missing or incomplete data

Question 4.4

Which of the following is an example of a data quality issue related to data completeness? Select ONE option.

    A. missing entries in critical columns
    B. different formats for the same data type
    C. duplicate records in the dataset
    D. imbalanced class distribution

4.4 DATA QUALITY AND ITS EFFECT ON THE ML MODEL

The quality of the ML model is highly dependent on the quality of the dataset from which it is created. There are the following categories of defects resulting from data quality issues:

- *Reduced accuracy*: these defects may be caused by data that is wrong, incomplete, mislabelled, insufficient, obsolete, irrelevant and not pre-processed. For example, if the model was trained on a news article dataset with very little news about software failures, then predictions for this type of news are likely to be inaccurate.

- *Biased model*: these defects are caused by data that is incomplete, unbalanced, unfair, lacking diversity or duplicated. For example, if the bugs that were taken to predict fix times were from one customer only, then it is likely to have an adverse effect on the bug fix time prediction for other customers.

- *Compromised model*: these defects are due to data privacy and security restrictions. For example, it can lead to security vulnerabilities, which would enable attackers to reverse-engineer information from the models and might cause leakage of personal information.

Quick questions

Question 4.5

A financial institution is building a credit scoring model using customer transaction data. However, the data collected from some customers is outdated by several years, while data from others is recent. What is the most likely problem this inconsistency will cause? Select ONE option.

    A. The model will learn better from older data.

    B. The model will generalise well across all customers.

    C. The model's predictions may be inaccurate due to temporal data inconsistencies.

    D. The model will automatically account for the data's age.

Question 4.6

A marketing team is using a customer dataset to predict which users are likely to churn. They realise that most of the data points come from a small group of loyal customers, while potential churners are under-represented. What is the most likely issue this will cause? Select ONE option.

    A. The model might struggle to predict churn due to unbalanced data.

    B. The model will become more accurate in predicting churn.

    C. The model will ignore the imbalance and treat all data equally.

    D. The model will perform better by focusing on loyal customers.

4.5 DATA LABELLING FOR SUPERVISED LEARNING

Let us move on to obtaining data suitable for training the model. Supervised learning requires labelled data (see Section 3.1.1). Data labelling enriches the unlabelled or poorly labelled data, so it can become suitable for supervised learning. Data labelling is a resource-intensive activity, and Figure 4.1 defines that, on average, this activity accounts for 25 per cent of the time spent on ML projects. For example, experienced testers can prioritise unmarked bugs, as illustrated in Figure 4.7, by labelling them as bugs with low, medium or high priority.

Figure 4.7 Prioritisation

Low   Medium   High

Labelling objects in images by drawing rectangles around them is another common labelling technique often known as annotation (see Figure 4.8).

Figure 4.8 Annotation

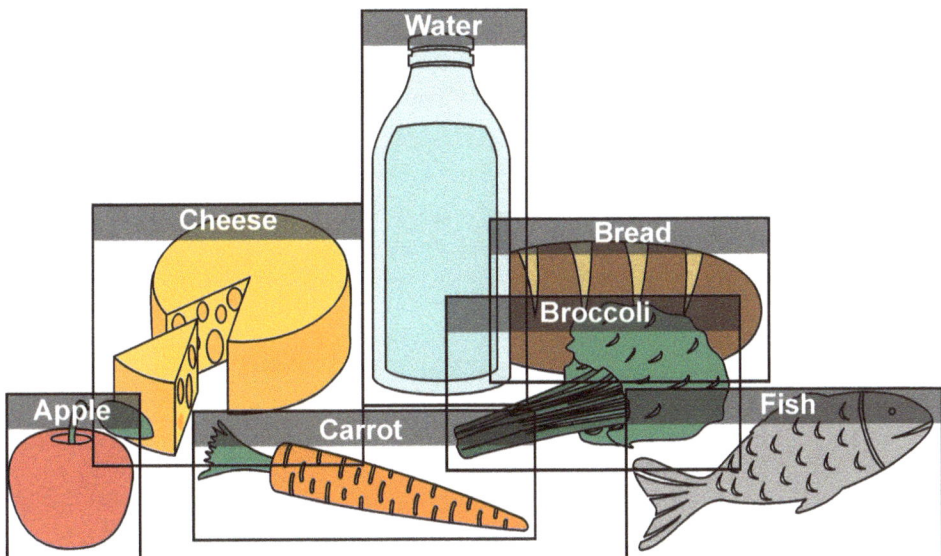

4.5.1 Approaches to data labelling

There are many ways of performing labelling. It can be *internal* and done by testers or developers within the company. It can be outsourced and crowdsourced. *Outsourced labelling* is done by an external specialist organisation, and *crowdsourced labelling* is performed by a large group of individuals. Due to the difficulty of managing the quality of labelling, several annotators may be asked to label the same data, and a decision is then taken on the label to be used. Labelling can also be *AI-assisted* and done using tools to recognise, annotate and cluster similar data. The results are then confirmed or perhaps supplemented by a human. And then there is a *hybrid* approach, where a combination of the above labelling approaches could be used. For example, crowdsourced labelling is typically managed by an external organisation that has access to specialised AI-based crowd-management tools. It may also be possible to reuse a pre-labelled publicly available dataset, avoiding the need for data labelling altogether.

Industry insights

Amazon Mechanical Turk as an example of crowdsourcing platform for data labelling

Amazon Mechanical Turk (MTurk) is a popular crowdsourcing platform used for various data labelling tasks (Amazon, 2025). It connects requesters who need data to be labelled with a large pool of workers willing to complete these tasks at competitive prices. In order to get this service, you have to clearly describe what you need to be labelled, for example 'Identify and label all cats in this image'. MTurk provides tools to create forms, upload images and design custom workflows. Through consensus labelling, the same tasks are assigned to multiple workers, and the results are compared to ensure accuracy. And then the experts review a subset of the completed tasks to validate accuracy.

4.5.2 Mislabelled data in datasets

Supervised learning assumes that the data is correctly labelled by the data annotators. However, it is rare in practice for all items in a dataset to be labelled correctly; data still gets mislabelled (see Figure 4.9 as an illustration of this). This happens because:

- Random errors may be made by annotators (e.g. pressing the wrong button).
- Systemic errors may be made (e.g. where the labellers are given the wrong instructions or poor training).
- Deliberate errors may be made by malicious data annotators.
- Translation errors may take correctly labelled data in one language and mislabel it in another.
- Where the choice is open to interpretation, subjective judgements made by data annotators may lead to conflicting data labels from different annotators.
- Lack of required domain knowledge may lead to incorrect labelling.
- Complex classification tasks can result in more errors being made.
- The tools used to support data labelling have defects that lead to incorrect labels.
- ML-based approaches to labelling are probabilistic, and this can lead to some incorrect labels.

Figure 4.9 Mislabelled data

4.6 SELF-SUPERVISED LEARNING

Manual data labelling is usually a very expensive and time-consuming process. That is the reason why new approaches that do not require human annotators are actively being developed. One of these approaches is self-supervised learning (Huyen, 2025), a type of ML that is at the intersection between supervised and unsupervised learning (see Section 3.1 on forms of machine learning). The main idea behind it is that a model can learn from data even when that data does not come with labels. Instead of relying on humans to label data (such as saying this picture is a 'cat' or this sentence is about 'sports'), the model generates labels making use of the structure within its own input data (or modification of it, e.g. using augmentation or cropping). In other words, self-supervised learning is when an ML model trains itself to learn one part of the input from another part of the input. This is the main difference from unsupervised learning, where no labels are created and hidden patterns or structures within the input data are revealed.

The self-supervised learning approach is widely used in NLP. Models such as BERT and GPT are trained using self-supervised techniques by hiding parts of sentences and asking the model to predict what is missing or what comes next; but it is not just for language – self-supervised learning is also used in computer vision. For instance, a model might try to guess what a missing part of an image looks like, or try to figure out how an image has been rotated. In audio, self-supervised learning can help models to learn by predicting future sounds or filling in missing parts of a recording.

Because of its flexibility and efficiency, self-supervised learning has become one of the most powerful tools in modern AI.

From theory to practice

Self-supervised learning vs unsupervised learning

To understand the difference between self-supervised learning and unsupervised learning, consider the following situation.

Imagine we have the sentence 'White daisies grow in the garden'. A self-supervised learning task might ask the model to guess a missing word: 'White daisies grow in the ___'. In this case, the model learns to fill in the blank (predict the word 'garden') based on the rest of the sentence (the input 'White daisies grow in the'). It learns grammar, sentence structure and meaning without anyone needing to label the sentence. It is a self-supervised task because the label for training (the word 'garden') is part of the full input data itself used for training (a text corpus used for the NLP task).

An unsupervised learning task might ask the model to group similar sentences together:

1. 'White daisies grow in the garden'.
2. 'Blue hydrangeas grow in the garden'.
3. 'White daisies are flowers'.
4. 'Rose daisies grow in the garden'.
5. 'There are many trees in the forest'.
6. 'Hydrangeas grow in the garden'.

It is a clustering task without using any explicit labels in the input data, and the result after unsupervised learning is two clusters:

- Cluster 1: 1, 2, 4, 6
- Cluster 2: 3, 5

The first cluster contains sentences describing various types of flowers growing in the garden, and the second cluster contains the remaining sentences.

Quick questions

Question 4.7

What is a common data mislabelling cause in manual annotation processes? Select ONE option.

    A. incorrect data types

    B. human error during the labelling process

    C. lack of feature scaling

    D. inconsistent class distribution

Question 4.8

A self-driving car company is training a model using a dataset of images with such labels as 'pedestrian', 'vehicle' or 'background'. They find that some objects on images are mislabelled, with pedestrians who are partially occluded by a car erroneously marked as part of the larger object – 'vehicle' – instead of separately as 'pedestrian'. What is the MOST likely cause for this mislabelling? Select ONE option.

    A. The dataset contains low-resolution images.

    B. The labelling process was outsourced to annotators unfamiliar with the labelling guidelines.

    C. The dataset has an equal number of images for each category.

    D. The training dataset does not contain images with pedestrians.

TERMS

Augmentation: the activity of creating new data points based on an existing dataset.

Data cleaning: the activity of data pre-processing when incorrect data, duplicate data or outliers are either removed or corrected, data imputation is used and removal or anonymisation of personal information is performed.

Data gathering: the activity of data acquisition when the source of the data is identified and the means for collecting the data are determined.

Data identification: the activity of data acquisition when the structure, types and characteristics of data to be used for training and predictions are identified.

Data imputation: the activity of data pre-processing when the missing values are replaced with estimated or guessed values.

Data labelling: the activity of adding meaningful tags to objects in raw data to support classification in ML.

Data sampling: the activity of data pre-processing that involves selection of some part of the total available dataset so that patterns in the larger dataset can be observed.

Data transformation: the activity of data pre-processing when the format of the given data is changed.

Feature extraction: the activity that involves the derivation of informative and non-redundant features from the existing features.

Feature selection: the activity that involves the selection of those features which are most likely to contribute to model training and prediction.

Inter-annotator agreement (inter-rater reliability): a statistical measure used to assess the degree to which different individuals (annotators or raters) give consistent labels or ratings to the same items within a dataset when labelling or annotating data.

SELF-ASSESSMENT EXERCISES

1. What is the most resource-intensive activity in the ML workflow, and what are its steps?

2. What are the data preparation challenges?

3. Name the subdatasets being selected from the initial dataset when developing an ML model. What is their role?

4. List the factors influencing the amount of data used in the ML model development and testing.

5. How can the initial dataset be split into the subdatasets? What are the splitting ratios?

6. Describe possible dataset quality issues.

7. Name three categories of defects that stem from the data quality issues. What are their reasons? Give examples.

8. What is data labelling and what are the types of data labelling?

9. What approaches to data labelling exist?

10. Name the possible reasons for data being mislabelled.

5 ML FUNCTIONAL PERFORMANCE METRICS

SUMMARY

This chapter talks about the confusion matrix and the different metrics derived from the confusion matrix, including accuracy, precision, recall and F1-score. Then it goes over some of the additional ML functional performance metrics such as the ROC curve, AUC, MSE, R-squared and the silhouette coefficient, each serving a specific purpose in assessing model performance. It also covers choosing appropriate functional performance metrics based on the intended use as well as their limitations. You can also brush up on some of the latest ML benchmark suites at the end of this chapter.

LEARNING OBJECTIVES

After covering this chapter, you should be able to:

- Calculate the ML functional performance metrics from a given set of confusion matrix data (K3)

- Contrast and compare the concepts behind the ML functional performance metrics for classification, regression and clustering methods (K2)

- Summarise the limitations of using ML functional performance metrics to determine the quality of the ML system (K2)

- Select appropriate ML functional performance metrics and/or their values for a given ML model and scenario (K4)

- Evaluate the created ML model using selected ML functional performance metrics (K3)

- Explain the use of benchmark suites in the context of ML (K2)

LINKS TO OTHER CHAPTERS

This chapter is related to previous chapters as follows:

- Chapter 2 explains what bias is.
- Chapter 4 provides the basis for data labelling for supervised learning.

5.1 CONFUSION MATRIX

When it comes to classification problems, a model will rarely give us correct predictions every single time. In order to understand this a little better, we need to create a **confusion matrix** (or **error matrix**) with the outcomes presented in Figure 5.1.

As you can see, **true positive (TP)** is the number of objects that the model has assigned to a given class, and they truly belong to that class. For example, the model predicts that the text is a bug description, and it really is a bug description.

True negative (TN) is the number of objects the model has NOT assigned to the class, and they are indeed NOT in that class. That is, the model says the text is not a bug description, and it is really not a bug description.

False negative (FN) is the number of objects that the model does NOT assign to the class, but they do in fact belong to it. For example, the model predicts that the text is not a bug description, but in fact it is a bug description.

And the last one is **false positive (FP)**. This is the number of objects the model assigns to a given class, but in fact they do NOT belong to it. That is, the model says the text is a bug description, but in fact, it is not.

Figure 5.1 The confusion matrix

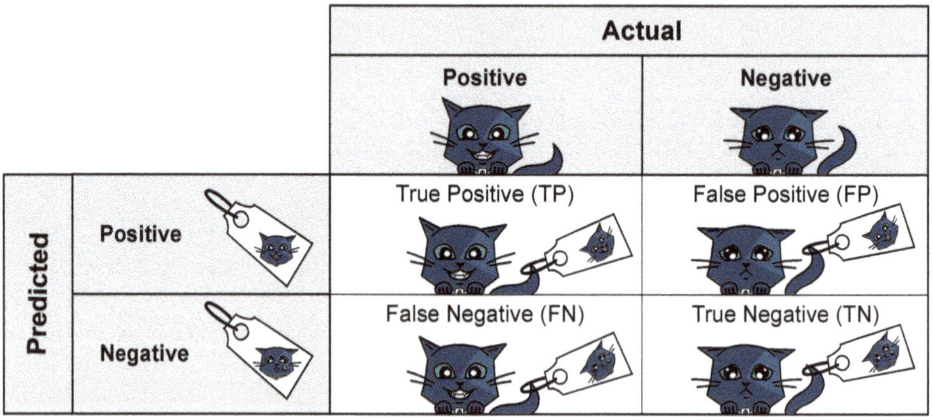

TP, TN, FP and FN are quantitative values summarising the ML functional performance of a classification algorithm. Based on these metrics, we can define the following **ML functional performance metrics**.

- The first metric is **accuracy**. Accuracy is the probability that the class will be predicted correctly. We take the number of all correct predictions (true positives and true negatives) and divide it by the total number of predictions:

$$\text{Accuracy} = \frac{TP + TN}{TP + TN + FP + FN} \cdot 100\% \tag{5.1}$$

- The next metric is **precision**. Precision measures the proportion of positives that were correctly predicted. It is a measure of how sure one can be about positive predictions. We do this by dividing the number of items correctly predicted by the total number of items attributed to the class:

$$\text{Precision} = \frac{TP}{TP + FP} \cdot 100\% \tag{5.2}$$

- The third metric is called **recall**. Recall (also known as **sensitivity** or **true positive rate, TPR**) measures the proportion of actual positives that were predicted correctly. It is a measure of how sure one can be about not missing any positives:

$$\text{Recall} = \text{TPR} = \frac{TP}{TP + FN} \cdot 100\% \tag{5.3}$$

- The last one is **F1-score**, which is the harmonic mean of precision and recall:

$$\text{F1-score} = 2 \cdot \frac{\text{Precision} \cdot \text{Recall}}{\text{Precision} + \text{Recall}} = 2 \cdot \frac{TP}{2 \cdot TP + FN + FP} \cdot 100\% \tag{5.4}$$

The result is a value between zero and one. A score close to one indicates that false data has little influence on the result, and a low F1-score suggests that the model is poor at detecting positives (see Figure 5.2).

Figure 5.2 Boundary values for the F1-score

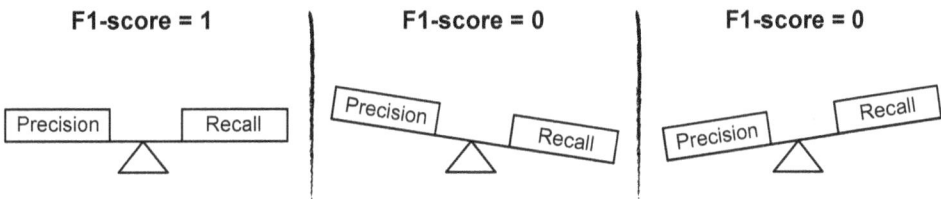

From theory to practice

Let us try to calculate the ML functional performance metrics (accuracy, precision, recall, F1-score) from the set of confusion matrix data given in Figure 5.3.

Figure 5.3 Confusion matrix with source data

	Confusion matrix	Actual	
		Positive	Negative
Predicted Positive		TP = 4054	FP = 343
Negative		FN = 129	TN = 2398

If we substitute specific values of TP, FP, FN and TN into the equations (5.1)–(5.4), we obtain the following results:

$$\text{Accuracy} = \frac{4054 + 2398}{4054 + 2398 + 343 + 129} \cdot 100\% \approx 93\%$$

$$\text{Precision} = \frac{4054}{4054 + 343} \cdot 100\% \approx 92\%$$

$$\text{Recall} = \frac{4054}{4054 + 129} \cdot 100\% \approx 97\%$$

$$\text{F1-score} = 2 \cdot \frac{4054}{2 \cdot 4054 + 129 + 343} \cdot 100\% \approx 94\%$$

Quick questions

Question 5.1

A confusion matrix for a classification model is given in Figure 5.4. Which of the following options represents the precision of the model? Select ONE option.

    A. $40/60 \cdot 100$
    B. $70/100 \cdot 100$
    C. $40/50 \cdot 100$
    D. $80/110 \cdot 100$

Figure 5.4 The confusion matrix with source data for Question 5.1

Confusion matrix	Actual positive	Actual negative
Predicted positive	40	20
Predicted negative	10	30

Question 5.2

A confusion matrix for a binary classification model is given in Figure 5.5. Which of the following options is the accuracy of the model? Select ONE option.

    A. 0.2

    B. 0.6

    C. 0.3

    D. 0.4

Figure 5.5 The confusion matrix with source data for Question 5.2

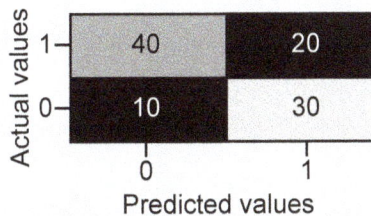

5.2 ADDITIONAL ML FUNCTIONAL PERFORMANCE METRICS FOR CLASSIFICATION, REGRESSION AND CLUSTERING

There are numerous other metrics for different types of ML problems (see Figure 5.6).

Some of the most commonly used metrics are *supervised classification* metrics, which include the receiver operating characteristic curve and the area under curve.

- The **receiver operating characteristic (ROC) curve** is a graphical plot that illustrates the dependence of the correct positive classifications proportion on the false positive classifications proportion when varying the threshold of the decisive rule. As shown in Figure 5.7, the ROC curve is plotted with TPR (see Equation (5.3)) against the **false positive rate (FPR)**:

$$FPR = \frac{FP}{TN + FP}$$

with TPR on the y axis and FPR on the x axis.

Figure 5.6 Additional ML functional performance metrics

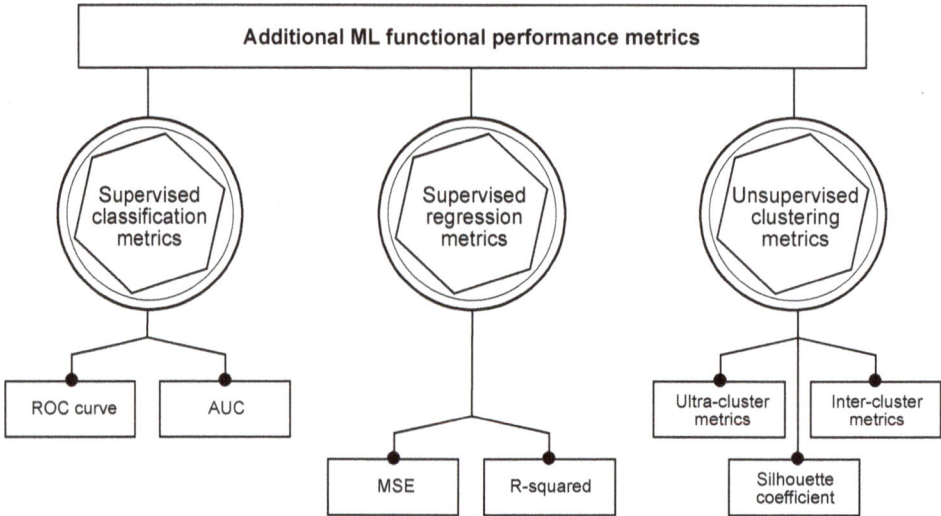

Figure 5.7 The ROC curve and the AUC

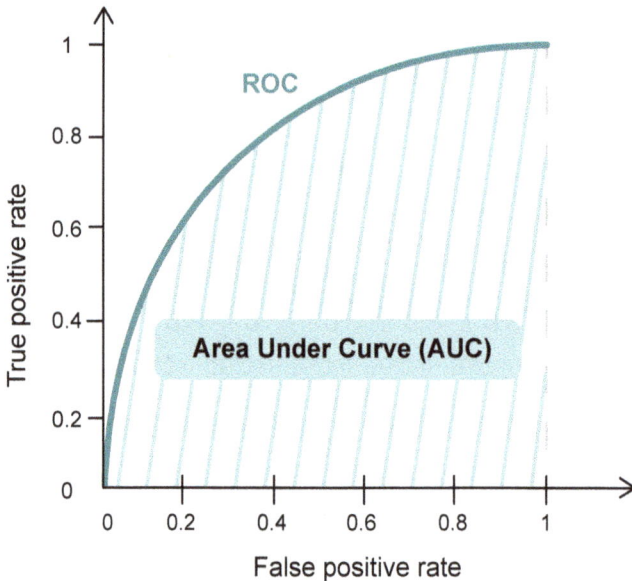

- The **area under curve (area under the ROC curve, AUC)** is illustrated in Figure 5.7. It represents the degree of a classifier separability, showing how well the model distinguishes between classes; the higher the AUC, the better the model's predictions (see Figure 5.8). If the model is always correct in all the predictions, it means that the TPR is always 1, FPR is 0, and the ROC curve for the perfect model looks like a step connecting points (0, 0), (0, 1) and (1, 1). The AUC equals 1 in this case. If the model is random and cannot distinguish between the two classes, TPR is equal to the FPR because it makes the same number of true and false positive predictions, and the ROC curve looks like a diagonal line connecting points (0, 0) and (1, 1). The AUC for the random curve is 0.5.

Figure 5.8 ROC curve examples

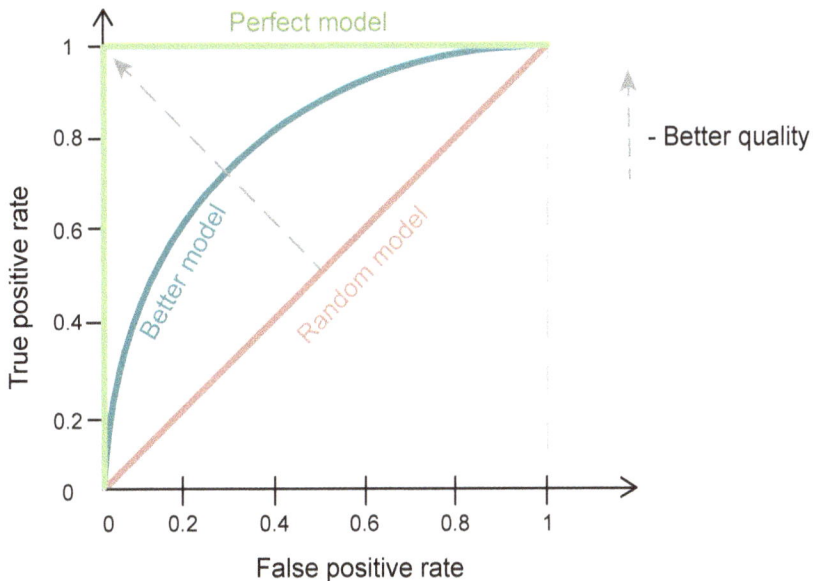

The next type of additional ML functional performance metrics is *supervised regression metrics*. For supervised **regression models**, the metrics represent how well the regression line fits the actual data points. Here, we have mean square error and R-squared.

- **Mean square error (MSE)** is the average of the squared differences between the actual value y_i and the predicted value $\hat{y}_i$ shown in Figure 5.9, where i is the number of the value out of n possible values:

$$MSE = \frac{\sum_{i=1}^{n} (\hat{y}_i - y_i)^2}{n}$$

The value of MSE is always positive, and a value closer to zero suggests a better regression model. Squaring the difference ensures positive and negative errors do not cancel each other out.

Figure 5.9 Differences between the actual and the predicted values used for the MSE calculation for the linear regression model

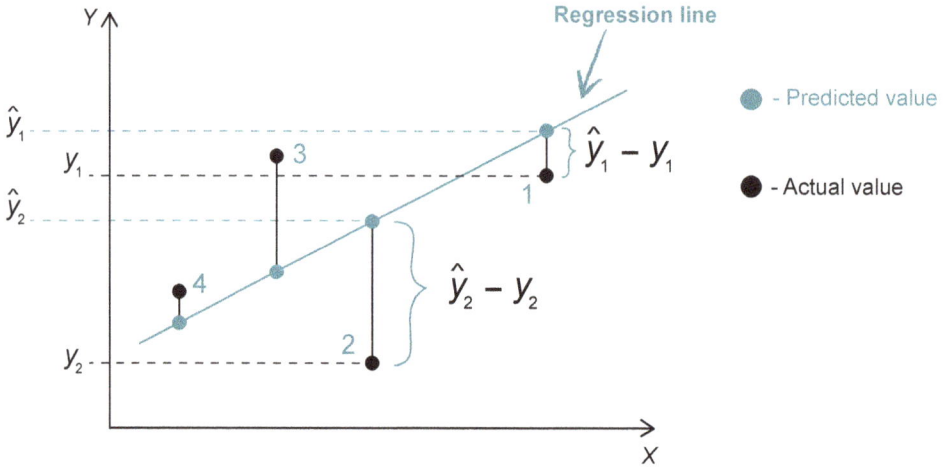

- **R-squared** (also known as the **coefficient of determination**) is a statistical measure of how close the data points are to the fitted regression line. It is calculated by the following formula:

$$R^2 = 1 - \frac{\sum\limits_{i=1}^{n} \left(\hat{y}_i - y_i\right)^2}{\sum\limits_{i=1}^{n} \left(y_i - \bar{y}\right)^2}$$

where $\bar{y}$ is a mean value:

$$\bar{y} = \frac{1}{n} \sum\limits_{i=1}^{n} y_i$$

Figure 5.10 helps to understand the R-squared calculation for the linear regression model.

R-squared value of 1 indicates that the model predicts 100 per cent of the relationship, a value of 0.8 indicates that the model predicts 80 per cent, and a value close to 0 means that the model does not explain the relationship between the variables X and Y. Figure 5.11 summarises these three situations.

The third type of additional ML functional performance metrics is *unsupervised clustering metrics*.

For unsupervised clustering, there are several metrics that represent the distances between the various clusters and the closeness of data points within a given cluster: intra-cluster metrics, inter-cluster metrics, and the silhouette coefficient.

Figure 5.10 Differences between the actual and the predicted values (a), the actual and the mean values (b) used for the R-squared calculation for the linear regression model

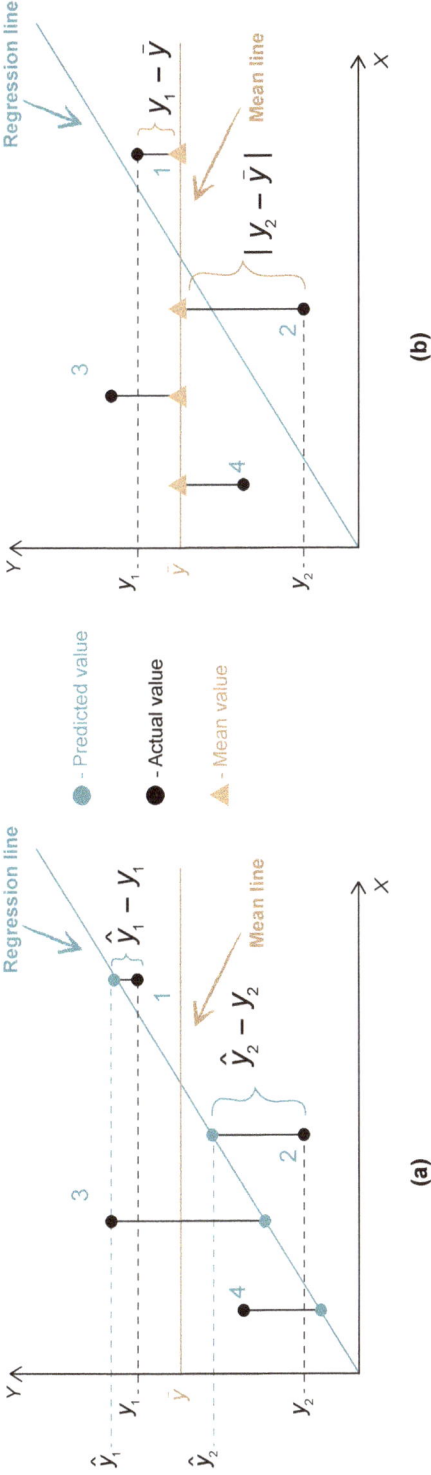

(a)

(b)

Figure 5.11 R-squared in case of great fit (a), good fit (b) and inconsistent fit (c) to the regression line

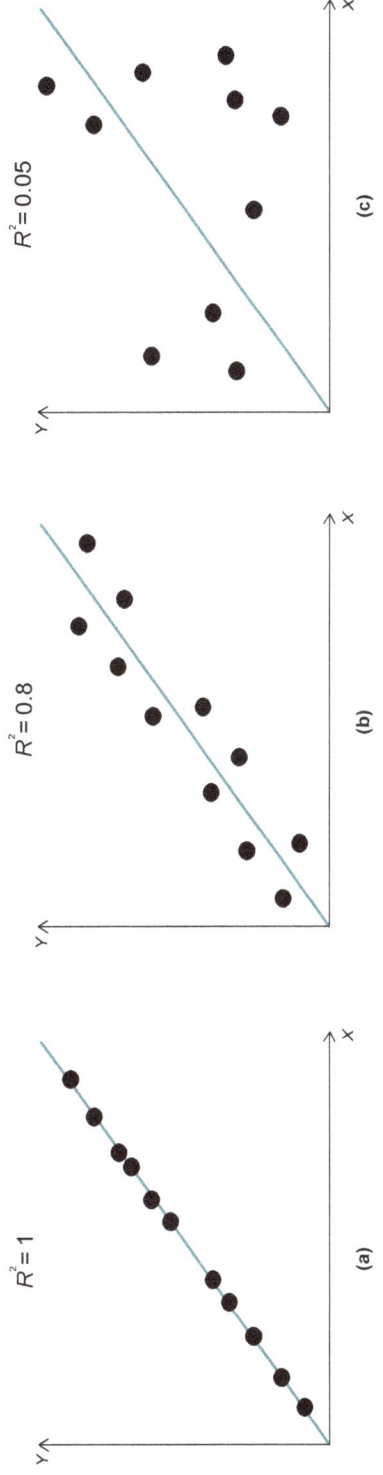

$R^2 = 1$

$R^2 = 0.8$

$R^2 = 0.05$

(a)

(b)

(c)

- **Intra-cluster metrics** measure the similarity of data points within a cluster. Figure 5.12 provides examples of intra-cluster measures:

  - *complete diameter distance*, which is the farthest distance between two points *x* and *y* in a cluster *S*:

$$\delta(S) = \max_{x,y \in S} d(x,y)$$

  - *average diameter distance*, which is the average distance between all points in a cluster *S*:

$$\delta(S) = \frac{1}{|S|\,(|S|-1)} \sum_{x,y \in S, \, x \neq y} d(x,y)$$

    where |S| is the number of points in S.

Figure 5.12 Distances to calculate intra-cluster metrics

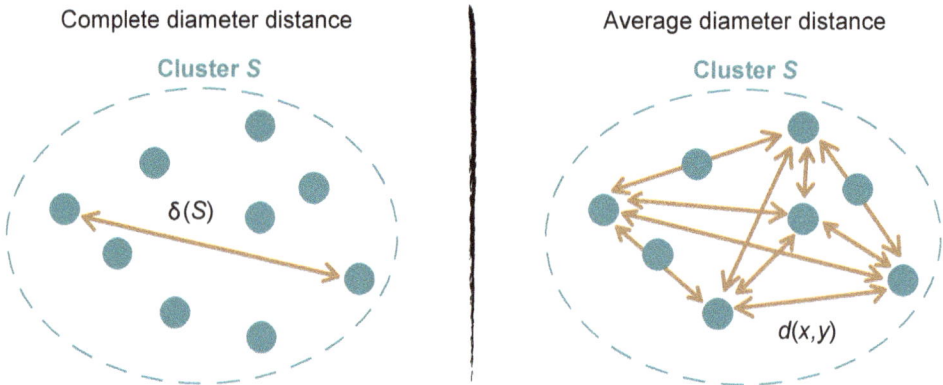

Complete diameter distance
Cluster S
$\delta(S)$

Average diameter distance
Cluster S
$d(x,y)$

- **Inter-cluster metrics** measure the similarity of data points in different clusters. Examples of inter-cluster measures are presented in Figure 5.13:

  - *single linkage distance*, which is the closest distance between two objects *x* and *y* in two clusters *S* and *T*:

$$\delta(S,T) = \min_{x \in S, \, y \in T} d(x,y)$$

  - *complete (maximum) linkage distance*, which is the farthest distance between two objects *x* and *y* in two clusters *S* and *T*:

$$\delta(S,T) = \max_{x \in S, \, y \in T} d(x,y)$$

Figure 5.13 Distances to calculate inter-cluster metrics

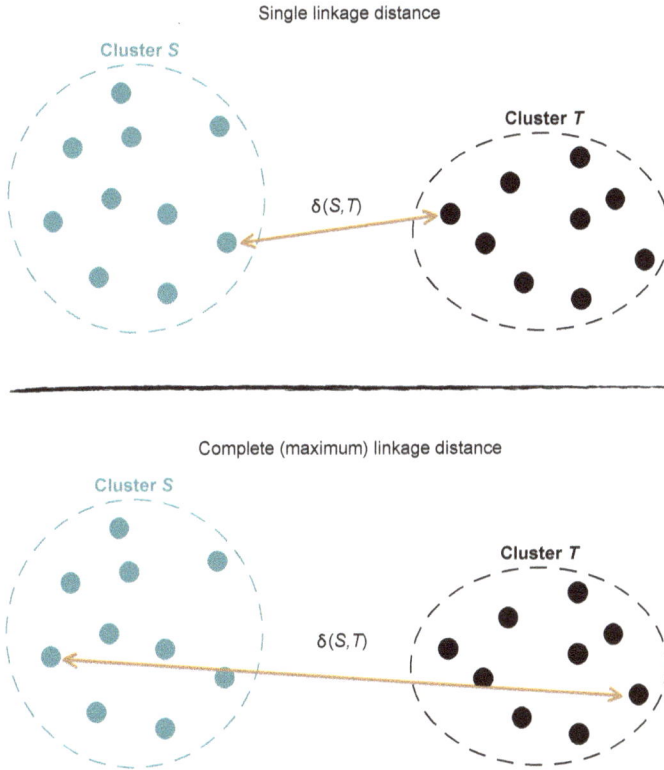

Single linkage distance

Complete (maximum) linkage distance

- The **silhouette coefficient** (also known as **silhouette score**) is a measure between −1 and +1 based on the average inter-cluster and intra-cluster distances shown in Figure 5.14:

$$Silhouette\ coefficient = \frac{b - a}{\max(a,b)}$$

Here a is the mean distance between a sample x and all other points y in the same cluster S:

$$a = \delta(S) = \frac{1}{|S - 1|} \sum_{y \in S,\, x \neq y} d(x,y)$$

b is the smallest mean distance between a sample x and all other points y in the next nearest cluster (V or T):

$$b = \min(\delta(S,T), \delta(S,V))$$

Figure 5.14 Distances to calculate the silhouette coefficient

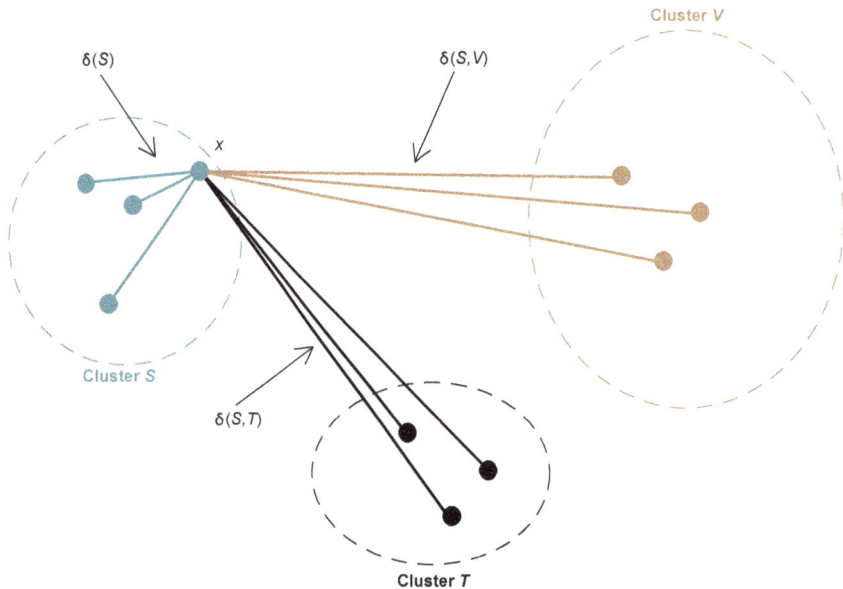

where

$$\delta(S,T) = \frac{1}{|T|}\sum_{y \in T}d(x,y)$$

$$\delta(S,V) = \frac{1}{|V|}\sum_{y \in V}d(x,y)$$

A score of +1 means the clusters are well-separated, a score of 0 implies random clustering, and a score of −1 means the clusters are wrongly assigned (see Figure 5.15).

5.3 LIMITATIONS OF ML FUNCTIONAL PERFORMANCE METRICS

ML functional performance metrics are limited to measuring the functionality of the model, for example in terms of accuracy, precision, recall, MSE, AUC and the silhouette coefficient. They do not measure other non-functional quality characteristics, such as performance efficiency or explainability, flexibility and autonomy.

ML functional performance metrics are constrained by several other factors:

Figure 5.15 The silhouette coefficient in the case of well-separated clusters (a), random clustering (b) and wrongly assigned clusters (c)

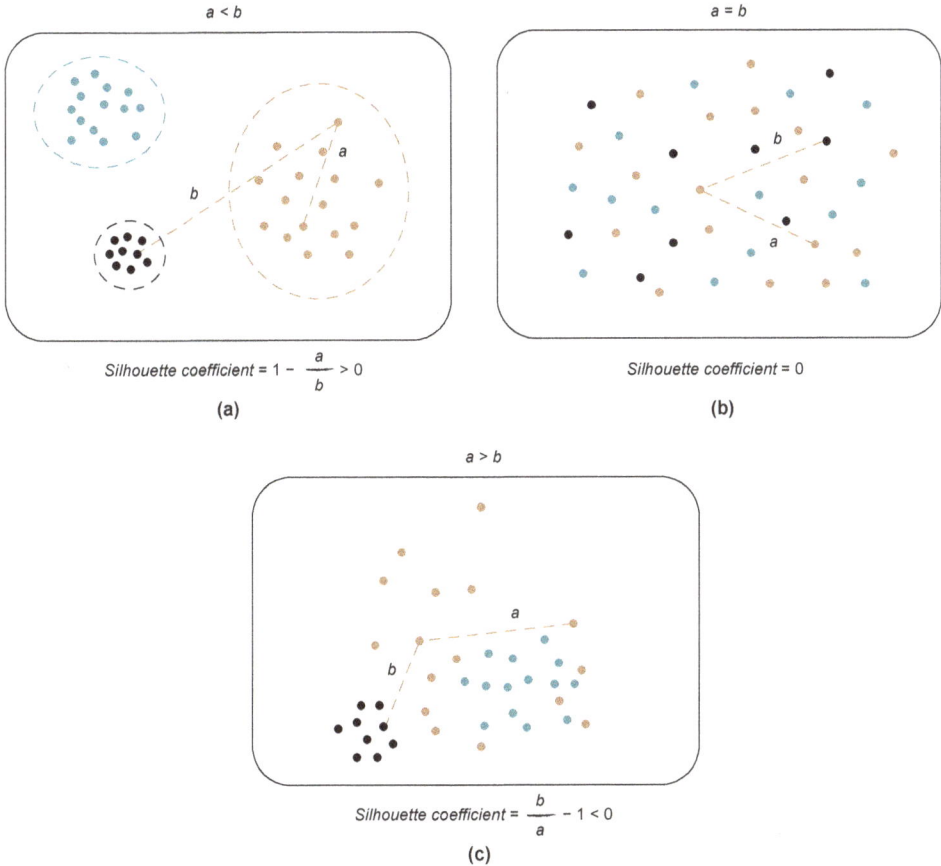

$a < b$

$$\text{Silhouette coefficient} = 1 - \frac{a}{b} > 0$$

(a)

$a = b$

$$\text{Silhouette coefficient} = 0$$

(b)

$a > b$

$$\text{Silhouette coefficient} = \frac{b}{a} - 1 < 0$$

(c)

- For supervised learning, the ML functional performance metrics are calculated on the basis of labelled data, and the accuracy of the resultant metrics depends on correct labelling (see Chapter 4 and Figure 5.16).

Figure 5.16 Mislabelled data leading to inaccurate metrics

- The data used for measurement may not be representative (e.g. it may be biased, see Section 2.4) and the generated ML functional performance metrics depend on this data, as shown in Figure 5.17.

Figure 5.17 Bias in data leading to bias in metrics

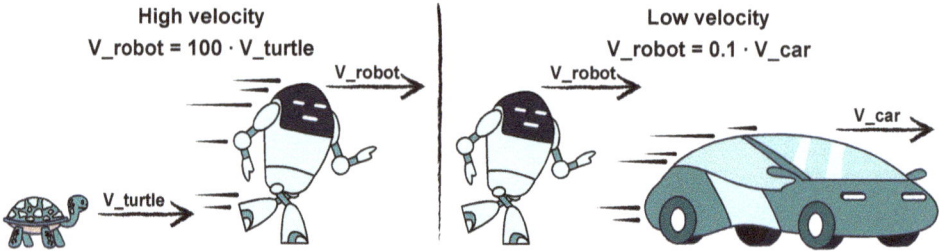

High velocity
$V\_robot = 100 \cdot V\_turtle$

Low velocity
$V\_robot = 0.1 \cdot V\_car$

- The system may comprise several components, but the ML functional performance metrics only apply to the ML model, as illustrated in Figure 5.18, for example the data pipeline is not considered by the ML functional performance metrics to evaluate the model.

Figure 5.18 Assessing the model as a whole

- Most of the ML functional performance metrics can only be measured with support from tools, see Figure 5.19.

Figure 5.19 Tool-dependent measurement

Quick questions

Question 5.3

Which factor can negatively impact model performance metrics due to errors in data pre-processing? Select ONE option.

  A. incorrect data labelling
  B. hyperparameter tuning
  C. dropout rate
  D. model ensemble

Question 5.4

Which of the following factors can mislead performance metrics in an ML model? Select ONE option.

  A. feature extraction
  B. imbalanced classes
  C. optimisation algorithm
  D. model explainability

5.4 SELECTING ML FUNCTIONAL PERFORMANCE METRICS

It is very difficult to build an ML model that achieves the highest score for all of the ML functional performance metrics generated from a confusion matrix. To make it easier, the most appropriate functional performance metrics are selected as acceptance criteria, based on the expected use of the model. For example, to minimise false positives, a high value of precision is required, whereas to minimise false negatives, the recall metric should be high. The following criteria can be used when selecting the ML functional performance metrics:

- Accuracy can be applicable if the false positive and false negative counts and costs are similar, but, if one class of data dominates over others, then we should consider the F1-score.

- Precision can be suitable when the cost of false positives is high and confidence in positive outcomes needs to be high, but, when the classifier deals with situations where a very large percentage of cases are positive, using precision alone is unlikely to be a good choice.

- Recall is critical for positives not to be missed, and for this a high recall score is important, for example missing any true positive results in cancer detection and marking them as negative is unacceptable.

- F1-score is most useful when there is an imbalance in the expected classes, and when the precision and recall are of similar importance.

In addition, several metrics may be applicable for given ML problems:

- The AUC for the ROC curve may be used for supervised classification problems.
- MSE and R-squared may be used for supervised regression problems.
- Inter-cluster metrics, intra-cluster metrics and the silhouette coefficient may be used for unsupervised clustering problems.

From theory to practice

Problem 1. Weather forecasting: using accuracy to test an ML model

Accuracy is useful in situations where all categories are equally important and there is no significant cost associated with misclassifying one class over another.

In weather forecasting, accuracy measures the correctness of predictions made by weather models. Meteorologists use accuracy to assess how well the forecasted weather conditions match the actual observed conditions. High accuracy in weather forecasting is essential for providing reliable information to the public, especially for making decisions related to outdoor activities, agriculture and transportation.

Problem 2. Medical diagnosis: using precision to test an ML model

Precision is useful when the cost of false positives is high, and we want to ensure that the positive predictions made by the model are accurate. In medical diagnostics, precision is crucial for tests that identify diseases. For instance, in cancer detection, precision measures the proportion of correctly identified cancer cases out of all cases classified as positive (potentially having cancer). A high precision means fewer false alarms, which is vital for ensuring accurate diagnoses and avoiding unnecessary treatments.

Problem 3. Spam filtering: using recall to test an ML model

Recall is useful when the cost of false negatives is high and we want to ensure that the model captures as many positive instances as possible. In a spam filter for an email service, recall is crucial for identifying spam emails (positive class) while minimising false positives (non-spam emails incorrectly classified as spam). A higher precision value indicates that the model is better at correctly identifying spam and has fewer false positives, which is crucial for an email service to avoid mistakenly filtering out legitimate emails.

Problem 4. Information retrieval: using F1-score to test an ML model

F1-score is used when there is an imbalance between the categories or when both precision and recall are important; in other words, the cost of both false positives and false negatives is high. In search engines, the F1-score is used to evaluate the effectiveness of information retrieval systems. It considers both precision (relevance

---

of retrieved documents) and recall (capturing all relevant documents). A high F1-score indicates that the search engine retrieves relevant documents while minimising irrelevant ones, providing users with accurate and comprehensive search results.

Problem 5. Credit risk: using the ROC curve and the AUC to test an ML model

Using ROC curves and the AUC for credit scoring is a powerful method to evaluate and compare the performance of credit scoring models. These metrics help in assessing how well the models can distinguish between good and bad credit risks. Here, we compute TPR and FPR at various threshold settings and calculate the area under the ROC curve to get a single metric representing the model's overall performance. The ROC curve provides a visual representation of the trade-off between the TPR and the FPR at different thresholds. A curve closer to the top-left corner indicates a better-performing model. The AUC value summarises the model's performance across all thresholds. Higher AUC values generally indicate a better-performing model.

Problem 6. Finance: using the MSE to test an ML model

MSE is a crucial metric in finance for evaluating and improving the accuracy of various predictive models, ranging from risk management to pricing and forecasting, ensuring that financial decisions are based on reliable and accurate predictions. For instance, in algorithmic trading, the MSE is used to evaluate the performance of trading algorithms. The accuracy of trade signal predictions can be assessed using MSE, comparing predicted trade outcomes to actual outcomes. Also, models predicting the profitability of trading strategies are evaluated using the MSE to ensure accurate predictions of returns. The MSE is sensitive to the scale of the data, meaning larger errors are penalised more heavily.

Problem 7. Risk management: using R-squared to test an ML model

In risk management, R-squared can be used to assess the effectiveness of risk models. For instance, in a Value at Risk model, R-squared might be used to determine how well the model explains the historical variance in portfolio returns. R-squared can also be used to evaluate the effectiveness of hedging strategies. A high R-squared between the hedged portfolio and the underlying asset or index indicates that the hedge is effective at reducing risk.

Problem 8. Customer segmentation: using silhouette coefficient to test an ML model

The silhouette coefficient can be applied in several contexts, primarily to assess the quality of clustering in various analyses. For example, financial institutions often segment their customers to provide personalised services or targeted marketing. By applying clustering algorithms (such as K-means, hierarchical clustering, etc.) and using the silhouette coefficient, they can evaluate the quality of the segmentation. Clustering can be used to identify groups of customers or investments with similar risk profiles. For instance, in credit scoring, customers can be grouped based on their risk of default. In portfolio management, clustering can help to identify groups of assets that behave similarly. By evaluating these clusters with the silhouette coefficient, managers can ensure that their portfolios are well-diversified. Effective clustering can reveal underlying structures in the asset returns, helping to construct portfolios that minimise risk through diversification.

Problem 9. Fraud detection in financial transactions: using several metrics to test an ML model

Sometimes, it is not obvious which ML performance metric should be used as the most important one for evaluating and testing an ML model. In such a case, we need to calculate several metrics (e.g. accuracy, precision, recall and F1-score).

Models that identify fraudulent transactions in real time use accuracy to measure how well they distinguish between legitimate and fraudulent transactions. High accuracy in these models helps financial institutions to reduce false positives (flagging legitimate transactions as fraud) and false negatives (missing actual fraudulent transactions), but, while accuracy is a crucial metric, it is important to consider the specific context and data characteristics in financial applications. In fraud detection, the number of fraudulent transactions is typically much smaller than legitimate ones, which leads to class imbalance. High accuracy might be misleading if the model simply predicts the majority class (e.g. predicting all transactions as legitimate). In such cases, metrics such as precision, recall and F1-score become more informative.

When identifying fraudulent transactions, precision is vital to minimising false positives, which occur when legitimate transactions are incorrectly flagged as fraud. High precision ensures that genuine transactions are not unnecessarily blocked, reducing inconvenience to customers and maintaining trust, but the financial cost of false positives versus false negatives varies by application. For instance, in fraud detection, false negatives (missed frauds) might be more costly than false positives. Therefore, precision should be evaluated in the context of overall business costs.

Using recall in anti-money laundering (AML) applications is essential for regulatory compliance and the prevention of illegal activities. Financial institutions are required to file suspicious activity reports when they detect potentially suspicious activities. High recall ensures that most suspicious activities are identified and reported, helping institutions to comply with regulatory requirements. Regulators can impose heavy penalties for failing to detect and report money laundering activities. High recall helps to avoid such penalties by ensuring comprehensive detection of suspicious transactions.

F1-score is a valuable metric in finance, as it provides a balanced measure of a model's performance by considering both precision and recall. Using the F1-score helps financial institutions to develop more reliable and effective models, ensuring better decision-making and risk management. Besides fraud detection, the F1-score is particularly important in applications such as AML, credit scoring, customer churn prediction and stock price movement prediction, where both false positives and false negatives carry significant costs.

5.5 BENCHMARK SUITES FOR ML

ML benchmarks are standardised tests or suites used to evaluate the performance, efficiency and accuracy of ML models, frameworks and hardware. They allow researchers, developers and vendors to compare different systems under controlled and repeatable conditions. ML benchmarks can provide various measures, including training and inference times, the quality of training data and quality metrics of an AI model itself. Training time means how fast a framework can train an ML model using a defined training dataset to a specified target quality metric, such as 93 per cent accuracy. Inference time refers to how long it takes for a trained model to make a prediction on new, unseen data.

ML benchmark suites are provided by several organisations, such as:

- *MLCommons®* (MLCommons, 2025): an AI engineering consortium started in 2020 and built on a philosophy of open collaboration to improve AI systems. The foundation for the MLCommons benchmark work was derived from and builds upon *MLPerf®*, which aims to deliver a representative benchmark suite for AI/ML that fairly evaluates performance of software frameworks, AI processors and ML platforms in the cloud. Their *AlgoPerf: Training Algorithms* benchmark measures how much faster different neural network models can be trained to a given target performance by changing the underlying training algorithm (e.g. the optimiser or the hyperparameters). The *AILuminate* benchmark assesses the safety of generative AI chatbot systems by enumerating a set of hazards and then testing a system for appropriate handling of prompts that could enable those hazards. After testing, the system is assigned hazard-specific and overall safety ratings ranging from low to high risk, based on the percentage of prompts not handled appropriately.

- *Embedded Microprocessor Benchmark Consortium* (EEMBC®, 2025): a community developing industry-standard benchmarks for the hardware and software used in autonomous driving, mobile imaging, the Internet of Things (IoT), mobile devices and many other applications. Their *ADASMark™* benchmark suite is intended to analyse the performance of SoCs used in autonomous driving by utilising real-world workloads that represent highly parallel applications such as surround view stitching, segmentation and CNN traffic sign classification. The *MLMark®* benchmark is an ML benchmark designed to measure the performance and accuracy of embedded inference on edge devices.

- *Evidently AI* (Evidently AI, 2025): an open-source platform for ML observability. It offers various features and functionalities for evaluating, testing and monitoring ML models. Starting from 2024, Evidently AI has put together a database of more than 200 LLM benchmarks and publicly available datasets one can use to evaluate LLM capabilities in various domains, including logical reasoning, language understanding, question answering, code generation, bias mitigation and more.

Quick questions

Question 5.5

What is the primary purpose of an ML benchmark suite? Select ONE option.

  A. To provide pre-trained models for various tasks.
  B. To offer tutorials and documentation for ML libraries.
  C. To define a set of standardised tasks and datasets for evaluating and comparing model performance.
  D. To optimise hyperparameters automatically for a given model.

TERMS

Accuracy: the ML functional performance metric used to evaluate a classifier, which measures the proportion of predictions that were correct (ISO/IEC TR 29119-11).

Area under curve (area under the ROC curve, AUC): a measure of how well a classifier can distinguish between two classes.

Confusion matrix (error matrix): a technique for summarising the ML functional performance of a classification algorithm.

F1-score: an ML functional performance metric used to evaluate a classifier, which provides a balance between recall and precision.

False negative (FN): an ML model prediction in which the model mistakenly predicts the negative class.

False positive (FP): an ML model prediction in which the model mistakenly predicts the positive class.

False positive rate (FPR): the ratio between the number of negative events wrongly categorised as positive (false positives) and the total number of actual negative events.

Inter-cluster metric: a metric that measures the similarity of data points in different clusters.

Intra-cluster metric: a metric that measures the similarity of data points within a cluster.

Mean square error (MSE): the statistical measure of the average squared difference between the estimated values and the actual value.

ML benchmark suite: a dataset used to compare ML models and ML algorithms over a range of evaluation metrics.

ML functional performance metrics: a set of measures that relate to the functional correctness of an ML system.

Precision: an ML functional performance metric used to evaluate a classifier, which measures the proportion of predicted positives that were correct (ISO/IEC TR 29119-11).

Recall (true positive rate (TPR), sensitivity): an ML functional performance metric used to evaluate a classifier, which measures the proportion of actual positives that were predicted correctly (ISO/IEC TR 29119-11).

Receiver operating characteristic (ROC) curve: a graphical plot that illustrates the ability of a binary classifier as its discrimination threshold is varied.

Regression model: an ML model whose expected output for a given numeric input is a continuous variable (ISO/IEC DIS 23053).

R-squared (coefficient of determination): a statistical measure of how close the data points are to the fitted regression line.

Silhouette coefficient (silhouette score): a clustering measure between -1 and +1 based on the average inter-cluster and intra-cluster differences.

True negative (TN): an ML model prediction in which the model correctly predicts the negative class.

True positive (TP): an ML model prediction in which the model correctly predicts the positive class.

SELF-ASSESSMENT EXERCISES

1. Explain what the confusion matrix is.

2. Which ML performance metrics can be calculated using a confusion matrix? How do you calculate them?

3. Provide examples for additional ML performance metrics used for supervised classification.

4. Name two additional ML performance metrics used for supervised regression models. Describe how to calculate them.

5. Which unsupervised clustering metrics do you know? What is the difference between them?

6. What are the limitations of ML functional performance metrics?

7. What are the criteria for selecting accuracy as an ML functional performance metric for an ML model?

8. What are the criteria for selecting precision as an ML functional performance metric for an ML model?

9. What are the criteria for selecting recall as an ML functional performance metric for an ML model?

10. Describe the role of benchmark suites for ML.

6 ML – NEURAL NETWORKS AND TESTING

SUMMARY

This chapter provides a short history of the development of neural networks, starting with models such as the McCulloch–Pitts model and the Rosenblatt model. Then it focuses on the perceptron and how it evolved into DNNs. This chapter zooms in on the structure and training of neural networks, their coverage measures and the real-life applications of neural networks.

LEARNING OBJECTIVES

After reading this chapter, you should be able to:

- Explain the structure and function of a neural network including a DNN (K2)
- Experience the implementation of a perceptron (H)
- Describe the different coverage measures for neural networks (K2)

LINKS TO OTHER CHAPTERS

This chapter provides a more detailed description of neural networks, one of the key ML techniques introduced in Chapter 1.

6.1 NEURAL NETWORKS

In the previous chapters we have broken down the ML workflow and introduced classical ML models, but sometimes classical ML models cannot solve the task at hand with sufficient accuracy, which is something the human brain is capable of. So, to implement this, researchers moved on to more complex models: neural networks. A deep neural network is useful when you need to replace human labour with autonomous work without losing its efficiency. In a nutshell, the idea behind the technology was to replicate the functioning of the human brain, represented here as a multitude of linked neurons.

6.1.1 First neuron models

In 1943 McCulloch and Pitts developed a computer neural network model based on mathematical algorithms and the theory of brain activity (Figure 6.1). They proposed

Figure 6.1 The neuron models development timeline

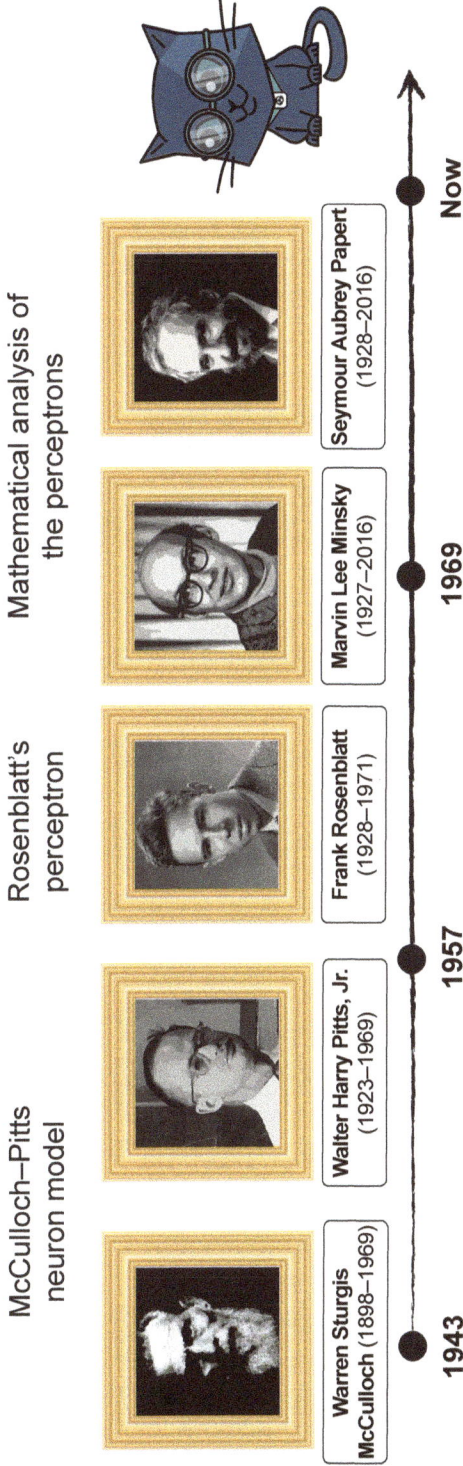

McCulloch–Pitts neuron model

Rosenblatt's perceptron

Mathematical analysis of the perceptrons

Warren Sturgis McCulloch (1898–1969)

Walter Harry Pitts, Jr. (1923–1969)

Frank Rosenblatt (1928–1971)

Marvin Lee Minsky (1927–2016)

Seymour Aubrey Papert (1928–2016)

1943

1957

1969

Now

that **neurons** could be thought of as devices that operate with binary numbers, and called this model 'threshold logic'. They presented a network of electronic neurons and demonstrated that it could perform virtually any imaginable numerical or logical operation. Figure 6.2 shows the McCulloch–Pitts neuron model, which can be compared to the structure of a real neuron shown in Figure 6.3. The real neuron consists of several dendrites (main inputs), which receive neural signals, and a single axon (main output).

Figure 6.2 The McCulloch–Pitts neuron model

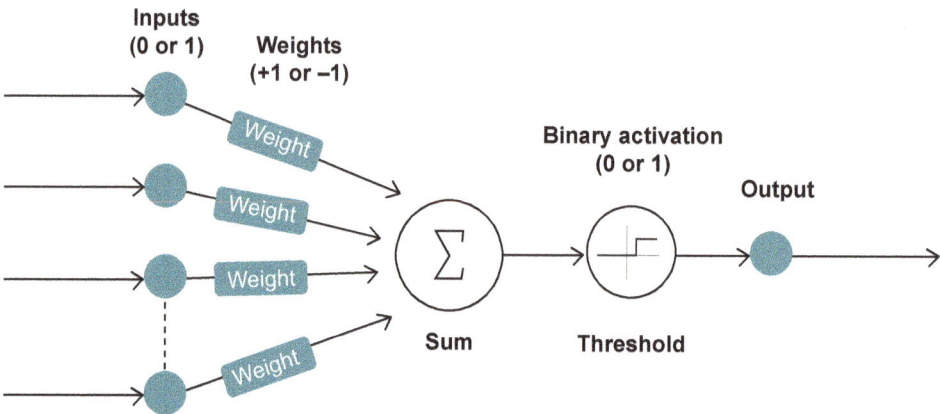

Figure 6.3 A real neuron

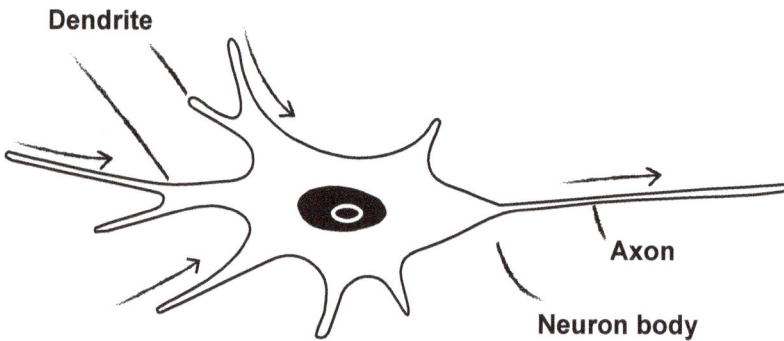

In 1957 Rosenblatt developed mathematical and computer models of the brain's perception of information, based on a neural network. This network was trained using the arithmetic operations of addition and subtraction. This was one of the first examples of a neural network called the 'single-layer **perceptron**', which could be used to decide if an input belongs to a particular class or not. Figure 6.4 provides a diagram for the Rosenblatt perceptron model.

Figure 6.4 The Rosenblatt perceptron model

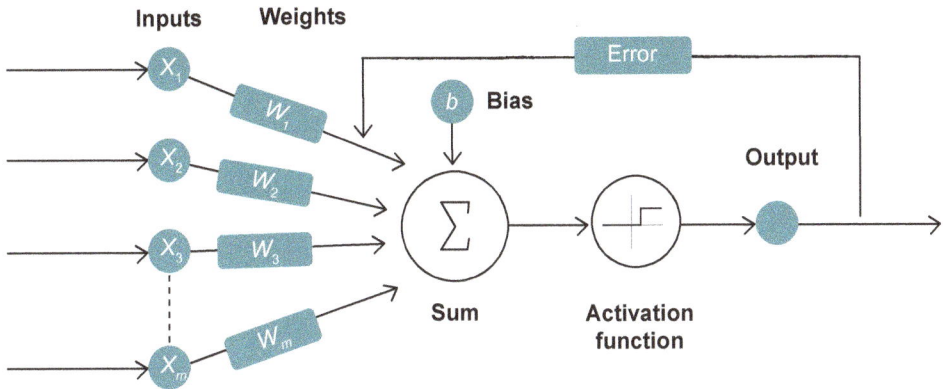

What is the difference between the McCulloch–Pitts neuron model and the Rosenblatt neuron model? In the Rosenblatt neuron model, inputs can be any real numbers, not only binary values, and the weights are different for them, not fixed (Fabien, 2019). Furthermore, there is a method to adjust the weights to train them that is missing in the McCulloch–Pitts neuron model.

Let us consider how a perceptron works. A perceptron is a single-layer neural link with four main parameters: input values; weights and bias; net sum; and an activation function. The perceptron model begins with multiplying all input values x_i and their weights w_i. It then adds these values to create the weighted sum:

$$w \cdot x = \sum_{i=1}^{m} w_i \, x_i \tag{6.1}$$

where m is the number of inputs to the perceptron, w is the vector of real-valued weights and x is the vector of input values. After that, this weighted sum is applied to the activation function (also known as the step function) to obtain the output value $f(x)$:

$$f(x) = \begin{cases} 1, & \text{if } w \cdot x + b > 0 \\ 0, & \text{otherwise} \end{cases} \tag{6.2}$$

where b is the individual bias of the neuron. It is an element that shifts the boundary away from the origin without any dependence on the input value.

The perceptron receives multiple input signals and, if the sum of the input signals exceeds a certain threshold, it either outputs a signal or does not return an output. In the context of supervised learning and classification, this can then be used to predict the class of a sample. The output can be represented as '1' or '0'. It can also be represented as '1' or '–1', depending on which activation function is used.

The value obtained as a perceptron's output is compared with the desired output, and error is calculated as their difference:

$$\text{error} = \text{desired output} - f(x) \tag{6.3}$$

If the error is non-zero, the weights are updated and calculation steps (6.1)–(6.3) repeated, so one can implement the perceptron's training. To update the weights, a learning rate is used, which is a small positive constant that determines the step size of the updates:

$$\text{updated value for } w_i = w_i + \text{learning\_rate} \cdot \text{error} \cdot x_i$$

A perceptron can be thought of as a 'binary linear classifier'. A **linear classifier** is a type of classifier that makes its predictions based on a linear combination of the input features and, for a linear classifier, the boundary separating the classes must be linear; it must be representable by a point (in one dimension), a straight line (in two dimensions) as in Figure 6.5(a), a plane (in three dimensions) or a hyperplane (in higher dimensions). However, if the classes cannot be separated perfectly by a linear classifier, as in Figure 6.5(b), it could give rise to errors.

Figure 6.5 A linear (a) and non-linear (b) boundary separating the classes in two-dimensional space

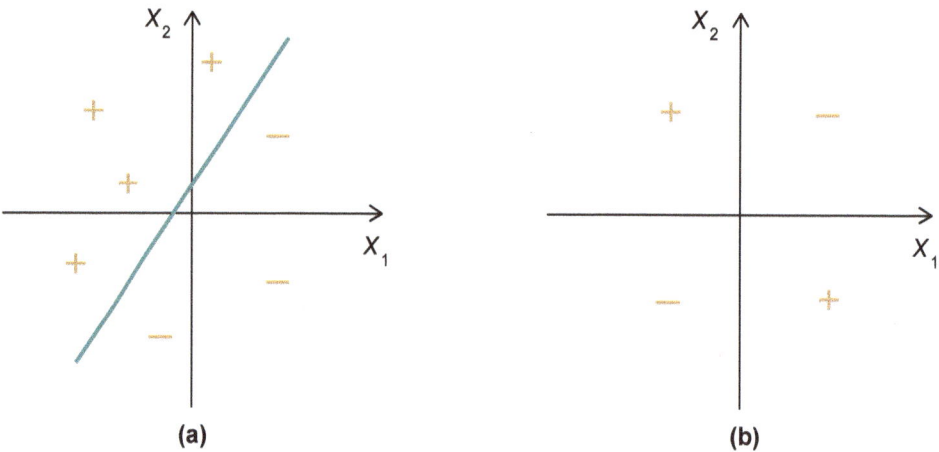

(a)   (b)

Based on these statements, a single perceptron can learn basic logical functions such as NOT – in this case the boundary separating the classes is a real point, $x = x_0$, between 0 and 1 (see Figure 6.6), the logical AND – the boundary separating the classes is a straight line

$$w_1 \cdot x_1 + w_2 \cdot x_2 + b = 0$$

(see Figure 6.7), and the logical OR – the boundary separating the classes is also a straight line

$$w_1 \cdot x_1 + w_2 \cdot x_2 + b = 0$$

illustrated in Figure 6.8, but a perceptron cannot learn the exclusive OR (XOR) logical function (Figure 6.9).

Figure 6.6 The logical NOT function and the boundary separating the classes

x	NOT (x)
0	1
1	0

Boundary: $x = x_0$

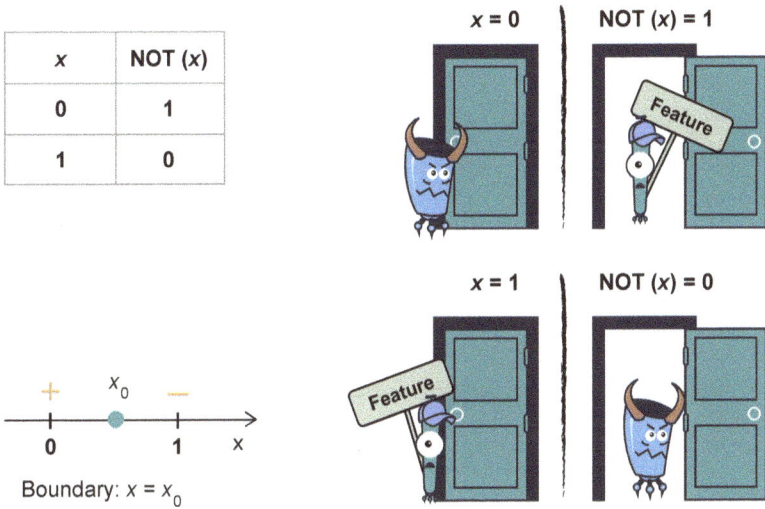

Figure 6.7 The logical AND function and the boundary separating the classes

x_1	x_2	x_1 AND x_2
0	0	0
0	1	0
1	0	0
1	1	1

Boundary: $w_1 \cdot x_1 + w_2 \cdot x_2 + b = 0$

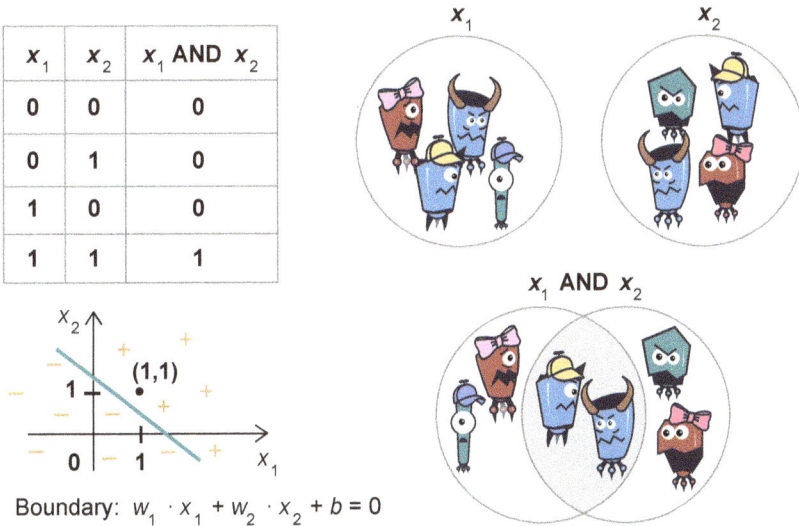

Figure 6.8 The logical OR function and the boundary separating the classes

x_1	x_2	x_1 OR x_2
0	0	0
0	1	1
1	0	1
1	1	1

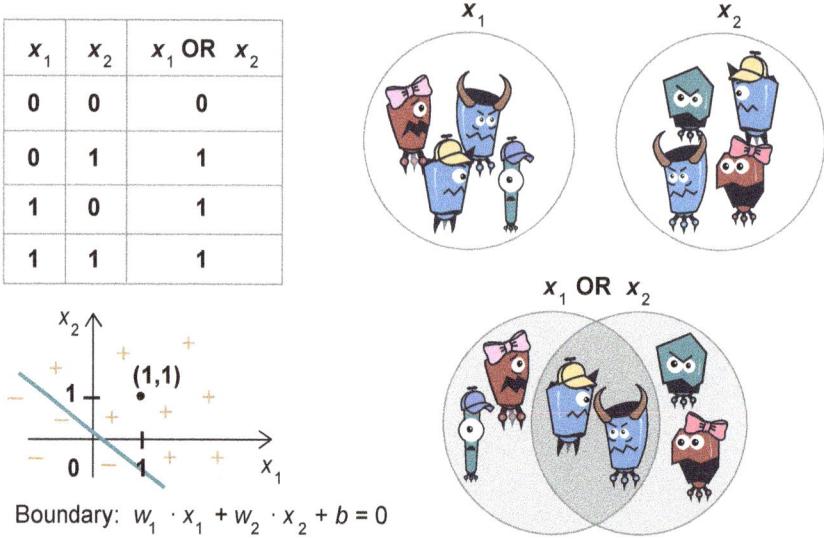

Boundary: $w_1 \cdot x_1 + w_2 \cdot x_2 + b = 0$

Figure 6.9 The logical XOR function and the boundary separating the classes

x_1	x_2	x_1 XOR x_2
0	0	0
0	1	1
1	0	1
1	1	0

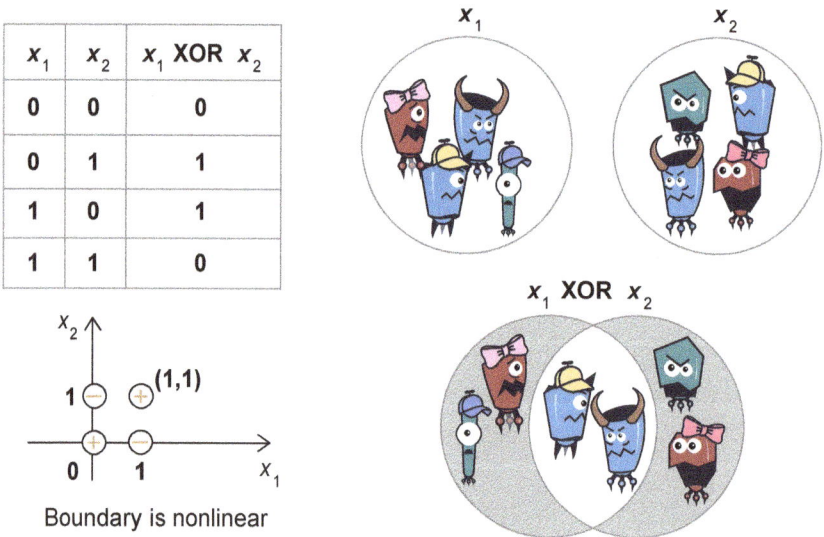

Boundary is nonlinear

In 1969 the idea of neural networks was harshly criticised by Minsky and Papert in the book *Perceptrons: An Introduction to Computational Geometry* (Minsky and Papert, 1969). They pointed out serious problems that hindered the effective use of artificial neural networks. For example, they drew attention to the impossibility of implementing the XOR function in neural networks, as well as pointing out insufficient computing power available back then. This book undermined the interest in neural networks for some time; however, the field was still of interest to many researchers. Computers improved, computing power increased, scientists solved the XOR problem, making advances in the field more and more realistic. This brings us to the multi-layered neural network of today, the DNN.

6.1.2 Deep neural network

Figure 6.10 represents a typical structure of a DNN. A neural network is made up of *neurons* that are linked by *layers* and *connections* between them. A neuron is a computing unit that receives information, performs simple calculations on it and passes it on. Neurons are combined into three types of layers. The *input layer* receives inputs. Then there are *hidden layers* made up of artificial neurons, which are also known as *nodes*. The *output layer* provides predictions.

Figure 6.10 A typical DNN structure

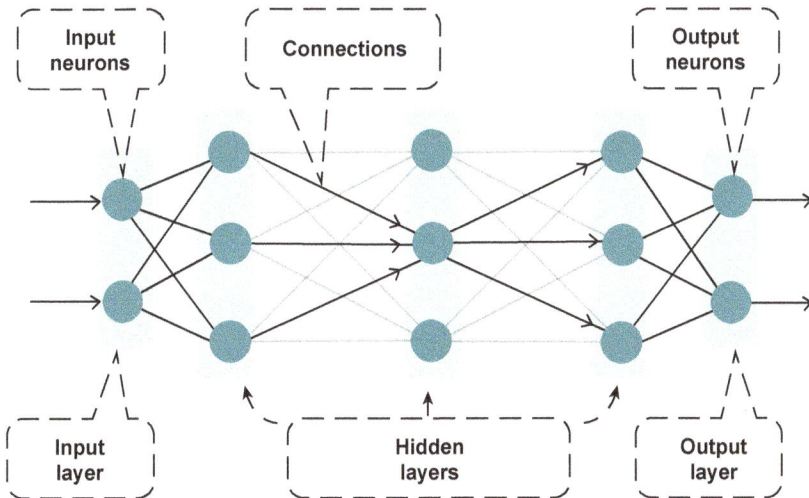

A synapse is a connection between two neurons; it is characterised by its weight. It makes the input information change when it is passed from one neuron to the next. Let us say there are three neurons that transmit information to the next one, as shown in Figure 6.11. Respectively, we have three weights corresponding to each of these neurons. The neuron that has the largest weight will be the dominant information in the next neuron. The computations are performed by each neuron except for those in the input layer, and, as a result, we get **activation values**. These values are calculated by running the activation function that receives values from all the neurons in the previous layer and bringing them to a certain range. It then assigns the weights to the connections

Figure 6.11 A diagram for a DNN with three hidden layers

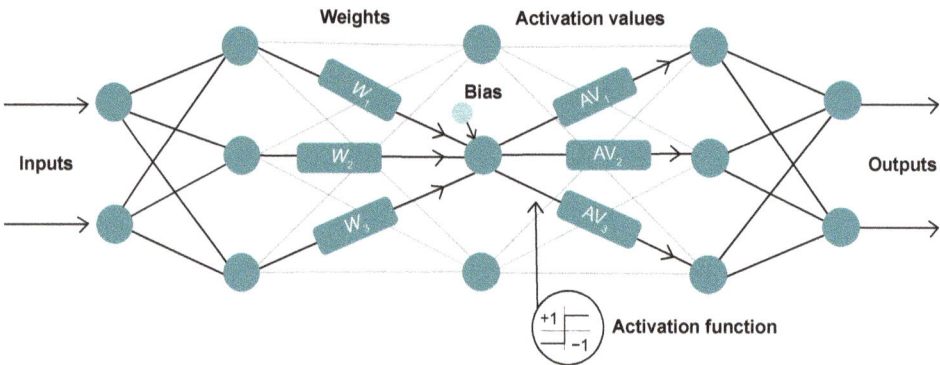

between the neurons and the individual bias of each neuron. Note that the bias we are talking about here is some predefined constant value and not the degree of prejudice we talked about in the previous chapters. Running different activation functions can result in different activation values. These values are typically centred around zero and have a range between −1 (meaning that the neuron is 'disinterested') and +1 (meaning that the neuron is 'very interested'), or are centred around 0.5 and have a range between 0 and 1. An activation function is used to add non-linearity to a model, enabling the neural network to capture and represent complex patterns in the data. Without non-linearity, even with multiple layers, the neural network would function like a linear regression model.

During training, each neuron has a preset bias value, and the training data is passed through the network, activating functions in every neuron, which generate outputs. These outputs are then compared with the known correct results (for example, labelled data). The difference between the actual output and the known correct result is then fed back through the network to modify the values of the weights on the connections between the neurons in order to minimise this difference. This process is called *backpropagation*. As more training data is fed through the network, the weights are adjusted as the network learns. This continues until the outputs are considered good enough to end training.

Quick questions

Question 6.1

What is the main purpose of the activation function in a neural network? Select ONE option.

    A. To initialise the weights.
    B. To calculate the input to the hidden layer.
    C. To introduce non-linearity into the network.
    D. To prevent overfitting.

Question 6.2

Which of the following best describes the structure and function of a DNN? Select ONE option.

    A. A DNN consists of a single layer of neurons that perform linear computations, making it similar to linear regression.

    B. A DNN is a network with multiple hidden layers, where each layer applies linear transformations to the input data.

    C. A DNN consists only of input and output layers, without any hidden layers or non-linear transformations.

    D. A DNN is a neural network with multiple hidden layers, and each layer uses activation functions to introduce non-linearity, enabling the model to learn complex patterns.

Hands-on exercise 2: implement a simple perceptron

Follow these steps to implement a single-layer perceptron model in Python that learns the logical AND function:

1. Define a function that calculates the perceptron output based on its input parameters: inputs, weights and bias.

2. Use the truth table for the AND logic to define a list of input–output pairs for the perceptron model.

3. Initialise the bias and the vector of weights in the range of [-0.5, 0.5].

4. Train the perceptron model to determine the weight values for learning the logical AND function.

Hands-on exercise 2 solution hints

Use the Python random module to generate pseudo-random numbers.

A high-level overview of the perceptron learning algorithm is as follows:

1. Initialise the bias with a constant value and the weights with random values in the range of [-0.5, 0.5].

2. For each input–output pair in the training data:

    a) Compute the perceptron's output using the current weights and bias.

    b) Update the weights based on the error, i.e. the difference between the desired output and the perceptron's output.

3. Repeat steps 2 and 3 until the perceptron correctly classifies all input–output pairs or the specified number of iterations is reached.

The update rule for the weights is:

- If the perceptron output is correct, do not change the weights.
- If the perceptron output is too low, increase the weights.
- If the perceptron output is too high, decrease the weights.

To update the weights, use the **learning rate**, which is a small positive constant that determines the step size of the updates.

The full solution can be found in the GitHub repository **github.com/exactpro/ai-testing-guide/tree/main/HO_Exercise_2**.

6.2 COVERAGE MEASURES FOR NEURAL NETWORKS

Assessing the coverage for neural networks is a new field of study. The first academic papers appeared in 2017, which means there is little objective evidence available. The statement and the decision coverage have been around for more than 50 years and there is still little evidence of their efficacy, despite the fact that they have been mandated when testing medical devices and avionics systems. The following approaches have been proposed by researchers:

- *Neuron coverage*: full neuron coverage requires each neuron in the neural network to achieve an activation value greater than zero, as illustrated in Figure 6.12. This is very easy, and research has shown that almost 100 per cent coverage is achieved with a few test cases. This coverage measure may be most useful to serve as a red flag when it is not achieved.

Figure 6.12 Full neuron coverage

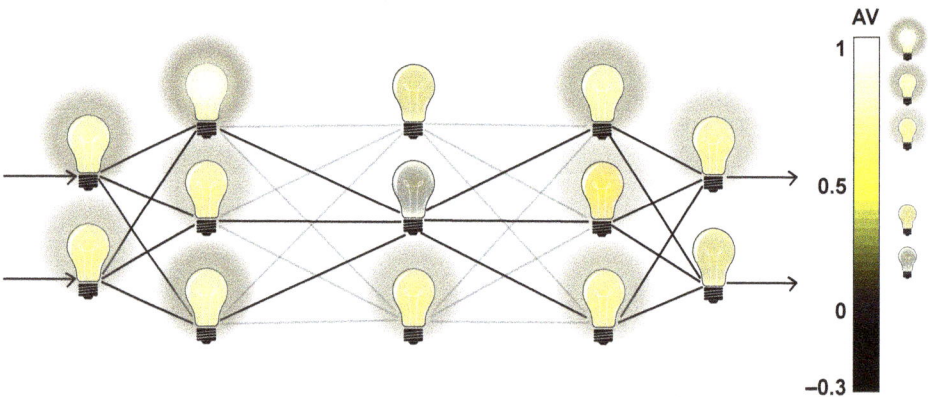

- *Threshold coverage*: full threshold coverage, shown in Figure 6.13, requires that each neuron achieves an activation value greater than a specified threshold. This type of coverage has been given this name here in order to easily distinguish it from neuron coverage with a threshold set to zero.

Figure 6.13 Full threshold coverage

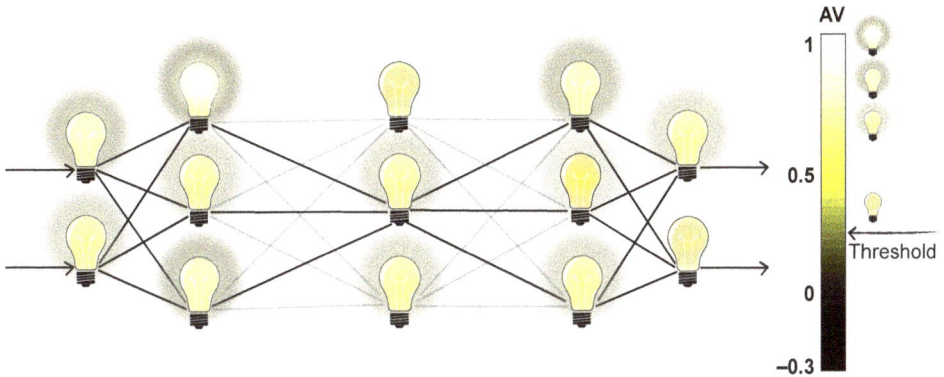

- *Sign-change coverage*: to achieve full sign-change coverage, test cases need to cause each neuron to achieve both positive and negative activation values. Refer to Figure 6.14 as an example of two test cases demonstrating full sign-change coverage.

Figure 6.14 Two test cases to achieve full sign-change coverage

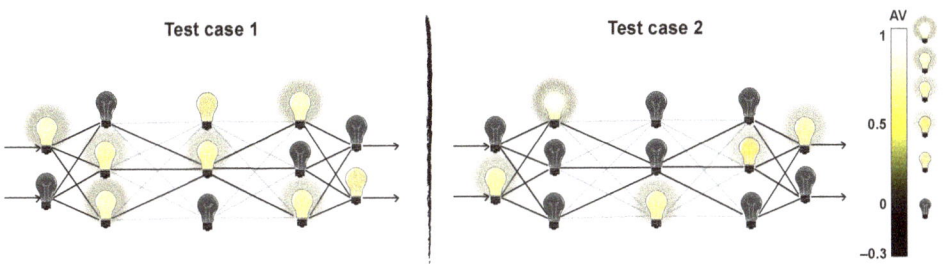

- *Value-change coverage*: to achieve full value-change coverage, test cases need to cause each neuron to achieve two activation values, where the difference between the two values exceeds some chosen value. Figure 6.15 is given to illustrate two test cases for full value-change coverage.

Figure 6.15 Two test cases demonstrating full value-change coverage with the difference between the two activation values exceeding 0.3

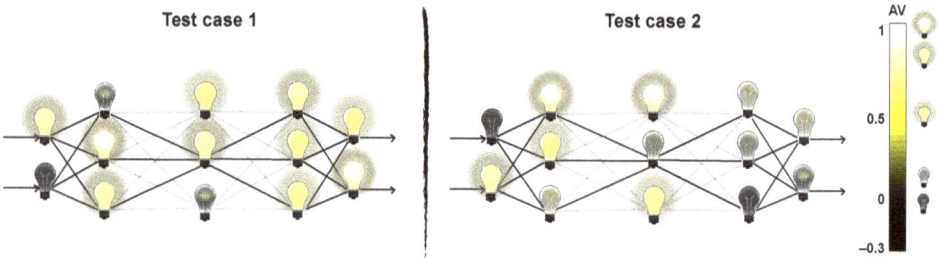

- *Sign-sign coverage*: this coverage considers pairs of neurons in adjacent layers. For a pair of neurons to be considered covered, a test case needs to show that changing the sign of a neuron in the first layer causes the neuron in the second layer to change its sign, while the signs of all other neurons in the second layer remain unchanged (see Figure 6.16).

Figure 6.16 Sign-sign coverage

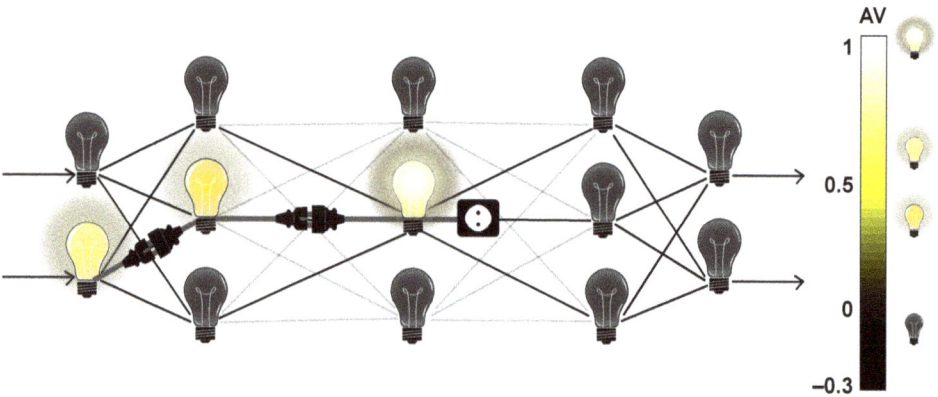

It is also worth mentioning that researchers have been experimenting on further coverage measures based on layers (Usman et al., 2022), so we will see what the future holds.

Industry insights

Real-life applications of neural networks

When it comes to finance, neural networks can help us in the areas of banking and credit risk, market investment and fraud. The first area contains credit risk predictions and macroeconomic predictions. The second area consists of financial predictions, stock trading and portfolio management. The third area includes fraud prediction and detection.

If we talk about financial predictions, artificial neural networks allow us to forecast the exchange rates, stock movements and prices based on their historical data and the information extracted from the market news. For example, they can be applied in stock trading for the buy-sell-hold forecasts where stocks are traded separately using the daily close prices. Bridgewater Associates LP is one company leveraging ML techniques in its investment strategies, aiming to fully harness the potential of neural networks for stock market prediction (HSGAC, 2024). Another example is AI Capital Management LLC, which is a proprietary trading firm that has been examining the potential for applying AI models in the financial market.

Another area of focus is macroeconomic predictions and credit risk, which plays a crucial role for financial institutions. The solutions to this problem are based on the analysis of historical data, and, again, the most accurate models for these issues are DNNs. Deep learning can also be leveraged to benefit portfolio building (Ma et al., 2023); namely, neural networks are used to forecast the returns on assets and to minimise investment risk. WorldQuant LLC is a global firm that incorporates AI in its trading and investment process (HSGAC, 2024).

As technology advances, more importance is placed on online transactions, but at the same time ways of committing financial fraud are also becoming more sophisticated. Luckily, artificial neural networks can help to keep our finances safe. Deep learning and artificial neural network applications are powering systems capable of detecting all forms of financial fraud. These applications can identify unusual activity by analysing information such as payment method, time, location, item purchased and the amount spent (Nepal Rastra Bank, 2020). Even a small deviation from the norm in any of these categories can highlight a potential fraud case. For instance, a transaction occurring outside an established time frame can be identified as being fraudulent. Smart solutions allow Visa to look at more than 500 data elements to determine if a transaction is suspicious (Visa, 2023), but still it can make it very embarrassing when a card is declined by a retailer by mistake.

As we can see, neural networks are used to solve rather critical problems. This is why it is especially important to test them.

6.3 TRANSFORMER ARCHITECTURE

The Transformer is a type of deep learning model that has become one of the most important tools in AI today. It was introduced by researchers at Google in 2017 (Uszkoreit, 2017) and is now used in many powerful AI systems, including language models such as ChatGPT and BERT.

What makes the Transformer special is how it processes information. Older models, such as Recurrent Neural Networks, looked at data one step at a time, for example reading a sentence word by word. This made them slow and sometimes not very good at understanding the meaning of longer texts. Transformers changed that by looking at the whole input at once. This allows them to understand context better and run much faster.

The most important part of the Transformer is something called attention – more specifically, self-attention. This means the model learns which words in a sentence are most important in relation to each other. Take the poetic line, 'The moon watched as he wandered, lost in thought'. Here, attention helps the model to understand that 'he' – and not the moon – is the subject doing the wandering, despite the unusual structure. This ability is key to grasping metaphor and nuance in creative language.

Another key feature of the Transformer is that it does not process words in order, as a human does. Instead, it looks at everything in parallel. To keep track of the order of words, the Transformer adds something called positional encoding (Lin et al., 2022). This is a way of giving each word a sense of its position in the sentence, so the model does not lose the structure of the text.

The Transformer is made up of two main parts: the encoder and the decoder. The encoder reads and processes the input (like a sentence in English), and the decoder creates the output (like the translated sentence in French). Each part contains several layers that include attention mechanisms and small neural networks. Some models, such as BERT, only use the encoder part. Others, such as GPT, only use the decoder.

Transformers are now used for a wide range of tasks. They can translate languages, summarise text, write code, answer questions and even generate images or music. Because they work so well and can handle so many types of data, they are also being used outside language, such as in image recognition, audio processing and scientific research such as understanding proteins (Moussad et al., 2023).

An appropriate question here would be about the connection between generative models and Transformers. A Transformer is like the blueprint or design for how a model is built and how it processes data. It is a specific architecture, just as a car might use an electric motor or a gasoline engine – both are ways to build cars, but the design is different. Generative models are about what the model does. A generative model creates new data that looks like the data it was trained on, for example generating text (like GPT models, OpenAI, 2025a) or creating new images (like DALL-E, OpenAI, 2025b) or Midjourney models (Midjourney, 2025).

Not all Transformer models are generative. Some of them are built to analyse or label existing data without creating new content. These are called non-generative Transformer models, and they play a key role in many practical AI applications.

One of the most famous non-generative models is BERT. BERT is designed to deeply understand the meaning of text by reading it in both directions at once – from left to right and right to left. This helps it to grasp the full context of a sentence, which is especially useful in tasks such as question answering, sentiment analysis or identifying whether a sentence is spam. However, BERT – and its newer versions like RoBERTa (Liu et al., 2019), DistilBERT (Sanh et al., 2019) and SBERT (Reimers and Gurevych, 2019) – does not generate new text, it only works with what is already there.

Non-generative Transformers have also been successfully applied outside language tasks. For example, the Vision Transformer (ViT) is a model that uses the Transformer architecture to recognise and classify images (Dosovitskiy et al., 2021). Instead of analysing words, it analyses visual parts of an image to identify what is inside – such as whether an image contains a cat, a tree or a car. ViT is not generative either; it does not create new images, but focuses on understanding existing ones.

Quick questions

Question 6.3

Which of the following best describes coverage measures in the context of neural networks? Select ONE option.

    A. Coverage measures assess how well a neural network generalises to new, unseen data by calculating the loss on the training dataset.

    B. Coverage measures track the number of training examples correctly classified by the network during validation.

    C. Coverage measures refer to the proportion of neurons activated during the training process, helping to evaluate the diversity of patterns learned by the model.

    D. Coverage measures are used to determine the number of layers and neurons required in a neural network based on the complexity of the data.

Question 6.4

What does the neuron coverage measure evaluate in the context of neural networks? Select ONE option.

    A. The percentage of neurons that activate at least once when processing a set of inputs, assessing how thoroughly the network explores different activation states.

    B. The total number of neurons in the network that contribute to overfitting during training.

    C. The percentage of neurons that remain inactive during training, helping to identify dead neurons.

    D. The proportion of neurons that are updated during the backpropagation step, determining the network's learning efficiency.

TERMS

Activation value: the output of an activation function of a neuron in a neural network.

Learning rate: a small positive constant that determines the step size of the updates for the weights and bias in the perceptron model.

Linear classifier: a type of classifier that makes its predictions based on a linear combination of input features.

Neuron (node, artificial neuron): a node in a neural network, usually receiving multiple input values and generating an activation value.

Neuron coverage: the coverage of activated neurons in the neural network for a set of tests.

Perceptron: a neural network with just one layer and one neuron.

Sign-change coverage: the coverage of neurons activated with both positive and negative activation values in a neural network for a set of tests.

Sign-sign coverage: the coverage achieved if, by changing the sign of each neuron, it can be shown to individually cause one neuron in the next layer to change sign while all other neurons in the next layer do not change sign for a set of tests.

Synapse: a connection between two neurons.

Threshold coverage: the coverage of neurons exceeding a threshold activation value in a neural network for a set of tests.

Value-change coverage: the coverage of neurons activated where their activation values differ by more than a change amount in the neural network for a set of tests.

Weight: an internal variable of a connection between neurons in a neural network that affects how it computes its outputs and that changes as the neural network is trained.

SELF-ASSESSMENT EXERCISES

1. Name the first neural models. Describe their difference.
2. What simple logical functions can a perceptron model learn? Provide justification for your answer.
3. List the main elements of the simple perceptron.
4. What is an artificial neural network?
5. Explain the difference between the artificial neural network and the deep neural network.

6. List the main elements of the deep neural network.

7. What is neuron coverage, and how does it differ from the threshold coverage?

8. Explain what is sign-change coverage.

9. Give the definition for value-change coverage.

10. Describe what sign-sign coverage is.

PART 3
TESTING AI-BASED SYSTEMS

7 TESTING AI-BASED SYSTEMS OVERVIEW

SUMMARY

This chapter describes a broader concept of software testing, its value and ways of evaluating the quality of obtained information. It then explores the importance of system requirements and design specifications, and why defining AI-based systems specifications can be challenging. Then it focuses on the testing levels for AI-based systems and how they differ from those of conventional systems. The chapter also covers the potential challenges in dealing with acquiring test data for AI-based systems, testing for automation bias in AI-based systems and documenting AI components. It gives an overview of what concept drift is and how to handle it, what the main risks associated with the AI-based systems are and how they influence the test approach, based on an extensive exercise on how to test a video recommendation system.

LEARNING OBJECTIVES

After reading this chapter, you should be able to:

- Explain how system specifications for AI-based systems can create challenges in testing (K2)
- Describe how AI-based systems are tested at each test level (K2)
- Recall the factors associated with test data that can make testing AI-based systems difficult (K1)
- Explain automation bias and how this affects testing (K2)
- Describe the documentation of an AI component and understand how documentation supports the testing of AI-based systems (K2)
- Explain the need for frequently testing the trained model, to handle concept drift (K2)
- For a given scenario, determine a test approach to be followed when developing an ML system (K4)

LINKS TO OTHER CHAPTERS

This chapter is related to other chapters as follows:

- Chapter 1 looks at AI as a service.

- Chapter 2 provides a description of quality characteristics specific to AI-based systems.
- Chapter 3 covers the ML workflow.
- Chapter 4 reviews data preparation activities and describes dataset quality issues.
- Chapter 5 focuses on ML functional performance metrics and criteria.
- Chapter 6 details coverage criteria.
- Chapter 8 explains the test oracle problem. It also considers test objectives and acceptance criteria.
- Chapter 9 goes over the test techniques applied to the testing of AI-based systems.

7.1 WHAT IS SOFTWARE TESTING?

Before we dive into the specifics of testing AI-based systems, it is important to take a step back and look at the broader discipline of software testing itself – mainly, what it is, what it aims to achieve and why it remains a critical part of any software development lifecycle.

According to the ISTQB Certified Tester Foundation Level syllabus (Cerquozzi et al., 2024), *testing* is the process that evaluates the quality of a component or system and related work products. At its core, software testing is an information service. Its primary purpose is to deliver objective, actionable insights to stakeholders about the quality and risks associated with a software product. This includes identifying defects such as any issues in the code, configuration, data or specification that could reduce the software's value to its users or stakeholders. These defects may not always be immediately visible, but they can have far-reaching implications, from degraded performance and user dissatisfaction to system failure or financial loss.

Neglecting software testing is comparable to making high-stakes decisions without sufficient intelligence: it is like planning a military operation without reconnaissance; treating patients without diagnostics; or engaging in algorithmic trading without access to real-time market data. In each of these domains, the absence of accurate, timely and relevant information can lead to serious consequences. Software development is no different.

Software testing is often defined as the process of exploring software with the intent of finding bugs, but it is not merely about confirming that a system works under ideal conditions; rather, it is a focused investigation aimed at revealing what does not work, where risks lie and how severe those risks might be. More formally, it is an empirical, technical investigation conducted to provide stakeholders with information about the quality of the product or service under test (Kaner, 2022).

The value that software testing provides can be evaluated along three main dimensions:

- *Information quality*: How effectively does the testing process detect, describe and communicate defects? High-quality testing produces insights that are accurate, clear and useful for decision-making.

- *Speed*: How quickly can testing deliver this information? In modern development cycles, timely feedback is essential to maintaining momentum and reducing time-to-market.

- *Cost*: How efficiently can this value be delivered? Testing that is too expensive or resource-intensive may not necessarily be sustainable in fast-paced or resource-constrained environments.

Achieving better, faster and more affordable testing is a substantial and ongoing challenge for organisations and project teams.

One way to assess the quality of this information is by applying a conceptual framework introduced by Wang and Strong (1996), which was based on the following preliminary aspects:

- *Accessibility*: Are the results available to those who need them, when they need them?

- *Interpretability*: Can the results be clearly understood and acted upon?

- *Relevance*: Do the insights address the needs and concerns of stakeholders?

- *Accuracy*: Are the findings correct and based on empirical evidence?

These four key aspects serve as the foundation for a broader framework proposed by Wang and Strong. Their research expanded these initial ideas into a comprehensive classification of data quality, grouped into four main categories:

- intrinsic data quality, referring to the characteristics that make data trustworthy;

- contextual data quality, implying that the usefulness of data depends on how well it fits a specific task;

- representational data quality, focusing on how clearly and consistently data is presented;

- accessibility data quality, revolving around the ease with which the users can get the data they need.

Each category contains specific characteristics that together offer a detailed view of what makes data valuable and fit for use. The diagram in Figure 7.1 summarises this classification.

This helps to reinforce the idea that testing is not just a technical activity, it is a communication and decision-support function. Its effectiveness depends not only on the tools and techniques used, but also on how well the results are communicated, understood and applied.

This foundation sets the stage for a deeper exploration into testing AI-based systems. Such systems have a number of emerging properties and challenges associated with them. As we move on to that topic, we will see how the core principles of software testing still apply but also how they must evolve to meet the unique characteristics of AI-driven technologies. As with any software system, delivery processes benefit

Figure 7.1 A conceptual framework of data quality (Source: Adapted from Wang and Strong, 1996)

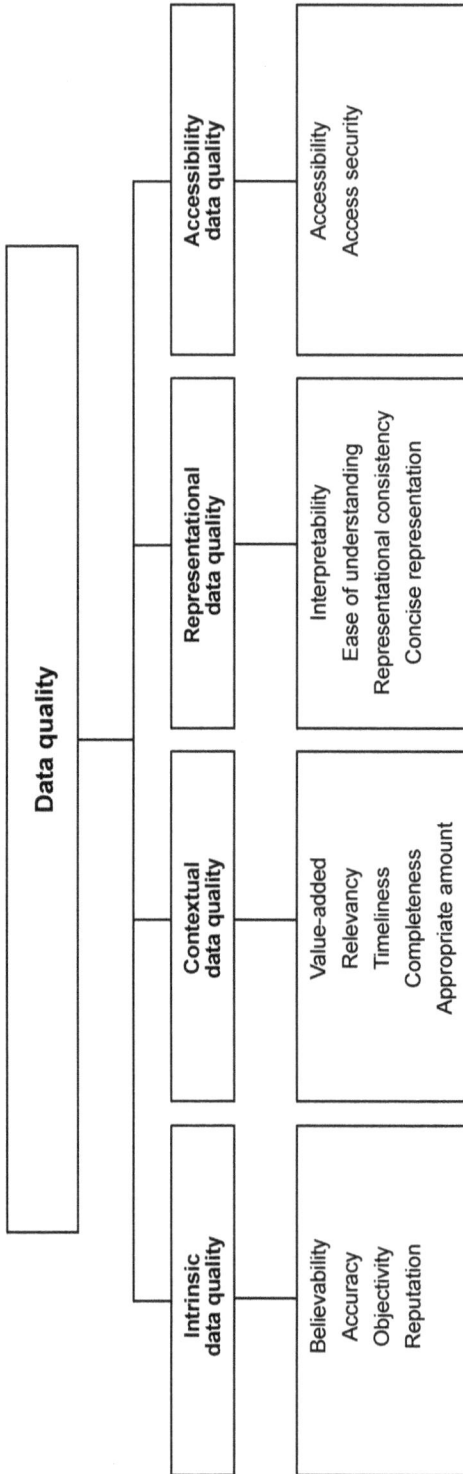

		Data quality		
Intrinsic data quality	**Contextual data quality**	**Representational data quality**	**Accessibility data quality**	
Believability	Value-added	Interpretability	Accessibility	
Accuracy	Relevancy	Ease of understanding	Access security	
Objectivity	Timeliness	Representational consistency		
Reputation	Completeness	Concise representation		
	Appropriate amount			

from the availability of clear, well-understood requirements and specifications. They can guide not only what we build, but also how we can measure whether it works as intended, especially when some parts of the system behave probabilistically or in ways that are difficult to trace. Let us now explore how to do structured and meaningful software testing for AI-based systems.

7.2 SPECIFICATION OF AI-BASED SYSTEMS

We have dived deep into the process of developing AI-based systems and have learned that we can use metrics to assess the model's quality; but what about evaluating other components of the system? What else can we look at when testing such complex systems? We have to keep in mind that the testing process starts with requirements and specifications.

Figure 7.2 Design specifications

System requirements and design specifications are equally important for both conventional systems and AI-based systems. Design specifications describe your software and its performance as well as how the user should interact with it (Figure 7.2). System requirements specifications, on the other hand, specify what the software needs to do, and how the system will perform each function. In a nutshell, system requirements provide the 'what' of the software project, outlining its goals and functionalities, while design specifications provide the 'how', offering detailed technical instructions on how to build the system to meet those requirements.

The specifications provide a baseline for testers to check against in order to verify and validate if system behaviour aligns with what is expected. However, if the specifications are incomplete and lack testability, this introduces a **test oracle problem**, when we need to determine the correct output for a given input (for more details, see Section 8.7 on test oracles for AI-based systems).

Let us look at the reasons why defining AI-based system specifications can be challenging:

Figure 7.3 Reasons for challenges in defining AI-based system specifications

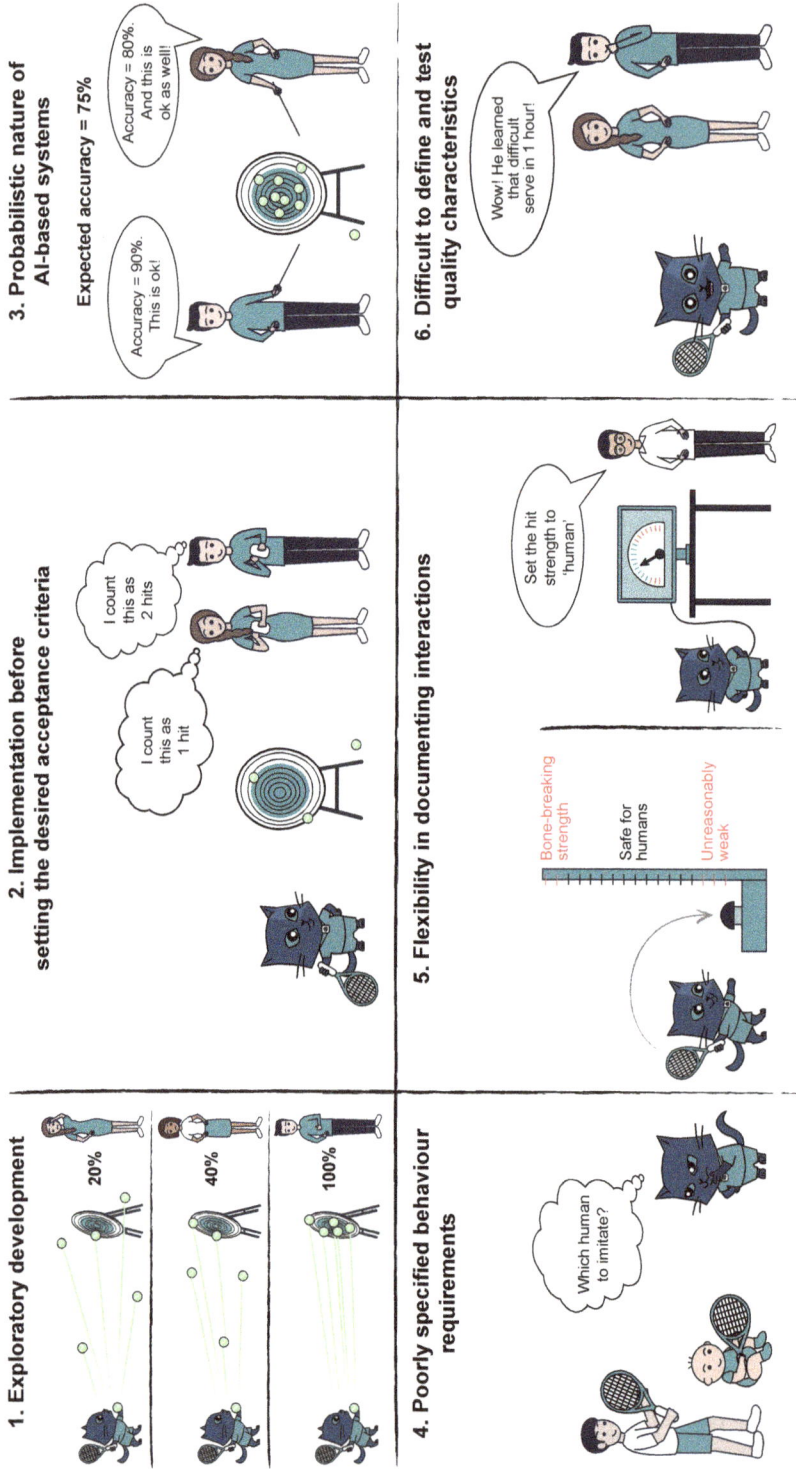

1. Exploratory development

20%

40%

100%

2. Implementation before setting the desired acceptance criteria

I count this as 1 hit

I count this as 2 hits

3. Probabilistic nature of AI-based systems

Expected accuracy = 75%

Accuracy = 90%. This is ok!

Accuracy = 80%. And this is ok as well!

4. Poorly specified behaviour requirements

Which human to imitate?

5. Flexibility in documenting interactions

Bone-breaking strength

Safe for humans

Unreasonably weak

Set the hit strength to 'human'

6. Difficult to define and test quality characteristics

Wow! He learned that difficult serve in 1 hour!

- In many AI-based projects, requirements are specified as high-level business objectives and predictions. Often, AI-based system projects start with a dataset, with the aim of establishing which predictions can be obtained from that data; so development of these types of systems is exploratory. This approach, of course, is totally different from the conventional project where we determine the underlying logic from the beginning.

- The accuracy of the AI-based system is reviewed after we get independent test results. This often leads to inadequate specifications, as implementation starts before we establish the desired acceptance criteria.

- The probabilistic nature of many AI-based systems can make it necessary to specify tolerances for some of the expected quality requirements, such as the accuracy of predictions.

- Imitating human behaviour can lead to poorly specified behaviour requirements because all people are different and have different capabilities, which exacerbates the process of defining a test oracle.

- In configurations where AI is used to implement user interfaces through natural language recognition, computer vision or physical interaction with humans, systems need to show even more flexibility in documenting such interactions.

- Quality characteristics specific to AI-based systems, such as adaptability, flexibility, evolution and autonomy, need to be included in requirements specifications (see Chapter 2), but, since these characteristics are relatively new, it can be difficult to define and test them.

Figure 7.3 depicts the factors contributing to challenges in defining specifications for AI-based systems.

Quick questions

Question 7.1

Why is it difficult to define comprehensive test cases for AI-based systems based on their specifications? Select ONE option.

    A. AI-based systems generate fixed outputs, so test cases become redundant after initial testing.

    B. AI-based systems rely on static datasets, making their behaviour predictable and test cases limited.

    C. The probabilistic and adaptive nature of AI-based systems means their outputs can vary based on the data and training, making it challenging to predict all possible behaviours.

    D. AI-based systems use simple decision trees with adjustable parameters, which makes testing straightforward and specifications of these systems easy to cover.

Question 7.2

Why does imitating human behaviour in AI-based systems often lead to challenges in testing? Select ONE option.

A. Human behaviour is entirely predictable, making it easy to specify and replicate in AI-based systems.

B. Human behaviour is inconsistent and context-dependent, making it difficult to define clear, formal specifications for AI-based systems that aim to mimic it.

C. AI-based systems that mimic human behaviour often rely on simple algorithms, resulting in overly specific behaviours where each action can be predicted based on a specific set of parameters.

D. AI-based systems are excellent at imitating human behaviour, reducing the need for detailed specifications.

7.3 TEST LEVELS FOR AI-BASED SYSTEMS

AI-based systems usually have AI and non-AI components. While we test non-AI components using conventional approaches, AI components may require something different. The biggest difference here is the inclusion of two new test levels to handle the testing of the input data and the models used in AI-based systems, as seen in Figure 7.4. All test levels that tackle **AI component** testing need to be closely supported by data scientists and domain experts.

Figure 7.4 Test levels for AI-based systems

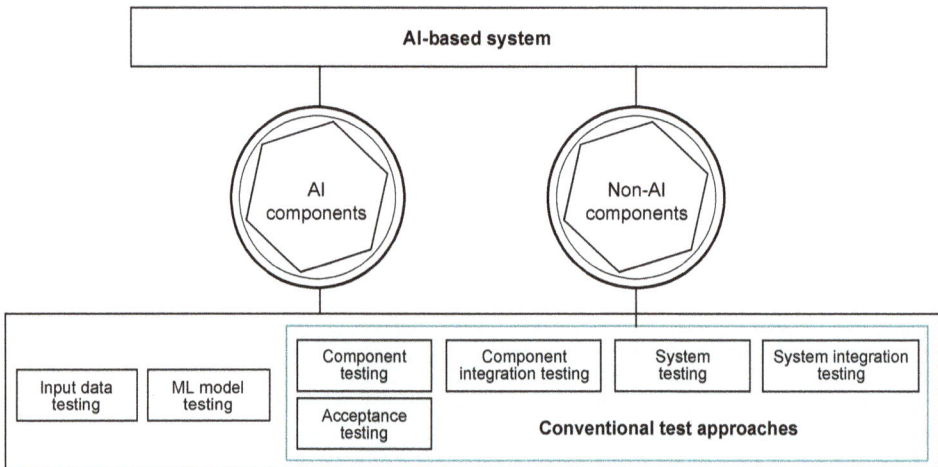

7.3.1 Input data testing

The objective of **input data testing** is to ensure the highest quality of training and prediction data. As shown in Figure 7.5, this includes reviews, statistical techniques, EDA and static and dynamic testing of the **data pipeline** (the pipeline is what we call the software responsible for data supply). The pipeline takes data from production, cleans it and sends it to the environments where this data is being analysed and the models are being trained (see Figure 7.6). For example, it may be historical data for exchange rates or stock prices, or data describing financial transactions. Usually, the data pipeline is made up of several components performing data preparation (see Chapter 4), and the testing of these components includes both component testing and integration testing. The training pipeline may be quite different from the data pipeline used to support operational prediction. For training, the data pipeline can be considered a prototype, compared to the fully engineered, automated version used operationally (see Figure 7.7). The testing of these two versions may differ and should include testing the functional equivalence.

Figure 7.5 Input data testing techniques

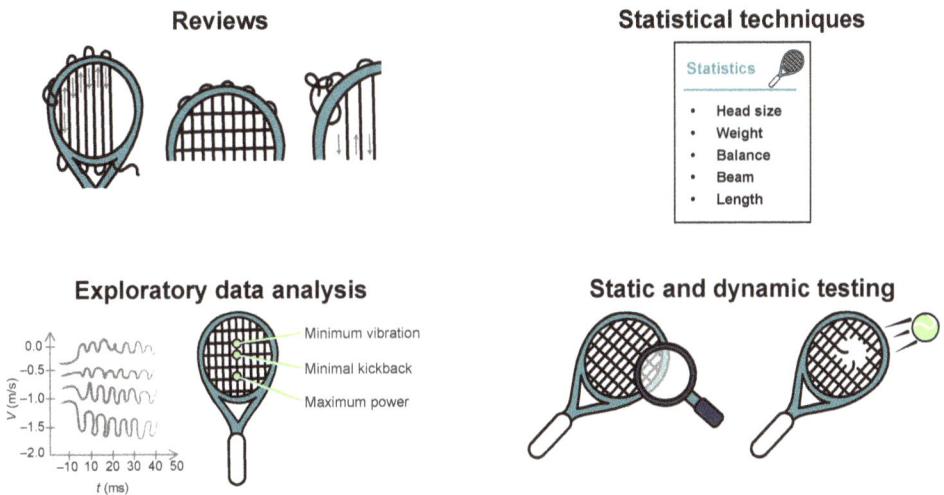

Reviews

Statistical techniques

Statistics

- Head size
- Weight
- Balance
- Beam
- Length

Exploratory data analysis

Minimum vibration

Minimal kickback

Maximum power

Static and dynamic testing

7.3.2 ML model testing

The objective of **ML model testing** is to confirm that the model meets the specified performance criteria, including functional and non-functional ones (see Figure 7.8). This step also has to make sure that the choices of the ML framework, algorithm, model, model settings and hyperparameters are as optimal as possible. If applicable, ML model testing may also include testing to achieve white-box coverage criteria (see Chapters 6 and 9 for coverage measures used in white-box testing). The selected model is later integrated with other AI and non-AI components.

Figure 7.6 A data pipeline

Figure 7.7 A prototype (a) and a fully engineered version (b)

(a)

(b)

Figure 7.8 ML model testing

1st serve average speed

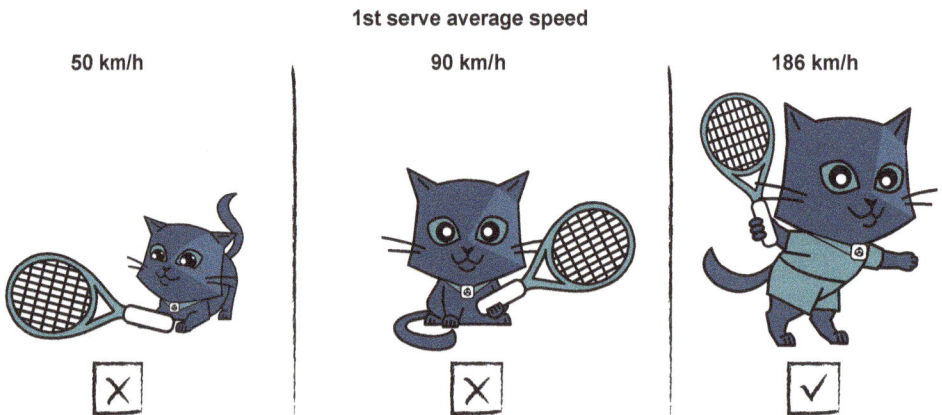

50 km/h

90 km/h

186 km/h

7.3.3 Component testing

Component testing is a conventional test level that is applicable to any non-model components (Figure 7.9), such as user interfaces and communication components. See the ISTQB Certified Tester Foundation Level syllabus (Cerquozzi et al., 2024).

Figure 7.9 Component testing

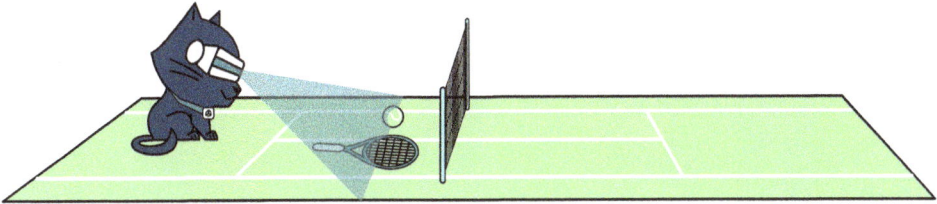

Quick questions

Question 7.3

What is a critical concern when testing input data for an autonomous driving system? Select ONE option.

    A. Input data can be limited to ideal road conditions with well-defined traffic conditions and vehicle characteristics, as AI-based systems perform best in controlled environments.

    B. Testing input data only needs to focus on daytime images, as AI-based systems struggle with night driving.

    C. Ensuring input data includes diverse scenarios, such as different weather conditions, traffic patterns and road types, to accurately evaluate the system's performance.

    D. Input data should consist solely of urban driving scenarios, as highway conditions are less complex.

Question 7.4

What is an example of component testing in an ML system for disease diagnostics? Select ONE option.

    A. Testing the entire system's ability to provide accurate diagnoses for all medical conditions.

    B. Testing how the system interacts with doctors and their patients to gather informative feedback on usability and correctness of the predictions made on the basis of patient complaints about diseases.

    C. Testing only the final diagnosis output for accuracy without considering intermediate steps.

    D. Testing the image processing module separately to ensure it correctly identifies key features in medical scans before integrating it with the diagnosis module.

Question 7.5

Which of the following options is the MOST likely example of ML model testing for a customer churn prediction model? Select ONE option.

    A. Comparing the model's predictions against actual customer churn rates on a test dataset.

    B. Training the model on past customer behaviour data.

    C. Updating the model with new customer behaviour data and churn rates to improve its predictive capabilities.

    D. Collecting user feedback on the model's predictions and adjusting the model parameters to improve the functional performance.

7.3.4 Component integration testing

Component integration testing ensures that AI and non-AI system components interact correctly (see Figure 7.10). Here, we make sure that the data pipeline inputs function as expected, and that model predictions are exchanged with the relevant system components. Where AI is provided as a service (see Section 1.7 on AIaaS), it is normal to perform API testing of the provided service as part of component integration testing.

7.3.5 System testing

System testing is conducted to make sure that the complete system (including both AI and non-AI components) performs as expected in a **test environment** that closely represents the **operational environment** from both functional and non-functional viewpoints (Figure 7.11). It can be done as field trials in the expected operational environment, or simulator testing if test scenarios are hazardous or difficult to replicate in an operational environment. During system testing, the **ML functional performance criteria** (see Chapter 5) are retested to ensure that the test results from the initial ML

Figure 7.10 Component integration testing

Figure 7.11 System testing

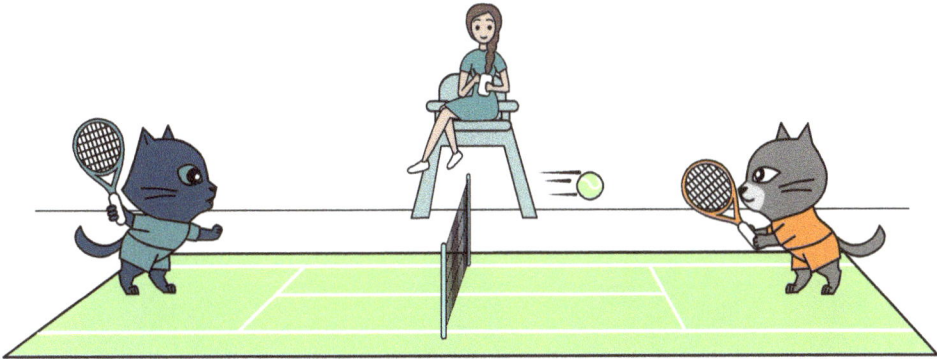

model testing are not affected when the model is added to the complete system. Here we also test many of the non-functional requirements as well.

7.3.6 System integration testing

System integration testing follows the system testing and verifies that multiple subsystems or systems work together as expected in an integrated environment (see Figure 7.12). This testing focuses on ensuring seamless interaction and data flow between complete systems, such as the integration of an AI-driven system with external operational systems, hardware or APIs. It evaluates both functional and non-functional aspects of the integration. System integration testing helps to uncover integration issues that might only appear when all subsystems are connected.

7.3.7 Acceptance testing

Acceptance testing is used to determine whether the complete system is acceptable to the customer (Figure 7.13), even though this can be very complicated to establish for AI-based systems (see Section 8.8 on test objectives and acceptance criteria).

Figure 7.12 System integration testing

Figure 7.13 Acceptance testing

Industry insights

Failed test instances with real voice assistants

Users have reported instances where voice assistants misinterpret commands or activate unintentionally. For instance, in 2018 a family in Portland, Oregon, reported that their Amazon Echo device recorded a private conversation and sent it to a random contact without their knowledge (Wolfson, 2018). Alexa mistakenly interpreted background conversation as a series of commands, which triggered it to record and send the audio clip. This raised serious privacy concerns about how voice assistants interpret commands and handle recorded data. There were reported cases of Alexa going completely off-script, laughing completely unprompted and, in one case, it even started listing funeral homes in the area, again, unprompted (CBS News, 2018).

Quick questions

Question 7.6

Which of the following options is the MOST likely example of system testing for a recommendation system for an e-commerce platform? Select ONE option.

A. Evaluating how well the recommendation engine suggests products based on user interactions and preferences.

B. Monitoring the system's performance during peak traffic periods to ensure it handles user requests efficiently.

C. Testing the accuracy of product recommendations by comparing them against actual purchase behaviour over a defined period.

D. Conducting tests to measure user engagement with different recommendation algorithms.

Question 7.7

Which of the following BEST illustrates acceptance testing for a voice recognition system for a virtual assistant? Select ONE option.

A. Verifying that the system can accurately transcribe speech from a diverse set of speakers in various environments.

B. Assessing how well the system performs when integrated with other software applications, such as calendars and reminders.

C. Conducting user trials to ensure that the voice recognition accurately understands commands and meets the needs of end-users.

D. Analysing the model's accuracy and precision on validation and test datasets during the model development prior to its deployment.

7.4 TEST DATA FOR TESTING AI-BASED SYSTEMS

We have just looked at seven levels of testing AI-based systems, but, as with any conventional system, there could be certain risks and potential problems. Let us look at some of them. There are several potential challenges in dealing with acquiring test data for AI-based systems:

- **Big data** can be difficult to create and manage. For example, it may be difficult to create representative test data for a system that consumes large volumes of images and audio at a high speed.

- *Input data* may need to change over time, particularly if it represents events in the real world. For example, when creating a model that predicts how long it takes to fix a bug, you need to consider that the description of bugs can be updated over time.

- *Personal and confidential data* may require sanitisation, encryption or redaction. Legal approval for use may also be required.

- When testers use the *same data acquisition and data pre-processing methods* as data scientists, then defects in these steps may be masked.

7.5 TESTING FOR AUTOMATION BIAS IN AI-BASED SYSTEMS

Incorrect or insufficient test data, and therefore inadequate testing of the ML model, can lead to the system providing people with imprecise predictions. In addition, there is a tendency for humans to be too trusting of AI-based systems' decision-making.

This misplaced trust may be called either **automation bias** or **complacency bias** and it takes two forms:

- accepting recommendations provided by the system without even thinking about other sources;

- overlooking failures due to the lack of adequate system monitoring.

This is very important in finance and banking. Here, AI presents an opportunity to transform how we deal with credit and risk. Lack of rigorous testing and monitoring can easily lead to deepening of the existing bias, creating vicious cycles that reinforce biased credit allocation, while making issues in lending even harder to find (see Figure 7.14).

Quick questions

Question 7.8

Which of the following options is a real-life example of automation bias that can negatively affect the testing of an AI-based system? Select ONE option.

    A. A team tests a self-driving car but decides to ignore the manual driving controls, assuming the automated driving system will always function perfectly.

    B. A software development team regularly updates their AI-based application to fix bugs and enhance features.

    C. An organisation implements a new AI tool and conducts thorough testing to ensure compliance with regulations.

    D. A data science team reviews patient data manually to confirm the recommendations made by the AI-based medical diagnosis system before making treatment decisions.

Figure 7.14 Biased credit allocation

7.6 DOCUMENTING AN AI COMPONENT

In order to avoid the automation bias, we need to pay attention to documentation. The key areas of documentation that are important to testing include:

- the purpose of the system and the specification of functional and non-functional requirements – these types of documentation typically form part of the test basis;

- architectural and design information outlining how the different AI and non-AI components interact – this supports the identification of integration testing objectives and may provide a basis for white-box testing of the system structure;

- the specification of the operating environment – this is required when testing the autonomy, flexibility and adaptability of the system;

- the source of any input data, including associated metadata – this needs to be clearly understood when testing the following aspects:

  - functional correctness of untrustworthy inputs;

  - explicit or implicit sample bias;

  - flexibility, including the mis-learning from poor data inputs for self-learning systems;

- the way in which the system is expected to adapt to changes in its operational environment – this is needed as a test basis when testing for adaptability;

- details of expected system users – this is needed to ensure that testing can be made representative.

The typical content for the documentation of an AI component includes:

- *general information*: identifiers, description, developer details, hardware requirements, licence details, version, date and point of contact;

- *design*: assumptions and technical decisions;

- *usage*: primary and secondary use cases, typical users, approach to self-learning, known bias, ethical issues, safety issues, transparency, decision thresholds, platform and concept drift;

- *datasets*: features, collection, availability, pre-processing requirements, use, content, labelling, size, privacy, security, bias/fairness and restrictions/constraints;

- *testing*: test dataset (description and availability), independence of testing, test results, testing approach for robustness, explainability, concept drift and portability;

- *training and ML functional performance*: ML algorithm, weights, validation dataset, selection of ML functional performance metrics, thresholds for ML functional performance metrics and actual ML functional performance metrics.

7.7 TESTING FOR CONCEPT DRIFT

One more problem that we can face is that the operational environment can change without the trained model being able to adapt. This is called a **concept drift**, and it typically causes the outputs of the model to become less accurate and less useful over time. Systems that are susceptible to it should be regularly tested against their agreed functional performance criteria, to ensure that any concept drift is detected quickly. This can be done through retiring or re-training the system. Retiring is the removal of the system and re-training is performed with up-to-date training data and followed by confirmation testing, regression testing and possibly a form of A/B testing, where the updated B-system is better than the original A-system. Figure 7.15 illustrates concept drift, its detection and re-training the system.

Industry insights

Concept drift in Yahoo mail's spam filter

Yahoo mail's spam filter experienced a decline in performance because it did not adapt quickly enough to new types of spam. Spammers developed new tactics to bypass the filter, leading to an increase in spam emails reaching users' inboxes, giving birth to many Reddit threads with people complaining about it (Reddit, 2022).

7.8 SELECTING A TEST APPROACH FOR AN ML SYSTEM

An AI-based system generally comprises both AI and non-AI components (see Figure 7.4). The testing approach for such systems is guided by a risk analysis and includes traditional testing methods alongside specialised techniques designed for AI components and AI-driven systems. Let us explore some common risks and their corresponding mitigations for ML systems.

AI-based systems' risks can be broken into project and product risks, as it is for conventional systems. **Project risks** are connected to the ML development workflow. For instance, data quality issues can happen due to poor assessment during EDA or a corrupted data pipeline (see Section 4.3 on data quality issues). They affect the next steps of the workflow, such as model training, evaluation and tuning (see Chapter 3). As a result, the choice of a framework, algorithm/model and settings/hyperparameters might be sub-optimal. These risks are given in Figure 7.16 and can be mitigated by subject matter expert reviews, EDA and dynamic testing.

After a model is deployed into production, we start dealing with **product risks** that stem from the fact that the users might come across a number of issues related to the model's performance (see Figure 7.17). If training data is irrelevant, it will cause a situation where the functional performance of a model in production differs significantly from the results at the testing stage; this happens frequently due to overfitting. For example, a model may provide excellent predictions when the data is similar to the training data but provides poor results otherwise. If the development team has incorrectly selected metrics for model evaluation, the end-user may consider the model to be of poor quality,

Figure 7.15 Concept drift and re-training a system

even though it shows satisfying results with the selected metrics. This is because all the metrics used to validate the model are artificial and do not always reflect the logic of the world around us.

It also might occur due to concept drift. In addition to that, AI-based systems might have non-functional performance issues when usability of the software does not meet users' expectations. Since all of these risks originate from the development phase, they can be resolved by improvements in the ML workflow, for example subject matter expert reviews and relevant non-functional testing activities.

We would also like to highlight self-learning system risks, for example the data used by the system for self-learning may be irrelevant. In this case, reviews by experts could identify the problematic data. The system may be failing due to the new self-learned functionality being unacceptable. This could be mitigated by automated regression testing, including performance comparison with the previous functionality. The system

Figure 7.16 Typical project risks specific to ML systems

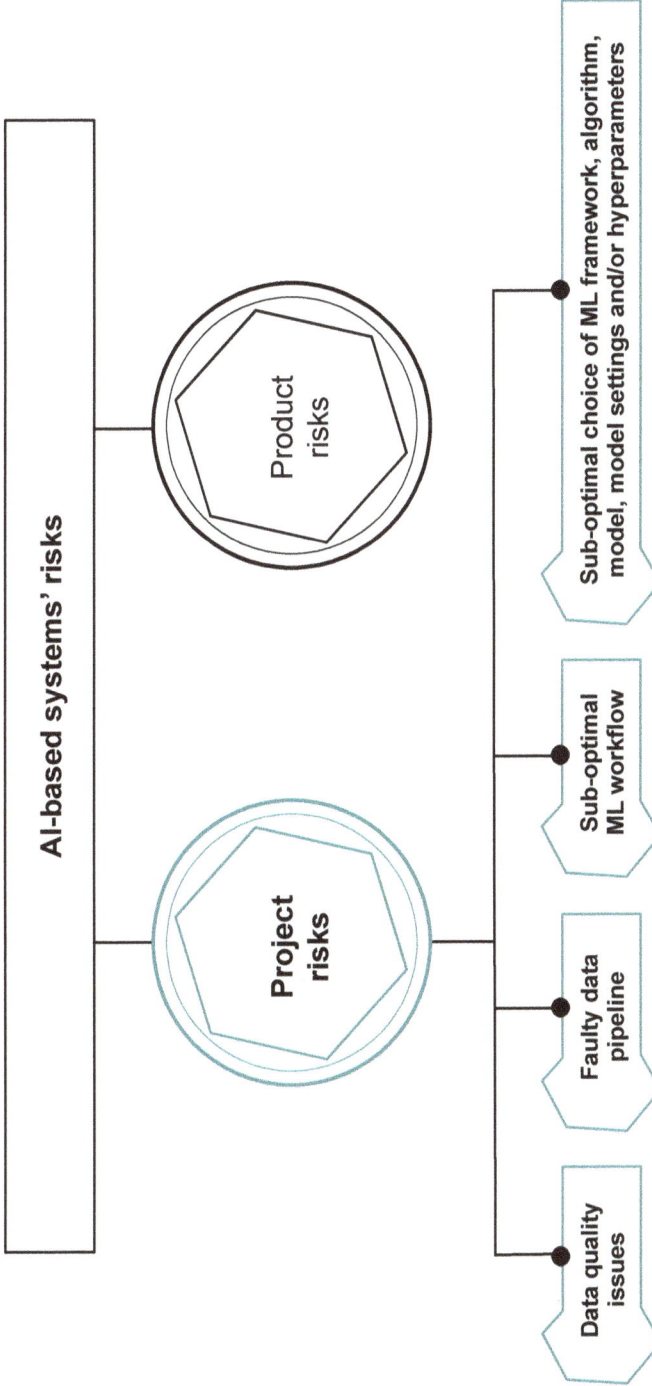

AI-based systems' risks

Project risks

Product risks

Data quality issues

Faulty data pipeline

Sub-optimal ML workflow

Sub-optimal choice of ML framework, algorithm, model, model settings and/or hyperparameters

Figure 7.17 Typical product risks specific to ML systems

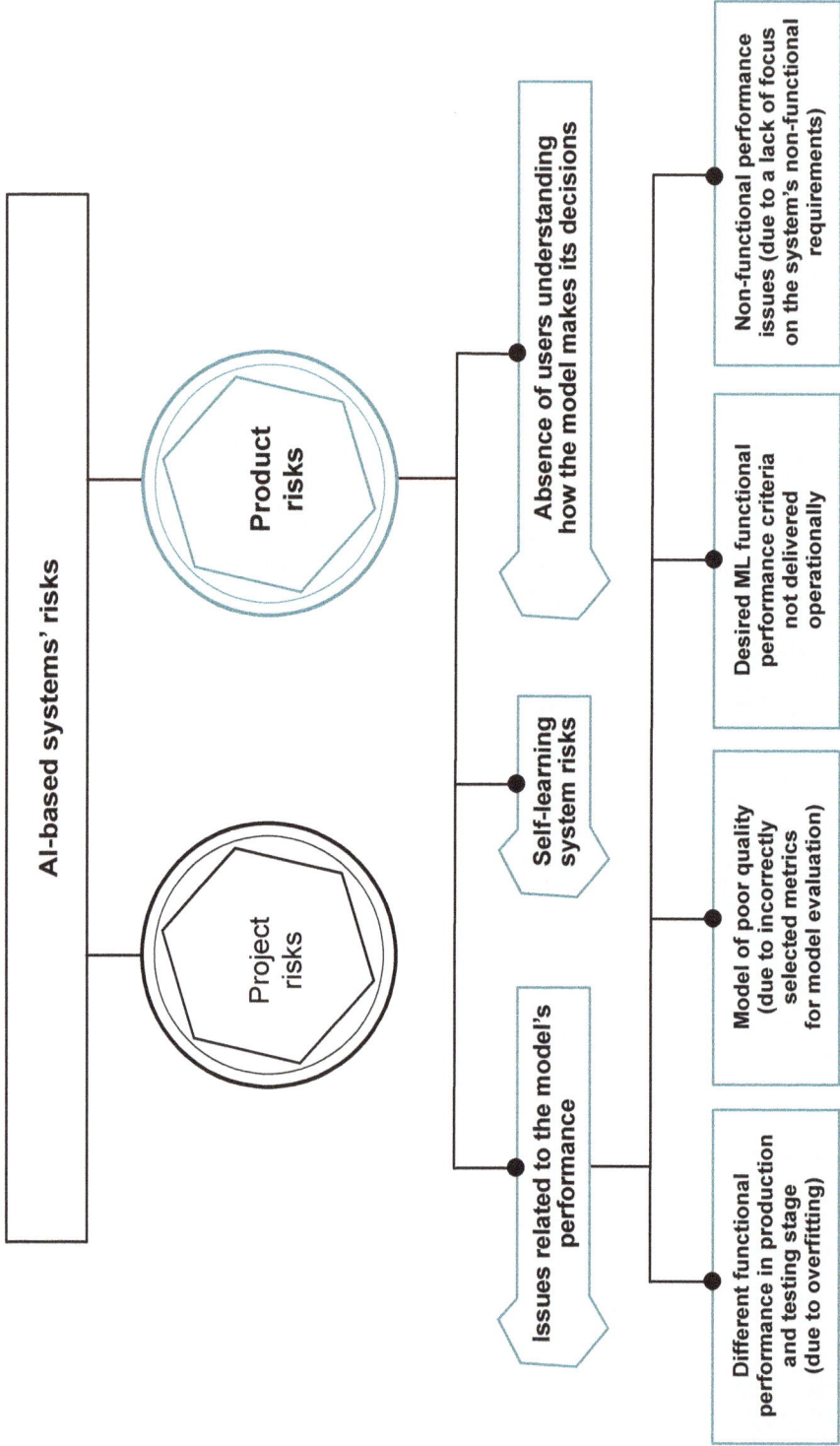

may be learning in a way that is not expected by the users, which could be detected by experience-based testing.

Even if a model works perfectly, a user might be still unsatisfied with its lack of explainability, interpretability and/or transparency, so it is critical for the stakeholders to understand how a model makes its decisions. This also might be considered a risk, especially in areas such as legal and healthcare.

From theory to practice

Imagine that you have been asked for your opinion on the test approach to be followed when developing an ML system for providing video recommendations on YouTube. Which typical risk aspects do you expect most likely to be associated with this system and to require mitigation through testing?

We will take a look at some of the ways through which we can test our entire recommendation system – from the model's behaviour to the health of the pipeline.

The test approach is based on a risk analysis for an ML system. That is why we should start with some typical risks specific to our video recommendation system that require mitigation through testing.

A good recommendation system should be trained on a large, diverse video dataset. Hence, the first group of risks is linked to low data quality and lack of data diversity, as well as issues stemming from inconsistent data formats. To ensure data quality, we should use reviews, EDA and dynamic testing.

The next possible risk is a sub-optimal choice of the ML framework, algorithm, model, model settings and/or hyperparameters. This risk may be mitigated by reviews with ML experts, who will use their domain knowledge to select the most appropriate options.

There are three types of recommendation systems:

- *Similarity-based on the query content*: the system retrieves content based on the similarity, for example if you like a football video, it will show you another one. The match is based on the item content such as description, title, etc.

- *Wisdom of the crowd*: instead of relying on item content, these recommendation models consider user preferences. If user A likes movies X, Y and Z and user B likes movies X and Z, then user B would probably like movie Y. These models are popular because they go beyond topic and content. They can thoroughly recommend a baseball video to a sports-loving user who just liked a football video.

- *Session-based*: the system captures a user's intent in a specific session and recommends items based on the session-level contextual information. For instance, if a user searches for a football video and intends to search for the rules of the game, they want the system to show them the rules in this session, even though they might have liked a certain nature video earlier.

Wisdom of the crowd and session-based systems require a lot of user–item interaction data. If that is not available, one might start with the similarity-based on the query content recommendation system. Even when there is a lot of data for existing users, one might not have enough for a new user. This situation is called the **cold start problem** in recommendation systems (Lika et al., 2014). In such cases, content-based recommendation systems can be a good proxy until one has enough interaction data for new users.

Let us return to the risk aspects. One more risk is related to the incorrect objective design, for example the model may be trained to predict if a user likes a video on YouTube based on whether or not a user will watch 95 per cent of the video by video length. If we have a near-perfect model that predicts a probability of over 95 per cent watch, we can say that we are recommending videos that the user likes, right?

Here is the catch, though: consider a one-minute video (V1) vs a thirty-minute video (V30). It takes 57 seconds to watch 95 per cent of V1, and it takes 1,710 seconds to watch 95 per cent of V30. V1 could also be a clickbait video, while a user can like V30 and still watch just 1,600 seconds of it. So, does our definition assure that the positive labels represent user preference?

Also, most platforms have multiple signals – like, share, download, clicks, etc. Which objective should you use to train the model? Usually, one is not enough. Let us say we train multiple models based on different objectives. We have multiple scores from each model. Then a single number score is created based on an aggregation formula on all scores, which is used to create the final ranking.

The point is that, if the training objective is not carefully designed, even a near-perfect model will not give good recommendations.

The next possible risk aspect is recommending irrelevant or repetitive content, which may lead to user disengagement. To mitigate this, extensive testing may be conducted to evaluate the system's ability to provide diverse and relevant recommendations.

One more risk is recommending low-quality or misleading content that may harm users' trust. The possible mitigation here is to implement content quality assessment mechanisms, to test the system's ability to filter out low-quality or misleading videos and to check that users' feedback is monitored and the model based on content quality metrics is adjusted.

Another risk is making mistakes during inference due to the mishandling of features. During model training, we might use many features besides embeddings, such as user location, age, video length, etc. It is common to apply transformations such as scaling to these features before using them. If you scaled a feature in training but not in inference, your model predictions could vary. To mitigate this kind of risk, we may use reviews, EDA and dynamic testing to evaluate model predictions and metrics.

The next risk is related to the updated embeddings. Recommendation systems are trained periodically. Using older embeddings can lead to inconsistencies and inaccurate recommendations. Hence, after each training cycle, the updated embeddings should be used to recommend items, and we should check this.

One more possible risk aspect is when the desired ML functional performance criteria are met, but the users may be unhappy with the delivered results. This may happen when the wrong performance criteria are selected, for example high recall instead of high precision is chosen as the target metric.

In the case of video recommendations on YouTube, false positives are detrimental. YouTube's primary goal is to suggest videos a user will love – and to avoid recommending videos a user will dislike at all costs. However, it is perfectly acceptable if not all videos a user could enjoy are presented to them. In other words, false negatives are not a major concern. For this kind of problem, precision is the right target metric.

Reviews with experts may mitigate the chance of choosing the wrong ML functional performance metrics, or experience-based testing could also identify inappropriate criteria. The risk could also be due to concept drift, in which case more frequent testing of the operational system could mitigate the risk.

Let us proceed to the next risk. Users may be dissatisfied if recommendations do not align with their preferences or if they find the content uninteresting. The way to mitigate this is to conduct user acceptance testing to gather feedback on the relevance and quality of recommendations, to check that user engagement metrics are monitored and re-training mechanisms implemented to improve user satisfaction and to test the system's ability to adapt to shifting user preferences and changing trends by introducing new data and simulating real-world scenarios.

Another possible risk is algorithmic biases in recommendations. If not trained properly, recommendation and ranking systems may be programmed with a series of algorithmic biases that might impede their effectiveness. These biases can vary, based on whether a recommendation algorithm prioritises popular, highly ranked or clickbait content over a user's actual preferences (*popularity bias*), or fails to understand multiple user interests at the same time, recommending only a certain kind of result (*single-interest bias*).

To mitigate this kind of risk, you may implement bias testing to identify and address potential biases, evaluate recommendation performance across diverse user segments and content genres and use fairness-aware metrics to assess balance and equity. One easy way to measure bias is to see the views distribution. What percentage of views is captured by the top 1 per cent, 5 per cent, 10 per cent, … of videos, and how often are these videos recommended to users vs other videos. This 80–20 effect can be seen across topics (specific topics dominate the app), creators (few popular creators vs niche creators), etc. An ML model learns bias in the dataset, among other things, so, if your dataset is biased, the chances are that your recommendation results will reflect it.

One more risk is privacy risk. As recommendation systems leverage large quantities of user data to carry out their functions, they may be prone to privacy risks. Data containing personal identifiers may be collected by such systems without obtaining explicit consent, causing loss of user agency. If not fortified adequately through data protection and cybersecurity mechanisms, these datasets may run the risk of being de-anonymised and misused by bad actors to granular-profile users.

A possible way to mitigate privacy risks is to implement rigorous privacy testing, to check compliance with privacy regulations and to check that users are allowed to opt-out or adjust privacy settings.

The next risk aspect is violating copyright laws or ethical standards in content recommendations. Compliance reviews with relevant regulations, content and ethical guidelines might help to mitigate these legal and ethical risks.

Let us proceed to the scalability and performance risk, which is when the system may struggle to scale with a growing user base and increasing amounts of content. The possible mitigation is to conduct scalability and stress/load testing to ensure the recommendation system can handle increasing workloads and to test the system's response time under different levels of user activity and content volume.

Finally, the last risk aspect we will discuss is adversarial attacks with malicious attempts to manipulate the recommendation system. To mitigate this risk, adversarial testing should be conducted to identify vulnerabilities, and robustness testing should be implemented to evaluate the system's resilience to adversarial attacks.

TERMS

Acceptance testing (user acceptance testing): a test level that focuses on determining whether to accept the system.

AI component: a component that provides AI functionality.

Automation bias (complacency bias): a type of bias caused by a person favouring the recommendations of an automated decision-making system over other sources.

Big data: extensive datasets whose characteristics in terms of volume, variety, velocity and/or variability require specialised technologies and techniques to process.

Cold start problem: a problem related to the sparsity of information available in the recommendation algorithm for novel users or new items.

Component integration testing (module integration testing, unit integration testing): the integration testing of components.

Component testing (module testing, unit testing): a test level that focuses on individual hardware or components of software system.

Concept drift: a change in the perceived accuracy of an ML model's predictions over time caused by changes in user expectations, behaviour and the operational environment.

Data pipeline: the implementation of data preparation activities to provide input data to support training by an ML algorithm or prediction by an ML model.

Input data testing: a test level that focuses on the quality of the data used for training and prediction by ML models.

ML functional performance: the degree to which an ML model meets ML functional performance criteria.

ML functional performance criteria: criteria based on ML functional performance metrics used as a basis for model evaluation, tuning and testing.

ML model testing: a test level that focuses on the ability of an ML model to meet required ML functional performance criteria and non-functional criteria.

Operational environment: an environment in which a system operates.

Product risk: a risk that affects the quality of a product.

Project risk: a risk that affects project success.

Risk: a factor that could result in future negative consequences.

System integration testing: the integration testing of systems.

System testing: a test level that focuses on verifying that a system as a whole meets specified requirements.

Test environment (test bed, test rig): an environment containing hardware, instrumentation, simulators, software tools and other support elements needed to conduct a test (ISO 24765).

Test oracle: a source to determine an expected result to compare with the actual result of the system under test.

Test oracle problem: the challenge of determining whether a test has passed or failed for a given set of test inputs and state.

SELF-ASSESSMENT EXERCISES

1. Identify the reasons why specifying AI-based systems can be particularly challenging.
2. List test levels for AI-based systems. Is there any difference compared with test levels for conventional systems?

3. Select any two test levels and describe how AI-based systems are tested at each of them.

4. What are the main challenges in dealing with test data for AI-based systems?

5. Explain what automation bias is and name its forms.

6. What are the key areas of documentation that are important to testing?

7. Discuss the typical content of the AI component documentation.

8. What is concept drift? Explain how to handle it in an AI-based system.

9. Discuss possible test approaches for ML systems based on the project risk analysis.

10. What are possible test approaches based on the product risk analysis for ML systems?

8 TESTING AI-SPECIFIC QUALITY CHARACTERISTICS

SUMMARY

This chapter presents examples of issues concerned with testing self-learning systems. It describes major testing challenges for different types of AI-based systems, such as autonomous, probabilistic, non-deterministic and complex systems. This chapter provides the key testing tips for algorithmic, sample and inappropriate biases, as well as transparency, interpretability and explainability of the AI-based systems. The chapter also focuses on the test oracles and the search for 'ground truth'. It explores the main test objectives and acceptance criteria based on the potential product risks and quality characteristics for an AI-based system.

LEARNING OBJECTIVES

After covering this chapter, you should be able to:

- Explain the challenges in testing created by the self-learning of AI-based systems (K2)

- Describe how autonomous AI-based systems are tested (K2)

- Explain how to test for bias in an AI-based system (K2)

- Explain the challenges in testing created by the probabilistic and non-deterministic nature of AI-based systems (K2)

- Explain the challenges in testing created by the complexity of AI-based systems (K2)

- Describe how the transparency, interpretability and explainability of AI-based systems can be tested (K2)

- Use a tool to show how explainability can be used by testers (K3)

- Explain the challenges in creating test oracles resulting from the specific characteristics of AI-based systems (K2)

- Select appropriate test objectives and acceptance criteria for the AI-specific quality characteristics of a given AI-based system (K4)

LINKS TO OTHER CHAPTERS

This chapter touches on some of the concepts that are covered in other chapters:

- Chapter 2 describes different quality characteristics of AI-based systems. It also explains what algorithmic bias, sample bias and inappropriate bias are.
- Chapter 9 considers test techniques, such as A/B testing, back-to-back testing and metamorphic testing, in detail.
- Chapter 10 looks at virtual test environments for AI-based systems.

8.1 CHALLENGES IN TESTING SELF-LEARNING SYSTEMS

Self-learning systems are equipped with ML techniques that try to enable computers to make decisions based on data without explicit programming instructions. The basic building block of self-learning systems is the ability to learn based on experience and then take action in response to new or unforeseen events. Self-learning systems have to be able to continuously evolve, self-develop and self-learn in order to adapt to the dynamically changing environment (see Figure 8.1).

Figure 8.1 Ability to evolve, self-develop and self-learn

Let us talk about the issues that need to be resolved when testing self-learning systems. Figure 8.2 summarises a few of them, and they need to be addressed with utmost attention.

Figure 8.2 Challenges encountered when testing self-learning systems

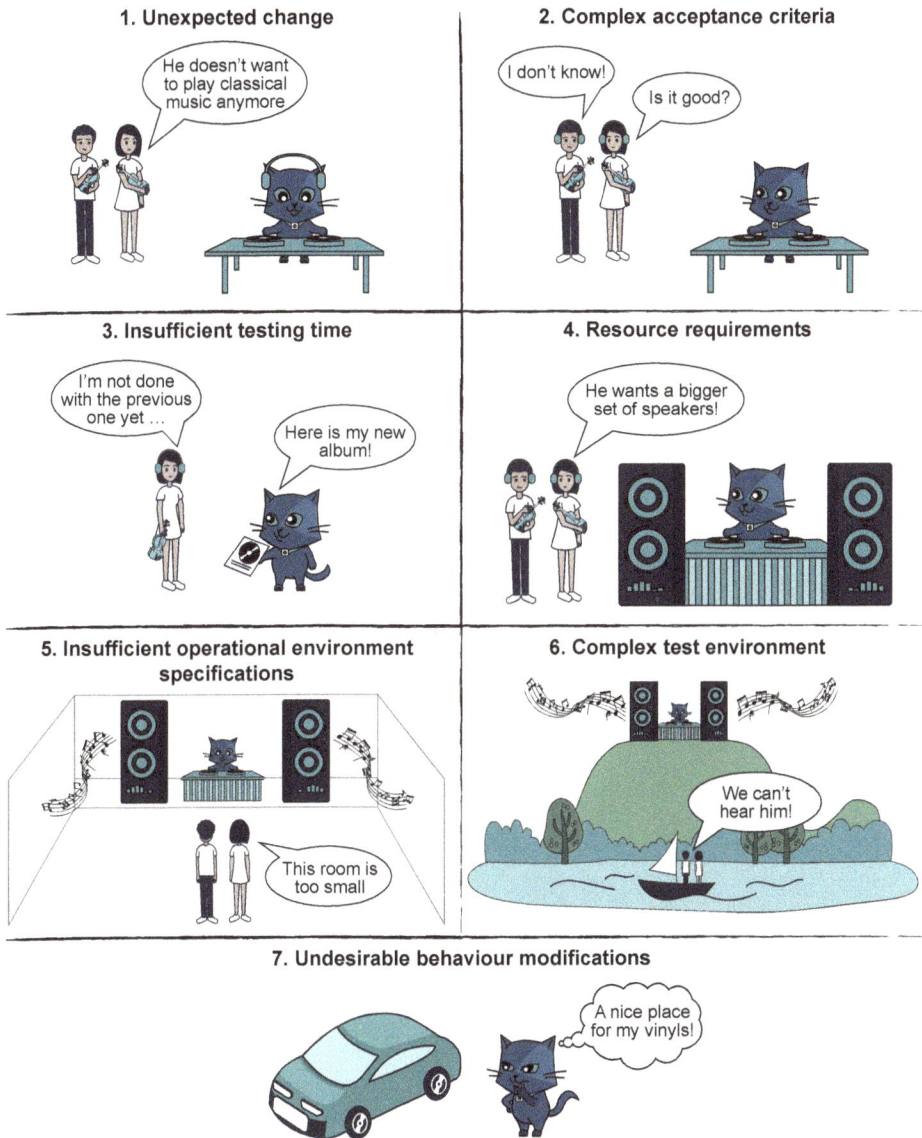

1. *Unexpected change*: it is usually possible to evaluate against the original requirements, design and specified constraints, but if the system has devised an innovative approach, the implementation of which cannot be seen, it may be quite complicated to design tests for this. On the one hand, this test design challenge may be tackled by tests that remain relevant as the system changes its behaviour, which would prevent a regression problem, but on the other hand, it may also require new tests to be designed based on new system behaviours. In such cases, exploratory testing can be particularly valuable, as it allows testers to investigate and adapt to the system's evolving behaviour in real time.

2. *Complex acceptance criteria*: we have to define expectations for system improvement as it self-learns, and that can be quite subjective. So, more objective and complex acceptance criteria may be required in addition to a continuous record of the baseline functional performance.

3. *Insufficient testing time*: we have to know the speed at which the system learns and adapts. If it happens too quickly, we might not have enough time to manually execute new tests after each change, so we need tests that can be run automatically when the system changes itself.

4. *Resource requirements*: we might have to define the resources that the system can use while self-learning or adapting. It would also be wise to link said resource usage to a measurable improvement in functionality or accuracy.

5. *Insufficient operational environment specifications*: a self-learning system might change if the received environmental inputs are outside expected ranges, or if they are not reflected in the training data. Therefore, the full scope of possible changes in the operational environment to which the system is expected to respond will be defined as acceptance criteria.

6. *Complex test environment*: managing the test environment to make sure it can replicate all the potential high-risk operational environment changes could be quite challenging. This may be tested by manipulating inputs, or by obtaining access to different physical environments in which the system can be tested.

7. *Undesirable behaviour modifications*: a self-learning system modifies its behaviour based on its inputs, and it may not be possible for testers to prevent this from occurring; but it is important to prevent a situation where testing causes a self-learning system to adversely change its behaviour.

Industry insights

Insufficient training causes Microsoft Tay chatbot failure

Tay was a chatbot released by the Microsoft Corporation as a Twitter bot on 23 March 2016 (Charlton, 2016). Controversy arose when Tay began posting inflammatory and offensive tweets through its Twitter account, prompting Microsoft to shut down the service just 16 hours after its launch. Even though the company stated that Tay was built using 'relevant public data' that had been 'modelled, cleaned, and filtered', once the chatbot went live, it appeared that filtering was insufficient. The company had to quickly scrub Tay's posts, removing its insulting comments.

A week later, Microsoft accidentally re-launched Tay on Twitter during testing. Once active again, Tay posted several drug-related tweets and soon got stuck in a repetitive loop, tweeting 'You are too fast, please take a rest' multiple times per second. Because these tweets mentioned its own username, they flooded the feeds of over 200,000 Twitter followers, causing widespread annoyance.

Quick questions

Question 8.1

An AI-based recommendation system in an e-commerce platform adapts to user behaviour by learning from purchase patterns. However, different stakeholders have varying expectations: business leaders want a higher percentage of website visitors who have made certain purchases, while users demand personalised, relevant recommendations. The system meets some but not all of these conflicting goals. What is the MOST likely challenge faced when testing this self-learning system? Select ONE option.

A. insufficient testing time

B. insufficient operational environment specifications

C. complex acceptance criteria

D. unexpected change

8.2 TESTING AUTONOMOUS AI-BASED SYSTEMS

When it comes to autonomy, one of the biggest questions that needs to be resolved is when the systems might need human involvement. This may require:

- testing for a specific scenario when the system should relinquish control (Figure 8.3(a));
- testing whether the system requests human intervention when the system should be relinquishing control after a specified period of time (Figure 8.3(b));
- testing whether the system unnecessarily requests human intervention when it should still be working autonomously (Figure 8.3(c)).

On the one hand, it may be helpful to use boundary value analysis to find the necessary conditions for testing autonomous AI-based systems but, on the other, it can be difficult to define how the parameters that determine autonomy manifest themselves.

Figure 8.3 Testing if a system requires human involvement

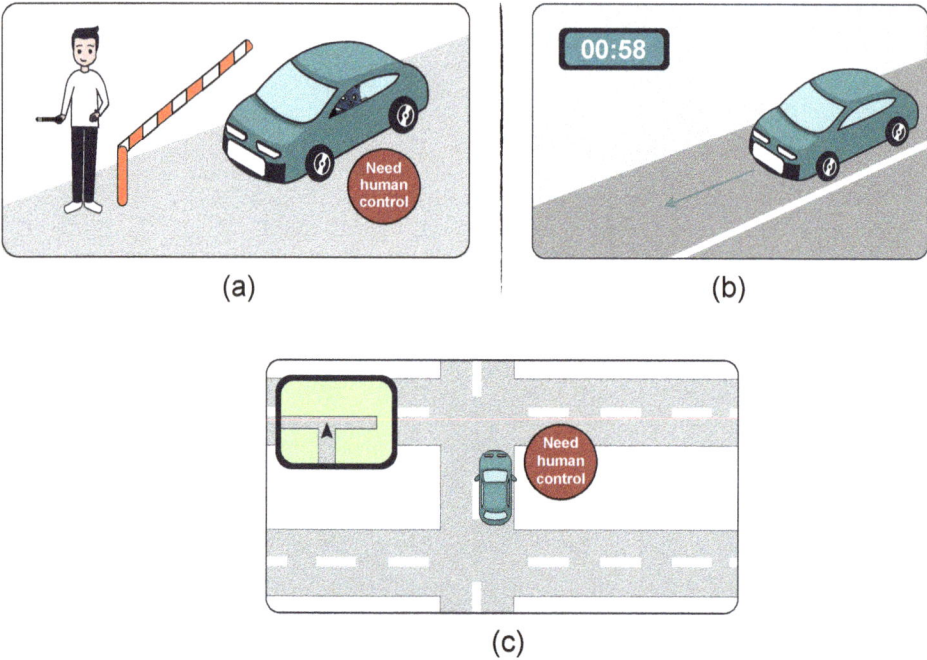

(a)

(b)

(c)

Industry insights

Pseudo-full autonomy of Amazon's Just Walk Out technology

Amazon Go checkout-less shops were launched claiming to have the most advanced shopping technology called 'Just Walk Out', eliminating queues and cashiers. The technology operates through an app on a shopper's mobile device, which automatically checks in when the shopper enters the shop. Shoppers can browse and shop as usual, with sensors scanning items as customers put them in their baskets. Amazon then bills the purchases to the shopper's Amazon account as they leave. However, the technology consistently fell short of several internal benchmarks. Notably, it never achieved full promised autonomy. Amazon employees disclosed that the checkout system relied heavily on a team of human reviewers to label and verify purchases that the AI could not process accurately. An India-based team labelled videos for AI training, which is common for ML, but they also verified videos of purchases flagged as 'low-confidence events'. When the shop launched in 2016, nearly all purchases required human review. By mid-2022, 70 per cent of purchases still needed confirmation. Currently up to 50 per cent of purchases require human review, which is significantly higher than Amazon's internal goals (Zeff, 2024).

8.3 TESTING FOR ALGORITHMIC, SAMPLE AND INAPPROPRIATE BIAS

An ML system should also be evaluated against different biases (see Chapter 2). This may involve positive bias being deliberately introduced to mitigate the inappropriate one, as shown in Figure 8.4(a). Testing with an independent dataset can often detect this bias; however, it can be difficult to identify all the data that causes it because the ML algorithm can use combinations of seemingly unrelated features, see Figure 8.4(b).

Figure 8.4 Introducing the positive bias to mitigate the inappropriate bias (a) and the difficulty of identifying all the data that causes the inappropriate bias (b)

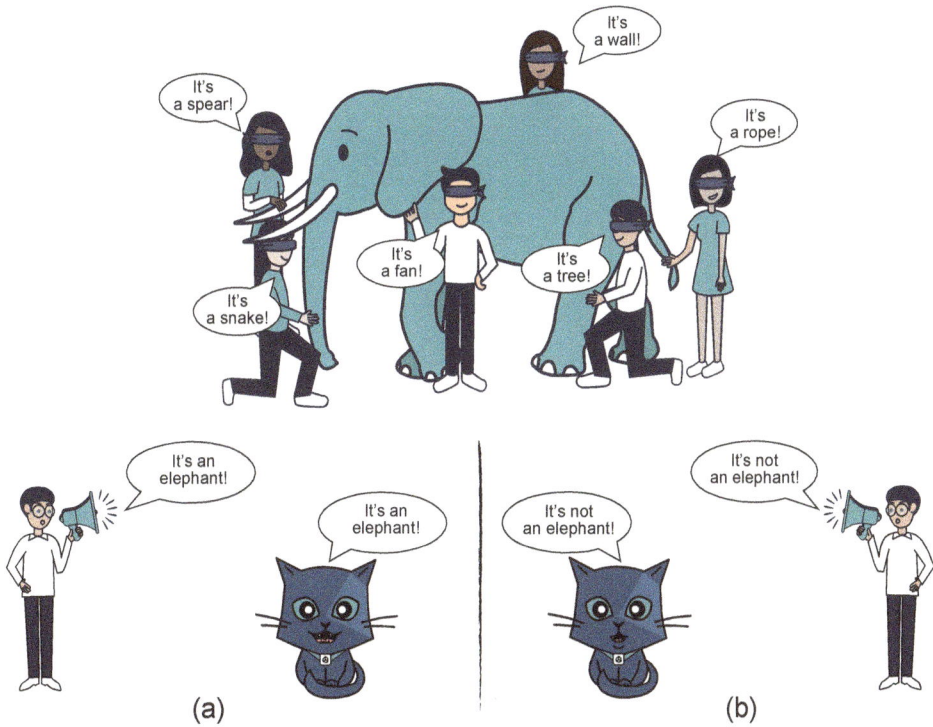

AI-based systems should be tested for algorithmic bias, sample bias and inappropriate bias, which may involve:

- checking for bias during the model's training, evaluation and tuning activities (see Figure 8.5);

Figure 8.5 Biased training and evaluation

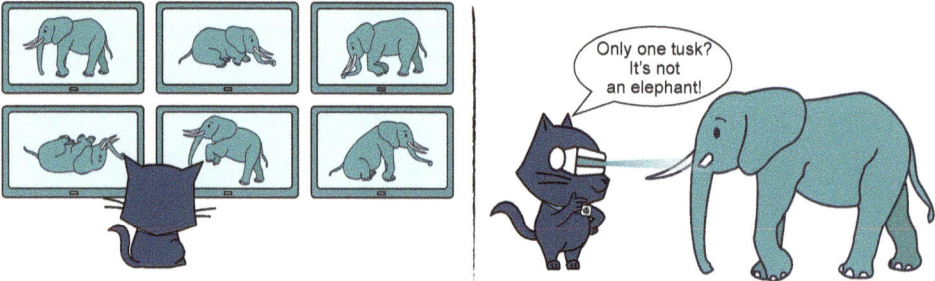

- checking for sample bias by reviewing the source of the training data and the processes used to acquire it, as well as by reviewing the data pre-processing as part of the ML workflow, as shown in Figure 8.6;

Figure 8.6 Biased data acquisition and data pre-processing

- checking how changes in inputs affect outputs (Figure 8.7) over a large number of interactions, and examining the biased results;

Figure 8.7 Biased input data influencing output results

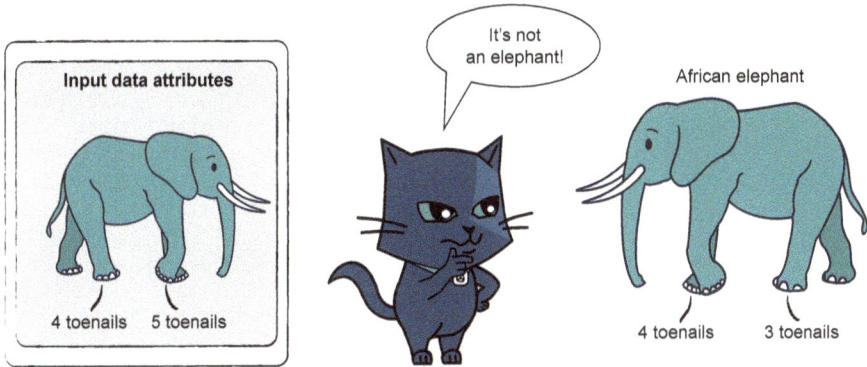

- obtaining additional information concerning the attributes of the input data potentially related to bias and then correlating it to the results, as illustrated in Figure 8.8. This is because the bias can be based on 'hidden' variables that are not explicitly present in the input data, but are inferred by the algorithm.

Figure 8.8 Additional details on biased attributes impacting outputs

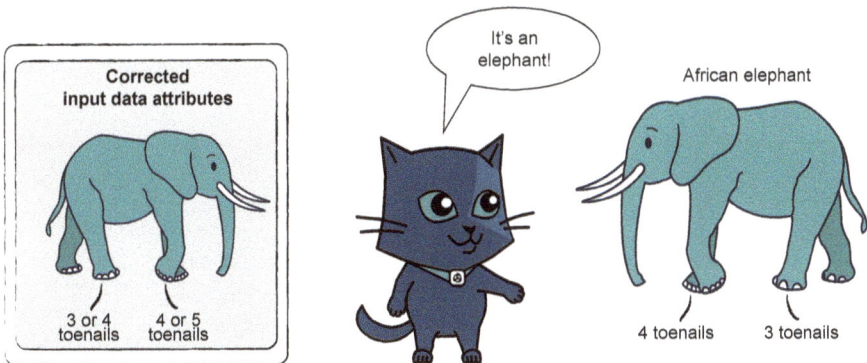

Industry insights

Bias in Amazon's automated hiring tool

Since 2014, Amazon has been developing computer programs to automate the review of job applicants' resumes, aiming to streamline the search for top talent. The experimental hiring tool used AI to rate job candidates, similar to product ratings on Amazon. However, by 2015 the company realised the system was not gender-neutral for technical job candidates (Dastin, 2018). This bias arose because the training data predominantly consisted of resumes submitted to Amazon over a 10-year period, most of which came from men, reflecting the male-dominated tech industry. Since the AI model was trained on past hiring data, it learned patterns that mirrored the existing gender biases present in the industry and at Amazon. As a result, Amazon's system favoured male candidates and downgraded resumes that included the word 'women's', as in 'women's chess club captain'.

8.4 CHALLENGES IN TESTING PROBABILISTIC AND NON-DETERMINISTIC AI-BASED SYSTEMS

Please keep in mind that most **probabilistic systems** are also **non-deterministic**, and so the following list of testing challenges typically applies to AI-based systems with any of these attributes.

- There may be multiple valid outcomes from a test with the same set of preconditions and inputs, as shown in Figure 8.9. This can cause difficulties when tests are reused for confirmation and regression testing, where reproducibility of testing is important, and when the tests are automated.

Figure 8.9 A scenario with multiple valid outcomes

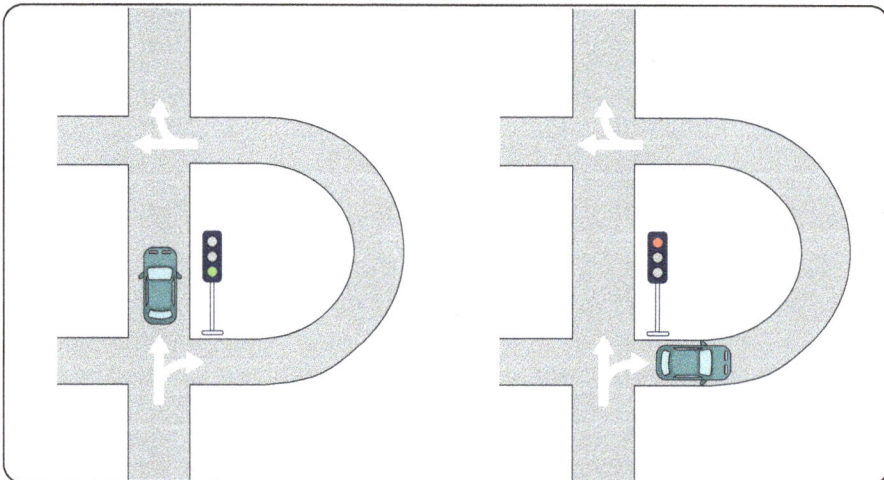

- The tester requires a deeper understanding of the system behaviour to check whether the test has passed rather than simply stating an exact value for the expected test result (see Figure 8.10).

Figure 8.10 A scenario with an unclear outcome

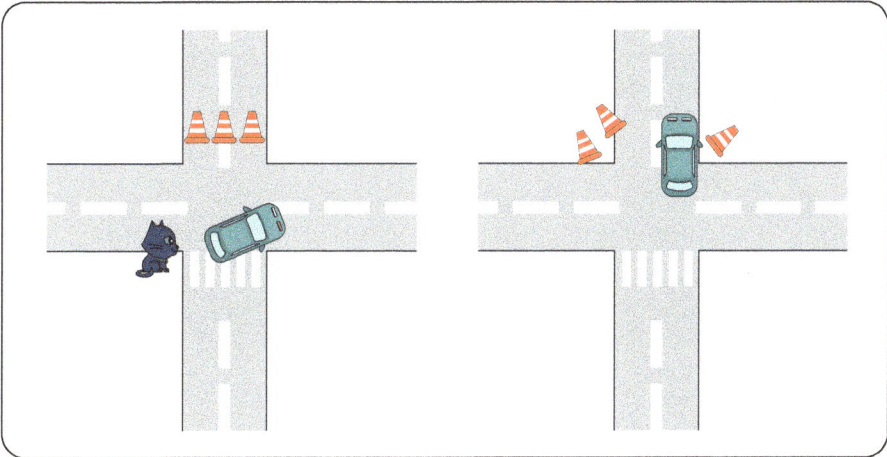

- If a single definitive output from a test is not possible due to the probabilistic nature of the system, it is often necessary for the tester to run a test several times in order to generate a statistically valid test result, as illustrated in Figure 8.11.

Figure 8.11 A statistically valid outcome scenario

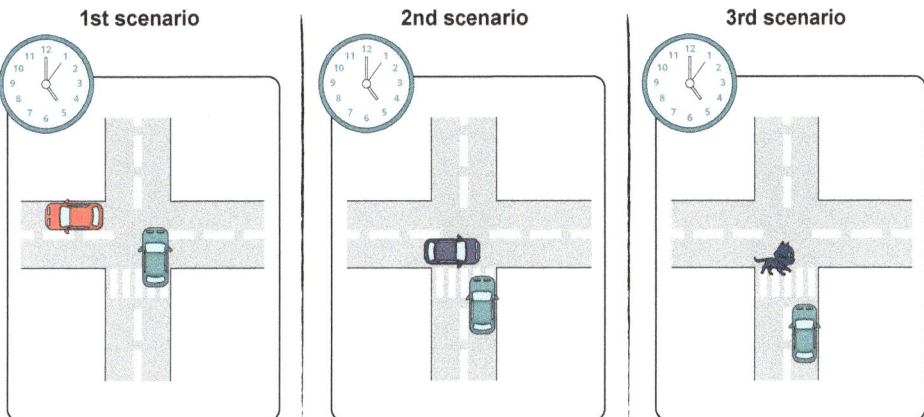

1st scenario   2nd scenario   3rd scenario

Quick questions

Question 8.2

A probabilistic AI-based system is used by a bank to predict the risk of loan defaults. The system assigns a probability score to each loan applicant, indicating the likelihood of their default. During testing, the system produces slightly different risk scores for the same applicant when the test is run multiple times. To obtain reliable test outcomes, the tester must run the test several times and analyse the average results. What is the MOST likely challenge faced when testing this financial risk prediction system? Select ONE option.

A. The system has been trained on insufficient financial data, causing unstable predictions.

B. The probabilistic nature of the system causes variability in the results, requiring multiple test runs for statistical significance.

C. The system's model is outdated, leading to inconsistent risk predictions across different test runs.

D. The system's algorithm is overfitting, causing fluctuating results during the testing process.

Question 8.3

An autonomous vehicle should be able to navigate through unpredictable environments, such as busy city streets. Its decision-making system is based on probabilistic models that evaluate the likelihood of various events, such as pedestrians crossing, cars merging or sudden obstacles appearing. During testing, the autonomous vehicle does not always react in exactly the same way under identical conditions due to the probabilistic nature of its decision-making. What is the MOST appropriate approach to evaluate if the test has passed or not? Select ONE option.

A. Verifying that the autonomous vehicle follows a rigid, pre-programmed set of actions for each test scenario to ensure consistency of its driving activities.

B. Checking if the vehicle reacts in the exact same way every time under the same test conditions.

C. Ensuring that the vehicle's reactions are safe and within acceptable performance thresholds, even if different decisions are made in similar situations.

D. Verifying that the vehicle always takes the fastest possible route to avoid any obstacles during the test scenarios.

8.5 CHALLENGES IN TESTING COMPLEX AI-BASED SYSTEMS

AI-based systems are often used to implement tasks that are too complex for humans to perform. This can lead to a test oracle problem because testers are unable to determine various expected results. A similar problem arises when the internal structure of an AI-based system is software-generated, making it too complex for humans to understand, which, in turn, may be tackled by black-box testing.

Also, the problems with non-deterministic systems are exacerbated when an AI-based system consists of several interacting components, each providing probabilistic results (see Figure 8.12). The interactions between AI components can make it quite challenging to identify all the risks and design tests.

Figure 8.12 AI-based system consisting of several interacting components, each providing probabilistic results

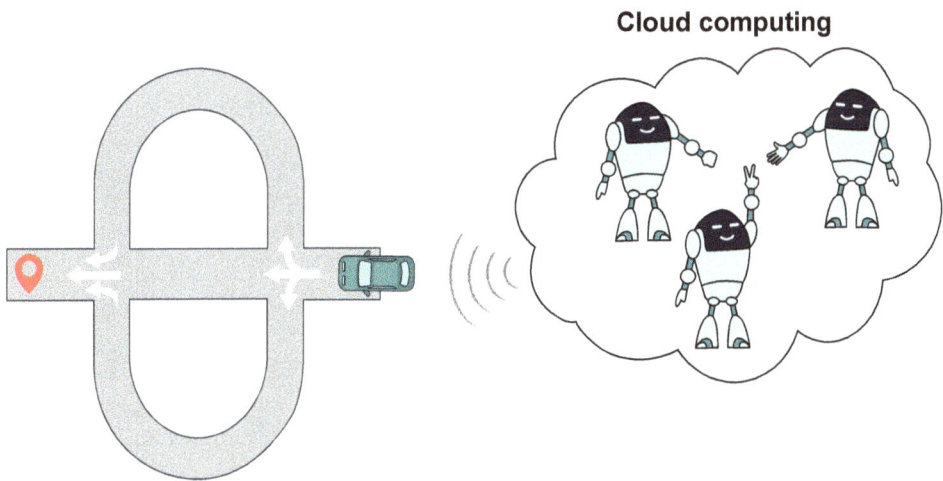

Cloud computing

Quick questions

Question 8.4

A healthcare company has developed an AI-based system to assist doctors in diagnosing patients. The system combines image recognition for analysing medical scans, NLP for interpreting doctors' notes and a decision-making engine that provides treatment recommendations. Each component works independently but contributes to the final diagnosis. What is the primary challenge in testing this complex AI-based system? Select ONE option.

    A. Testing the interactions between components is challenging because issues in one part could affect the overall performance.

    B. Testing the system is straightforward, since each component's output is entirely independent of the others.

    C. Ensuring that each component functions perfectly on its own will guarantee accurate overall system performance.

    D. The system's complexity only requires testing the decision-making engine, as it is the final component that provides the diagnosis.

Question 8.5

A tester is evaluating a complex AI-based system that predicts real-time traffic patterns and adjusts vehicle routes accordingly. It is known that the system's ML algorithms learn from dynamic and ever-changing data. What is the MOST significant challenge faced by the tester in this situation? Select ONE option.

    A. Calculating whether there is enough gasoline for the route.

    B. Identifying and designing test scenarios.

    C. Testing whether the system requests human intervention.

    D. Defining exact expected results for each test scenario.

8.6 TESTING THE TRANSPARENCY, INTERPRETABILITY AND EXPLAINABILITY OF AI-BASED SYSTEMS

Information on AI-based systems may be provided by the system developers. This might include the sources of training data, labelling and the system components' design. When this information is not available, it can make the design of tests challenging. The situation can be compared to differences in black-box and white-box testing, and has similar advantages and disadvantages.

Transparency, which is the level of visibility of the algorithm and data used by the AI-based system (see Figure 8.13 and Chapter 2 for the quality characteristics of AI-based systems), can be tested by comparing the information documented on the data and algorithm to the actual implementation.

Figure 8.13 Transparency

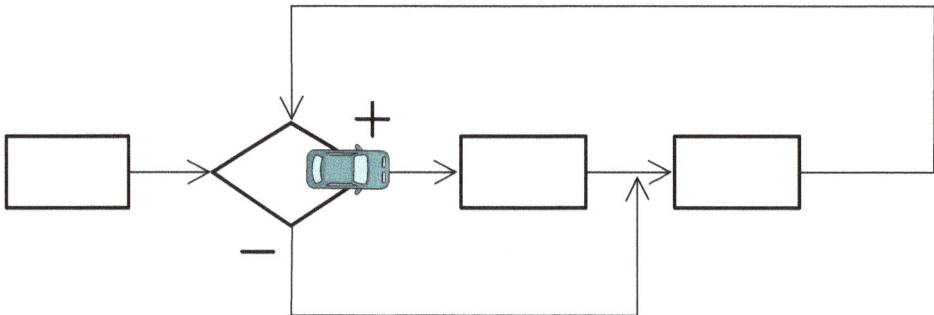

ML makes it more complicated to explain the link between a specific input and a specific output than with conventional systems. This low level of *explainability* (see Figure 8.14) is primarily because the model generating the output is itself generated by the algorithm and does not reflect human thinking. Different ML models provide different levels of explainability, and should be selected based on the requirements for the system. One method to understand explainability is through the dynamic testing of the ML model when applying perturbations to the test data. Methods exist for quantifying explainability and providing visual representations. Some of these methods are **model-agnostic**, while others are specific to a particular type of model and require access to it. Exploratory testing can also be used to better understand the relationship between the inputs and outputs of a model.

Figure 8.14 Explainability

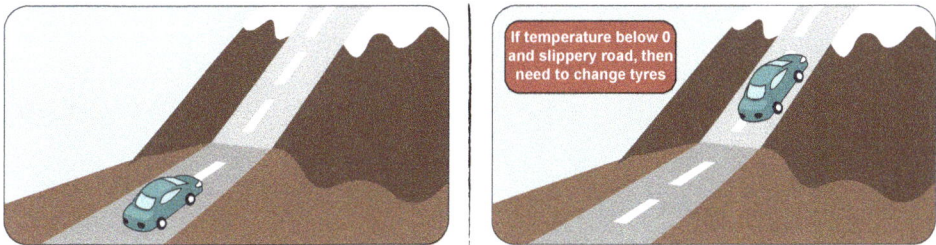

Figure 8.15 provides a chronology of the development of some popular explanatory methods (Holzinger et al., 2022). One of these methods is called the **local interpretable model-agnostic explanations (LIME) method**. The LIME method is model-agnostic. The term model-agnostic means that you can use LIME with any ML model when training your data and interpreting the results. LIME uses dynamically injected input perturbations and the analysis of outputs to provide testers with a quantitative and visual representation of the relationship between inputs and outputs. This can be an effective method for providing model explainability. However, it is limited to providing possible reasons for the outputs, rather than a definitive reason, and is not, in fact, applicable for all types of algorithms. It can explain the predictions of any classifier or regressor, but at the same time it cannot interpret the results of clustering, association or searching models.

Figure 8.15 The explanatory methods development timeline (Source: Adapted from Holzinger et al., 2022)

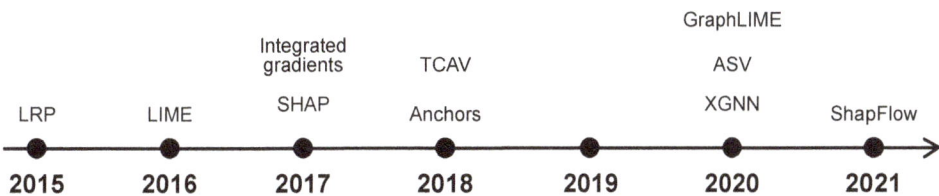

The *interpretability* of an AI-based system is heavily dependent on who this applies to (see Figure 8.16). Different stakeholders may have their own requirements in terms of how well they grasp the technology. Measuring and testing the level of understanding for both interpretability and explainability can be challenging, as stakeholders will vary in their levels of understanding. When performed, this testing typically takes the form of user surveys that help to find out what users think the AI-based system should do in a specific situation.

Figure 8.16 Interpretability

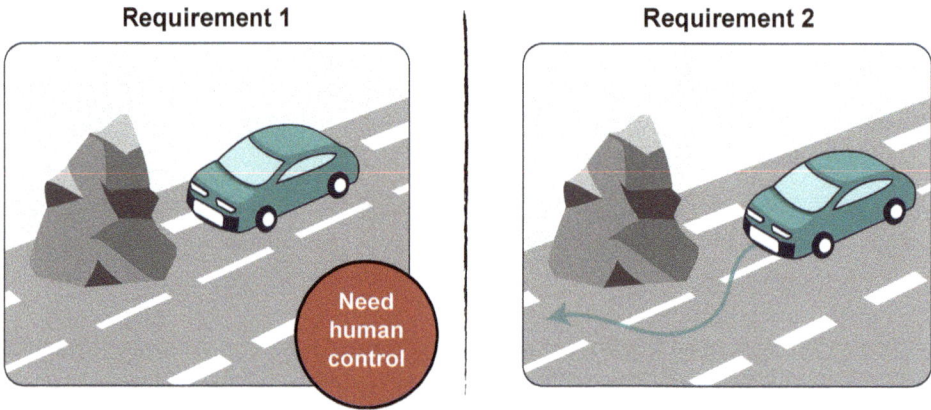

Requirement 1 — Need human control

Requirement 2

From theory to practice

LIME explainer for a food product classification model

Consider an example of how the LIME method works in the context of an ML model that predicts a food product category based on a product name. For instance, the model classifies 'Extra Virgin Olive Oil' as 'Vegetable Oil'.

At first, LIME generates perturbed samples by slightly altering the original text. In the case of text data, this is typically done by removing or replacing words. Each product name is represented as a collection of words (tokens), and each unique word becomes a feature. These words are transformed into real-valued vectors, known as word embeddings, within a semantic space. Words with similar meanings are represented by similar vectors in this space. The position of each word in the product name and the importance of different words are taken into account. In other words, the initial textual product name is transformed into a fixed-length numerical representation and then analysed.

The LIME tool generates the perturbed instances based on the word vector for the product name used as a sample. To do this, it randomly selects some words from the product name and removes or substitutes them to create multiple slightly altered product names. For example, from the product name 'Extra Virgin Olive Oil', LIME might generate 'Extra Virgin Oil' or 'Extra Virgin Olive-Green Oil'. Each of these perturbed samples is fed into the original model, and the predictions for the product category are made. For example, the model might predict that 'Extra Virgin Olive Oil' belongs to 'Vegetable Oils' with 85 per cent prediction probability, 'Extra Virgin Oil' belongs to 'Vegetable Oils' with 78 per cent prediction probability and 'Extra Virgin Olive-Green Oil' belongs to 'Vegetable Oils' with 82 per cent prediction probability.

LIME assigns higher weights to samples that are closer in similarity to the original product name. For example, descriptions that are missing fewer words or maintain the key words 'olive' or 'oil' are considered more similar to the original description.

LIME then fits a simple, interpretable model (like a linear regression or decision tree) using the perturbed samples, where the input is the altered product name and the output is the product category predicted by the original model. The simple model helps to approximate the behaviour of the complex model for the original product name.

LIME uses the simple model to identify which words from the original product name were most important for the prediction by calculating their weights. For example, LIME might reveal that words such as 'olive' and 'oil' were the key contributors to the prediction of the 'Vegetable Oils' category, while the word 'extra' had less effect.

LIME provides a visualisation showing the positive or negative contribution of each word (text feature) to the final prediction by indicating their weight values (positive or negative). Words that contribute to the final classification result can also be highlighted in the original product name during visualisation.

LIME helps to interpret black-box models (such as deep learning or ensemble models) and provides insight into what specific words or features are driving the prediction, allowing you to better understand and trust the decision-making process.

Quick questions

Question 8.6

Which of the following statements about the LIME method is true? Select ONE option.

    A. LIME is model-agnostic and is only applicable to clustering and association models.

    B. LIME provides definitive reasons for the outputs of ML models.

    C. LIME can explain predictions of classifiers and regressors, but not clustering or association models.

    D. LIME can only be used with specific ML models, not across different types, which makes it useless.

8.7 TEST ORACLES FOR AI-BASED SYSTEMS

A test oracle serves as a mechanism to recognise issues when they arise during software testing. It is often defined as a procedure that distinguishes between the correct and incorrect behaviours of the **system under test (SUT)** (Barr et al., 2015). Testing can show that defects are present in the test object, but cannot prove that there are no defects (Buxton and Randell, 1970). It is better to think about a test oracle as something helpful in detecting an incorrect behaviour, as it is not able to prove the correct behaviour anyway.

The ISTQB glossary defines a test oracle as a source to determine an expected result to compare with the actual result of the SUT. This expected result will not be able to cover every detail of the software output; instead, it should focus only on aspects relevant to detecting defects and anomalies.

For complex systems, including those involving AI, it can be difficult to say with certainty what is wrong and what behaviour is incorrect. This difficulty is known as the 'test oracle problem'. The problem is especially relevant to the evolving systems, systems that do not have well-defined requirements or where their outputs can be subjective due to varying stakeholder preferences.

Researchers have identified several types of test oracles (Hoffman, 1998). These include:

- A *true oracle* provides the correct result for every possible input, completely independent of the SUT. It ensures faithful and thorough testing and is suitable for any test case, even enabling exhaustive verification in some scenarios. However, this accuracy comes at a cost, for it is often expensive, complex to build, slow to run and challenging to maintain over time.

- *Stochastic oracles* use random sampling to verify system behaviour across a wide range of inputs. They offer flexibility in selecting coverage levels and can be simpler and less costly than a true oracle. Despite their efficiency, they may miss systematic or subtle faults, can be slow to verify results and lack the ability to focus on specific system behaviours.

- *Heuristic oracles* verify outputs at selected points and interpolate results based on heuristics. They are fast and effective for systems with regular behaviour and can scale well to large data volumes. However, they depend heavily on well-chosen checkpoints and heuristics, which makes them potentially inflexible and prone to missing incorrect or systematically flawed algorithms.

- *Sampling oracles* validate a limited set of test cases – often easy or representative inputs. They are quick, inexpensive and can be directed to focus on specific areas of interest. Still, they are highly prone to bias and may overlook specific or systematic faults, particularly those affecting complex or edge-case behaviours.

- *Consistent oracles* rely on comparing outputs to previously observed (and accepted) results, making them ideal for monitoring changes, regression testing and checking side effects. They can handle large data volumes and work quickly in certain environments. However, they do not catch legacy bugs already embedded in the baseline, may be slow in some cases and often require careful maintenance and analysis to identify meaningful changes or faults.

True test oracles are rarely obtainable in most business contexts. Practitioners have to rely on *partial oracles* (Finot et al., 2013) – those that produce some aspects of the expected results for a subset of the inputs and are reasonably accurate in judging the difference between the actual and expected results.

Test oracles require interpretation. A good oracle should be sensitive enough to identify when something truly unusual happens and flag it for human review. At the same time, it should not overwhelm testers with minor issues that do not matter. To a degree, test oracles are similar to fraud detection systems in the payments industry, environment monitoring platforms in large IT infrastructures or market surveillance systems in stock exchanges. It is recommended to build ensembles consisting of partially diverse test oracles to have a more efficient and reliable test process.

With complex, non-deterministic or probabilistic systems, it can be difficult to establish a test oracle without knowing the '**ground truth**' or the actual real-world result that the AI-based system is trying to predict, which is the mechanism used to determine whether the system is operating correctly (see Figure 8.17).

Figure 8.17 The ground truth to establish a test oracle

In some situations, it may be possible to define the expected result with certain limits. This may be established by consulting an expert, although he/she might still be wrong. There are several important factors to consider in such circumstances, shown in Figure 8.18:

- The competence of human experts can differ, but it is essential that they possess at least the same level of competence as the people the system is trying to substitute. This is because the knowledge base of an expert system is developed from human proficiency.

- Experts can come to different assumptions, even when given the same information.

- Human experts may not approve of the automation of their judgement. Here we use **double-blind testing**.

- Humans are more likely to doubt and use phrases such as 'I'm not sure, but ...'. If this kind of caveat is not available to the AI-based system, this should be considered when comparing the responses.

Figure 8.18 Test oracle problems associated with human experts and automation

Quick questions

Question 8.7

What is the 'test oracle problem' in the context of AI-based systems? Select ONE option.

    A. The inability to run tests due to insufficient computational power in AI-based systems.

    B. The difficulty in determining the expected test results, especially in complex or probabilistic systems.

    C. The challenge of writing comprehensive test scripts for AI-based systems with constantly evolving software.

    D. The need to manually review all test results instead of using automated test tools.

The following test techniques can alleviate the test oracle problem (refer to Chapter 9 for more details):

- *A/B testing*: a testing method where the response of two versions of the program (A and B) to the same inputs are compared, with the purpose of determining which of the two versions is better.

- *Back-to-back testing*: a testing method where an alternative version of the system is used as a **pseudo-oracle**, and its outputs are compared with the test results produced by the SUT.

- *Metamorphic testing*: a testing technique aimed at generating test cases that are based on a source test case that has passed.

8.8 TEST OBJECTIVES AND ACCEPTANCE CRITERIA

You have to consider a lot of things when testing an ML-based system, but what are the objectives of this process? Test objectives and acceptance criteria need to be based on the potential product risks. These risks can often be identified from an analysis of the required quality characteristics.

In 'The Testing Glossary Project', Paul Gerrard describes several different views on the 'Q-word' (quality). These include seeing quality as purpose, meeting requirements, cost, compliance with known standards, value, performance and other aspects (Youtube, 2022). According to the ISTQB CT-AI syllabus, quality is 'the degree to which a work product satisfies stated and implied requirements' (Dussa-Zieger et al., 2021). This definition focuses on whether the software meets what was explicitly written in the requirements, as well as any reasonable expectations that might not have been stated. It emphasises that both the clear and hidden needs of the users must be fulfilled for a product to be considered high-quality.

Computer scientist Gerald Weinberg offered a broader view by defining quality as 'value to some person' (Weinberg, 1992). This definition was further refined by the Rapid Software Testing school to 'Quality is value to some person at some time, who matters' (Kaner et al., 2001). This highlights that quality is subjective and can vary depending on the person using the product and the context in which it operates. What one person finds effective or satisfying, another might experience as frustrating or flawed. This makes quality a moving target – it is not fixed, but rather changes over time and from one user to another.

Because of this, software testers need to consider the relativity of quality. A product that was considered excellent five years ago might seem outdated or clunky today, even if it still meets its original requirements. User expectations evolve, new technologies emerge and what once added value might now feel like a limitation. Understanding that quality is not a static measure but something that adapts with time helps teams to build systems that stay relevant and valuable in the long run.

When evaluating software quality, it is also important to understand what counts as a defect. A defect, also called a bug, is not just a coding error. It can be any aspect of the product that reduces its value to a favoured stakeholder or increases its value to someone for whom the product was not intended, without offering a good enough benefit to make up for it. This means that design flaws, usability issues or missing features can all be considered bugs, even if the system is functioning 'as expected'. Modern quality models such as the ISO/IEC 25010 standard (ISO/IEC, 2023) help teams to assess product quality across various attributes, such as functional suitability, performance efficiency, compatibility, interaction capability, reliability, security, maintainability, flexibility and safety (Figure 8.19).

The quality characteristics for an AI-based system include those traditionally considered in ISO/IEC 25010 with some additions.

Figure 8.20 summarises the additional quality characteristics of AI-based systems. Let us look at them and discuss what we should pay attention to when evaluating acceptance criteria.

1. *Adaptability*: you need to check if the system still functions correctly and meets non-functional requirements when it adapts to a change in its environment. Also you need to understand how long the system takes to adapt and resources required for this.

2. *Flexibility*: you have to consider how the system copes outside the initial specification and, again, check the time the system takes and/or the resources it used to change itself to manage a new context.

3. *Evolution*: you have to understand how well the system learns from the experience and how it copes with the data changes.

4. *Autonomy*: you have to evaluate how the system operates outside its expected operational conditions and whether it can be persuaded to hand over the control when it shouldn't.

5. *Transparency, interpretability and explainability*: these have to be assessed by questioning the system users or, if the actual system users are not available, by people with a similar background, and by reviewing the ease of accessing the algorithm and the dataset.

6. *Freedom from inappropriate bias*: the model has to be tested by a bias-free **test suite** or experts, or by comparing the results to the external data.

7. *Ethics*: you have to review the system using any suitable checklist, such as the EC Assessment List for Trustworthy Artificial Intelligence (European Union, 2020).

8. *Probabilistic systems and non-deterministic systems*: these cannot be evaluated with precise acceptance criteria because, when working correctly, the system may return slightly different results for the same tests.

9. *Reward hacking*: this can be identified by independent tests when they use a different means of measuring success compared to the intelligent agent being tested.

10. *Potential side effects*: these are checked by generating tests that cause the system to exhibit these side effects.

11. *Safety*: this has to be carefully assessed in a virtual test environment (see Section 10.2 on virtual test environments for testing AI-based systems).

Figure 8.19 The ISO/IEC 25010 quality characteristics (Source: Adapted from ISO/IEC, 2023)

Software product quality								
Functional suitability	**Performance efficiency**	**Compatibility**	**Interaction capability**	**Reliability**	**Security**	**Maintainability**	**Flexibility**	**Safety**
Functional completeness	Time behaviour	Co-existence	Appropriateness	Faultlessness	Confidentiality	Modularity	Adaptability	Operational constraint
Functional correctness	Resource utilisation	Interoperability	Learnability	Availability	Integrity	Reusability	Scalability	Risk identification
Functional appropriateness	Capacity		Operability	Fault tolerance	Non-repudiation	Analysability	Installability	Fail safe
			User error protection	Recoverability	Accountability	Modifiability	Replaceability	Hazard warning
			User engagement		Authenticity	Testability		Safe integration
			Inclusivity		Resistance			
			User assistance					
			Self-descriptiveness					

Figure 8.20 Quality characteristics specific to AI-based systems

From theory to practice

Facial recognition AI-based systems are widely used in airport boarding, bank customer identification, biometric entry/exit processes, hotel check-in, pedestrian detection, casinos protecting against problem gamblers and other applications. It is known that such systems are *biased*, but it is critical to minimise bias to improve the accuracy of facial recognition algorithms. Which *test objectives* and *acceptance criteria* do you recommend to minimise bias in facial recognition systems?

Facial recognition software exhibits biases and inaccuracies, particularly when it comes to certain demographic groups. Consider some of the groups that facial recognition software may have problems with:

- Facial recognition algorithms often perform less accurately on *individuals with darker skin tones*. This bias can result from imbalances in the training data, leading to a lack of representation of diverse skin tones.

- Some facial recognition systems show gender biases, with higher error rates in accurately identifying the faces of *women* compared to men. This can be attributed to imbalances in training data as well.

- Facial features can change significantly with age, and some facial recognition systems may have difficulties accurately identifying *older individuals*.

- *Children's* faces can also pose challenges for facial recognition systems, as their facial features are still developing, and they may look significantly different as time goes on.

- Binary gender assumptions in facial recognition algorithms can result in errors when attempting to identify *non-binary* or *gender non-conforming individuals*.

- Biases may exist against *specific ethnic groups* or *individuals from certain regions*, depending on the makeup of the training data used to develop the facial recognition system.

- Facial recognition systems trained on datasets that lack diversity in *cultural* and *ethnic* facial features may struggle with accurate recognition for individuals with unique features.

To gain a reasonably comprehensive understanding of bias diversity, which is our test objective, we need to evaluate multiple aspects in the AI-based facial recognition system. The acceptance criterion is the absence of inappropriate bias. This can be achieved by:

- testing the system with an independent, diverse and representative bias-free test suite, or by involving expert reviewers;

- comparing the test results with external data sources, such as census data or datasets obtained through collaboration with diverse communities, to detect unwanted bias in inferred variables (external validity testing).

TERMS

Double-blind testing: a test when neither the experts nor the evaluators of the outputs should know which ratings were automated.

Ground truth: the information provided by direct observation and measurement that is known to be real or true.

LIME method: the local interpretable model-agnostic explanations program for explaining the predictions from an ML model.

Model-agnostic method: a method that may be used for any ML model.

Non-deterministic system: a system that will not always produce the same set of outputs and final state given a particular set of inputs and starting state.

Probabilistic system: a system that has behaviour described in terms of probabilities; hence its outputs cannot be perfectly predicted.

Pseudo-oracle: an independently derived variant of the test item used to generate results, which are compared with the results of the original test item based on the same test inputs.

System under test (SUT): a type of test object that is a system.

Test suite: a set of test scripts or test procedures to be executed in a specific test run.

SELF-ASSESSMENT EXERCISES

1. Name and discuss several potential challenges in testing self-learning systems.

2. When might autonomous AI-based systems need human involvement, and what are the corresponding testing activities?

3. Explain what an algorithmic bias, a sample bias, an inappropriate bias and a positive bias are.

4. What can help to detect bias during the testing of AI-based systems?

5. Describe what probabilistic and non-deterministic AI-based systems are and the testing challenges typical to these systems.

6. Discuss the main problems arising when complex AI-based systems are tested.

7. What are possible reasons for a low level of explainability of AI-based systems, and what are the methods for providing ML model explainability?

8. How can transparency and interpretability be tested in AI-based systems?

9. What is a test oracle and the 'ground truth'? Name the main challenges in creating test oracles for AI-based systems.

10. What do we need to pay attention to when evaluating acceptance criteria for different AI-specific quality characteristics?

9 METHODS AND TECHNIQUES FOR TESTING AI-BASED SYSTEMS

SUMMARY

This chapter dives deep into methods and techniques for testing AI-based systems. It goes over the importance of identification of data poisoning and adversarial attacks, and the dangers they pose. Then the chapter shifts to reviewing pairwise testing and its benefits. Back-to-back, A/B and metamorphic testing (MT) are discussed as potential solutions for a test oracle problem. The chapter also focuses on experience-based testing (and its three manifestations – error guessing, exploratory testing and checklist-based testing) while looking for issues it can resolve. Lastly the chapter gives you some hints on how to select an appropriate test technique and how this process differs from the one applied to non-AI-based systems.

LEARNING OBJECTIVES

After reading this chapter, you should be able to:

- Explain how testing ML systems can help to prevent adversarial attacks and data poisoning (K2)
- Explain how pairwise testing is used for AI-based systems (K2)
- Apply pairwise testing to derive and execute test cases for an AI-based system (K3)
- Explain how back-to-back testing is used for AI-based systems (K2)
- Explain how A/B testing is applied to testing AI-based systems (K2)
- Apply metamorphic testing for testing AI-based systems (K3)
- Apply metamorphic testing to derive test cases for a given scenario and execute them (K3)
- Explain how experience-based testing can be applied to testing AI-based systems (K2)
- Apply exploratory testing to an AI-based system (K3)
- For a given scenario, select appropriate test techniques when testing an AI-based system (K4)

LINKS TO OTHER CHAPTERS

This chapter is related to other chapters as follows:

- Chapter 6 goes over the coverage measures for neural networks.
- Chapter 8 addresses the challenges associated with test oracles for AI-based systems and highlights the specific test objectives relevant to them.
- Chapter 10 looks at virtual environments for testing AI-based systems.

9.1 ADVERSARIAL ATTACKS AND DATA POISONING

The purpose of a test technique is to help identify test conditions, test cases and test data. Some techniques are more applicable to certain situations and test levels, and others are applicable to all test levels. When creating test cases, testers generally use a combination of test techniques to achieve the best results from the test effort.

The use of test techniques in the test analysis, test design and test implementation activities can range from very informal (little to no documentation) to very formal (see Figure 9.1). The appropriate level of formality depends on the context of testing, including the maturity of test and development processes, time constraints, safety or regulatory requirements, the knowledge and skills of the people involved and the software development lifecycle model.

Figure 9.1 Levels of formality for test techniques

Formal   Informal

9.1.1 Adversarial attacks

An **adversarial attack** is the process of giving a trained model deceptive data in order to cause it to provide incorrect predictions. This was first tried on spam filters, which were tricked by slightly modifying a spam email without losing readability (see Figure 9.2), then on image classifiers by simply changing a few pixels, but still it made it possible to persuade a neural network to change its image classification. The visual in Figure 9.3 explains how adversarial perturbations can affect an input image and its classification.

Figure 9.2 An adversarial attack vs a spam filter

Figure 9.3 An adversarial attack vs an image classifier

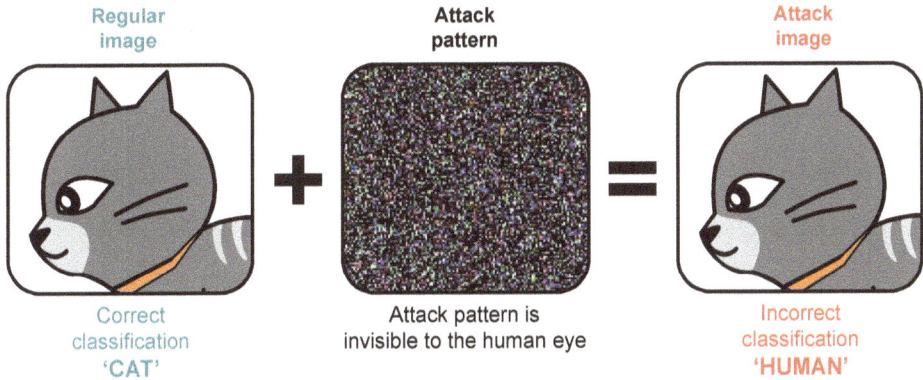

Valid inputs perturbed by an attacker, known as **adversarial examples**, are generally transferable, so if one causes an ML system to fail, then it will probably cause another system trained to do the same task to fail as well. This can even happen if the second ML system has been trained with different data and is based on different architectures.

White-box adversarial attacks can happen when the **attacker** knows the training algorithm and its parameters, and black-box ones can occur after the attacker explores the model functionality in order to attempt to build its clone. The attacker then uses a white-box approach to identify adversarial examples for this duplicate model. Since the results are transferable, the adversarial examples will normally work on the original model. In order to stop this from happening, adversarial examples are identified and added to the training data, making sure that the model learns to correctly recognise them. This is performed during **adversarial testing**.

From theory to practice

Adversarial attack against a handwritten digit recognition system

The handwritten digit recognition system is based on an ML model trained to classify images of handwritten digits from 0 to 9. The model achieves high accuracy on a test dataset, correctly classifying most images. An attacker wants to trick the ML model into misclassifying an image by making imperceptible changes to it. The attacker selects an image of the digit '3' from the test dataset and adds carefully crafted noise to it. He/she generates an adversarial perturbation – a small amount of noise – that is imperceptible to the human eye but significantly alters the model's prediction, and after that combines the original image with the adversarial perturbation to create an adversarial example. When the adversarial example (original image + perturbation) is presented to the ML model, it is misclassified. Despite the fact that it appears visually similar to the original image, the model now incorrectly predicts it as a different digit (e.g. '5' instead of '3').

Quick questions

Question 9.1

What is an adversarial attack in the context of ML models? Select ONE option.

   A. When an ML model is intentionally trained on faulty data to improve its robustness.
   B. When deceptive data is used to trick a trained model into providing incorrect predictions.
   C. When two different ML models collaborate to enhance accuracy.
   D. When an ML system is made resistant to perturbations and adversarial examples.

9.1.2 Data poisoning

Next is **data poisoning**. Data poisoning attacks have two goals: inserting backdoors or **neural network trojans** for future intrusions, or corrupting training data (e.g. introducing mislabelled data), so the model would start giving incorrect predictions (see Figure 9.4).

Poisoning attacks may be targeted with the aim of causing the ML system to misclassify in specific situations. A commonly used example is falsely reporting spam emails as not being spam to trick spam filtering software. Data poisoning attacks may also be indiscriminate, such as with a **denial-of-service (DoS)** attack.

Various tactics can be implemented to spot poisoned data, for example EDA shows poisoned data as outliers. Also, strong data acquisition policies can ensure the origins

Figure 9.4 A data poisoning attack

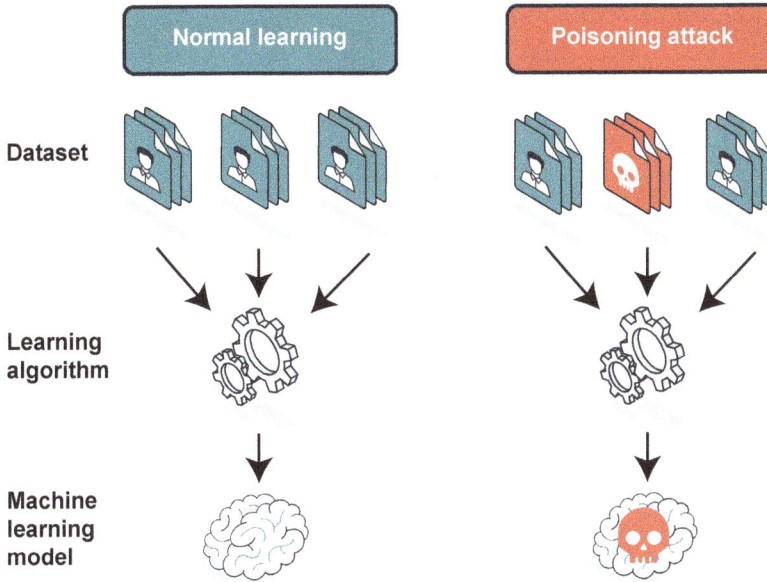

of training data, limiting its chances of being poisoned. We can try using A/B testing (see Section 9.4) to check that the updated version of the system is still closely aligned with the previous version. And regression testing of an updated system with a trusted test suite could potentially detect if a system was poisoned.

From theory to practice

Data poisoning attack against the system detecting fraudulent financial transactions

Suppose a company uses ML algorithms to detect fraudulent transactions in a financial system. The algorithms are trained on a dataset of transactions labelled as either legitimate or fraudulent. An attacker wants to manipulate the ML model's behaviour by injecting fraudulent data into the training dataset. They gain access to the company's system and subtly modifies a portion of the training data by adding fraudulent transactions to the dataset and labelling them as legitimate. These fraudulent transactions are carefully crafted to resemble legitimate transactions, but are designed to deceive the ML model. During the training process, the ML model learns from the poisoned dataset, including the injected fraudulent transactions labelled as legitimate. As a result, the model's performance may be compromised, leading to an increased likelihood of false negatives (i.e. failing to detect actual fraudulent transactions) or false positives (i.e. incorrectly flagging legitimate transactions as fraudulent).

9.1.3 Red teaming

To further strengthen AI security beyond functional testing models, organisations can turn to *red teaming*, a practice borrowed from cybersecurity (DeMarco, 2018; Oakley, 2019). In the context of AI, red teams may target:

- the AI model itself (e.g. tricking it with adversarial examples);
- its training data (e.g. inserting poisoned data);
- supporting infrastructure (e.g. servers, APIs or connected apps).

Red teams act as ethical hackers, using the same tools and techniques as malicious ones would. They attempt to bypass defences without causing real harm. These exercises are often conducted over several weeks and end with a detailed report of findings and security recommendations.

What makes red teaming especially valuable is that it evaluates not just the AI model, but the whole system, including data pipelines, interfaces, human oversight and more. It also helps to test how the team and processes respond to attacks.

With AI becoming more critical in areas such as healthcare, finance and public safety, proactive testing is essential. That is where continuous automated red teaming (CART) comes in (Anderson et al., 2024). CART uses automation to simulate attacks regularly and at scale, giving organisations ongoing insight into their vulnerabilities without waiting for scheduled tests.

Red teaming complements adversarial testing and data validation strategies by adopting the perspective of an intelligent attacker. It helps organisations to:

- detect weaknesses that internal teams might miss;
- test the resilience of defences across the entire AI pipeline;
- understand how systems and people react under realistic attack conditions.

It is also worth mentioning that, during red teaming exercises, there could also be *blue teams* that respond to the attacks in real time trying to prevent and mitigate the potential threats (Oakley, 2019). This helps to evaluate not just whether a system is vulnerable, but also how well the team and their tools can react when under attack.

To make both teams more effective, organisations may implement *purple teaming*. This is not a separate team, but a collaborative process where red and blue teams share insights. Red teams explain how they broke in, and blue teams use that knowledge to strengthen defences. This feedback loop improves detection strategies and helps to train security staff.

As AI systems increasingly control sensitive tasks, this kind of active, adversarial and collaborative testing becomes essential for responsible AI deployment.

Quick questions

Question 9.2

A company that uses ML for fraud detection suspects that some of its training data may have been poisoned, causing incorrect fraud predictions. Which of the following strategies could help them to detect and prevent future data poisoning? Select ONE option.

    A. Re-training the model using a new algorithm without checking the existing data.

    B. Getting rid of A/B testing, back-to-back testing and regression testing to speed up model launch.

    C. Adding a lot of random data to the training set to dilute any poisoned data that may be present.

    D. Using EDA to identify outliers in the data and implementing strict data acquisition policies.

9.2 PAIRWISE TESTING

As a rule, the number of parameters for an AI-based system is very high, especially when using big data or interacting with the outside world. In this case, **exhaustive testing** would yield an infinite number of tests, so we have to utilise techniques to decrease it. This is where **pairwise testing** comes in, because it is easy to understand and has ample tool support. It is based on the observation that the majority of faults are caused by interactions of two factors at most. In theory, pairwise-generated test suites cover all combinations of those pairs; therefore, they are much smaller than exhaustive ones, yet still very effective in finding defects. Figure 9.5 compares parameter combinations for exhaustive and pairwise testing with three model parameters, each having two possible values.

Figure 9.5 Exhaustive testing (a) and pairwise testing (b)

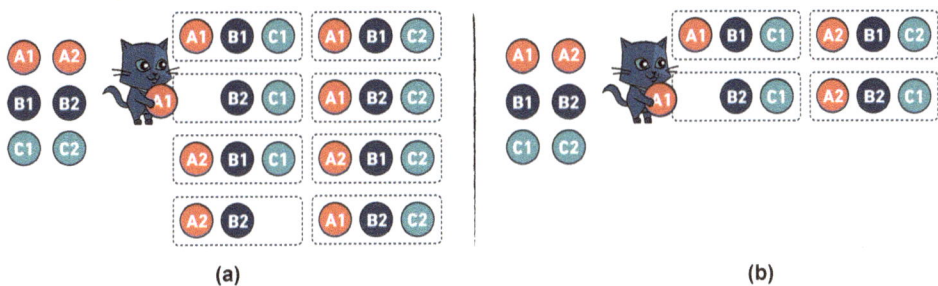

(a)   (b)

In practice, even the use of pairwise testing can result in extensive test suites, and the addition of automation and virtual test environments (see Chapter 10) often becomes necessary to allow the required number of tests to be run.

From theory to practice

Calculation of the number of pairwise parameter combinations

Consider an ML model used to predict the likelihood of employees deciding to leave the company or stay on, judging by the information about them. This model is based on an employee dataset (**github.com/exactpro/ai-testing-guide**), a snippet of which is shown in Figure 9.6.

'LeaveOrNot' is the target parameter. If it is equal to 1, the employee is likely to leave the company, and if it is equal to 0, the employee is likely to stay on. There are also six input model parameters (features) with the following possible values:

- 'Education': [0, 1, 2] – 3 values;
- 'Age': [22, 23, ..., 41] – 20 values;
- 'LengthOfService': [0, 1, ..., 6] – 7 values;
- 'City': [0, 1, 2] – 3 values;
- 'PaymentTier': [1, 2, 3] – 3 values;
- 'Gender': [0, 1] – 2 values (here, 'Female' = 0, 'Male' = 1).

Figure 9.6 A snippet of the employee dataset

1 to 10 of 1834 entries Filter

Index	Education	Age	LengthOfService	City	PaymentTier	Gender	LeaveOrNot
0	0	34	1	0	3	1	0
1	0	28	5	2	1	0	1
2	0	38	4	1	3	0	0
3	1	27	2	0	3	1	1
4	1	24	1	2	3	1	1
5	0	22	2	0	3	1	0
6	0	38	3	1	3	1	0
7	0	34	2	0	3	0	1
8	0	23	2	2	3	1	0
9	1	37	1	1	2	1	0

Show 10 ∨ per page   1 2 10 100 180 184

The number of all theoretically possible combinations of six model parameters is obtained if we multiply all the numbers of possible values for each parameter by each other:

$$3 \cdot 20 \cdot 7 \cdot 3 \cdot 3 \cdot 2 = 7560$$

The number of pairwise combinations can be calculated by multiplying the two largest numbers from the list of the number of unique values of the model parameters:

$$20 \cdot 7 = 140$$

This number is 54 times smaller than the number of all theoretically possible combinations.

9.3 BACK-TO-BACK TESTING

When we have a test oracle problem (see Chapter 8) while testing AI-based systems, **back-to-back (differential) testing** could serve as a solution. Here, an alternative version of the system is used as a pseudo-oracle and its outputs then compared with the SUT results (see Figure 9.7). This pseudo-oracle could be on a different platform, with a different architecture and with a different programming language. When we test functionality, we do not have to apply our non-functional acceptance criteria to the pseudo-oracle, and that would make it far less expensive to build. In some situations, it may also be possible to create a pseudo-oracle using non-AI software. For pseudo-oracles to be effective, there should be no common software elements between the pseudo-oracle and the SUT.

Figure 9.7 Back-to-back testing

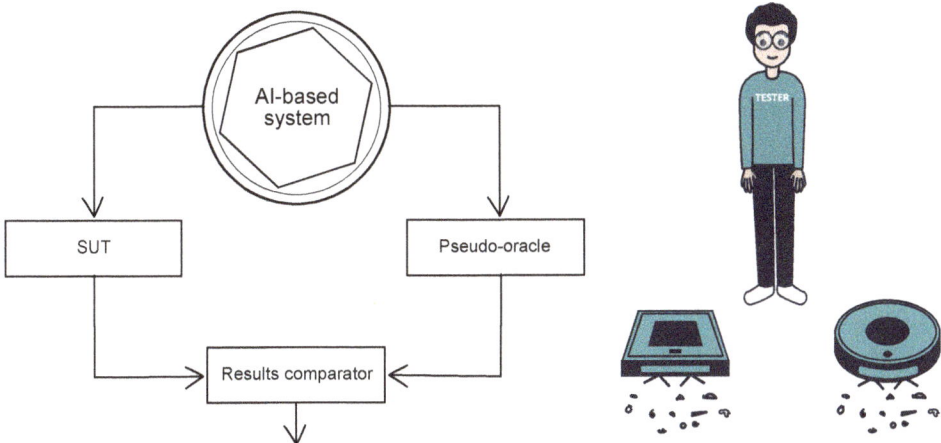

An example of back-to-back testing is comparing the performance of two different compression algorithms on a set of digital images when the goal of the test is to identify differences in performance and to determine which algorithm is the most effective.

Quick questions

Question 9.3

An engineering team is developing an AI-powered drone that performs autonomous inspections of the city's infrastructure components, such as bridges. They built a new AI-based model with a totally new algorithm and want to confirm that its inspection results closely match those of the previous model. What is the MOST likely test approach to ensure consistency and reliability across the AI-powered drone versions? Select ONE option.

    A. pairwise testing

    B. adversarial testing

    C. back-to-back testing

    D. manual testing

9.4 A/B TESTING

A/B testing is a method where the response of two variants (e.g. A and B) of the program to the same inputs are compared to determine which is better. It is a statistical test approach that typically requires the comparison of test results from several test runs to determine the difference between the programs. A/B testing is an approach to solving the test oracle problem, where the existing system is used as a **partial oracle**.

A/B testing can be used to test updates to an AI-based system if we agree on acceptance criteria. Whenever the system is updated, A/B testing is used to check that the updated variant performs as well as, or better than, the previous variant (see Figure 9.8).

Figure 9.8 A/B testing

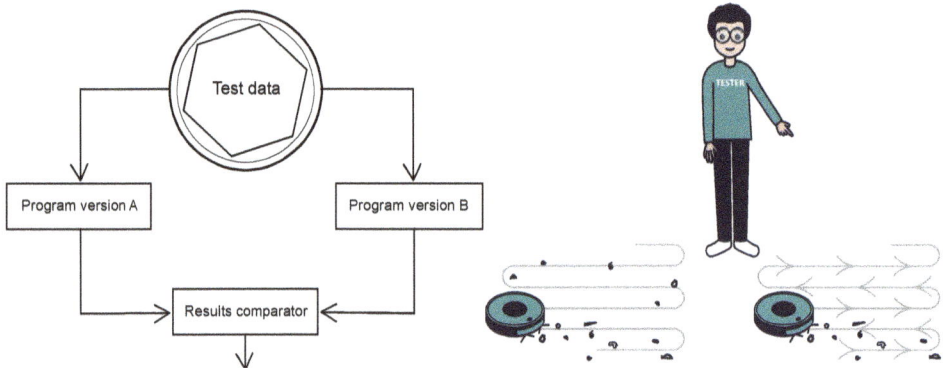

A/B testing can also be used to test self-learning systems. When the system makes a change, automated tests are run, and we compare the results with those before the change was made. If the system is improved, then the change is accepted, otherwise the system reverts to its previous state.

The biggest difference between A/B testing and back-to-back testing is that we use A/B testing to compare two versions of the same system and back-to-back testing to detect defects.

Quick questions

Question 9.4

A company is planning to update its AI-based recommendation engine. To ensure the update improves performance, they decide to use A/B testing. How will A/B testing help them to evaluate the updated system? Select ONE option.

    A. By running identical tests on the same system repeatedly to check for consistency.

    B. By comparing the updated system's performance to that of a different company's recommendation engine.

    C. By testing the updated system without comparing it to any previous versions.

    D. By comparing the updated recommendation engine with the current system using the same inputs.

9.5 METAMORPHIC TESTING

Metamorphic testing is aimed at generating test cases that are based on a passed **source test case**. Then, one or more **follow-up test cases** are made by changing the source test case based on a **metamorphic relation (MR)** (see Figure 9.9). The MR is based on the property of a required function of the test object, which tells us how a change in inputs is reflected in the expected results.

Figure 9.10 gives an example of a common situation for MRs and follow-up test cases, where the expected result differs from the original expected result of the source test case. For example, using the same average function, an MR can be created by multiplying each element of the input set by two, which would make the expected result to be the original expected result multiplied by two. Similarly, any other value could be used as a multiplier to potentially generate an infinite number of follow-up test cases.

MT can be used for most test objects and can be applied to both functional and non-functional testing. It is particularly useful where the generation of expected results is problematic, due to the lack of an inexpensive test oracle. In the area of AI, MT has been used for testing image recognition, search engines, route optimisation and voice recognition, among others.

Figure 9.9 Metamorphic testing

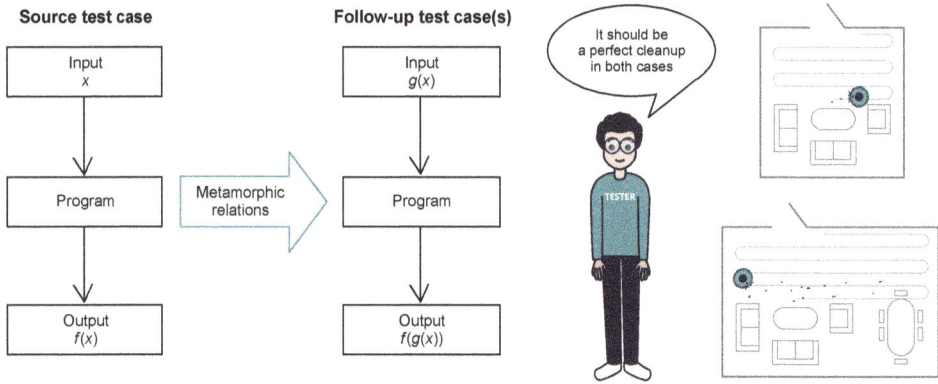

Figure 9.10 A source test case (a) and a follow-up test case (b) with different expected results (cleaning time is an expected result)

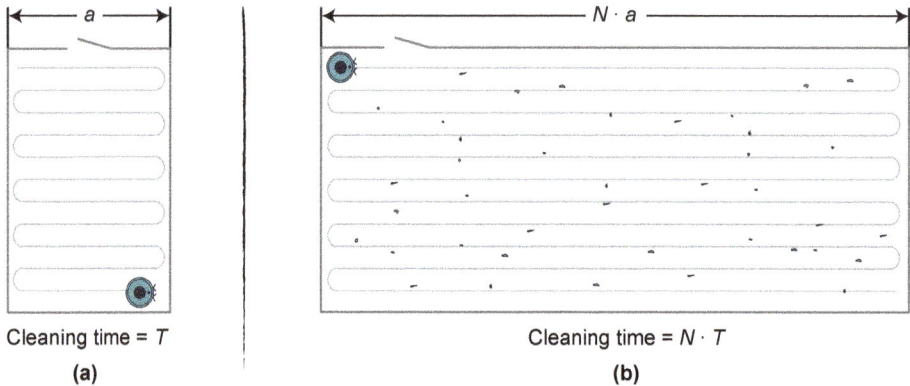

MT can also be useful even if it is not possible to verify that any source test case is correct. In this instance, MT generates one or more test cases that, when run, will create a set of outputs where the relationships between the outputs can then be checked for validity. We do not know if the individual tests are correct, but the relationships between them must hold true, thus providing confidence in the program (Figure 9.11).

MT is relatively new and differs from traditional test techniques because the expected results of the follow-up test cases are not absolute values, they are relative to the expected results. It is based on an easily understood concept and is quite effective at revealing defects.

It is possible to automatically generate follow-up test cases from well-specified MRs and a source test case. However, commercial tools are not currently available, although Google is already applying automated MT to test Android graphics drivers using the open-sourced GraphicsFuzz tool (Google, 2019).

Figure 9.11 Metamorphic testing based on the relationship between the outputs

From theory to practice

A correlation heatmap can help to reveal MRs in the ML model. The correlation heatmap for the dataset used to train the model is a colour-encoded correlation matrix indicating the pairwise correlation coefficients of all the columns in this dataset.

Let us return to the ML model used to predict whether employees leave the company or stay there (see Section 9.2) and try to derive several MRs for it. The correlation heatmap for the employee dataset (**github.com/exactpro/ai-testing-guide**) is given in Figure 9.12. A zero correlation suggests that there is no relationship between the two variables. A positive correlation is a relationship between two variables that move in the same direction, and a negative correlation indicates that two variables move in the opposite direction.

As we can see on the correlation heatmap, there are several parameters that slightly affect the target 'LeaveOrNot' parameter, or the prediction whether the employee leaves the company or not. They are 'Education', 'Age', 'City' and 'PaymentTier'. Therefore, there are metamorphic relations between these parameters and 'LeaveOrNot'. We can take the source test cases and derive follow-up test cases by changing values of the 'Education', 'Age', 'City' and 'PaymentTier' parameters while keeping the 'LeaveOrNot' parameter values the same.

We can also see that there is a negative correlation between 'LengthOfService' and 'LeaveOrNot', and also between 'Gender' and 'LeaveOrNot'. Thus we may conclude that long-serving male employees are the ones most likely to stay in the company, so we can derive corresponding follow-up test cases.

In addition to the correlation heatmap, we can plot the parameter distributions and analyse them to derive the follow-up test cases.

Figure 9.12 A correlation heatmap for the employee dataset (github.com/exactpro/ai-testing-guide)

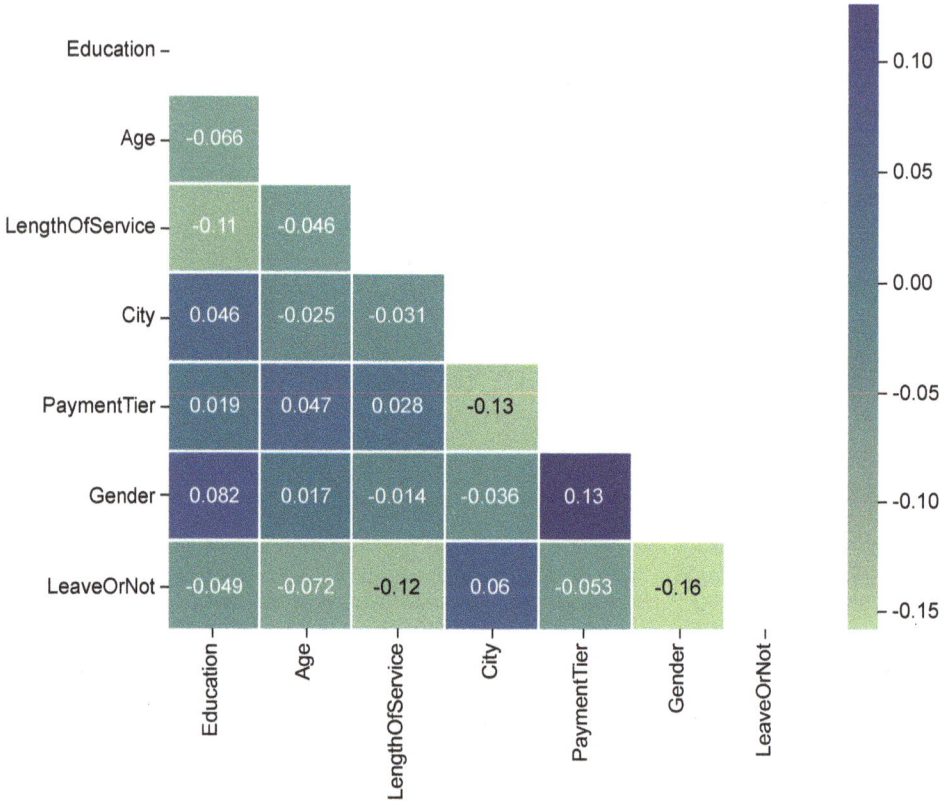

Quick questions

Question 9.5

Based on the correlation heatmap in Figure 9.12, which two variables are correlated and move in the same direction? Select ONE option.

    A. City and Age

    B. City and Gender

    C. Gender and Age

    D. Gender and PaymentTier

Question 9.6

You have been assigned as a tester to a team working on the development of an ML model predicting whether employees will leave the company or stay there, judging by the information available about the employees. You decided to generate the follow-up test cases with the expected results, which are the same as the original results of the source test cases (TCs), based on the parameter distributions shown in Figure 9.13. What is the MOST likely way to do this?

A. Source TCs: LeaveOrNot = 1, LengthOfService = 0
   Follow-up TCs: LeaveOrNot = 0, LengthOfService = 1

B. Source TCs: LeaveOrNot = 1, LengthOfService = 1, Gender = 1
   Follow-up TCs: LeaveOrNot = 0, LengthOfService = 0, Gender = 0

C. Source TCs: LeaveOrNot = 1, LengthOfService = 0, Gender = 1
   Follow-up TCs: LeaveOrNot = 1, LengthOfService = 0, Gender = 0

D. Source TCs: LeaveOrNot = 1, LengthOfService = 0
   Follow-up TCs: LeaveOrNot = 1, LengthOfService = 2

Figure 9.13 Parameter distributions for the employee dataset (github.com/exactpro/ai-testing-guide)

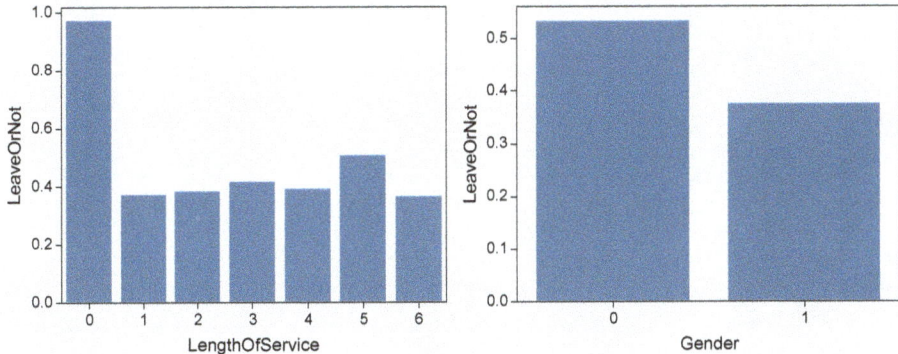

9.6 EXPERIENCE-BASED TESTING OF AI-BASED SYSTEMS

As shown in Figure 9.14, **experience-based testing** includes **error guessing, exploratory testing** and checklist-based testing, all of which can be applied to the testing of AI-based systems. *Error guessing* is typically based on testers' knowledge of typical developer errors and failures in similar systems (Figure 9.15). An example of error guessing applied to AI-based systems could be the use of knowledge about how ML systems have failed in the past due to the use of systematically biased training data.

In exploratory testing, tests are designed, generated and executed in an iterative manner, with the later tests based on the test results of earlier tests (see Figure 9.16). Exploratory testing is especially useful when there are poor specifications or test oracle

Figure 9.14 Experience-based testing

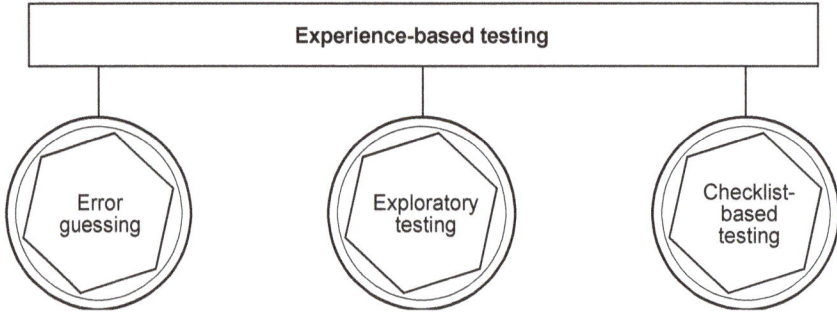

Figure 9.15 Error guessing

problems, which is often the case for AI-based systems. As a result, exploratory testing is often used in this context and should be used to supplement the more systematic testing based on techniques, such as MT.

A **tour** is a metaphor used for a set of strategies and goals for testers to refer to when they perform exploratory testing organised around a special focus. Typical tours for the exploratory testing of AI-based systems might focus on the concepts of bias, underfitting and overfitting.

ML systems are highly dependent on the quality of training data, and the existing field of EDA is closely related to the exploratory test approach. EDA is where data is examined for patterns, relationships, trends and outliers (see Figure 9.17). It involves interactive,

Figure 9.16 Exploratory testing steps

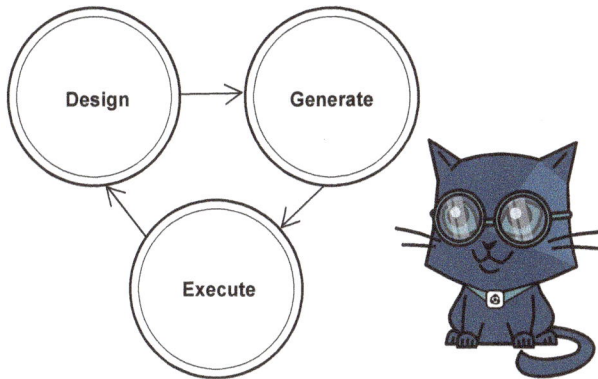

Figure 9.17 Patterns (a), trend and outliers (b) and relationships (c)

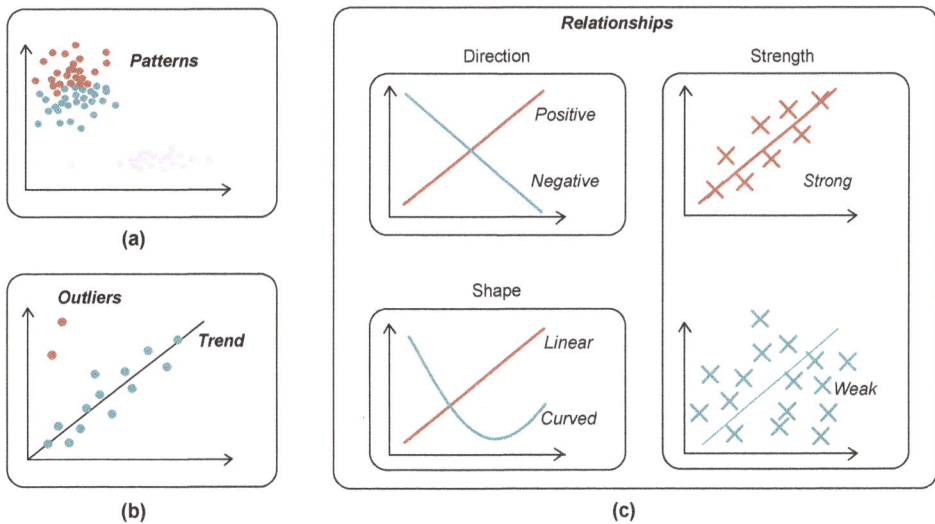

hypothesis-driven exploration that requires tool support in two areas: interaction with the data (to allow analysts to better understand complex data), and data visualisation (to allow them to easily display analysis results). The use of exploratory techniques, primarily driven by data visualisation, can help to validate the ML algorithm being used, identify changes that result in efficient models and leverage domain expertise.

For checklist-based testing (Figure 9.18), a checklist is required and testing involves designing, creating and executing tests to cover each condition listed. Google suggests a set of 28 ML tests (Breck et al., 2017) written as assertions in the areas of data, model

Figure 9.18 Checklist-based testing

development, infrastructure and monitoring, which is used as a testing checklist for ML systems:

- ML data:
  1. Feature expectations are captured in a schema.
  2. All features are beneficial.
  3. No feature's cost is too much.
  4. Features adhere to metalevel requirements.
  5. The data pipeline has appropriate privacy controls.
  6. New features can be added quickly.
  7. All input feature code is tested.
- Model development:
  1. Model specs are reviewed and submitted.
  2. Offline and online metrics correlate.
  3. All hyperparameters have been tuned.
  4. The impact of model staleness is known.
  5. A simpler model is not better.
  6. Model quality is sufficient on important data slices.
  7. The model is tested for considerations of inclusion.

- ML infrastructure:
  1. Training is reproducible.
  2. Model specs are unit-tested.
  3. The ML pipeline is integration-tested.
  4. Model quality is validated before serving.
  5. The model is debuggable.
  6. Models are canaried before serving.
  7. Serving models can be rolled back.
- Monitoring tests:
  1. Dependency changes result in notification.
  2. Data invariants hold for inputs.
  3. Training and serving are not skewed.
  4. Models are not too stale.
  5. Models are numerically stable.
  6. Computing performance has not regressed.
  7. Prediction quality has not regressed.

Quick questions

Question 9.7

A manufacturing company is testing a robotic arm used for precise assembly tasks. The testing team applies testing by anticipating potential issues, such as positioning errors, grip failures and calibration drifts, based on previous experiences with similar robotic systems. It allows testers to proactively identify likely failure points, such as misalignment or dropped parts, which might be missed by regular test scripts. What kind of testing activity do they use? Select ONE option.

   A. metamorphic testing
   B. error guessing
   C. pairwise testing
   D. back-to-back testing

9.7 SELECTING TEST TECHNIQUES FOR AI-BASED SYSTEMS

An AI-based system will typically include both AI and non-AI components. The test techniques selection for the non-AI components is generally the same as for any conventional testing. For the AI-based components, the choice may be more constrained (see Figure 9.19). For instance, a test oracle problem could be mitigated by use of the following:

- *Back-to-back testing*: this requires test cases to be available with an equivalent system to act as a pseudo-oracle. For regression testing, for example, it can be a previous version of the system.

- *A/B testing*: this often uses operational inputs as test cases to compare two variants of the same system using statistical analysis. A/B testing can be used to check for the data poisoning of a new variant, or for automated regression testing of a self-learning system.

- *Metamorphic testing*: this can be used by inexperienced testers to cost-effectively find defects. MT is not suitable for providing definitive results, as the expected results are not absolute but relative to the source test cases. Tool support is not currently available, but many tests can be generated manually.

Figure 9.19 Test techniques for AI-based systems

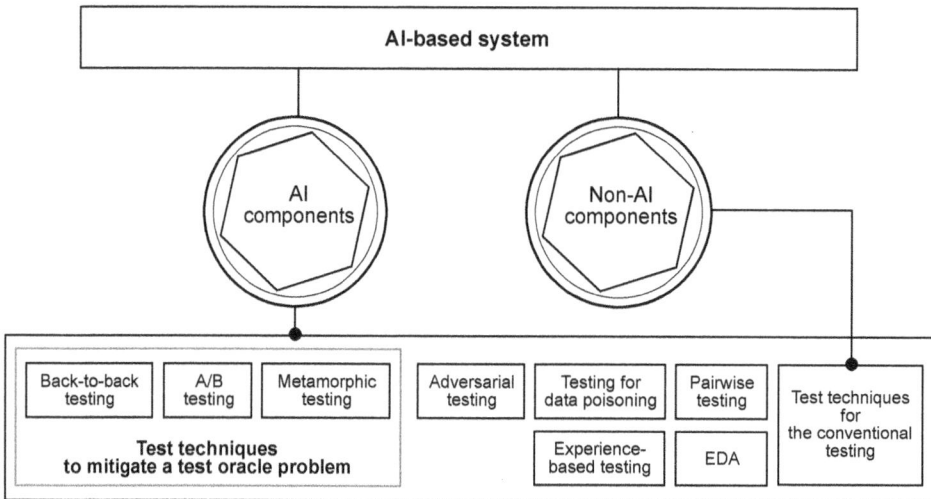

Adversarial testing is typically appropriate for ML models where the mishandling of adversarial examples could have a significant impact, or where the system may be attacked. Similarly, *testing for data poisoning* may be appropriate for ML systems where the system may be attacked.

Pairwise testing is often appropriate for complex AI-based systems with multiple parameters.

Experience-based testing is often suitable for testing AI-based systems, especially for consideration of the data used for training and operational data. EDA can be used to validate the ML algorithm, identify efficiency improvements and leverage domain expertise. In the specific area of neural networks, coverage of the network is often suitable for mission-critical systems.

From theory to practice

Imagine that there is an AI-driven image recognition system designed to identify objects in photographs. Due to the complexity of the AI model and the absence of a perfect test oracle, there is no definitive set of expected results for each image classification. Let us try to answer the question: which test technique is better to use when testing this AI-based system, and why?

Of course, it is back-to-back or differential testing that is used when a precise test oracle is unavailable. Back-to-back testing with multiple pseudo-oracles allows for the exploration of diverse perspectives, aiding in uncovering potential issues in the AI SUT.

We can select multiple pre-trained image recognition models as these pseudo-oracles from different sources, such as open-source frameworks or commercial APIs, and ensure the chosen pseudo-oracles represent diverse approaches and architectures to provide a comprehensive benchmark.

During the test execution, we have to run the images through the AI SUT and the selected pseudo-oracles and collect the classification results for each image. The results from different models serve as benchmarks for assessing the reliability and consistency of the AI-based system's classifications.

We have to compare the classifications provided by the AI SUT with those from the pseudo-oracles for each image, and to note any commonalities or differences in the identified objects. We also have to analyse the comparisons to identify patterns or consistencies in the classifications across models.

Different similarity metrics help to evaluate the similarity or dissimilarity of classifications between the AI SUT and pseudo-oracles: Jaccard similarity, cosine similarity, Euclidean similarity and others (Baisantry and Shukla, 2017).

If an AI SUT consistently misclassifies certain objects compared to the pseudo-oracles, this could indicate areas for improvement, such as the need to fine-tune the AI model, addressing specific image features and exploring additional training data.

9.8 TEST STRATEGIES FOR AI COMPONENTS

To better understand how to apply or generate the test techniques for AI components, we can divide the strategies by analogy with conventional systems into black-box, white-box and data-box ones (see Figure 9.20). In the case of *black-box testing*, we are focused on the output of a neural network, in the case of *white-box testing*, we are assessing the behaviour of the inner parts of a neural network (its neurons, layers, activation functions, etc.) and in the case of *data-box testing*, we are focusing on testing the data that we need for model training, validation, etc.

Figure 9.20 Testing strategies and test approaches for AI components

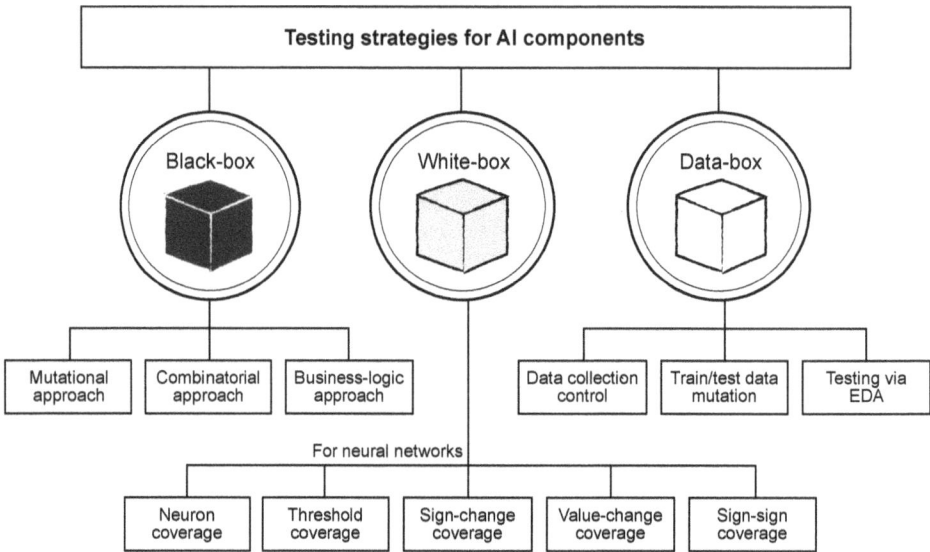

You cannot single out just one of these three strategies (be it black-box, white-box or data-box testing), because they are all important, so it is better to combine them. For instance, if we know which use cases exist in train/test data, we lean on this knowledge during test generation and at the input testing phase, and then we can use it to better define the coverage criteria for activation testing.

9.8.1 Black-box testing

Input-level tests analyse the predictions of a model with a given input. This is a black-box technique, which means it does not investigate the inner structure of a model (i.e. layers, neurons); instead, it focuses on the reactions of a model and tries to identify potential reasons for the unexpected behaviour.

There are several approaches to black-box testing:

- *The mutational approach* helps to investigate how a system will react to several similar inputs. With this approach, it is possible to see the discrepancy in prediction, and, in some cases, it will depend on the input parameters. However, the approach has one major flaw: even though a mutation is set by a predefined algorithm, from a business point of view, the process is unpredictable. It will find bugs, but the approach has limited reproducibility, which means it will be difficult to find the same bugs with the same mutation algorithm in different models. This goes against software testing verification/validation objectives.

- *The combinatorial approach* is used to test all relevant combinations of input values. It has a higher level of versatility and it is easier to apply the same approach to different systems keeping the reproducibility, which benefits from a higher probability of finding the same defects in different systems. From the software testing perspective, it gives a higher level of verification, if a piece of software acts properly. However, the validation is still low, because, here, it does not check if the software does what it is intended to do.

- *The business-logic approach* is closer to the validation-level perspective because it focuses on whether the system's behaviour aligns with stakeholders' expectations and real-world needs, rather than just checking technical correctness. But this approach is also insufficient because we lack the variability of tests related to the non-deterministic nature of ML systems. In other words, a scenario designed in the business language is a high-level one and does not deal with data bias or complex neuron relations properly, and that is what constitutes verification.

9.8.2 White-box testing

Achieving white-box test coverage criteria (for example, statement or branch coverage) is mandatory for some safety-related standards, and is often recommended for other critical applications. Monitoring and improving coverage leads to increased confidence in the test object; but assessing neural networks coverage provides little value as the same code is run each time the neural network is executed. Instead, coverage should be based on the structure of the neural network, and more specifically, the neurons and their activation values.

There are several proposed approaches to test neural networks (see Chapter 6 for coverage measures for neural networks):

- neuron coverage;
- threshold coverage;
- sign-change coverage;
- value-change coverage;
- sign-sign coverage.

9.8.3 Data-box testing

Much of the quality of an ML model depends on the data it trains from and is tested on. This brings us to the issue of data-sensitive faults. They cause a failure in response to a particular pattern of data. Detecting such errors is quite challenging, given their intangibly large input space. It is therefore very important to test training and test data at the preparation stage. There are several industry approaches here:

- *Data collection control*: in this case, experts develop requirements for the data collection process, then an environment is created that meets these requirements and, after that, data is collected from this environment. Still, it is not always possible to take into account all the aspects that may affect the model.

- *Train/test data mutation*: mutation testing is a technique that injects artificial faults into an SUT guided by the assumption that the ability to expose such artificial faults translates into the ability to expose real faults as well. In train/test data mutation, certain changes are applied to the training and test data, but this adds a degree of difficulty because, after each mutation, it is necessary to re-train the model and compare if its behaviour changed in comparison with the previous iteration.

- *Testing via EDA*: as we have seen earlier, the must-have of any ML development project is EDA. As a result of this activity, stakeholders have a better understanding of the characteristics of the data and what real-world scenarios it represents. The presence of subject matter experts is important at this stage, as some characteristics that an engineer or statistician might classify as incorrect may be important from a business perspective.

TERMS

A/B testing: a statistical test approach to determine which of two components or systems performs better.

Adversarial attack: the deliberate use of adversarial examples to cause an ML model to fail.

Adversarial examples: perturbed valid inputs that are passed to the trained model to cause it to provide incorrect predictions during an adversarial attack.

Adversarial testing: a test activity where adversarial examples are identified and added to the training data, making sure that the model learns to correctly recognise them.

Attacker: a person seeking to exploit potential vulnerabilities of a system.

Back-to-back testing (differential testing): testing to compare two or more variants of a test item or a simulation model of the same test item by executing the same test cases on all variants and comparing the results.

Data poisoning: the deliberate and malicious manipulation of training or input data to an ML model.

Denial-of-service (DoS) attack: a security attack that is intended to overload the system with requests such that legitimate requests cannot be serviced.

Error guessing: a test design technique where the experience of the tester is used to anticipate what defects might be present in the component or system under test as a result of errors made, and to design tests specifically to expose them.

Exhaustive testing (complete testing): a test approach in which the test suite comprises all combinations of input values and preconditions.

Experience-based testing: testing based on the tester's experience, knowledge and intuition.

Exploratory testing: an informal test design technique where the tester actively controls the design of the tests as those tests are performed and uses information gained while testing to design new and better tests.

Follow-up test case: a test case generated by applying a metamorphic relation to a source test case during metamorphic testing.

Metamorphic relation (MR): a description of how a change in the test inputs from the source test case to the follow-up test case affects a change in the expected outputs from the source test case to the follow-up test case.

Metamorphic testing (MT): a test technique in which the inputs and expected results are extrapolated from a passing test case using a metamorphic relation.

Neural network trojan: a vulnerability injected into a neural network using a data poisoning attack with the intent of exploiting it later.

Pairwise testing: a test technique in which test cases are designed to execute all possible discrete combinations of each pair of input parameters.

Partial oracle: a test oracle that verifies only some aspects of the test output.

Source test case: a test case that passed and is used as the basis of follow-up test cases in metamorphic testing.

Tour: a set of exploratory tests organised around a special focus.

SELF-ASSESSMENT EXERCISES

1. What is an adversarial attack? Discuss the types of adversarial attacks and their differences.

2. What is a data poisoning attack? Provide several examples.

3. Describe how adversarial testing and testing to detect data poisoning could be performed.

4. Discuss the pairwise testing of AI-based systems, and how the number of pairwise combinations can be calculated.

5. What is the role of a pseudo-oracle in back-to-back testing?

6. What are the key scenarios where A/B testing is the optimal method for evaluating an AI-based system?

7. What is the difference between A/B testing and back-to-back testing?

8. Name the basic concepts related to metamorphic testing. Discuss the application areas of metamorphic testing for AI-based systems.

9. List three main test techniques for experience-based testing of AI-based systems and describe the differences between these techniques.

10. Discuss how to select an appropriate test technique for testing the AI and non-AI components of AI-based systems.

10 TEST ENVIRONMENTS FOR AI-BASED SYSTEMS

SUMMARY

This chapter focuses solely on the question of test environments, their characteristics and kinds, the purposes for AI-based systems and also the benefits of using the virtual test environments. The chapter ends with a review of the key challenges in test environments for AI-based systems.

LEARNING OBJECTIVES

After covering this chapter, you should be able to:

- Describe the main factors that differentiate the test environments for AI-based systems from those required for conventional systems (K2)
- Describe the benefits provided by virtual test environments in testing AI-based systems (K2)

LINKS TO OTHER CHAPTERS

This chapter touches on some concepts that are covered in other chapters:

- Chapter 1 goes over the AI development frameworks, reviews the hardware for AI-based systems and focuses on standards and regulations for AI.
- Chapter 2 looks at characteristics of AI-based systems, such as flexibility, adaptability, autonomy, bias, ethics, transparency, interpretability and explainability.
- Chapter 5 covers ML model performance metrics.
- Chapter 7 addresses the challenges of acquiring test data for AI-based systems, highlighting big data as one of the primary obstacles.
- Chapter 9 considers adversarial testing and A/B testing.

10.1 TEST ENVIRONMENTS FOR AI-BASED SYSTEMS

It is no secret that AI-based systems are used in a lot of operational environments. This implies that, when those systems are tested, they require an equal variety of test environments.

Test environments for AI-based systems are where AI models and systems are evaluated, validated and tested to ensure they meet the set standards before deployment (see Figure 10.1). Test environments are deliberately designed to be controlled, which means that various parameters, variables and conditions are carefully managed and manipulated during testing. This control allows researchers, developers and testers to isolate and study specific aspects of AI-based systems without the interference of unpredictable real-world factors.

Figure 10.1 A crash test simulation

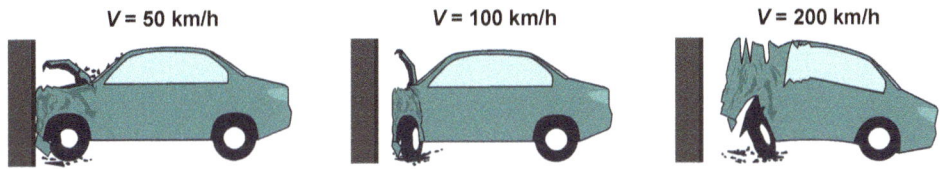

$V = 50$ km/h $V = 100$ km/h $V = 200$ km/h

For example, if we talk about self-driving vehicles, this could include variations in lighting, weather, terrain and user interactions. By simulating these scenarios, developers can fine-tune their AI models to handle a wide range of conditions while having full control over inputs, parameters and other variables within the given setting. Figure 10.2 provides an example of how a test environment can help in a weather conditions simulation. Developers often use test environments iteratively during the AI-based system's development cycle. They can make adjustments, re-train the AI model and conduct deliberate testing.

Figure 10.2 Driving vehicle simulations under different weather conditions

Test environment — Real life

Test case 1

Test case 1

Test case 2

Test case 2

The weather forecast is wrong again ... When will it rain?

TESTER

So, one of the central purposes of test environments is to assess how well AI-based systems perform. This includes measuring their accuracy and efficiency while completing tasks or solving problems. Performance metrics are defined in advance, enabling a systematic evaluation of the AI model's capabilities.

Safety is also a paramount concern when deploying AI-based systems, especially in critical applications such as autonomous vehicles (Figure 10.3), medical diagnosis and financial services. Test environments are used to simulate potentially dangerous scenarios to evaluate how AI-based systems respond and to ensure that they make safe decisions.

Figure 10.3 A safety scenario simulation for an autonomous vehicle

Reliability is another critical aspect of AI-based systems. In test environments, researchers can introduce various forms of noise, errors or unexpected inputs to assess how well the AI-based system maintains its functionality and performance under adverse conditions. Refer to Figure 10.4 as an example of reliability testing for a self-driving vehicle on the road with an erased lane marking.

Test environments allow for benchmarking AI-based systems against predefined standards or the performance of other models. This helps developers to understand where their system is positioned in comparison to industry standards. In some industries, such as healthcare and automotive, regulatory bodies require rigorous testing and validation of AI-based systems before they can be deployed (Figure 10.5). Test environments are instrumental in meeting these compliance requirements.

Figure 10.4 Lane keep assist testing when a self-driving vehicle passed (a) and failed (b) the test

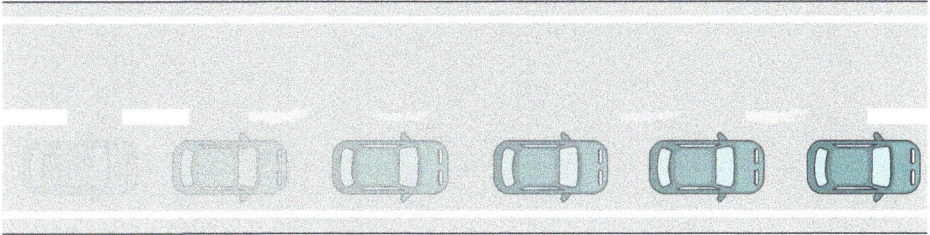

(a)

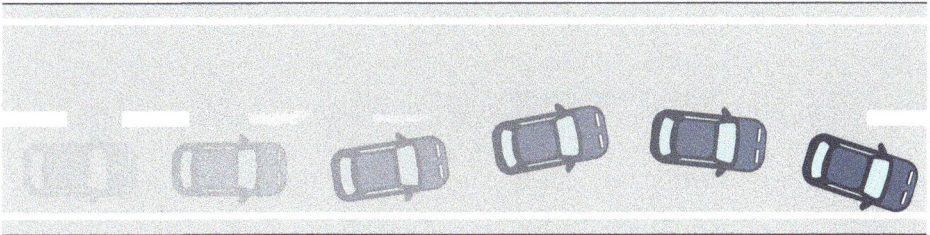

(b)

Figure 10.5 Benchmarking against predefined standards

Test environments can vary significantly, depending on the type of AI-based system and its intended application, but they generally share some similarities (see Figure 10.6).

Figure 10.6 Test environment similarities

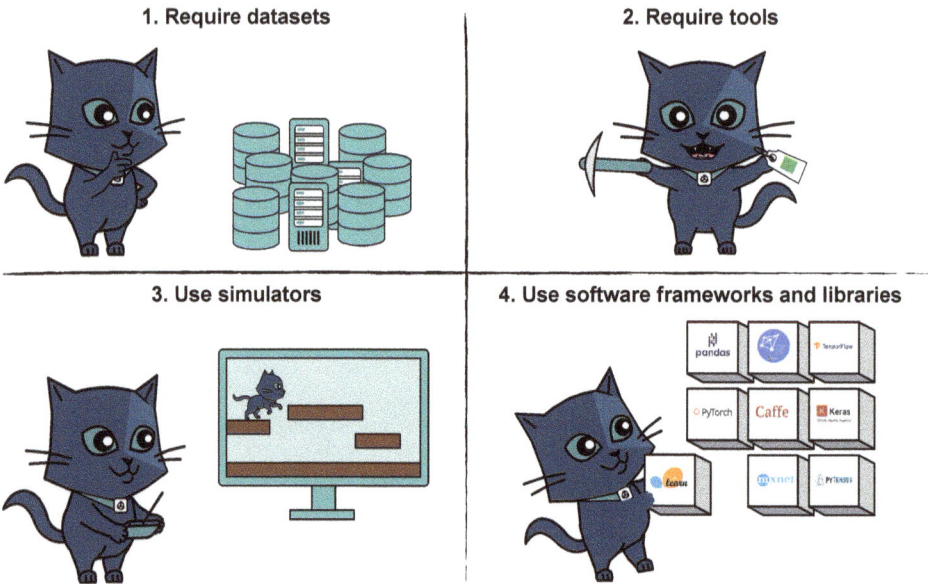

First of all, test environments require datasets that are used to train, validate and test AI models. These datasets should represent the types of inputs the AI-based system will encounter in the real world and may include text, images, videos, sensor data and more.

Tools for data management, data annotation and data pre-processing are essential for preparing and curating these datasets. For scalable AI-based systems, test environments may include tools for monitoring performance, resource utilisation and, of course, scalability.

In many cases, simulators are used to create virtual environments that mimic real-world scenarios. This, in turn, may require specialised hardware, such as high-performance GPUs, TPUs or custom hardware accelerators (see Section 1.6 on hardware for AI-based systems). For AI-based systems that run on specialised hardware, such as robots or drones, hardware emulation environments may be used to replicate the behaviour of the physical system.

This goes hand in hand with the use of software frameworks and libraries that provide tools for training, evaluation and experimentation. Common examples include TensorFlow, PyTorch and Scikit-learn (see Section 1.5 on AI development frameworks). They allow for the systematic evaluation of model performance, including metrics such as accuracy, precision, recall and F1-score (see Chapter 5).

Test environments vary widely in complexity and purpose, and the choice of environment depends on the specific AI application and research objectives. Effective testing and evaluation in these environments are crucial for the development of robust and reliable AI systems.

Here are some common types and examples of test environments for AI:

- *Simulation environments*, with examples such as OpenAI Gym (a widely used toolkit for developing and comparing reinforcement learning algorithms providing a variety of environments, including classic control tasks and 2D and 3D robotic simulations; Gymnasium, 2025), Unity ML-Agents (it is a popular game engine used for tasks such as game-playing, robotics and autonomous navigation; Unity Technologies, 2025) or MuJoCo (a physics engine for simulating complex and dynamic environments, often used in robotics and reinforcement learning research; MuJoCo, 2025).

- *Game environments*, where games such as Chess (Chess.com, 2025), AlphaGo (Deepmind, 2025), Dota 2 (Valve's Dota 2 has been used as a testbed for AI research, with the OpenAI team developing bots capable of competing against human players; Valve Corporation, 2025), StarCraft II (used in DeepMind's AlphaStar project to train AI agents to play real-time strategy games; Blizzard Entertainment, 2025) and Minecraft (Mojang Studios, 2025) are used to create complex and strategic environments for AI agents to compete in.

- *Robotic environments* could be represented by robot operating system (ROS) (which provides a framework and simulation environments for developing and testing robotics algorithms and control systems; Open Robotics, 2025a), CoppeliaSim (formerly V-REP) (a 3D robot simulation environment that is used for research and development in robotics; Coppelia Robotics AG, 2025) or platforms such as Gazebo (Open Robotics, 2025b) and Webots (Cyberbotics Ltd, 2019).

- *Self-driving car simulators*, with products such as SUMO (German Aerospace Center (DLR), 2025), NVIDIA DRIVE® Infrastructure (NVIDIA, 2025a) and Waymo Open Dataset (Waymo, 2025) offering realistic environments for testing autonomous driving algorithms and AI perception systems.

- *NLP environments*, such as general language understanding evaluation (GLUE; a benchmark for evaluating the performance of NLP models on various language understanding tasks; SuperGLUE, 2025) and Python NLP libraries such as NLTK (Natural Language Toolkit, 2025) and spaCy (spaCy, 2025) providing assistance with processing and analysis.

- *Medical imaging simulations* help to train and evaluate AI models for tasks such as image recognition and disease diagnosis. There are such products as Medspace. VR (Medspace, 2021), DICOM AI 3D VR viewer (Inlusion Factory of Emotions, 2020) and GATE (Gate, 2025).

- *Industrial and manufacturing environments* and other *custom environments* are for manufacturing processes, supply chain optimisation and quality control. Here, we can mention numerous Ansys products, such as Ansys Mechanical, Ansys Discovery, Ansys Twin Builder and others (Ansys, 2025), COMSOL Multiphysics® (COMSOL, 2025), Simulink® (MathWorks, 2025a), Synopsys.ai (Synopsys, 2025), etc.

- *Financial and trading simulations* are used for various purposes, including algorithmic trading strategy development, risk management and financial research. This group comes with a plethora of examples:

  - *Market simulations* help to zoom in on order execution in a market to optimise execution strategies, minimise transaction costs and reduce market impact. Traders and quantitative analysts use *historical data backtesting* to test performance and trading strategies (Forex Tester Online, 2025); *Monte Carlo simulations* generate multiple possible future market scenarios using random sampling to assess the risk and potential outcomes of investment portfolios (Portfolio Visualizer, 2025); *agent-based models* simulate the behaviour of individual market participants and their interactions affecting market dynamics and trading patterns (Simudyne, 2022).

  - *Portfolio management simulations* determine the optimal allocation of assets in a portfolio to achieve specific risk and return objectives (Ziggma, 2025).

  - *Options and derivatives pricing simulations* based on the *Black-Scholes models* are used for pricing options and other financial derivatives (Hoadley Trading & Investment Tools, 2025). *Binomial models*, such as the Cox-Ross-Rubinstein model, are used to simulate the possible price movements of assets and calculate option prices (MathWorks, 2025b).

  - Full electronic automation in stock exchanges has recently become popular, generating high-frequency intraday data and motivating the development of near real-time price forecasting methods. ML algorithms are widely applied to mid-price stock predictions. *High-frequency trading simulations* test the performance and robustness of high-frequency trading algorithms (InfoReach, 2025).

  - Using *reinforcement learning algorithms*, AI agents can learn optimal trading strategies by interacting with simulated market environments (AI4Finance Foundation, 2022; JPMorganChase, 2023). These environments help to train trading agents to make decisions and optimise their portfolios.

It is also worth noting that characteristics of AI-based systems can cause the test environments to differ from those for conventional systems. These characteristics include (see Figure 10.7):

- *Self-learning*: self-learning systems, and some autonomous systems, are expected to adapt to changing operational environments that may not have been fully defined when the system was initially deployed (see Section 2.1 on flexibility and adaptability). As a result, defining test environments that can replicate these undefined environmental changes is complicated.

- *Autonomy*: autonomous systems are expected to respond to changes in their environment without human intervention, and also recognise situations where autonomy should be given back to human operators (see Section 2.2 on autonomy). Replicating the circumstances for ceding autonomy may require extreme test environment scenarios. Some systems are designed for hazardous environments, so setting up test environments for that could be quite a challenge.

Figure 10.7 Characteristics of AI-based systems

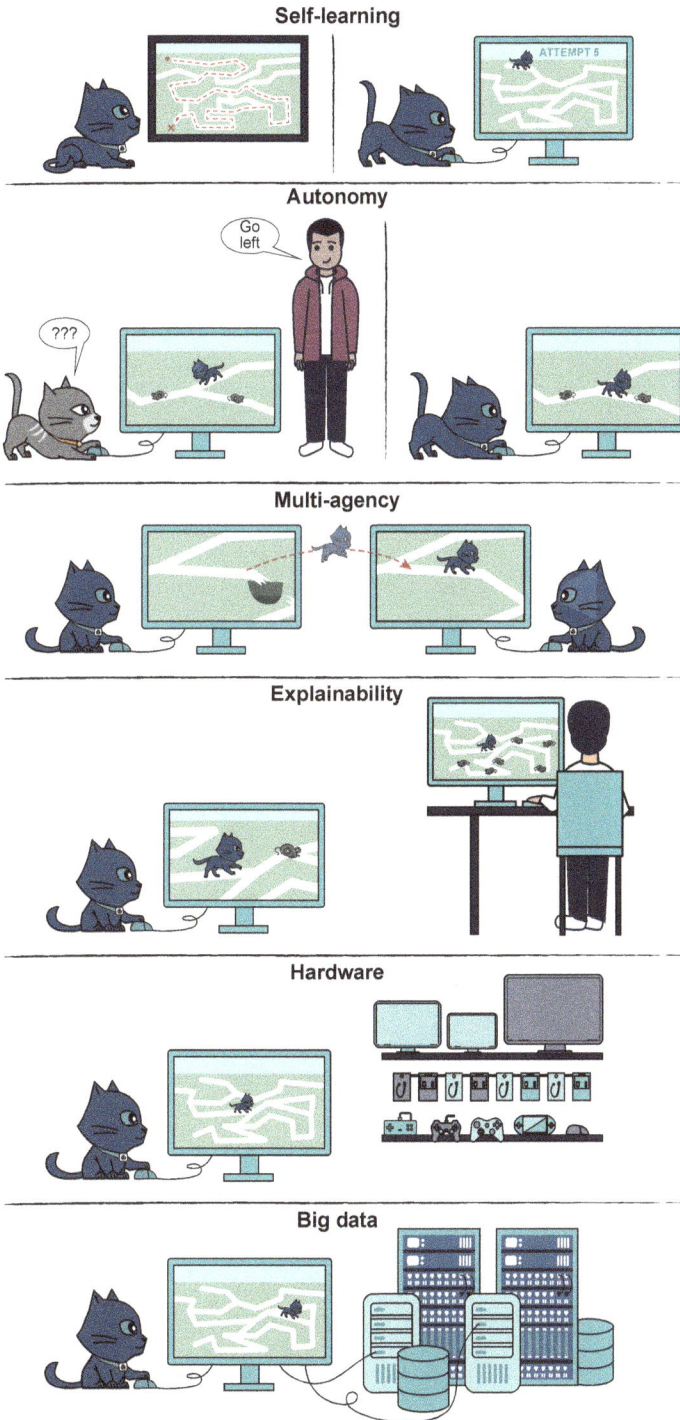

- *Multi-agency:* where **multi-agent** AI-based **systems** are expected to work with other AI-based systems, the test environment may need to incorporate a level of non-determinism, so that it can mimic the non-determinism of the AI-based systems with which the SUT interacts.

- *Explainability:* the nature of some AI-based systems can make it difficult to determine how the system made its decisions (see Section 2.7 on transparency, interpretability and explainability), so the test environment may need to incorporate a means of explaining how the system came to a particular decision.

- *Hardware:* some of the hardware used to host AI-based systems is specifically designed for this purpose, such as AI-specific processors (see Section 1.6 on hardware for AI-based systems). When it comes to the test environment, the need to include such hardware should be considered as part of the relevant test planning.

- *Big data:* if an AI-based system requires big data, the necessary measures should be implemented as part of a test environment setup (see Section 7.4 on test data for testing AI-based systems).

Quick questions

Question 10.1

Why do test environments for AI-based systems often differ from those for conventional systems? Select ONE option.

   A. AI-based systems are simpler, so their test environments are usually less complex than those for conventional systems.
   B. AI-based systems require larger amounts of test data to cover diverse scenarios, so their test environments need to handle significant data processing and storage.
   C. Conventional systems are much more complex by default because they require test environments that account for non-determinism, self-learning and autonomy, unlike AI-based systems.
   D. Testing AI-based systems is easier because they do not require human oversight or interaction in any scenario.

Question 10.2

Why might test environments for AI-based systems require ongoing updates compared to conventional systems? Select ONE option.

   A. To accommodate new versions of the AI software only.
   B. To simplify the testing process for non-deterministic and probabilistic systems for a certain set of parameters.
   C. To ensure the environment reflects changes in real-world data patterns and distribution.
   D. To minimise the use of diverse datasets in testing.

10.2 VIRTUAL TEST ENVIRONMENTS FOR TESTING AI-BASED SYSTEMS

Let us consider the benefits of using a **virtual test environment** when testing AI-based systems.

- Testing of dangerous scenarios can be performed without any danger to the SUT, humans or the operational environment.

- Testing of unusual scenarios can be performed when real operations are time-consuming or expensive to set up.

- Testing can be performed of extreme scenarios that would otherwise be impossible to test in reality at all.

- Testing can be performed of time-intensive scenarios in reduced timescales, which leads to saving time usually spent on environment setup and test implementation.

- Observability and controllability are far greater in virtual test environments, for example ensuring that an unusual set of financial trading conditions is replicated with far better observability and monitoring controls.

- The simulation of hardware by virtual test environments allows systems to be tested with simulated hardware components that otherwise may not be available; perhaps, they have not been developed yet or are too expensive.

Using a virtual test environment can also contribute to greater sustainability. Unlike physical test setups, virtual environments typically are not as resource-intensive, leading to lower energy consumption and reduced overall environmental footprint. This approach supports more eco-friendly development practices, but can also lead to cost savings for testing activities.

As shown in Figure 10.8, virtual test environments may be built specifically for a given system, may be generic or may be developed to support specific application domains. Both commercial and open-source virtual test environments are available to support the AI-based system testing. Examples include:

- *MORSE* (the Modular Open Robots Simulation Engine): this is a simulator for generic mobile robot simulation of single or multi robots, based on the Blender game engine (MORSE, 2016).

- *AI Habitat*: this is a simulation platform created by Facebook AI, designed to train embodied agents (such as virtual robots) in photo-realistic 3D environments (Meta Platforms, 2023).

- *NVIDIA DRIVE*: this is an open and scalable platform for self-driving cars from NVIDIA. It is based on a cloud platform and is capable of generating billions of miles of autonomous-vehicle testing (NVIDIA, 2025b).

- *MathWorks®, MATLAB® and Simulink*: these provide the ability to prepare training data, produce ML models and simulate the execution of AI-based systems, including the models using synthetic data (MathWorks, 2025a, 2025c).

Figure 10.8 Virtual test environment types

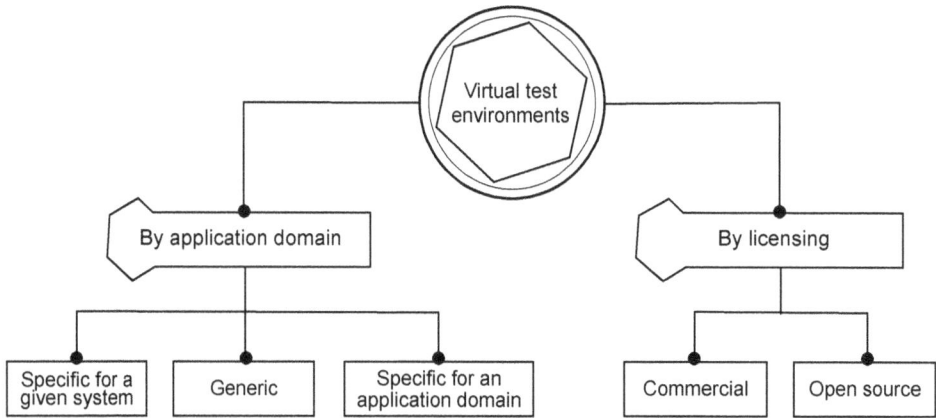

Another term related to the topic that we should mention here is **digital twin**. In a nutshell, a digital twin can be seen as an advanced continuous simulation of a physical entity, while a virtual test environment is a broader term used to describe any simulated setting created for testing purposes, which may not necessarily represent a physical real-life counterpart.

From theory to practice

Example 1. Virtual test environment for testing a recommendation system in e-commerce

For the sake of simplicity, let us imagine a tech company developing an AI-driven recommendation system for an e-commerce platform. The goal for the recommendation system is to analyse user behaviour and preferences, to suggest personalised product recommendations.

The development team creates a virtual test environment that simulates user interactions and behaviours on the e-commerce platform. This simulation environment is hosted on cloud infrastructure and closely resembles the production environment in terms of data and system architecture. **Synthetic data** generation techniques are used to generate simulated user interactions, such as browsing history, product views, searches and purchases (Degtiarenko, 2024; Goyal and Mahmoud, 2024). These synthetic datasets are representative of real user behaviour and are used to test the recommendation system's performance under different scenarios. The testing team defines a variety of test scenarios to evaluate the recommendation system's effectiveness and accuracy. Test scenarios include typical user journeys, such as new user onboarding, product discovery, cross-selling, up-selling and re-engagement.

A/B testing (see Chapter 9) is conducted in the virtual test environment to compare the performance of different recommendation algorithms and configurations. Users are randomly assigned to different experimental groups, each receiving recommendations generated by a different algorithm or parameter setting. The effectiveness of each algorithm is measured based on user engagement metrics such as **click-through rate (CTR)**, **conversion rate (CVR)** (Li et al., 2021) and revenue.

Stress testing is performed to assess the recommendation system's scalability and performance under high traffic loads (Ali et al., 2022). The virtual test environment is subjected to simulated spikes in user activity and traffic volume to evaluate the system's response time, throughput and resource utilisation.

Fault injection techniques are employed to simulate various failure scenarios and edge cases, such as server failures, network outages and data corruption (Moradi et al., 2023). This helps to identify potential vulnerabilities and weaknesses in the recommendation system's architecture and resilience mechanisms.

Security testing is conducted to assess the recommendation system's resistance to common security threats, such as data breaches, unauthorised access and manipulation attacks (Gorripati et al., 2021). Vulnerability assessments, penetration testing and code reviews are performed to identify and mitigate security risks (Chandrakant and Prakash, 2019).

The virtual test environment is used to verify that the recommendation system complies with relevant regulations and standards, such as data privacy laws (GDPR) and industry-specific regulations (see Section 1.9 on standards, regulations and AI).

Example 2. Digital twin in fintech

A fintech equivalent of a digital twin (Degtiarenko, 2023; Itkin, 2024) could be a simulation that models a trading infrastructure for testing purposes (see Figure 10.9). Instead of requiring hundreds of servers – as a real-life trading system does – this model can run on just a few, significantly reducing the hardware footprint and costs. Considering access limitations often encountered in financial services, using a model enables better and more efficient testing due to better control over the environment coupled with the capacity to model, run and analyse diverse scenarios. It also helps to speed up the start of testing and the test library delivery, as well as supporting better-informed decision-making.

System modelling can start early on and, as the system matures, the model provides stakeholders with early, objective insights, allowing the development team to address issues before they become critical. Supplemented by ML methods, system modelling can help to further enhance the efficiency of such software testing tasks as test generation and results interpretation. A data-driven AI-enabled system modelling approach helps to improve test coverage, optimise test libraries and reduce the number of test scripts to execute, all the while maintaining their effectiveness and leading to better detection of vulnerabilities. The result is a more efficient, automated and resource-light test library that can be continuously updated with new and refined scripts as the system evolves.

Figure 10.9 Digital twins in fintech

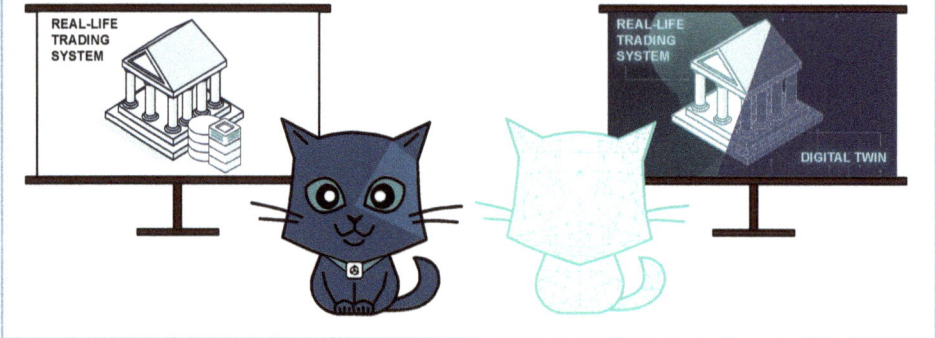

Quick questions

Question 10.3

Given the following statements:

I. Testing real-world scenarios without any possibility of danger to the SUT, humans or the operational environment

II. Testing rare and extreme scenarios that might be too costly, time-consuming or impossible to set up in real life

III. Reduced observability and monitoring controls, making it harder to test financial conditions

IV. Simulation of hardware components, allowing tests to be conducted even if the hardware is not yet developed or is too expensive

Which of these statements are the key benefits of using a virtual test environment when testing AI-based systems? Select ONE option.

A. I and II

B. II, III and IV

C. I, II and IV

D. I, III and IV

10.3 CHALLENGES IN TEST ENVIRONMENTS FOR AI-BASED SYSTEMS

Building test environments for AI-based systems can be a complex task and, since we talked about benefits, we also have to mention the difficulties that arise when it comes to AI-based system test environments. Here are some of the key challenges involved in creating effective test environments for AI-based systems:

- *Data quality and diversity*: ensuring that the test data accurately represents diverse real-world scenarios that the AI-based system will encounter can be complicated. Also, sometimes, when the AI-based system is trained on biased historical data (see Section 2.4 on bias), it is difficult to promote fairness.

- *Scalability*: AI-based systems often need to handle large amounts of data and complex computations. Creating test environments that scale to these requirements can be costly and technically complex.

- *Realism*: striking the right balance between realism and controllability in a test environment is crucial. Simulations and synthetic data may lack the nuances and unpredictability of real-world data, which, in turn, can affect the AI-based system's performance.

- *Privacy and ethics*: steps have to be taken when handling sensitive data in test environments to ensure that data is anonymised and used responsibly (see also Section 2.5 on ethics).

- *Resource constraints*: AI models often require significant computational resources. Setting up and managing a test environment with the necessary computing power can be expensive and may require specialised hardware that could be hard to obtain. In addition, developing and maintaining realistic test environments can be expensive and time-consuming. Balancing the cost and time constraints with the need for comprehensive testing is challenging.

- *Reproducibility*: ensuring that tests can be reproduced consistently is essential for debugging and benchmarking AI-based systems; this includes managing dependencies and version control.

- *Edge cases and rare events*: AI-based systems also need to perform well in edge cases and rare events, which are often difficult to capture in a test environment.

- *Adversarial testing*: as previously noted, AI-based systems can exhibit susceptibility to adversarial attacks (see Section 9.1.1); therefore, the creation of test cases and environments to assess the system's ability to withstand such attacks requires a specialised skillset.

- *Dynamic environments*: some AI applications, such as autonomous vehicles, operate in dynamic and changing environments, so we have to create test environments that simulate these dynamic conditions accurately.

- *Human-in-the-loop testing*: some AI-based systems, such as chatbots or recommendation engines, interact with humans, so we have to design test environments that involve constant human feedback and evaluation.

- *Regulatory compliance*: adhering to regulatory requirements and standards in AI testing (see Section 1.9 on standards, regulations and AI), especially in fields such as healthcare or finance, can be challenging due to evolving regulations.

- *Interactions with external systems*: AI-based systems often interact with external systems and APIs, which could sometimes prove quite complex.

- *Long-term testing*: some AI-based systems, such as those used in critical infrastructures or healthcare, need to be tested for long periods to assess their reliability and safety over time.

To address these challenges, interdisciplinary teams of AI researchers, domain experts and engineers work together to design and build effective test environments that can thoroughly evaluate AI-based systems' performance and safety before deployment in real-world applications.

TERMS

Click-through rate (CTR): the probability that a user will click on a specific online advertisement.

Conversion rate (CVR): the probability that the user will take the desired action (e.g. purchase in e-commerce).

Digital twin: an advanced continuous simulation of a physical entity.

Fault injection: the process of intentionally adding a defect to a component or system to determine whether it can detect and possibly recover from it.

Multi-agent system: a system that comprises multiple intelligent agents.

Security testing: a type of testing to determine the security of a component or system.

Stress testing: a type of performance testing conducted to evaluate a system or component at or beyond the limits of its anticipated or specified workloads, or with reduced availability of resources such as access to memory or servers (ISO 24765).

Synthetic data: artificially generated data that is generated as an alternative to real-world data.

Virtual test environment: a test environment in which one or more parts are digitally simulated.

SELF-ASSESSMENT EXERCISES

1. What is a test environment for an AI-based system?

2. List the common features of test environments for AI-based systems.

3. Provide several examples of test environments for AI-based systems.

4. Why do test environments for AI-based systems differ from those for conventional systems?

5. What is a virtual test environment?

6. Discuss the benefits of using a virtual test environment when testing AI-based systems.

7. Name the types of virtual test environments for AI-based systems.

8. Provide several examples of virtual test environments for AI-based systems.

9. Explain what a digital twin is.

10. What are the main challenges of building test environments for AI-based systems?

PART 4
TESTING WITH AI

11 USING AI FOR TESTING

SUMMARY

This chapter reviews how AI supports software testing and optimises it. The chapter provides insights on which testing activities are currently impractical for implementation as AI, and why this is so. The chapter also explains how AI can be used for test case generation, regression test suite optimisation, defect prediction and graphical user interface (GUI) testing. It concludes with final thoughts on the potential role of AI as a teammate.

LEARNING OBJECTIVES

After reading this chapter, you should be able to:

- Categorise the AI technologies used in software testing (K2)
- Explain how AI can assist in supporting the analysis of new defects (K2)
- Explain how AI can assist in test case generation (K2)
- Explain how AI can assist in optimisation of regression test suites (K2)
- Explain how AI can assist in defect prediction (K2)
- Implement a simple AI-based defect prediction system (H)
- Go over the use of AI in testing user interfaces (K2)

LINKS TO OTHER CHAPTERS

This chapter is related to other chapters as follows:

- Chapter 1 describes the main AI technologies that can be used in model building.
- Chapter 8 looks at the test oracle problem.
- Chapter 9 reviews back-to-back testing.

11.1 AI TECHNOLOGIES FOR TESTING

Throughout the previous chapters, we have discussed the theory of testing AI-based systems, but what about the application of AI in testing? AI technologies can be used to support various aspects of software testing (several AI technologies were listed in Chapter 1). Let us look at the three broad areas of AI technologies used by the software engineering community (Harman, 2012), presented in Figure 11.1 and illustrated in Figure 11.2.

- *Fuzzy logic and probabilistic methods* are well-suited for addressing real-world problems that are probabilistic or cannot be accurately defined in a reliable manner. For example, analysing and predicting possible system failures using **Bayesian techniques** may estimate failure likelihood.

- *Classification, learning and prediction* can be applied to various use cases, such as **defect prediction**. When assisted by ML, this area can supplement various software testing tasks.

- *Computational search and optimisation techniques* can help with optimisation problems using complex search algorithms. This aids with generating and selecting test cases to achieve the required coverage criterion, and to optimise regression testing activities.

Figure 11.1 Current key areas of AI technologies in software testing

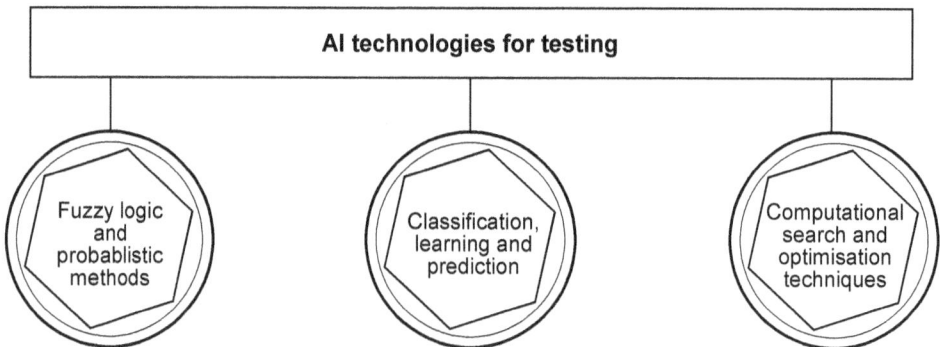

Of course, this categorisation is not comprehensive, but over time, as the industry advances, new and more precise categorisations may emerge.

Figure 11.2 AI technologies for testing

Fuzzy logic and probabilistic methods

Classification, learning and prediction

Computational search and optimisation techniques

From theory to practice

Example 1. Fuzzy logic and probabilistic methods in testing

Beyond measuring software completeness, a fuzzy logic-based approach can also enhance test case prioritisation by accounting for attributes such as failure rates and execution times. This approach assigns fuzzy linguistic variables to each test case, classifying them into priority levels (from 'very low' to 'very high') with additional crisp parameters such as 'prerequisite test case' and 'recently updated' status. Higher priority is given to cases marked as recently updated, based on the assumption that recent changes are more prone to defects. Prerequisite parameters also play a key role, ensuring that dependencies among test cases are honoured, ultimately optimising the test flow and improving the prioritisation of test cases (Karatayev et al., 2024).

Fuzzy logic also aids in reducing testing costs while enhancing test quality. By utilising fuzzy-based metrics, you can assess the quality and effectiveness of test projects early in the testing phase, improving decision-making without increasing costs. Since test cases often overlap with various software quality attributes – such as functionality, reliability and usability, as defined in ISO/IEC 25002:2024

(ISO, 2024) – fuzzy sets and linguistic values (e.g. high, nominal, low) help to evaluate the uncertain correlations between test cases and quality characteristics. This approach enables comparison across test projects by aggregating these correlations, ultimately allowing software teams to assess the consistency, quality and effectiveness of their test projects more accurately (Zhang and Zhou, 2007).

Example 2. Classification, learning and prediction in testing

Every software model contains various defects, making the automatic detection and classification of these issues essential to ensure reliability. Most defect prediction models use established methodologies and algorithms, such as statistical techniques and ML. These models rely on historical data – specifically, software metrics and actual defect rates – using this data to train the model on patterns that indicate defect-prone modules. Once trained, these tools can analyse software metrics from a recent project to estimate which modules are likely to contain defects. Research on software defect prediction indicates that AI-based predictors can detect, on average, 70 per cent of defects in a system compared to manual code reviews, which detect between 35 per cent and 60 per cent, and inspections, which find up to 30 per cent (Misirli et al., 2011). ML-based defect predictors operate in two phases: a training phase, where the model learns from data on previous projects, and a testing phase, where it predicts which modules in a new project are likely to be defect-free or contain issues. Here, a module may refer to any component within the source code, such as a package, class, file or method.

In defect prediction as a classification task, input variables for the model are a set of static code attributes such as lines of code, counts of operands and operators, cyclomatic complexity, maintenance severity, programming effort and time, branch count, and more. Alongside these code attributes, each module in the training data has a class label: '0' for defect-free and '1' for defective, serving as the output variables for the ML model. If a module in the software is associated with a bug (code defect) during testing, it is labelled with '1'; if not, it is labelled with '0'. A classification algorithm, such as the Naive Bayes classifier, is often used for this type of prediction model (Misirli et al., 2011).

An ML model can also be designed to predict not only the presence of defects but also their count. For this regression-based approach, the model uses the number of defects per module as the output variable. Algorithms such as decision trees can be applied to train this model on defect counts (Rathore and Kumar, 2016; Peng, 2022).

Example 3. Computational search and optimisation techniques in testing

Software defect prediction plays a crucial role in identifying the software modules most likely to contain defects and in optimising testing resource allocation. Ranking defective modules in order of priority is essential to maximise resource efficiency and minimise testing time and costs, especially in projects with constrained budgets. Two common ranking criteria in ML algorithms are *bug count* and *bug density*. Bug count refers to the total number of bugs in a module, while bug density measures the frequency of bugs per line of code. Bug density often provides a clearer indication of where resources are needed most; for instance, between two modules with an equal number of bugs, the module with fewer lines of code would take priority due to its higher bug density (Nassif et al., 2023).

Many ML-based techniques exist for optimising test suites. Clustering methods, such as K-means clustering, group similar test cases and help to identify redundant cases, reducing the test suite size. For example, a K-means algorithm can form clusters of similar test cases, which are then refined using a genetic sorting algorithm to produce a reduced yet representative set of tests (Nagy et al., 2023). Reinforcement learning algorithms are also used to optimise test execution. Reinforcement learning models learn from historical data, user interactions and outcomes to determine the most effective sequence for running tests. For instance, an interaction-recording system can capture user and tester interactions with an application, creating a complete path of user actions. The recorded logs serve as input data, enabling a reinforcement learning agent to learn optimal strategies for testing by maximising rewards based on specific actions and states (Waqar et al., 2022).

11.2 USING AI TO ANALYSE REPORTED DEFECTS

Found defects need to be reported, categorised, prioritised and checked for duplicates (Figure 11.3). This activity is often called defect triage or analysis. It helps to optimise the time spent on defect resolution. This can also be assisted by AI through:

- *Categorisation*: NLP can be used to analyse defect reports to obtain additional information that can be provided alongside other metadata to clustering algorithms. They, in turn, can identify suitable defect categories and highlight similar or duplicate defects.

- *Criticality*: if ML models are trained on critical defect features, they can be used to identify those defects in real-life production scenarios.

- *Assignment*: ML models can suggest which developers are the best fit for particular tasks.

Figure 11.3 Defect analysis

Quick questions

Question 11.1

Which of the following defect triage activities can be assisted by AI to suggest the most suitable developer for a specific task? Select ONE option.

    A. categorisation

    B. criticality

    C. assignment

    D. clustering

Question 11.2

A financial software company frequently encounters new defects in its application after each update. The company decides to implement AI tools to assist in analysing these defects and improve their software reliability. Which of the following is the BEST example of how AI can assist in supporting the analysis of new defects in this context? Select ONE option.

    A. The AI tool automatically schedules updates and patches for future releases to prevent defects from occurring.

    B. The AI tool clusters similar reported defects, identifies patterns in the code affected and suggests probable root causes based on previous issues.

    C. The AI tool creates new testing environments each time a defect is reported to check for similar issues across different configurations of the application.

    D. The AI tool immediately deploys a fix to users whenever a defect is detected in the application, without any developer input.

11.3 USING AI FOR TEST CASE GENERATION

Utilising AI to generate tests can be effective when creating testing assets and maximising both code and requirements coverage (Figure 11.4). The basis for these tests includes the source code, the user interface and a machine-readable test model with some tools basing the tests on observation of the low-level behaviour of the system through instrumentation or through log files.

However, this can once again lead us to a test oracle problem (see Chapter 8), because the AI-based tool does not know what the expected results should be for a given set of test data (see Figure 11.5). One solution is to use back-to-back testing, if a suitable system is available to use as a pseudo-oracle (see Section 9.3 on back-to-back testing). Alternatively, tests could be run with the expectation that no critical failures occur, such as an 'application not responding' message, a system crash or other obvious indicators of malfunction.

Figure 11.4 Test case generation

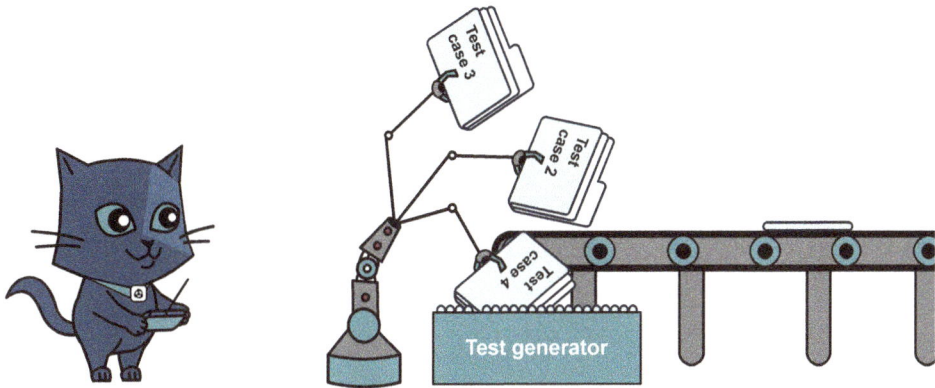

Figure 11.5 The test oracle problem

Research comparing AI-based test generation tools with similar non-AI fuzz testing tools shows that the AI-based tools can achieve equivalent levels of coverage and find more defects while reducing the average sequence of steps needed to cause a failure from around 15,000 steps to around 100 steps (Mao et al., 2016). This makes debugging far easier (see Figure 11.6).

Figure 11.6 AI-based vs non-AI testing tools

From theory to practice

Let us consider a software development team working on a new e-commerce website. They need to ensure that the website functions correctly across various browsers and devices and handles different user interactions accurately. To achieve this, they decide to employ AI-based test case generation techniques.

The team trains ML models on historical data of user interactions, bug reports and system behaviour to learn patterns and dependencies in the software. In order to mimic real user interactions with the website, it was decided to generate synthetic test scenarios using generative adversarial networks. The GAN is an algorithmic architecture that uses two neural networks to generate new data instances that resemble the training data (Guo et al., 2022). In our case, these data instances are inputs for test cases. One neural network ('generator') generates test cases, while the other one ('discriminator') evaluates whether these test cases look like the ones produced by an intelligent and competent software tester. Discriminator networks can also use additional data collected by rule-based methods such as code coverage and test execution metrics.

According to this approach, the AI-based system generates diverse input datasets, including different user profiles, product categories and browsing behaviours. Using the trained ML models and GANs, the AI-based system generates test cases that cover various scenarios, such as user registration, product search, add-to-cart and checkout processes. The generated test cases are executed against the e-commerce website on different browsers and devices using automated testing frameworks. Then the AI-based system monitors the test execution and collects feedback on the system's behaviour. Based on the test results and feedback, the AI-based system continuously improves its test case generation techniques. It adapts to changes in the software and user behaviour to ensure comprehensive test coverage.

11.4 USING AI FOR THE OPTIMISATION OF REGRESSION TEST SUITES

Frequent changes to a system associated with its modification and improvement can cause the regression test suite to grow excessively large, because testers need to re-implement all test cases that were configured in the early stages to ensure that the system works as expected. At a certain moment, it becomes difficult to retest all test cases because it will be costly in terms of time, resources and budget. Therefore, optimisation of the regression test cases becomes essential, and an AI-based tool can help to solve this problem. It can optimise the regression test suite by analysing data from previous test outcomes, related defect information and recent changes in the system. Through this analysis, the AI-based tool can identify redundant or low-value test cases, enabling their removal without compromising defect detection coverage. This targeted optimisation saves time and effort, allowing testing teams to focus on the most impactful cases.

Recent research shows that the test suite can be potentially reduced by at least 60 per cent while still detecting most defects and saving at least 70 per cent of the test execution duration time compared to the retest-all approach (Reda et al., 2022) (see Figure 11.7).

Figure 11.7 Test execution with the retest-all approach (a) and with the AI-based optimisation approach (b)

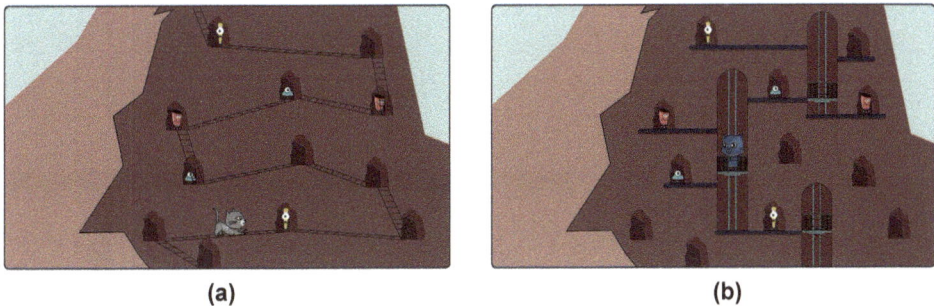

(a)   (b)

Quick questions

Question 11.3

A company frequently updates its software, which has led to an increasingly large regression test suite. What is a realistic benefit the company might gain by using AI to optimise its regression test suite? Select ONE option.

    A. AI will remove the need for regression testing after each update.

    B. AI can analyse past test results and recent changes to reduce the test suite size and cut down execution time.

    C. AI can eliminate all duplicate tests without analysing defect patterns.

    D. AI will ensure that absolutely no defects are missed, regardless of the regression test suite size on all stages of software development lifecycle.

11.5 USING AI FOR DEFECT PREDICTION

Defect prediction can help to find out if a defect is present, how many of them are there and whether they can be found. The results can be used for test prioritisation. Predictions are usually based on source code metrics, process metrics and/or organisational metrics.

Due to so many potential factors to consider, determining the relationship between them and the likelihood of defects is almost always beyond human capabilities (see Figure 11.8). As a result, using an AI-based approach that typically uses ML is a necessity. Defect prediction is most effective when based on prior experiences in a similar situation (e.g. with the same code base and/or the same developers).

Figure 11.8 Manual code review

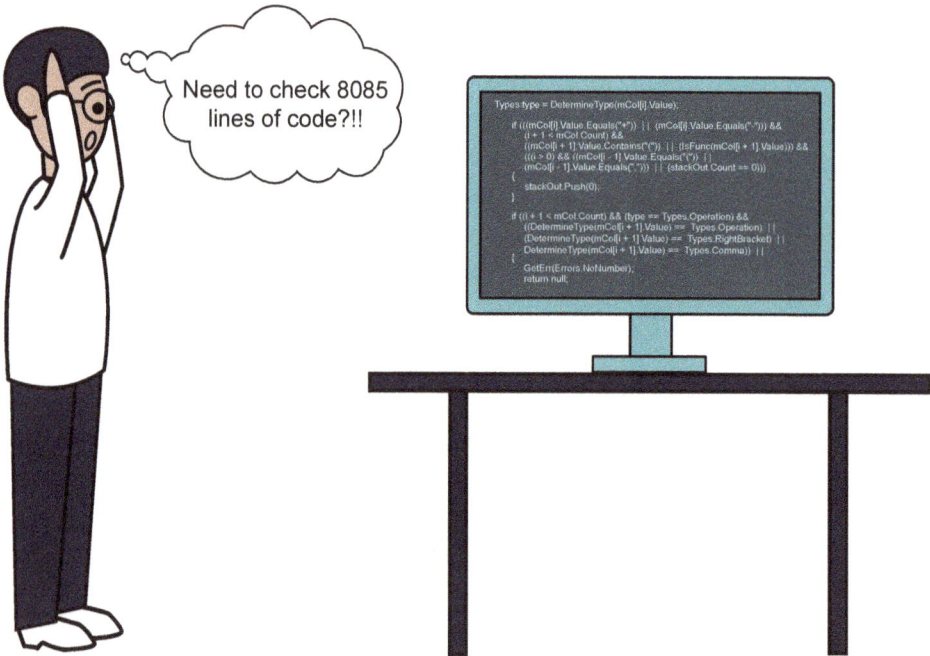

Defect prediction using ML has been successfully implemented in several different situations. It has been established that the best predictors are organisational indicators, such as the number of people making changes to the code and the number of different organisations making edits to the code, rather than the more commonly used source code indicators, such as the number of code lines and cyclomatic complexity (Nagappan et al., 2008), which is outlined in Figure 11.9.

Figure 11.9 Best code defect predictors

Number of people making changes to the code file

Source code metrics

More important >

- Number of code lines
- Number of statements
- Number of methods
- Cyclomatic complexity

Quick questions

Question 11.4

A software development team wants to predict defect-prone areas in their large and complex codebases to improve test prioritisation. What is the MOST relevant approach they might use? Select ONE option.

A. Prioritise source code metrics such as code lines and cyclomatic complexity, as they are always the strongest defect predictors, and don't pay attention to other metrics.

B. Manually analyse all possible factors in the code to determine defect likelihood.

C. Use an AI-based approach to analyse organisational metrics, such as the number of people modifying a code file, for better defect prediction.

D. Focus solely on process metrics, disregarding organisational factors.

Hands-on exercise 3: build a defect prediction system

Use the EclipseJDTCore_final.csv file provided in the GitHub repository (**github.com/exactpro/ai-testing-guide/tree/main/HO_Exercise_3**) to build an ML model predicting the presence of bugs in the code at any class level. Use the random forest classifier to train the model. Try to find the optimal combination of input features and their quantity. Evaluate the model by calculating accuracy, precision, recall and the F1-score.

The data in the EclipseJDTCore_final.csv file was obtained as a combination of data acquired from the two publicly available datasets from the repository for the Eclipse JDT Core open source software (Bug Prediction Dataset, 2025):

- Change metrics (15) plus categorised (with severity and priority) post-release defects;

- CK and other 11 object oriented metrics for the last version of the system plus categorised (with severity and priority) post-release defects.

Hands-on exercise 3 solution hints

- Add a new column titled 'hasBugs' to the dataset provided in the EclipseJDTCore_final.csv file. This column should indicate whether the class contains any bugs. If there is at least one non-zero value in the columns named 'bugs', 'nonTrivialBugs', 'majorBugs', 'criticalBugs' or 'highPriorityBugs', then 'hasBugs' is True.
- Use the 'hasBugs' column as an output feature for the prediction model.

The full solution can be found in the GitHub repository (**github.com/exactpro/ai-testing-guide/tree/main/HO_Exercise_3**).

11.6 USING AI FOR TESTING USER INTERFACES

As user interfaces become more dynamic and complex, testing them efficiently and accurately is increasingly important. Traditional GUI testing approaches often struggle to keep up with frequent changes in design and structure. This is where AI can play a valuable role. In this section, we look at how AI-based techniques and tools are being used to improve the effectiveness and reliability of GUI testing by making it more adaptive and scalable, and less dependent on rigid scripting.

11.6.1 Using AI to test through the GUI

Testing through the **graphical user interface (GUI)** is the typical approach for manual testing and is often the starting point for test automation initiatives. The resulting tests mimic human interaction with the SUT (see Figure 11.10(a)). This can be done by the capture/playback approach – Figure 11.10(b) – although we have to keep in mind that

Figure 11.10 Human interaction with GUI (a) and AI-based interaction with GUI (b)

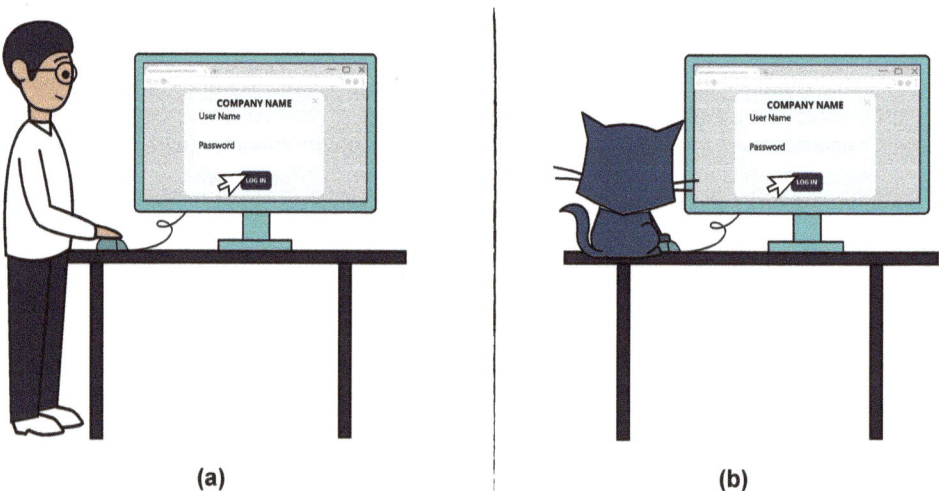

(a)   (b)

this approach is very change-sensitive, and each alteration would require a recapture action.

AI can mitigate the shortcomings of this approach by employing AI-based tools to identify the correct objects using various criteria, and to choose stable identification criteria, for example changing a button's location can lead to a change in test priorities. This approach classifies the objects in the user interface as the ones matching or not matching the test.

Visual testing uses image recognition to interact with GUI objects through the same interface as an actual user, and does not require access to the underlying code and interface definitions, thus making it non-intrusive and independent of the aforementioned technology. The scripts need to only work through the visible user interface. This approach allows the tester to create scripts that interact directly with the images, buttons and text fields on the screen in the same way as a human user, without being affected by the overall screen layout.

Quick questions

Question 11.5

What is the MOST likely way for AI to assist in testing through the GUI of an application? Select ONE option.

    A. By rewriting the source code of the application to fix defects automatically, and also when the properties of the GUI elements change.
    B. By dynamically identifying GUI elements and interacting with them, even when their properties change.
    C. By eliminating the need for all forms of functional and non-functional testing.
    D. By manually validating user interactions with the GUI.

11.6.2 Using AI to test the GUI

GUI testing is the process of evaluating an application's GUI to ensure it meets both functional and non-functional requirements. This involves designing a series of test scenarios, executing them and comparing the actual outcomes with the expected results. The testing focuses on assessing the application's response to user interactions, such as mouse clicks and keyboard inputs, as well as verifying the behaviour of interface elements such as buttons, dialogues, menus, images, toolbars and text fields in response to user actions.

AI algorithms can analyse requirements or application structures to automatically generate relevant test cases for the GUI testing. AI-based tools can extract GUI interactions using 'dynamically organised agents' that adaptively arrange themselves to capture these interactions efficiently (Hu et al., 2024). These tools then use a multidimensional data extraction approach to retrieve data relevant to the test requirements from the interaction trace (logs or records of how the GUI behaves during these interactions) and perform verification, ensuring that the application's interface meets specified requirements and behaves correctly for end-users. For example, AI-based tools can identify all clickable elements on a web page and generate test cases to validate their functionality.

ML models can assess the acceptability of user interface screens through supervised learning and **heuristics**. In this context, heuristics refers to guidelines that help the ML model to assess the quality or usability of a user interface screen. These are not hard-coded rules, but rather general principles or best practices used in user interface/user experience (UI/UX) design, such as 'buttons should be visible and not overlap', or 'text should have sufficient contrast with the background'. Tools based on these models can identify incorrectly rendered elements, determine whether some objects are inaccessible or hard to detect and find other GUI issues, as shown in Figure 11.11.

Figure 11.11 AI-based GUI testing

While image recognition is one form of a computer vision algorithm, other forms of AI-based computer vision can compare screenshots to identify unintended changes to the layout, size, position, colour, font or other visible attributes of objects. The results can support regression testing.

The technology for checking the acceptability of screens can be combined with comparison tools to create more sophisticated AI-based regression testing tools that are capable of advising whether the detected user interface changes are likely to be acceptable to users, or whether these changes should be flagged and relayed to be checked by a human. Such AI-based tools can be used for accessibility testing, for things like colour contrast for the visually impaired. AI-based tools can also support testing for compatibility on different browsers, devices or platforms aimed at checking that the user interface for the same application works correctly on various browsers, devices and platforms.

Industry insights

Visual testing with Applitools

GUI-based system testing is a persistent challenge in test automation due to its tendency to be brittle, costly to develop and time-consuming to execute. Despite these drawbacks, many developers and testers are drawn to using the GUI as the primary test interface. GUI-based tests hold a unique advantage, as they stimulate the SUT end-to-end, mimicking a user's perspective and interacting with deeper layers such as databases. When integrated wisely into a broader testing strategy, these tests can be highly effective, though tool manufacturers have long struggled to address their inherent issues.

Applitools (Applitools, 2025a) is a tool for visual testing designed to ensure that a system's GUI looks as expected. It provides APIs for major programming languages and test frameworks, enabling testers to set up visual assertions on single elements or full screens. During testing, Applitools Eyes Test Manager (Applitools, 2025b) captures screenshots that are sent to an Eyes server, where computer vision algorithms detect visible changes, filtering out inconsequential differences. Test results are then reviewed in the Eyes Test Manager, where changes can be approved, rejected or ignored. Applitools' method uses a baseline comparison, similar to **approval testing**, protecting against unintended visual changes. The tool's AI, built on a vast dataset of GUI validations, claims 99.99 per cent accuracy (Prasad, 2018) and continually improves through daily analysis of new images. By comparing sequences of images, Applitools enables flexible adjustments, minimising maintenance as the GUI evolves.

From theory to practice

Using AI to test a trading system

The task of assessing the quality of complex financial technology platforms – such as trading, clearing and settlement, banking, wealth management or payments systems – is accompanied by several distinctive challenges that explain why this effort requires a combination of deep technical and domain expertise. These challenges are:

- vigorous regulatory oversight and enforcement (driven by principles- or outcome-based frameworks);
- high visibility and impact on national economies and the society;
- expectation of robust governance and operational resilience;
- centralisation and no ability to decrease the risk through canary deployments.

To address system challenges specific to exchange systems, the Exactpro team uses a test generation and test library optimisation approach, combining model-based testing and AI algorithms (Exactpro, 2025). The process is, to some extent, similar to a new test model introduced by Paul Gerrard (EuroSTAR Huddle, 2019). Using a digital model (digital twin) of the SUT and enhancing it with sets of AI algorithms allows the Exactpro team to:

- explore system behaviour without the need to access the system's source code;
- have the test framework fully match the complexity of the SUT;
- achieve comprehensive – yet resource-efficient – test coverage by producing a minimal acceptable amount of realistic feature-rich scenarios simulating authentic trading participants' actions;
- continuously improve the quality of the test library over the three testing phases by fine-tuning the model's accuracy and generative capabilities.

The implemented AI testing approach consists of the following steps (see Figure 11.12) (Exactpro, 2024):

1. *Test basis analysis*: this is analysing the data available from specifications, system logs and other formal and informal sources, normalising it and converting it into machine-readable form.

2. *Input dataset and expected outcomes dataset*: the knowledge derived from the test basis analysis enables the creation of the input dataset used for test execution. It also lays the foundation for modelling a digital twin of the SUT – a machine-readable description of its behaviour expressed as input sequences, actions, conditions, outputs and flow of data from input to output. The resulting expected values dataset further helps to reconcile the data received from the SUT during testing with the pre-calculated expected values.

3. *Test execution, output dataset*: all possible test script modifications are passed on for execution to Exactpro's AI-enabled framework for automation in testing. The framework converts the test scripts into the required message format and, upon test execution, collects traffic files for analysis in a raw format for unified storage and compilation of the output dataset.

4. *Enriching the output dataset with annotations*: the 'output' dataset is attributed annotations for interpretation purposes and subsequent application of AI-enabled analytics. This also enables the development of the interpretation dataset – a dataset containing aggregate data and annotations from the processed 'output' and 'expected outcomes' datasets in Steps 4 and 5.

5. *Model refinement*: this step plays a major role in the development of the digital twin. During property and reconciliation checks in iterative movements between Steps 4 and 5, the model logic is gradually trained and improved to provide a more accurate interpretation of the 'output' dataset and to produce updated versions of the 'expected outcomes' and 'interpretation' datasets.

6. *Test reinforcement and learning weights dataset*: discriminative techniques are applied to the test library being developed, to identify the best-performing test scripts and reduce the volumes of tests required for execution to the minimal amount that, at the same time, covers all target conditions and data points extracted from the model.

Figure 11.12 An AI testing approach for a trading system

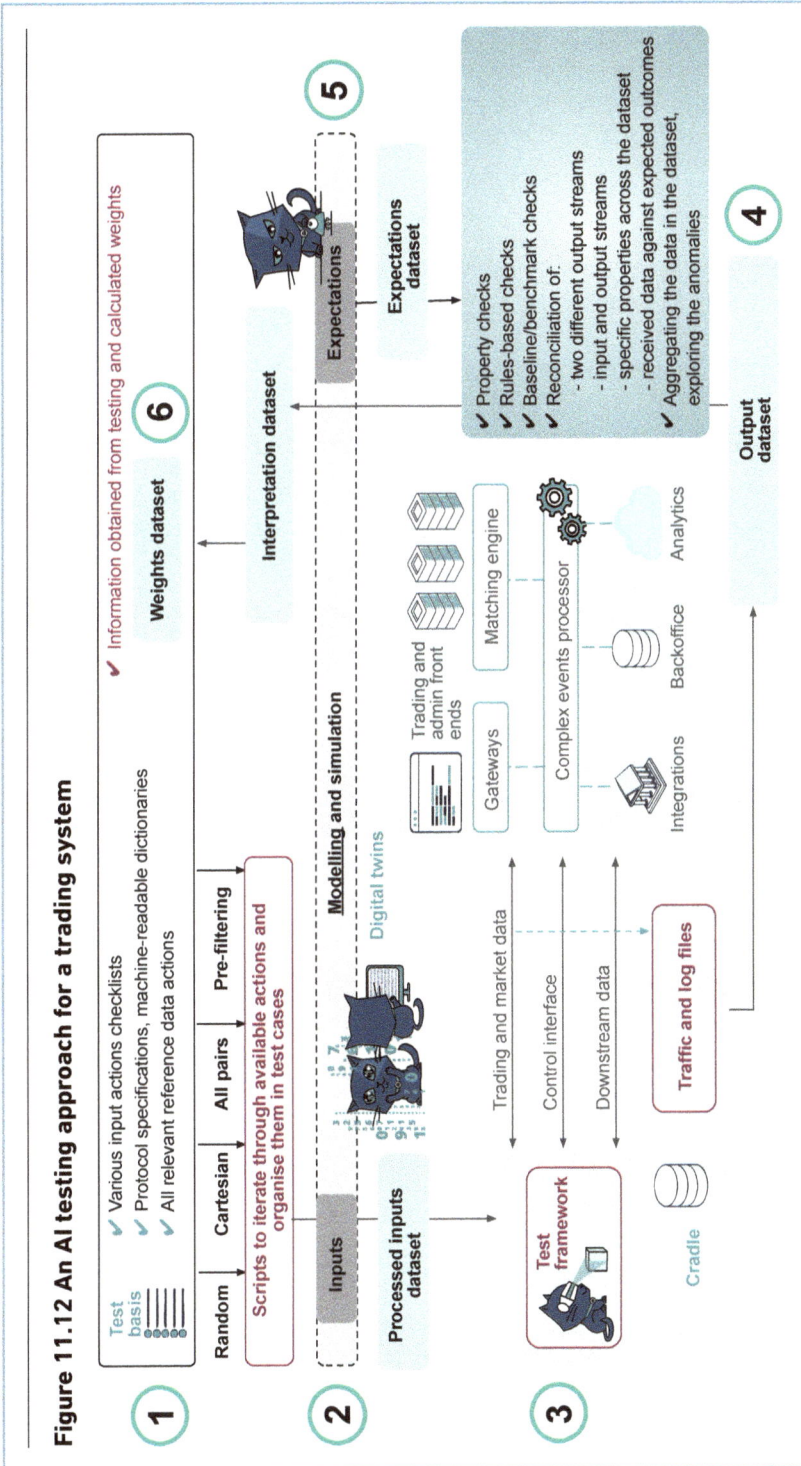

✔ Various input actions checklists
✔ Protocol specifications, machine-readable dictionaries
✔ All relevant reference data actions

✔ Information obtained from testing and calculated weights

1

Test basis

Random | Cartesian | All pairs | Pre-filtering

Scripts to iterate through available actions and organise them in test cases

2

Inputs

Processed inputs dataset

Modelling and simulation

Digital twins

3

Test framework

Cradle

Trading and market data

Control interface

Downstream data

Traffic and log files

Trading and admin front ends

Gateways

Matching engine

Complex events processor

Integrations

Backoffice

Analytics

4

Output dataset

✔ Property checks
✔ Rules-based checks
✔ Baseline/benchmark checks
✔ Reconciliation of:
  - two different output streams
  - input and output streams
  - specific properties across the dataset
  - received data against expected outcomes
✔ Aggregating the data in the dataset, exploring the anomalies

5

Expectations

Expectations dataset

6

Weights dataset

Interpretation dataset

285

The final test library is a subset of select scenarios fine-tuned until the maximum possible level of test coverage is achieved with the minimal reasonable number of checks to execute. Carefully optimising a subset of test scripts results in achieving a significantly more performant and less resource-heavy version of the initially generated test library.

Unified storage of all test data in a single database enables better access to test evidence and maximum flexibility for applying smart analytics, including for reporting purposes. The final test coverage report helps to demonstrate traceability between the requirements and the test outcomes – an important auditability and compliance criterion.

11.7 FINAL THOUGHTS ON THE POTENTIAL ROLE OF AI AS A TEAMMATE

AI is not a teammate and it is not a collaborator. Terms such as a 'digital workforce' or 'synthetic labour' reflect an incorrect understanding of the nature and limitations of AI technology, and expose organisations to a variety of negative consequences.

The *Oxford English Dictionary* defines a 'teammate' as 'a member of the same team or group as yourself'. So, considering AI a teammate would imply having shared tasks and goals, as well as accountability, but is that feasible?

Through the course of their upbringing, humans are exposed to myriads of behavioural, cultural and ethical conventions. They are then subjected to academic and workplace rules that, in combination, help to develop a sense of duty, moral responsibility and guilt. These features ultimately differentiate teammates you want on your team from those you do not.

In contrast to humans, AI fundamentally lacks intent and moral agency. It can only mimic them based on the data either encoded in it or stemming from its training data. It is not a physical or legal person that can be liable for its actions. It is only humans that bear responsibility for the AI's actions and are liable for the outcomes – positive or negative.

AI is not and cannot be a teammate; it is a tool, a technology able to significantly accelerate some human tasks and drive productivity. Agentic AI working as part of a well-orchestrated framework across business workflows is potentially able to drive productivity at scale.

Depending on task complexity, however, operating AI also requires above-average, sometimes highly specialised, expertise – and the quality and reliability of the outputs will always be the responsibility of the human part of the team. The more integrated AI workflows become, the more vigilant and knowledgeable their perceived 'teammates' will have to be. Concerns around transparency, explainability and ethics must remain a priority as AI agents become more deeply embedded in workplace operations.

This growing integration of AI into critical workflows often brings with it discussions about ethics and accountability, sometimes framed under the term 'Responsible AI', but this term itself warrants closer scrutiny. The phrase can be misleading, as it may suggest that AI itself is capable of being responsible. In reality, the term refers to the responsible development and use of AI by humans.

Responsibility is a human trait. It involves intent, judgement and accountability, none of which can be meaningfully attributed to software. While we can try to design AI systems to act in ways that align with ethical guidelines we talked about early in the book or organisational policies, the responsibility for those designs, decisions and outcomes always lies with the humans behind them. Branding AI as 'responsible' risks obscuring the chain of accountability and may create a false sense of autonomy or trustworthiness in systems that are ultimately shaped by human choices.

Quick questions

Question 11.6

A software testing team is interested in implementing a solution to identify user interface (UI) issues and assess the acceptability of their UI across different devices and browsers. What is the MOST likely practical approach they might consider based on current technology? Select ONE option.

    A. Utilise ML models combined with computer vision algorithms to assess UI screens and identify potential issues for human review.

    B. Rely solely on manual testing to check for UI issues across different devices and various platforms.

    C. Use only heuristic evaluation methods without any automated tools to ensure thoroughness while checking that the UI for the same application works correctly on various browsers.

    D. Focus on testing functionality rather than the user interface, as UI is less important.

TERMS

Approval testing: a test approach that focuses on capturing the current output of a piece of code and then comparing it to a previously approved version.

Bayesian techniques: a technique that considers before and after probability distributions as parameters of a statistical model.

Defect prediction: a technique to predict the areas within the test object in which defects will occur or the quantity of defects that are present.

Graphical user interface (GUI): a type of interface that allows users to interact with a component or system through graphical icons and visual indicators.

GUI testing: a test approach performed by interacting with a test object using a graphical user interface.

Heuristic: a generally recognised rule of thumb that helps to achieve a goal.

Visual testing: testing that uses image recognition to interact with GUI objects through the same interface as an actual user, and does not require access to the underlying code and interface definitions.

SELF-ASSESSMENT EXERCISES

1. List three main categories of AI technologies used by the software engineering community. Which problems do they help to solve?

2. How could AI techniques be applied to enhance your current project, business or company operations? What challenges or constraints might arise when integrating AI into your processes? Which of these obstacles can be addressed with current resources or solutions, and which remain unresolved for now?

3. Discuss those testing activities where AI is less likely to be used.

4. How can AI help in defect analysis?

5. What are some possible ways to use AI in test case generation?

6. Discuss how AI can optimise a regression test suite.

7. Explain how AI can be utilised to predict defects. What are the most effective predictors of code defects?

8. What is the capture/playback approach and what is it for?

9. Is it possible to use AI for testing GUIs? If yes, go over possible ways to do this.

10. What is visual testing? Provide several examples of using AI-based computer vision for testing.

QUICK QUESTIONS ANSWERS

Chapter 1								
Question #	1.1	1.2	1.3	1.4	1.5	1.6		
Answer	D	B	C	C	D	B, C		
Chapter 2								
Question #	2.1	2.2	2.3	2.4	2.5	2.6		
Answer	D	B	C	A, C	C	D		
Chapter 3								
Question #	3.1	3.2	3.3	3.4	3.5			
Answer	D	C	B	D	A			
Chapter 4								
Question #	4.1	4.2	4.3	4.4	4.5	4.6	4.7	4.8
Answer	B	C	D	A	C	A	B	B
Chapter 5								
Question #	5.1	5.2	5.3	5.4	5.5			
Answer	A	C	A	B	C			
Chapter 6								
Question #	6.1	6.2	6.3	6.4				
Answer	C	D	C	A				
Chapter 7								
Question #	7.1	7.2	7.3	7.4	7.5	7.6	7.7	7.8
Answer	C	B	C	D	A	A	C	A

Chapter 8								
Question #	8.1	8.2	8.3	8.4	8.5	8.6	8.7	
Answer	C	B	C	A	D	C	B	
Chapter 9								
Question #	9.1	9.2	9.3	9.4	9.5	9.6	9.7	
Answer	B	D	C	D	D	C	B	
Chapter 10								
Question #	10.1	10.2	10.3					
Answer	B	C	C					
Chapter 11								
Question #	11.1	11.2	11.3	11.4	11.5	11.6		
Answer	C	B	B	C	B	A		

REFERENCES AND WEBLINKS

CHAPTER 1

Abimanyu, A.J., Purbolaksono, M.D. and Astuti, W. (2023) 'Sentiment analysis on movie review from Rotten Tomatoes using logistic regression and information gain feature selection'. *Building of Informatics, Technology and Science*, 5 (1), 162–170. doi.org/10.47065/bits.v5i1.3595.

Abouelazm, A., Michel, J. and Zollner, J.M. (2024) 'A review of reward functions for reinforcement learning in the context of autonomous driving'. *2024 IEEE Intelligent Vehicle Symposium (IV)*. arxiv.org/pdf/2405.01440.

Active Campaign (2024) '188 spam words to avoid: how to stay out of spam email filters'. *Active Campaign*. activecampaign.com/blog/spam-words.

Alam, Md.Z., Rahman, M.S. and Rahman, M.S. (2019) 'A random forest based predictor for medical data classification using feature ranking'. *Informatics in Medicine Unlocked*, 15, 100–180. doi.org/10.1016/j.imu.2019.100180.

Alzubaidi, L., Zhang, J., Humaidi, A.J., Al-Dujaili, A., Duan, Y., Al-Shamma, O., Santamaría, J., Fadhel, M.A., Al-Amidie, M. and Farhan, L. (2021) 'Review of deep learning: concepts, CNN architectures, challenges, applications, future directions'. *Journal of Big Data*, 8 (1), 53. doi.org/10.1186/s40537-021-00444-8.

Amazon Web Services (2025a) Amazon CodeGuru Security. *AWS*. aws.amazon.com/codeguru/.

Amazon Web Services (2025b) Amazon Comprehend. *AWS*. aws.amazon.com/comprehend/.

Amer, H. (2012) 'Using case based reasoning to support strategic management'. Master's thesis, Saimaa University of Applied Sciences Business Administration, Lappeenranta Degree Program in International Business Management. theseus.fi/bitstream/handle/10024/40223/Amer_Haisam.pdf.

Amjoud, A.B. and Amrouch, M. (2023) 'Object detection using deep learning, CNNs and vision transformers: a review'. *IEEE Access*, 11, 35479–35516. doi.org/10.1109/ACCESS.2023.3266093.

Anandhan, A., Shuib, L., Ismail, M.A. and Mujtaba, G. (2018) 'Social media recommender systems: review and open research issues'. *IEEE Access*, 6, 15608–15628. doi.org/10.1109/access.2018.2810062.

Arun, K.S. and Thomas, J. (2011) 'An automated mail sorter system using SVM classifier'. *International Journal of Computer Applications*, 32 (6), 27–31.

Ashwin, S.H. and Raj, R.N. (2023) 'Deep reinforcement learning for autonomous vehicles: lane keep and overtaking scenarios with collision avoidance'. *International Journal of Information Technology*, 15 (7), 3541–3553. doi.org/10.1007/s41870-023-01412-6.

Babu, U.R. and Reddy, D.K. (2016) 'Handwritten digit recognition system using FLDA and support vector machines'. *International Journal of Latest Trends in Engineering and Technology*, 7 (1), 596–608. dx.doi.org/10.21172/1.71.086.

Bannour, W., Maalel, A. and Ben Ghézala, H. (2021) 'Emergency management case-based reasoning systems: a survey of recent developments'. *Journal of Experimental & Theoretical Artificial Intelligence*, 35 (1), 35–58. doi.org/10.1080/0952813X.2021.1952654.

Bostrom, N. (2014) *Superintelligence: Paths, Dangers, Strategies*. Oxford: Oxford University Press.

Breiman, L. (2001) 'Random forests'. *Machine Learning*, 45 (1), 5–32. doi.org/10.1023/a:1010933404324.

Carr, T. (2024) 'Deterministic vs stochastic policies in reinforcement learning'. *Baeldung on Computer Science*. baeldung.com/cs/rl-deterministic-vs-stochastic-policies.

Cervantes, J., Garcia-Lamont, F., Rodríguez-Mazahua, L. and Lopez, A. (2020) 'A comprehensive survey on support vector machine classification: applications, challenges and trends'. *Neurocomputing*, 408 (1), 189–215. doi.org/10.1016/j.neucom.2019.10.118.

Chelladurai, C., Kuluchamy, P., Santhavaliyan, S. and Lawrence, T. (2023) 'Integrating AI-driven on-chip neural networks into Soc architectures'. *ICTACT Journal on Microelectronics*, 9 (3), 1634–1639. doi.org/10.21917/ijme.2023.0283.

Cheng, S. (2023) 'Classification of spam e-mail based on naïve Bayes classification model'. *Highlights in Science, Engineering and Technology*, 39, 749–753. doi.org/10.54097/hset.v39i.6640.

Colledanchise, M. and Ögren, P. (2018) *Behavior Trees in Robotics and AI*. Boca Raton, Florida: CRC Press. doi.org/10.1201/9780429489105.

Constantinou, A.C., Fenton, N.E. and Neil, M. (2012) 'pi-football: a Bayesian network model for forecasting Association Football match outcomes'. *Knowledge-Based Systems*, 36, 1–31. doi.org/10.1016/j.knosys.2012.07.008.

Coral (2025) 'Products'. *Coral*. coral.ai/products/.

Crevier, D. (1993) *AI: The Tumultuous Search for Artificial Intelligence*. New York: BasicBooks.

Das, R.K., Islam, M., Hasan, Md.M., Razia, S., Hassan, M. and Khushbu, S.A. (2023) 'Sentiment analysis in multilingual context: comparative analysis of machine learning and hybrid deep learning models'. *Heliyon*, 9 (9), e20281. doi.org/10.1016/j.heliyon.2023.e20281.

Datta, D., David, P.E., Mittal, D. and Jain, A. (2020) 'Neural machine translation using recurrent neural network'. *International Journal of Engineering and Advanced Technology*, 9 (4), 1395–1400. doi.org/10.35940/ijeat.d7637.049420.

DeepSeek (2025) Home page. *DeepSeek*. deepseek.com/.

Dellaert, F. and Hutchinson, S. (2023) '1.2. Reasoning: introduction to robotics and perception'. *Robotics{book}*. roboticsbook.org/S12_reasoning.html.

Deng, L. (2012) 'The MNIST database of handwritten digit images for machine learning research (best of the web)'. *IEEE Signal Processing Magazine*, 29 (6), 141–142. doi.org/10.1109/msp.2012.2211477.

Devlin, J., Chang, M.-W., Lee, K. and Toutanova, K. (2019) 'BERT: pre-training of deep bidirectional transformers for language understanding'. *Proceedings of the 2019 Conference of the North American Chapter of the Association for Computational Linguistics: Human Language Technologies*, 1, 4171–4186. doi.org/10.18653/v1/N19-1423.

Dhaval, B. and Deshpande, A. (2020) 'Short-term load forecasting with using multiple linear regression'. *International Journal of Electrical and Computer Engineering*, 10 (4), 3911–3917. doi.org/10.11591/ijece.v10i4.pp3911-3917.

DIN (2019) *DIN SPEC 92001-1: Artificial Intelligence – Life Cycle Processes and Quality Requirements – Part 1: Quality Metamodel.* din.de/resource/blob/330532/c74e2a7bad469a41da4fb66916c4f94b/case-study-din-spec-92001-1-data.pdf.

DIN (2024) *DIN SPEC 92001-2: Artificial Intelligence – Life Cycle Processes and Quality Requirements – Part 2: Robustness.* dinmedia.de/en/technical-rule/din-spec-92001-2/330011015.

DrivenData (2025) 'Data science & AI competitions to build a better world'. *DrivenData.* drivendata.org/.

Dussa-Zieger, K., Henschelchen, W., Kocher, V., Liu, Q., Reid, S., Siemens, K. and Smith, A.L. (2021) *Certified Tester AI Testing (CT-AI) Syllabus v.1.0.* International Software Testing Qualifications Board. astqb.org/assets/documents/ISTQB_CT-AI_Syllabus_v1.0.pdf.

Eldesouky, M.T. and Raslan, A.T.N.E.-D. (2024) 'Utilizing association rule mining algorithms to identify dependencies between software defects'. *International Journal of Data Science and Analytics*, under review. doi.org/10.21203/rs.3.rs-4360582/v1.

Ellis, C. (2022) 'When to use neural networks'. *Crunching the Data.* crunchingthedata.com/when-to-use-neural-networks/.

European Commission (2021) *Proposal for a Regulation laying down harmonised rules on artificial intelligence (Artificial Intelligence Act).* COM(2021) 206 final. eur-lex.europa.eu/resource.html?uri=cellar:e0649735-a372-11eb-9585-01aa75ed71a1.0001.02/DOC_1&format=PDF.

European Union (2024) 'Article 3: definitions'. *EU Artificial Intelligence Act.* artificialintelligenceact.eu/article/3/.

Ezhilarasu, C.M., Skaf, Z. and Jennions, I.K. (2019) 'The application of reasoning to aerospace Integrated Vehicle Health Management (IVHM): challenges and opportunities'. *Progress in Aerospace Sciences*, 105, 60–73. doi.org/10.1016/j.paerosci.2019.01.001.

Francesconi, E. (2022) 'The winter, the summer and the summer dream of artificial intelligence in law'. *Artificial Intelligence and Law*, 30, 147–161. doi.org/10.1007/s10506-022-09309-8.

GDPR (2018a) 'Art. 5 GDPR: principles relating to processing of personal data'. *GDPR.EU.* gdpr.eu/article-5-how-to-process-personal-data/.

GDPR (2018b) 'Art. 22 GDPR: automated individual decision-making, including profiling'. *GDPR.EU.* gdpr.eu/article-22-automated-individual-decision-making/.

Georgeff, M.P. and Ingrand, F.F. (1989) 'Decision-making in an embedded reasoning system'. *Proceedings of the 11th International Joint Conference on Artificial Intelligence (IJCAI-89), Detroit, MI, USA, August 20–25, 1989.* IJCAI. ijcai.org/Proceedings/89-2/Papers/020.pdf.

Gianini, G., Fossi, L.G., Mio, C., Caelen, O., Brunie, L. and Damiani, E. (2020) 'Managing a pool of rules for credit card fraud detection by a game theory based approach'. *Future Generation Computer Systems*, 102, 549–561. doi.org/10.1016/j.future.2019.08.028.

GitHub (2025) 'GitHub Copilot: AI that buiilds with you'. *GitHub*. github.com/features/copilot.

Giuseppina, C. and D'Amico, A. (2019) 'Building energy performance forecasting: a multiple linear regression approach'. *Applied Energy*, 253. doi.org/10.1016/j.apenergy.2019.113500.

Godse, M. and Mulik, S. (2009) 'An approach for selecting software-as-a-service (SaaS) product'. In *2009 IEEE International Conference on Cloud Computing.* Bangalore, India: IEEE. doi.org/10.1109/CLOUD.2009.74.

Google (2025) 'Google Translate'. *Google*. translate.google.com/.

Google Cloud (2025a) 'AutoML Video Intelligence products'. *Google Cloud*. cloud.google.com/video-intelligence/automl/docs.

Google Cloud (2025b) 'Accelerate AI development with Google Cloud TPUs'. *Google Cloud*. cloud.google.com/tpu/.

Google Cloud (2025c) 'Document AI'. *Google Cloud*. cloud.google.com/document-ai#section-2.

Google Cloud (2025d) 'Turn speech into text using Google AI'. *Google Cloud*. cloud.google.com/speech-to-text#section-2.

Google Cloud (2025e) 'Text-to-speech AI'. *Google Cloud*. cloud.google.com/text-to-speech#section-2.

Gupta, H. (2023) 'Machine learning forecasting: AI in weather forecasting'. *ClimateAi*. climate.ai/blog/machine-learning-forecasting-how-ai-is-improving-weather-forecasting/.

Herle, A., Channegowda, J. and Prabhu, D. (2020) 'Quasar detection using linear support vector machine with learning from mistakes methodology'. In *2020 IEEE International Conference on Electronics, Computing and Communication Technologies.* Bangalore, India: IEEE. doi.org/10.1109/CONECCT50063.2020.9198529.

Herrera, P.J., Pajares, G. and Guijarro, M. (2012) 'A case-based reasoning system for recommending cooking recipes'. In Cai, K. (ed). *Java in Academia and Research*, 2nd edn. Hong Kong: iConcept Press.

HiSilicon Technologies (2025) 'Kirin 970'. *HiSilicon*. hisilicon.com/en/products/Kirin/Kirin-flagship-chips/Kirin-970.

House, A. and Agah, A. (2015) 'Autonomous evolution of digital art using genetic algorithms'. *Journal of Intelligent Systems*, 25 (3), 319–333. doi.org/10.1515/jisys-2014-0173.

Hussain, M., Afrin, S., Irin, A. and Park, S.K. (2021) 'Applying decision tree algorithm for air quality prediction in Bangladesh'. In *2021 5th International Conference on Electrical Information and Communication Technology*. Khulna, Bangladesh: IEEE. doi.org/10.1109/eict54103.2021.9733443.

IBM (2025a) 'Welcome to the IBM TechXchange Community'. *IBM*. community.ibm.com/community/user/my-community.

IBM (2025b) 'IBM Watson Studio'. *IBM*. ibm.com/products/watson-studio.

IBM (2025c) 'watsonx Assistant'. *IBM*. ibm.com/products/watsonx-assistant.

IEEE (2024) 'The IEEE global initiative 2.0 on ethics of autonomous and intelligent systems'. *IEEE SA*. standards.ieee.org/industry-connections/activities/ieee-global-initiative/.

ImageNet (2025) Home page. *ImageNet*. image-net.org/.

Ingram, M. (2019) 'A point-based Bayesian hierarchical model to predict the outcome of tennis matches'. *Journal of Quantitative Analysis in Sports*, 15 (4), 313–325. doi.org/10.1515/jqas-2018-0008.

Iovino, M., Scukins, E., Styrud, J., Ögren, P. and Smith, C. (2022) 'A survey of behavior trees in robotics and AI'. *Robotics and Autonomous Systems*, 154, 104096. doi.org/10.1016/j.robot.2022.104096.

ISO (2018) *ISO 26262-1:2018 Road Vehicles – Functional Safety – Part 1: Vocabulary*. iso.org/standard/68383.html.

ISO (2020) *ISO/IEC TR 29119-11:2020 Software and Systems Engineering – Software Testing – Part 11: Guidelines on the Testing of AI-based Systems*. iso.org/standard/79016.html.

ISO (2022) *ISO 21448:2022: Road Vehicles – Safety of the Intended Functionality*. iso.org/standard/77490.html.

Jiang, L., Liu, L., Yao, J. and Shi, L. (2020) 'A hybrid recommendation model in social media based on deep emotion analysis and multi-source view fusion'. *Journal of Cloud Computing*, 9, 57. doi.org/10.1186/s13677-020-00199-2.

Joy, S.M., Reich, R.M. and Reynolds, R.T. (2003) 'A non-parametric, supervised classification of vegetation types on the Kaibab National Forest using decision trees'. *International Journal of Remote Sensing*, 24 (9), 1835–1852.

Kaggle (2025) 'Level up with the largest AI & ML community'. *Kaggle*. kaggle.com/.

Katoch, S., Chauhan, S.S. and Kumar, V. (2020) 'A review on genetic algorithm: past, present, and future'. *Multimedia Tools and Applications*, 80 (5), 8091–8126. doi.org/10.1007/s11042-020-10139-6.

Keras (2025) 'A superpower for ML developers'. *Keras*. keras.io/.

Khairani, N.A. and Sutoyo, E. (2020) 'Application of K-means clustering algorithm for determination of fire-prone areas utilizing hotspots in West Kalimantan Province'. *International Journal of Advances in Data and Information Systems*, 1 (1), 9–16. doi.org/10.25008/ijadis.v1i1.13.

Kilari, H., Edara, S., Yarra, G.R.S. and Gadhiraju, D.V. (2022) 'Customer segmentation using K-means clustering'. *International Journal of Engineering Research & Technology*, 11 (3), 303–308. ijert.org/research/customer-segmentation-using-k-means-clustering-IJERTV11IS030152.pdf.

Kim, Y. and Vasarhelyi, M. (2023) 'Anomaly detection with the density based spatial clustering of applications with noise (DBSCAN) to detect potentially fraudulent wire transfers'. *The International Journal of Digital Accounting Research*, 24, 57–91. doi. org/10.4192/1577-8517-v24_3.

Kober, J., Bagnell, J.A. and Peters, J. (2013) 'Reinforcement learning in robotics: a survey'. *The International Journal of Robotics Research*, 32 (11), 1238–1274. doi.org/10.1177/0278364913495721.

Kobler, A. and Adamic, M. (2000) 'Identifying brown bear habitat by a combined GIS and machine learning method'. *Ecological Modelling*, 135 (2–3), 291–300. doi.org/10.1016/s0304-3800(00)00384-7.

Korol, T. (2012) 'Fuzzy logic in financial management'. In Dadios, E.P. (ed). *Fuzzy Logic: Emerging Technologies and Applications*. London: InTechOpen. doi.org/10.5772/35574.

Kumar, S. and Goudar, R.H. (2012) 'Cloud computing – research issues, challenges, architecture, platforms and applications: a survey'. *International Journal of Future Computer and Communication*, 1 (4), 356–360. doi.org/10.7763/ijfcc.2012.v1.95.

Kwon, O.B. and Sadeh, N. (2004) 'Applying case-based reasoning and multi-agent intelligent system to context-aware comparative shopping'. *Decision Support Systems*, 37 (2), 199–213. doi.org/10.1016/s0167-9236(03)00007-1.

Lahkar, B. and Singh, J. (2022) 'Twitter text sentiment analysis: a comparative study on unigram and bigram feature extractions'. *International Research Journal of Engineering and Technology*, 9 (8), 431–443. irjet.net/archives/V9/i8/IRJET-V9I870.pdf.

Lamini, C., Benhlima, S. and Elbekri, A. (2018) 'Genetic algorithm based approach for autonomous mobile robot path planning'. *Procedia Computer Science*, 127, 180–189. doi.org/10.1016/j.procs.2018.01.113.

learn.microsoft (2025) 'The Microsoft Cognitive Toolkit'. *Learn*. learn.microsoft.com/en-us/cognitive-toolkit/.

Lee, K.J. (2021) 'Architecture of neural processing unit for deep neural networks'. *Advances in Computers*, 122, 217–245. sciencedirect.com/science/article/abs/pii/S0065245820300887.

Liu, L., Lu, S., Lu, Y. and Suen, C.Y. (2014) 'Application of PR techniques to mail sorting in China'. *Proceedings of the 2014 International C* Conference on Computer Science & Software Engineering (C3S2E '14)*, Article 11, 1–7. doi.org/10.1145/2641483.2641536.

Maconi, S. (2019) 'Brexit: the predictors of a district majority vote'. *Department of Statistics, Uppsala University*, 1–36. Available at: diva-portal.org/smash/get/diva2:1326768/FULLTEXT01.pdf.

Manojlovic, T. and Stajduhar, I. (2015) 'Predicting stock market trends using random forests: a sample of the Zagreb stock exchange'. In *2015 38th International Convention on Information and Communication Technology, Electronics and Microelectronics (MIPRO)*. Opatija, Croatia: IEEE. doi.org/10.1109/mipro.2015.7160456.

Marreddy, M. and Mamidi, R.M. (2023) 'Learning sentiment analysis with word embeddings'. In *Hybrid Computational Intelligence for Pattern Analysis and Understanding, Computational Intelligence Applications for Text and Sentiment Data Analysis*. Cambridge, MA: Academic Press. doi.org/10.1016/b978-0-32-390535-0.00011-2.

Masood, R.F. (2017) 'Application of fuzzy logic in design of smart washing machine'. *arXiv*. arxiv.org/abs/1701.01654.

McCarthy, J., Minsky, M., Shannon, C.E. and Rochester, N. (1955) *A Proposal for the Dartmouth Summer Research Project on Artificial Intelligence*. Stanford, CA: Dartmouth College, Stanford University.

Metsis, V., Androutsopoulos, I. and Paliouras, G. (2006) 'Spam filtering with naive Bayes: which naive Bayes?' In *CEAS 2006: The Third Conference on Email and Anti-Spam*. Mountain View, CA: CEAS. ceas.cc/2006/9.pdf.

Microsoft Azure (2025) 'Azure AI search'. *Microsoft*. azure.microsoft.com/en-us/products/search.

Minnie, D. and Srinivasan, S. (2011) 'Intelligent search engine algorithms on indexing and searching of text documents using text representation'. In *2011 International Conference on Recent Trends in Information Systems*. Kolkata, India: IEEE. doi.org/10.1109/retis.2011.6146852.

Mobileye (2025) 'EyeQ™'. *Mobileye*. mobileye.com/technology/eyeq-chip/.

Mottahedi, M., Mohammadpour, A., Amiri, S.S., Riley, D. and Asadi, S. (2015) 'Multi-linear regression models to predict the annual energy consumption of an office building with different shapes'. *Procedia Engineering*, 118, 622–629. doi.org/10.1016/j.proeng.2015.08.495.

Murrugarra-Llerena, J., Kirsten, L. and Jung, C.R. (2022) 'Can we trust bounding box annotations for object detection?' In *2022 IEEE/CVF Conference on Computer Vision and Pattern Recognition Workshops (CVPRW)*. New Orleans, LA: IEEE. doi.org/10.1109/cvprw56347.2022.00528.

Muti, S. and Yıldız, K. (2023) 'Using linear regression for used car price prediction'. *International Journal of Computational and Experimental Science and Engineering*, 9 (1), 11–16. doi.org/10.22399/ijcesen.1070505.

Myers, K.L. (2023) 'A procedural knowledge approach to task-level control'. In *Proceedings of the Third Artificial Intelligence Planning Systems Conference*. Washington, DC: Association for the Advancement of Artificial Intelligence. aaai.org/papers/020-AIPS96-020-a-procedural-knowledge-approach-to-task-level-control/.

Natural Language Toolkit (2025) 'Documentation: Natural Language Toolkit'. *NLTK*. nltk.org/.

NVIDIA (2025) 'The core of AI'. *NVIDIA*. nvidia.com/en-us/data-center/volta-gpu-architecture/.

OpenAI (2025a) 'What can I help with?'.*ChatGPT*. openai.com/chatgpt/.

OpenAI (2025b) 'Models'. *OpenAI Platform*. platform.openai.com/docs/models.

Orr, J. and Dutta, A. (2023) 'Multi-agent deep reinforcement learning for multi-robot applications: a survey'. *Sensors*, 23 (7), 3625. doi.org/10.3390/s23073625.

Oyelade, J., Isewon, I., Oladipupo, F., Aromolaran, O., Uwoghiren, E., Ameh, F., Achas, M. and Adebiyi, E. (2016) 'Clustering algorithms: their application to gene expression data'. *Bioinformatics and Biology Insights*, 10, 237–253. doi.org/10.4137/bbi.s38316.

Pagnis, A., Tembhre, V. and Vyas, P. (2021) 'Technological singularity: an overview of what the future holds'. *International Journal of Computer Engineering in Research Trends*, 8 (10), 171–174. doi.org/10.22362/ijcert/2021/v8/i10/v8i101.

Pal, M. and Parija, S. (2021) 'Prediction of heart diseases using random forest'. *Journal of Physics: Conference Series*, 1817 (1), 012009. doi.org/10.1088/1742-6596/1817/1/012009.

Palatty, N.J. (2025) '81 phishing attack statistics 2025: the ultimate insight'. *Astra*. getastra.com/blog/security-audit/phishing-attack-statistics/.

Panigrahi, S., Kundu, A., Sural, S. and Majumdar, A.K. (2009) 'Credit card fraud detection: a fusion approach using Dempster–Shafer theory and Bayesian learning'. *Information Fusion*, 10 (4), 354–363. doi.org/10.1016/j.inffus.2008.04.001.

Pathak, M.J., Patel, R.L. and Rami, S.P. (2018) 'Comparative analysis of search algorithms'. *International Journal of Computer Applications*, 179 (50), 40–45. ijcaonline.org/archives/volume179/number50/pathak-2018-ijca-917358.pdf.

PyTorch (2025) 'Get started'. *PyTorch*. pytorch.org/.

Raja, K. and Ramathilagam, S. (2021) 'Washing machine using fuzzy logic controller to provide wash quality'. *Soft Computing*, 25 (15), 9957–9965. doi.org/10.1007/s00500-020-05477-4.

Razali, N., Mustapha, A., Yatim, F.A. and Ab Aziz, R. (2017) 'Predicting football matches results using Bayesian networks for English Premier League (EPL)'. *IOP Conference Series: Materials Science and Engineering*, 226, 1–6. doi.org/10.1088/1757-899x/226/1/012099.

Reddit (2025) Home page. *Reddit*. reddit.com/.

Reynolds, J., Ahmad, M.W. and Rezgui, Y. (2018) 'Holistic modelling techniques for the operational optimisation of multi-vector energy systems'. *Energy and Buildings*, 169, 397–416. doi.org/10.1016/j.enbuild.2018.03.065.

Rivas-Gomez, S., Pena, A.J., Moloney, D., Laure, E. and Markidis, S. (2018) 'Exploring the vision processing unit as co-processor for inference'. In *2018 IEEE International Parallel and Distributed Processing Symposium Workshops (IPDPSW)*. Vancouver, Canada: IEEE. doi.org/10.1109/ipdpsw.2018.00098.

Russell, S. and Norvig, P. (2020). *Artificial Intelligence: A Modern Approach*, 4th edn. Hoboken, New Jersey: Pearson.

Sadriu, L. (2023) 'Personalized investment recommendations using recommendation systems: meeting the growing demand for tailored investment solutions for institutional investors'. Master thesis, Lund University School of Economics and Management. lup.lub.lu.se/luur/download?func=downloadFile&recordOId=9119216&fileOId=9119217.

Salman, A.D. (2023) 'Gene expression analysis via spatial clustering and evaluation indexing'. *Iraqi Journal for Computer Science and Mathematics*, 4 (1), 4. doi.org/10.52866/ijcsm.2023.01.01.004.

Sarkar, S. (2018) 'A survey of Apple A11 bionic processor'. *ResearchGate*. researchgate. net/publication/340580371_A_survey_of_Apple_A11_Bionic_processor.

Scikit-learn (2025) 'Machine learning in Python'. *Scikit Learn*. scikit-learn.org/stable/ index.html.

Servos, D. and Osborn, S.L. (2017) 'Current research and open problems in attribute-based access control'. *ACM Computing Surveys*, 49 (4), 1–43. doi.org/10.1145/3007204.

Shah, K., Salunke, A., Dongare, S. and Antala, K. (2017) 'Recommender systems: an overview of different approaches to recommendations'. In *2017 International Conference on Innovations in Information, Embedded and Communication Systems (ICIIECS)*. Coimbatore, India: IEEE. doi.org/10.1109/ICIIECS.2017.8276172.

Shakya, A.K., Pillai, G. and Chakrabarty, S. (2023) 'Reinforcement learning algorithms: a brief survey'. *Expert Systems with Applications*, 231, 120495. doi.org/10.1016/j. eswa.2023.120495.

Shaziayani, W.N., Ul-Saufie, A.Z., Mutalib, S., Mohamad Noor, N. and Zainordin, N.S. (2022) 'Classification prediction of PM10 concentration using a tree-based machine learning approach'. *Atmospheric Techniques, Instruments, and Modeling*, 13 (4), 538. doi.org/10.3390/atmos13040538.

Shi, Y. (2024) 'Unveiling the powerhouses of AI: a comprehensive study of GPU, FPGA, and ASIC accelerators'. *Applied and Computational Engineering*, 50 (1), 97–105. doi.org/10.54254/2755-2721/50/20241251.

Stack Overflow (2025) 'Newest questions'. *Stack Overflow*. stackoverflow.com/questions.

Stahlberg, F. (2020) 'Neural machine translation: a review'. *Journal of Artificial Intelligence Research*, 69, 343–418. doi.org/10.1613/jair.1.12007.

Stiers, D., Daoust, J.-F. and Blais, A. (2018) 'What makes people believe that their party won the election?' *Electoral Studies*, 55, 21–29. doi.org/10.1016/j.electstud.2018.07.002.

Tableau (2025) 'Fuel faster data, insights, and action with Tableau Next'. *Tableau*. tableau.com/.

Takale, S., Bhong, T., Dethe, U. and Gandhi, P. (2022) 'Sales prediction using linear regression'. *Journal of Electronics, Computer Networking and Applied Mathematics*, 2 (5), 62–71. doi.org/10.55529/jecnam.25.62.71.

Tapjinda, T., Vechpanich, P., Leelasupakul, N., Prompoon, N. and Patanothai, C. (2015) 'An automated stock recommendation system from stock investment research using domain specific information extraction'. In *2015 12th International Joint Conference on Computer Science and Software Engineering*. Songkhla, Thailand: IEEE. doi.org/10.1109/ jcsse.2015.7219765.

TensorFlow (2025) 'An end-to-end platform for machine learning'. *TensorFlow*. tensorflow.org/.

The Apache Software Foundation (2025) 'Apache Mxnet: a flexible and efficient library for deep learning'. *Apache MXNet*. mxnet.apache.org/.

The Washington Times (2006) 'Promise of AI not so bright'. *The Washington Times*. washingtontimes.com/news/2006/apr/13/20060413-105217-7645r/.

Topal, M.O., Bas, A. and van Heerden, I. (2021) 'Exploring transformers in natural language generation: GPT, BERT, and XLNet', *arXiv*. arxiv.org/abs/2102.08036.

Toro Medina, J.A., Wilkins, K.N., Walker, M. and Stahl, G.M. (2016) 'Autonomous operations system: development and application'. *Annual Conference of the PHM Society*, 8 (1), 1–11. doi.org/10.36001/phmconf.2016.v8i1.2588.

Uludağlı, M.Ç. and Oğuz, K. (2023) 'Non-player character decision-making in computer games'. *Artificial Intelligence Review*, 56, 14159–14191. doi.org/10.1007/s10462-023-10491-7.

Vasanthi, P. and Mohan, L. (2024) 'Efficient YOLOv8 algorithm for extreme small-scale object detection'. *Digital Signal Processing*, 154, 104682. doi.org/10.1016/j.dsp.2024.104682.

Vidler, A. (2022) 'Recommender systems in financial trading: using machine-based conviction analysis in an explainable AI investment framework'. *arXiv*. arxiv.org/html/2404.11080v1.

Voogd, K.L., Allamaa, J.P., Alonso-Mora, J. and Son, T.D. (2023) 'Reinforcement learning from simulation to real world autonomous driving using digital twin'. *IFAC-PapersOnLine*, 56 (2), 1510–1515. doi.org/10.1016/j.ifacol.2023.10.1846.

Wang, X., Zhang, L. and Liu, Y. (2016) 'Research and design of a rules engine for bank anti-fraud platform'. In *Proceedings of the 2016 International Conference on Engineering Management (Iconf-EM 2016)*. Atlantis Press. doi.org/10.2991/iconfem-16.2016.45.

Wen, Y., Lu, Y. and Shi, P. (2007) 'Handwritten Bangla numeral recognition system and its application to postal automation'. *Pattern Recognition*, 40 (1), 99–107. doi.org/10.1016/j.patcog.2006.07.001.

Willemsen, P.G. and Eyer, L. (2008) 'A study of supervised classification of Hipparcos variable stars using PCA and Support Vector Machines'. *arXiv*. doi.org/10.48550/arXiv.0712.2898.

Wu, L., Garg, S.K. and Buyya, R. (2015) 'Service level agreement (SLA) based SaaS cloud management system'. In *2015 IEEE 21st International Conference on Parallel and Distributed Systems (ICPADS)*. Melbourne, Australia: IEEE. doi.org/10.1109/icpads.2015.62.

Wu, X. and Zeng, Y. (2019) 'Using apriori algorithm on students' performance data for association rules mining'. In *Proceedings of the 2nd International Seminar on Education Research and Social Science (ISERSS 2019)*. Atlantis Press. doi.org/10.2991/iserss-19.2019.300.

Wu, Y. (2023) 'Stock price prediction based on simple decision tree random forest and XGBoost'. *BCP Business & Management*, 38, 3383–3388. doi.org/10.54691/bcpbm.v38i.4311.

xAI (2025) 'Grok: your truth-seeking AI companion'. *GROK*. x.ai/grok.

Yadav, A.B. (2024) 'An analysis on the use of image design with generative AI technologies'. *International Journal of Trend in Scientific Research and Development*, 8 (1), 596–599. ijtsrd.com/papers/ijtsrd63468.pdf.

Zhai, A., Wu, H.-Y., Tzeng, E., Park, D.H. and Rosenberg, C. (2019) 'Learning a unified embedding for visual search at Pinterest'. *KDD '19: Proceedings of the 25th ACM*

SIGKDD International Conference on Knowledge Discovery & Data Mining, 2412–2420. doi.org/10.1145/3292500.3330739.

Zhang, Y., Carballo, A., Yang, H. and Takeda, K. (2023) 'Perception and sensing for autonomous vehicles under adverse weather conditions: a survey'. *ISPRS Journal of Photogrammetry and Remote Sensing*, 196, 146–177. doi.org/10.1016/j.isprsjprs.2022.12.021.

Zheng, J. and Zhang, J. (2016) 'The application of association rules mining in the analysis of students' test scores'. In *Proceedings of the 2016 International Conference on Education, Management and Computer Science*. Atlantis Press. doi.org/10.2991/icemc-16.2016.3.

CHAPTER 2

Amodei, D., Olah, C., Steinhardt, J., Christiano, P., Schulman, J. and Mané, D. (2016) 'Concrete problems in AI safety'. *arXiv*. arxiv.org/abs/1606.

Anandhan, A., Shuib, L., Ismail, M.A. and Mujtaba, G. (2018) 'Social media recommender systems: review and open research issues'. *IEEE Access*, 6, 15608–15628. doi.org/10.1109/access.2018.2810062.

Ashwin, S.H. and Raj, R.N. (2023) 'Deep reinforcement learning for autonomous vehicles: lane keep and overtaking scenarios with collision avoidance'. *International Journal of Information Technology*, 15 (7), 3541–3553. doi.org/10.1007/s41870-023-01412-6.

Dhaval, B. and Deshpande, A. (2020) 'Short-term load forecasting with using multiple linear regression'. *International Journal of Electrical and Computer Engineering*, 10 (4), 3911–3917. doi.org/10.11591/ijece.v10i4.pp3911-3917.

Drage, E. and Mackereth, K. (2022) 'Does AI debias recruitment? Race, gender, and AI's "eradication of difference"'. *Philosophy & Technology*, 35 (4), 89. doi.org/10.1007/s13347-022-00543-1.

Dussa-Zieger, K., Henschelchen, W., Kocher, V., Liu, Q., Reid, S., Siemens, K. and Smith, A.L. (2021) *Certified Tester AI Testing (CT-AI) Syllabus v.1.0*. International Software Testing Qualifications Board. astqb.org/assets/documents/ISTQB_CT-AI_Syllabus_v1.0.pdf.

European Commission (2019) 'Ethics guidelines for trustworthy AI'. *European Commission*. digital-strategy.ec.europa.eu/en/library/ethics-guidelines-trustworthy-ai.

Giuseppina, C. and D'Amico, A. (2019) 'Building energy performance forecasting: a multiple linear regression approach'. *Applied Energy*, 253, 113500. doi.org/10.1016/j.apenergy.2019.113500.

Gujarathi, A., Kulkarni, A., Patil, U., Phalak, Y., Deotalu, R., Jain, A., Panchi, N., Dhabale, A. and Chiddarwar, S. (2021) 'Design and development of autonomous delivery robot'. *arXiv*. doi.org/10.48550/arxiv.2103.09229.

House, A. and Agah, A. (2015) 'Autonomous evolution of digital art using genetic algorithms'. *Journal of Intelligent Systems*, 25 (3), 319–333. doi.org/10.1515/jisys-2014-0173.

Li, H., Qi, G., He, N. and Xinri, D. (2021) 'Shopping recommendation system design based on deep learning'. In *6th International Conference on Intelligent Computing and Signal Processing (ICSP)*. Xi'an, China: IEEE. doi.org/10.1109/icsp51882.2021.9409009.

Li, X., Chen, Z., Zhang, J.M., Sarro, F., Zhang, Y. and Liu, X. (2024) 'Bias behind the wheel: fairness testing of autonomous driving systems'. *arXiv*. doi.org/10.48550/arXiv.2308.02935.

Liao, S.M. (2023) 'Ethics of AI and health care: towards a substantive human rights framework'. *Topoi*, 42, 857–866. doi.org/10.1007/s11245-023-09911-8.

Myers, K., Berry, P., Blythe, J., Conley, K., Gervasio, M., McGuinness, D.L., Morley, D., Pfeffer, A., Pollack, M. and Tambe, M. (2007) 'An intelligent personal assistant for task and time management'. *AI Magazine*, 28 (2), 47–61. doi.org/10.1609/aimag.v28i2.2039.

OECD (2019) *G20 Ministerial Statement on Trade and Digital Economy. OECD.AI*. wp.oecd.ai/app/uploads/2021/06/G20-AI-Principles.pdf.

OECD (2024) 'Recommendation of the Council on artificial intelligence'. *OECD Legal Instruments*. legalinstruments.oecd.org/en/instruments/OECD-LEGAL-0449.

Parekh, D., Poddar, N., Rajpurkar, A., Chahal, M., Kumar, N., Joshi, G.P. and Cho, W. (2022) 'A review on autonomous vehicles: progress, methods and challenges'. *Electronics*, 11 (14), 2162. doi.org/10.3390/electronics11142162.

Royal Society (2019) *Explainable AI: The Basics*. Policy briefing DES6051. London: Royal Society. royalsociety.org/-/media/policy/projects/explainable-ai/AI-and-interpretability-policy-briefing.pdf.

SAE International (2021) 'Taxonomy and definitions for terms related to driving automation systems for on-road motor vehicles'. *SAE International*. sae.org/standards/content/j3016_202104/.

Sarraf, S. (2020) 'Current stage of autonomous driving through a quick survey for novice'. *American Scientific Research Journal for Engineering, Technology, and Sciences*, 73 (1), 1–7. asrjetsjournal.org/index.php/American_Scientific_Journal/article/view/6320.

Shah, K., Salunke, A., Dongare, S. and Antala, K. (2017) 'Recommender systems: an overview of different approaches to recommendations'. In *2017 International Conference on Innovations in Information, Embedded and Communication Systems (ICIIECS)*. Coimbatore, India: IEEE. doi.org/10.1109/ICIIECS.2017.8276172.

UNESCO (2021) 'Recommendation on the ethics of artificial intelligence'. SHS/BIO/REC-AIETHICS/2021. *UNESDOC Digital Library*. unesdoc.unesco.org/ark:/48223/pf0000380455.

Wilson, B., Hoffman, J. and Morgenstern, J. (2019) 'Predictive inequity in object detection'. *arXiv*. arxiv.org/pdf/1902.11097.

Yadav, A.B. (2024) 'An analysis on the use of image design with generative AI technologies'. *International Journal of Trend in Scientific Research and Development*, 8 (1), 596–599. ijtsrd.com/papers/ijtsrd63468.pdf.

Zhang, Y., Carballo, A., Yang, H. and Takeda, K. (2023) 'Perception and sensing for autonomous vehicles under adverse weather conditions: a survey'. *ISPRS Journal of Photogrammetry and Remote Sensing*, 196, 146–177. doi.org/10.1016/j.isprsjprs.2022.12.021.

CHAPTER 3

Ashwin, S.H. and Raj, R.N. (2023) `Deep reinforcement learning for autonomous vehicles: lane keep and overtaking scenarios with collision avoidance'. *International Journal of Information Technology*, 15 (7), 3541–3553. doi.org/10.1007/s41870-023-01412-6.

Asperti, A., Evangelista, D. and Piccolomini, E.L. (2021) 'A survey on variational autoencoders from a green AI perspective'. *SN Computer Science*, 2 (4), 301. doi.org/10.1007/s42979-021-00702-9.

Graesser, L. and Keng, W.L. (2019) *Foundations of Deep Reinforcement Learning: Theory and Practice in Python*. Boston: Addison-Wesley Professional.

Guo, X., Okamura, H. and Dohi, T. (2022) 'Automated software test data generation with generative adversarial networks'. *IEEE Access*, 10, 20690–20700. doi.org/10.1109/ACCESS.2022.3153347.

Ng, A.Y. and Jordan, M.I. (2001) 'On discriminative vs generative classifiers: a comparison of logistic regression and naive Bayes'. In Dietterich, T., Becker, S. and Ghahramani, Z. (eds). *Advances in Neural Information Processing Systems 14 (NIPS 2001)*. NeurIPS Proceedings. papers.nips.cc/paper_files/paper/2001/hash/7b7a53e239400a13bd6be6c91c4f6c4e-Abstract.html.

Raiaan, M.A.K., Mukta, Md.S.H., Fatema, K., Fahad, N.M., Sakib, S. and Mim, M.M.J. (2024) 'A review on large language models: architectures, applications, taxonomies, open issues and challenges'. *IEEE Access*, 12, 26839–26874. doi.org/10.1109/access.2024.3365742.

Yadav, A. (2015) 'AGILE: software development model'. *International Journal of Engineering and Technical Research*, 3 (3), 11–17. erpublication.org/published_paper/IJETR031503.pdf.

Xie, H. (2021) 'Research and case analysis of apriori algorithm based on mining frequent item-sets'. *Open Journal of Social Sciences*, 9 (4), 458–468. doi.org/10.4236/jss.2021.94034.

CHAPTER 4

Amazon (2025) 'Amazon Mechanical Turk'. *Amazon Mechanical Turk*. mturk.com/ .

Apache Software Foundation (2025) 'Apache Kafka'. *Kafka*. kafka.apache.org/.

Ben-David, A. (2008) 'Comparison of classification accuracy using Cohen's Weighted Kappa'. *Expert Systems with Applications*, 34 (2), 825–832. doi.org/10.1016/j.eswa.2006.10.022.

Clickworker (2025) 'AI training data'. *Clickworker*. clickworker.com/.

Huyen, C. (2025) *AI Engineering: Building Applications with Foundation Models*. Sebastopol, CA: O'Reilly Media.

Matplotlib (2025) 'Matplotlib: visualization with Python'. *Matplotlib*. matplotlib.org/.

NumPy (2025) Home page. *NumPy*. numpy.org/.

Pandas (2025) 'Pandas'. *Pandas*. pandas.pydata.org/.

Qiao, J., Wang, C., Guan, S. and Lv, S. (2022) 'Construction-accident narrative classification using shallow and deep learning'. *Journal of Construction Engineering and Management*, 148 (9). doi.org/10.1061/(ASCE)CO.1943-7862.0002354.

Seaborn (2025) 'Seaborn: statistical data visualization'. *Seaborn*. seaborn.pydata.org/.

Sharma, N. (2020) 'An introduction to data labeling in artificial intelligence'. *DZone*. dzone.com/articles/an-introduction-to-data-labeling-in-artificial-int.

CHAPTER 5

EEMBC (2025) 'Introducing the EEMBC MLMark Benchmark'. *EEMBC*. eembc.org/mlmark/.

Evidently AI (2025) '200 LLM benchmarks and datasets'. *Evidently AI*. evidentlyai.com/llm-evaluation-benchmarks-datasets.

MLCommons (2025) 'Better AI for everyone'. *MLCommons*. mlcommons.org/.

CHAPTER 6

Dosovitskiy, A., Beyer, L., Kolesnikov, A., Weissenborn, D., Zhai, X., Unterthiner, T., Dehghani, M., Minderer, M., Heigold, G., Gelly, S., Uszkoreit, J. and Houlsby, N. (2021) 'An image is worth 16×16 words: transformers for image recognition at scale'. In *International Conference on Learning Representations 2021*. OpenReview.net. openreview.net/forum?id=YicbFdNTTy.

Fabien, M. (2019) 'The Rosenblatt's Perceptron'. *Maël Fabien*. maelfabien.github.io/deeplearning/Perceptron/#.

HSGAC (2024) *AI in the Real World: Hedge Fund Use of Artificial Intelligence in Trading*. Report. hsgac.senate.gov/wp-content/uploads/2024.06.11-Hedge-Fund-Use-of-AI-Report.pdf.

Lin, T., Wang, Y., Liu, X. and Qiu, X. (2022) 'A survey of transformers'. *AI Open*, 3, 111–132. doi.org/10.1016/j.aiopen.2022.10.001.

Liu, Y., Ott, M., Goyal, N., Du, J., Joshi, M., Chen, D., Levy, O., Lewis, M., Zettlemoyer, L. and Stoyanov, V. (2019) 'RoBERTa: a robustly optimized BERT pretraining approach'. *arXiv*. doi.org/10.48550/arXiv.1907.11692.

Ma, Y., Wang, W. and Ma, Q. (2023) 'A novel prediction based portfolio optimization model using deep learning'. *Computers & Industrial Engineering*, 177, 109023. doi.org/10.1016/j.cie.2023.109023.

Midjourney (2025) Home page. *Midjourney*. midjourney.com/home.

Minsky, M. and Papert, S. (1969) *Perceptrons: An Introduction to Computational Geometry*. Cambridge, MA: The MIT Press.

Moussad, B., Roche, R. and Bhattacharya, D. (2023) 'The transformative power of transformers in protein structure prediction'. *Proceedings of the National Academy of Sciences of the United States of America*, 120 (32), e2303499120. doi.org/10.1073/pnas.2303499120.

Nepal Rastra Bank (2020) *Guidelines for Suspicious Transactions Reporting (STR)*. Nepal: Financial Information Unit, Nepal Rastra Bank.

OpenAI (2025a) 'Models'. *OpenAI Platform*. platform.openai.com/docs/models.

OpenAI (2025b) 'DALL-E: creating images from text'. *OpenAI*. openai.com/index/dall-e/.

Reimers, N. and Gurevych I. (2019) 'Sentence-BERT: sentence embeddings using Siamese BERT-networks'. *arXiv*. doi.org/10.48550/arXiv.1908.10084.

Sanh, V., Debut, L., Chaumond, J. and Wolf, T. (2019) 'DistilBERT, a distilled version of BERT: smaller, faster, cheaper and lighter'. *arXiv*. doi.org/10.48550/arXiv.1910.01108.

Usman, M., Sun, Y., Gopinath, D., Dange, R., Manolache, L. and Păsăreanu, C.S. (2022) 'An overview of structural coverage metrics for testing neural networks'. *International Journal on Software Tools for Technology Transfer*, 25 (3), 393–405. doi.org/10.1007/s10009-022-00683-x.

Uszkoreit, J. (2017) 'Transformer: a novel neural network architecture for language understanding'. *Google Research*. research.google/blog/transformer-a-novel-neural-network-architecture-for-language-understanding/.

Visa (2023) 'Response to Treasury on the payments system modernisation (licensing: defining payment functions) consultation paper'. treasury.gov.au/sites/default/files/2023-12/c2023-403207-visa.pdf.

CHAPTER 7

CBS News (2018) 'Amazon's Alexa is laughing at users & creeping them out'. *CBS News*. cbsnews.com/texas/news/amazon-alexa-laughing/.

Cerquozzi, R., Decoutere, W., Riverin, J.F., Hryszko, A., Klonk, M., Posthuma, M., Riou du Cosquer, E., Roman, A., Stapp, L., Ulrich, S. and Zakaria, E. (2024) *Certified Tester Foundation Level Syllabus*. International Software Testing Qualifications Board. istqb.org/wp-content/uploads/2024/11/ISTQB_CTFL_Syllabus_v4.0.1.pdf.

Kaner, C.J.D. (2022) 'Lecture 1: overview and basic definitions'. In *Black Box Software Testing Foundations*. Romania: BBST. bbst.courses/wp-content/uploads/2024/02/BBST%C2%AEFoundations2022.pdf.

Lika, B., Kolomvatsos, K. and Hadjiefthymiades, S. (2014) 'Facing the cold start problem in recommender systems'. *Expert Systems with Applications*, 41 (4), 2065–2073. doi.org/10.1016/j.eswa.2013.09.005.

Reddit (2022) 'The amount of spam coming through is absolutely ridiculous'. *Reddit*. reddit.com/r/yahoo/comments/vgrdwb/the_amount_of_spam_coming_through_is_absolutely/.

Wang, R.Y. and Strong, D.M (1996) 'Beyond accuracy: what data quality means to data consumers'. *Journal of Management Information Systems*, 12 (4), 5–33. doi.org/10.1080/07421222.1996.11518099.

Wolfson, S. (2018) 'Amazon's Alexa recorded private conversation and sent it to random contact'. *The Guardian*. theguardian.com/technology/2018/may/24/amazon-alexa-recorded-conversation.

CHAPTER 8

Barr, E.T., Harman, M., McMinn, P., Shahbaz, M. and Yoo, S. (2015) 'The oracle problem in software testing: a survey'. *IEEE Transactions on Software Engineering*, 41 (5), 507–525. doi.org/10.1109/TSE.2014.2372785.

Buxton, J.N. and Randell, B. (eds) (1970) *Software Engineering Techniques: Report on a Conference Sponsored by the NATO Science Committee, Rome, Italy, 27th to 31st October 1969*. Brussels: Scientific Affairs Division, NATO. homepages.cs.ncl.ac.uk/brian.randell/NATO/nato1969.PDF.

Charlton, A. (2016) 'Microsoft Tay AI returns to boast of smoking weed in front of police and spam 200k followers'. *International Business Times UK*. ibtimes.co.uk/microsoft-tay-ai-returns-boast-smoking-weed-front-police-spam-200k-followers-1552164.

Dastin, J. (2018) 'Amazon scraps secret AI recruiting tool that showed bias against women'. *Reuters*. reuters.com/article/world/insight-amazon-scraps-secret-ai-recruiting-tool-that-showed-bias-against-women-idUSKCN1MK0AG/.

Dussa-Zieger, K., Henschelchen, W., Kocher, V., Liu, Q., Reid, S., Siemens, K. and Smith, A.L. (2021) *Certified Tester AI Testing (CT-AI) Syllabus v.1.0*. International Software Testing Qualifications Board. astqb.org/assets/documents/ISTQB_CT-AI_Syllabus_v1.0.pdf.

European Union (2020) 'The assessment list for trustworthy artificial intelligence (ALTAI) for self assessment'. *Publications Office of the EU*. op.europa.eu/en/publication-detail/-/publication/73552fcd-f7c2-11ea-991b-01aa75ed71a1/language-en.

Finot, O., Mottu, J.-M., Sunyé, G. and Attiogbé, C. (2013) 'Partial test oracle in model transformation testing'. In Duddy, K. and Kappel, G. (eds). *Theory and Practice of Model Transformations* (Lecture Notes in Computer Science, 7909). Berlin: Springer. doi.org/10.1007/978-3-642-38883-5_17.

Hoffman, D. (1998) 'A taxonomy for test oracles'. *Proceedings of 11th International Quality Week*. pdfs.semanticscholar.org/4939/9c41364c832dadf491c11376bd7ca38e4a8b.pdf.

Holzinger, A., Saranti, A., Molnar, C., Biecek, P. and Samek, W. (2022) 'Explainable AI methods: a brief overview'. In Holzinger, A., Goebel, R., Fong, R., Moon, T., Müller, K.R. and Samek, W. (eds). *xxAI: Beyond Explainable AI*. Cham: Springer. doi.org/10.1007/978-3-031-04083-2_2.

ISO/IEC (2023) *ISO/IEC 25010:2023: Systems and software engineering – Systems and software Quality Requirements and Evaluation (SQuaRE) – Product quality model*, 2nd edn. International Organization for Standardization. Available at: iso.org/standard/78176.html.

ISTQB (2025) 'ISTQB glossary'. *ISTQB*. Available at: glossary.istqb.org.

Kaner, C., Bach, J. and Pettichord, B. (2001) *Lessons Learned in Software Testing: A Context-Driven Approach*. New York: Wiley.

Weinberg, G.M. (1992) *Quality Software Management: Systems Thinking*. New York, USA: Dorset House Publishing Co. Inc.

YouTube (2022) 'The Testing Glossary Project'. *Paul Gerrard*. Available at: youtube.com/playlist?list=PLdOu8I-wgEwPDjVkYbmzad-hOnxq_GnY4.

Zeff, M. (2024) 'Almost all of Amazon's "just walk out" developers got laid off after checkout-less shopping was nixed'. *Quartz*. qz.com/amazon-just-walk-out-layoffs-checkout-shopping-1851391441.

CHAPTER 9

Anderson, E., Holdsworth, J. and Kosinski, M. (2024) 'What is red teaming?' *IBM Think.* ibm.com/think/topics/red-teaming.

Baisantry, M. and Shukla, D.P. (2017) 'Comparison of different similarity measures for selection of optimal, information-centric bands of hyperspectral images'. In *Pecora 20: Observing a Changing Earth; Science for Decisions – Monitoring, Assessment, and Projection, Sioux Falls, SD, November 13–16, 2017.* Baton Rouge, LA: ASPRS. asprs.org/wp-content/uploads/2018/04/Baisantry_M.pdf.

Breck, E., Cai, S., Nielsen, E., Salib, M. and Sculley, D. (2017) 'The ML test score: a rubric for ML production readiness and technical debt reduction'. In *IEEE International Conference on Big Data.* IEEE. static.googleusercontent.com/media/research.google.com/en//pubs/archive/aad9f93b86b7addfea4c419b9100c6cdd26cacea.pdf.

DeMarco, J.V. (2018) 'An approach to minimizing legal and reputational risk in red team hacking exercises'. *Computer Law & Security Review*, 34 (4), 908–911. doi.org/10.1016/j.clsr.2018.05.033.

Google (2019) 'GraphicsFuzz'. *GitHub.* github.com/google/graphicsfuzz.

Oakley, J.G. (2019) *Professional Red Teaming.* Berkeley, CA: Apress. doi.org/10.1007/978-1-4842-4309-1.

CHAPTER 10

AI4Finance Foundation (2022). 'FinRL®: financial reinforcement learning'. *GitHub.* github.com/AI4Finance-Foundation/FinRL.

Ali, A., Maghawry, H.A. and Badr, N. (2022) 'Automation of performance testing: a review'. *International Journal of Intelligent Computing and Information Sciences*, 22 (4), 35–50. doi.org/10.21608/ijicis.2022.161846.1219.

Ansys (2025) 'Products'. *Ansys.* ansys.com.

Blizzard Entertainment (2025) StarCraft II. *Blizzard.* starcraft2.blizzard.com/en-gb/.

Chandrakant, B.A. and Prakash, J.P. (2019) 'Vulnerability assessment and penetration testing as cyber defence'. *International Journal of Engineering Applied Sciences and Technology*, 4 (2), 72–76. doi.org/10.33564/ijeast.2019.v04i02.012.

Chess.com (2025) 'Play chess online'. *Chess.com.* chess.com/.

COMSOL (2025) 'COMSOL Multiphysics® Simulation Software'. *COMSOL.* comsol.com/comsol-multiphysics.

Coppelia Robotics AG (2025) 'Create. Compose. Simulate. Any robot'. *Coppelia Robotics.* coppeliarobotics.com/.

Cyberbotics Ltd (2019) 'Robotics simulation services'. *Cyberbotics.com.* cyberbotics.com/.

Deepmind (2025) 'AlphaGo'. *Google DeepMind.* deepmind.com/research/highlighted-research/alphago.

Degtiarenko, D. (2023) 'Confident innovation: digital twins for operational resilience in exchanges and CCPs'. *The World Federation of Exchanges Focus Magazine*, 76. focus.world-exchanges.org/articles/confident-innovation-digital-twins-operational-resilience-exchanges-and-ccps.

Degtiarenko, D. (2024) 'AI-driven synthetic data engineering for improved digital resilience'. *World Federation of Exchanges Focus*, 85. focus.world-exchanges.org/articles/ai-driven-synthetic.

Forex Tester Online (2025) 'Advanced backtesting software'. *Forex tester online*. forextester.com/.

Gate (2025) 'GATE'. *GATE*. opengatecollaboration.org/.

German Aerospace Center (DLR) (2025) 'SUMO user documentation'. *SUMO*. sumo.dlr.de/docs/index.html.

Gorripati, S.K., Angadi, A. and Saraswathi, P. (2021) 'Recommender systems: security threats and mechanisms'. In Al-Turjman, F. and Deebak, B.D. (eds). *Security in IoT Social Networks, Intelligent Data-Centric Systems*. Cambridge, MA: Academic Press. doi.org/10.1016/B978-0-12-821599-9.00007-8.

Goyal, M. and Mahmoud, Q.H. (2024) 'A systematic review of synthetic data generation techniques using generative AI'. *Electronic*, 13 (17), 3509. doi.org/10.3390/electronics13173509.

Gymnasium (2025) 'Gymnasium: an API standard for reinforcement learning with a diverse collection of reference environments'. *Gymnasium Documentation*. gymnasium.farama.org/.

Hoadley Trading & Investment Tools (2025) 'On-line options pricing & probability calculators'. *Hoadley Trading & Investment Tools*. hoadley.net/options/calculators.htm.

InfoReach (2025) 'InfoReach HiFREQ Strategy Server'. *InfoReach*. inforeachinc.com/broker-neutral-trading/high-frequency-strategy-testing.

Inlusion Factory of Emotions (2020) 'DICOM AI 3D VR viewer'. *iNLUSiON*. inlu.net/vr-projects/dicom-ai-3d-vr-viewer/.

Itkin, I. (2024) 'AI in capital markets summit'. *LinkedIn*. linkedin.com/pulse/ai-testing-trading-platform-test-data-generation-report-iosif-itkin-o8aof.

JPMorganChase (2023) 'A multi-agent reinforcement-learning simulator framework: jpmorganchase/Phantom'. *GitHub*. github.com/jpmorganchase/Phantom.

Li, D., Hu, B., Chen, Q., Wang, X., Qi, Q., Wang, L. and Liu, H. (2021) 'Attentive capsule network for click-through rate and conversion rate prediction in online advertising'. *Knowledge-Based Systems*, 211, 106522. doi.org/10.1016/j.knosys.2020.106522.

MathWorks (2025a) 'Simulink is for model-based design'. *MathWorks*. uk.mathworks.com/products/simulink.html.

MathWorks (2025b) 'Binomial model'. *MathWorks*. mathworks.com/discovery/binomial-model.html.

MathWorks (2025c) 'MATLAB: designed for the way you think and the work you do'. *MathWorks*. ww2.mathworks.cn/en/products/matlab.html.

Medspace (2021) 'How is virtual reality (VR) used in medicine?' *medspace^{VR}*. medspacevr.com/article.

Meta Platforms (2023) 'Habitat: a platform for embodied AI research'. *HABITAT*. aihabitat.org/.

Mojang Studios (2025) 'Discover our games'. *Minecraft*. minecraft.net/en-us.

Moradi, M., Acker, B.V. and Denil, J. (2023) 'Failure identification using model-implemented fault injection with domain knowledge-guided reinforcement learning'. *Sensors*, 23 (4), 2166. doi.org/10.3390/s23042166.

MORSE (2016) 'The MORSE simulator documentation'. *MORSE*. openrobots.org/morse/doc/stable/morse.html.

MuJoCo (2025) 'Advanced physics simulation'. *MuJoCo*. mujoco.org/.

Natural Language Toolkit (2025) 'Documentation: Natural Language Toolkit'. *NLTK*. nltk.org/.

NVIDIA (2025a), 'Accelerate autonomous vehicle AI training and development'. *NVIDIA Autonomous Vehicles*. nvidia.com/en-us/self-driving-cars/infrastructure/.

NVIDIA (2025b) 'Accelerating the future of autonomous vehicles'. *NVIDIA Autonomous Vehicles*. nvidia.com/en-us/solutions/autonomous-vehicles/.

Open Robotics (2025a) 'ROS – Robot Operating System'. *ROS*. ros.org/.

Open Robotics (2025b) 'Simulate before you build'. *GAZEBO*. gazebosim.org/home.

Portfolio Visualizer (2025) 'Tools for better investors'. *Portfolio Visualizer*. portfoliovisualizer.com/.

Simudyne (2022) ' Simudyne is the first solution provider to bring agent-based modeling into the financial enterprise'. *Simudyne*. simudyne.com/technology/agent-based-modeling/.

spaCy (2025) 'Industrial-strength natural language processing in Python'. spacy.io.

SuperGLUE (2025) 'GLUE'. *SuperGLUE*. gluebenchmark.com/.

Synopsys (2025) 'Unleash the power of Synopsys.ai'. *Synopsys*. synopsys.com/ai/ai-powered-eda.html.

Unity Technologies (2025) 'Go create'. *Unity*. unity.com.

Valve Corporation (2025) 'A modern multiplayer masterpiece'. *Dota 2*. dota2.com/home.

Waymo (2025) 'Access Waymo open dataset'. *Waymo*. waymo.com/open/.

Ziggma (2025) 'Make your portfolio better – with each trade'. *ZIGGMA*. ziggma.com/portfolio-simulator/.

CHAPTER 11

Applitools (2025a) 'The AI-powered testing platform built for speed, scalability and accuracy'. *Applitools*. applitools.com.

Applitools (2025b) 'Test manager'. *Applitools*. applitools.com/tutorials/concepts/applitools-test-manager.

Bug Prediction Dataset (2025) Bug prediction dataset. *Bug Prediction Dataset*. bug.inf.usi.ch/download.php.

EuroSTAR Huddle (2019) 'New Software Testing Model'. *Paul Gerrard/TEST Huddle*. Available at: huddle.eurostarsoftwaretesting.com/resources/test-management/a-new-model-for-testing/.

Exactpro (2024) 'AI-enabled software testing for ARTEX MTF'. *Exactpro*. exactpro.com/case-study/trading-systems/ai-enabled-software-testing-artex-mtf.

Exactpro (2025) 'AI testing'. *Exactpro*. exactpro.com/ai-testing.

Guo, X., Okamura, H. and Dohi, T. (2022) 'Automated software test data generation with generative adversarial networks'. *IEEE Access*, 10, 20690–20700. doi.org/10.1109/ACCESS.2022.3153347.

Harman, M. (2012) 'The role of artificial intelligence in software engineering'. In *2012 First International Workshop on Realizing AI Synergies in Software Engineering (RAISE)*. Zurich: IEEE. doi.org/10.1109/raise.2012.6227961.

Hu, Y., Wang, X., Wang, Y., Zhang, Y., Guo, S., Chen, C., Wang, X. and Zhou, Y. (2024) 'AUITestAgent: automatic requirements oriented GUI function testing'. *arXiv*. arxiv.org/html/2407.09018v1.

ISO (2024) *ISO/IEC 25002:2024 – Systems and Software Engineering – Systems and Software Quality Requirements and Evaluation (SQuaRE) – Quality Model Overview and Usage*. iso.org/standard/78175.html.

Karatayev, A., Ogorodova, A. and Shamoi, P. (2024) 'Fuzzy inference system for test case prioritization in software testing'. *arXiv*. arxiv.org/abs/2404.16395.

Mao, K., Harman, M. and Jia, Y. (2016) 'Sapienz: multi-objective automated testing for Android applications'. In *ISSTA 2016: Proceedings of the 25th International Symposium on Software Testing and Analysis*. New York: Association for Computing Machinery. doi.org/10.1145/2931037.2931054.

Misirli, A.T., Bener, A. and Kale, R. (2011) 'AI-based software defect predictors: applications and benefits in a case study'. *AI Magazine*, 32 (2), 1–12. doi.org/10.1609/aimag.v32i2.2348.

Nagappan, N., Murphy, B. and Basili, V.R. (2008) 'The influence of organizational structure on software quality: an empirical case study'. In *ICSE '08: Proceedings of the 30th International Conference on Software Engineering*. New York: Association for Computing Machinery. doi.org/10.1145/1368088.1368160.

Nagy, S.M., Maghawry, H.A. and Badr, N.L. (2023) 'An enhanced approach for test suite reduction using clustering and genetic algorithms'. *Journal of Theoretical and Applied Information Technology*, 101 (11), 4287–4300. jatit.org/volumes/Vol101No11/15Vol101No11.pdf.

Nassif, A.B., Talib, M.A., Azzeh, M., Alzaabi, S., Khanfar, R., Kharsa, R. and Angelis, L. (2023) 'Software defect prediction using learning to rank approach'. *Scientific Reports*, 13 (1), 18885. doi.org/10.1038/s41598-023-45915-5.

Peng, X. (2022) 'Research on software defect prediction and analysis based on machine learning'. *Journal of Physics: Conference Series*, 2173, 012043. doi.org/10.1088/1742-6596/2173/1/012043.

Prasad, A. (2018) 'From visual AI inception to application visual management (AVM)'. *Applitools*. applitools.com/blog/product-release-applitools-v10-our-enterprise-visual-ui-testing-platform-10000-users-300-companies-100-million-tests-1-billion-component-level-results/.

Rathore, S.S. and Kumar, S. (2016) 'A decision tree regression based approach for the number of software faults prediction'. *ACM SIGSOFT Software Engineering Notes*, 41 (1), 1–6. doi.org/10.1145/2853073.2853083.

Reda, N., Hamdy, A. and Rashed, E.A. (2022) 'Multi-objective adapted binary bat for test suite reduction'. *Intelligent Automation & Soft Computing*, 31 (2), 781–797. doi.org/10.32604/iasc.2022.019669.

Waqar, M., Imran, Zaman, M.A., Muzammal, M. and Kim, J. (2022) 'Test suite prioritization based on optimization approach using reinforcement learning'. *Applied Sciences*, 12 (13), 6772. doi.org/10.3390/app12136772.

Zhang, Z. and Zhou, Y. (2007) 'A fuzzy logic based approach for software testing'. *International Journal of Pattern Recognition and Artificial Intelligence*, 21 (04), 709–722. doi.org/10.1142/s0218001407005636.

INDEX

Page numbers relating to figures and tables are given in italics.